AUTHENTIC RECIPES FROM CHINA & THAILAND

ASIAN FLAVORS
THE BEAUTIFUL
COOKBOOK

FISHERMAN ON RHONGU LAKE IN GUILIN, GUANGXI PROVINCE

ADAM WOOLFITT

SHREDDED CHICKEN AND TENDER CELERY *(see page 54)*

AUTHENTIC RECIPES FROM CHINA & THAILAND

ASIAN FLAVORS
THE BEAUTIFUL
COOKBOOK

RECIPES BY
CULINARY AUTHORITIES OF BEIJING, SHANGHAI, GUANDING, AND SICHUAN
PANURAT POLADITMONTRI
JUDY LEW

TEXT BY
WILLIAM WARREN

PHOTOGRAPHY BY
LUCA INVERNIZZI TETTONI
JOHN HAY

HarperCollins*Publishers*

Asian Flavors: The Beautiful Cookbook Copyright © 2003

First Edition

0-06-058028-3

President: John Owen
General Manager: Stuart Laurence
Co-editions Director: Derek Barton
Editorial Director: Elaine Russell
Managing Editor: Julia Roles
Text: Kevin Sinclair
Recipe Translators: Frances Ting Chiu Ling, Chen We Yei,
Cai You Qing, Kung Sen Wei De
Recipe Editors: Tan Lee Leng, Jacki Passmore
Picture Editor (China Landscapes): Mary-Dawn Earley
Calligraphy: Ethna Gallacher, Wong Chiu Tung
Map Illustrator: Linda Love
Designer: John Bull, Bull's Graphics

© 1986 Intercontinental Publishing Corporation Limited
© 1990 Weldon Owen Pty Limited
USA © 1990 Weldon Owen Inc.
Food photographs © 1982 Shufunotomo Co. Ltd.

ISBN 0-06-757588-9 (pbk.)

Printed by Toppan in China

A Weldon Owen Production

Copyright © 1992 Weldon Owen Inc., San Francisco

The Library of Congress has catalogued the hardcover
edition as follows:

Poladitmontri, Panurat.
    Thailand the beautiful cookbook; authentic recipes from
the regions of Thailand/recipes by Panurat Poladitmontri and
Judy Lew; text by William Warren; photography by Luca
Invernizzi Tettoni, John Hay.
        p.   cm.
    Includes index.
    ISBN 0-00-255029-6
    1. Cookery, Thai.   2. Thailand—Social life and customs.
    I. Lew, Judy.   II. Warren, William, 1930–   III. Title.
    TX724.5 T5P66 1992
641.59593—dc 20   91-33549

ISBN 0-06-757595-1 (pbk.)

Printed by Toppan in China

APPETISERS IN A LACQUER BOX (*see page 142*)

Contents

The Culinary Heritage

CHINA is more than just a country. It is a culture, a civilisation, a way of life that has developed through five thousand years of recorded history. It began when the Han people, forebears of the modern Chinese nation, started their long march to destiny from their ancient homeland near the modern city of Xian. Even before these fifty chronicled centuries of settled society, food played a vital role in the developing Chinese culture.

In the misty era before the Han tribes coalesced into the beginnings of the Chinese race, the first mythical hero to emerge was Fu Hsi. The main activities of this god-like fabled figure were hunting and fishing, and to him is attributed the invention of the kitchen and cooking. The next legendary figure in early Chinese mythology was Shen Nung, the Divine Husbandman. To him goes credit for the plough, the hoe and the care of farm animals. Huang Ti, the Yellow Emperor and the patron saint of Taoism, is worshipped still for the conception of planting grain and the invention of the pestle and mortar to crush it to make flour.

The hunter, the husbandman and the farmer; it is no accident that the first three objects of worship of the ancient Chinese should all have to do with food. Emperor Yu, the founder of the Xia Dynasty (twenty-first to sixteenth century BC), the first to unify the early Chinese, has been honoured over the centuries not so much for his political role as the earliest emperor but for his development of water control. This worthy step helped to stop the floods which ruined crops and encouraged the use of irrigation to improve yields. Since the days of the Great Yu, the overwhelming priority of every ruler of China has been to fill the rice bowls of the people. So it remains today. The fact that the billion people of China enjoy a healthy, satisfying, substantial diet with no rationing of basic foodstuffs is widely regarded as the single most vital achievement of the modern government in Beijing.

Things have not always been so auspicious. Throughout its long and turbulent history, the vast wealth of China, most of it created on the solid base built by the endless toil of peasants in the fields, has been a magnet for plunderers, adventurers and invaders. Nature, likewise, has taken a savage toll with drought and flood, earthquake and landslide, tidal wave and typhoon destroying the crops and herds so patiently built up at such a cost in sweat and tears. Not for nothing is the Yellow River, once tamed by Huang Ti, referred to as "China's Sorrow". Its floods over the centuries have left generations homeless, beggared whole provinces, destroyed crops over enormous areas and sentenced untold millions to death by famine.

But Chinese ingenuity, grit, vigour and endless toil have overcome all the obstacles. And when the time comes to give thanks to their many gods and beliefs, the

people of China do so while gathered around the dining table. Family feasts, celebratory banquets, birthdays, the summer and winter equinoxes, wedding anniversaries, celebrations of the birthday of Tin Hau, Goddess of Heaven, or of imported faiths like Christianity, Buddhism or Islam, the conclusion of one successful business deal or the agreement on launching a new one; all these and many more occasions call for glasses to be raised and chopsticks to be wielded. Any event can and is used as worthy excuse for a feast. It can be as simple as a home-cooked meal for an unexpected visit by friends, or as lavish as an imperial banquet that takes twenty chefs three weeks to prepare. Whatever the reason, and no matter how humble or splendid the surroundings, the way Chinese traditionally celebrate is by eating.

So food in all its aspects has, since the birth of Chinese civilisation, been a cornerstone of the national culture. In no other people has the preparation, preservation, cooking, cultivation and serving of food taken such a dominant and pervasive role. China's very history revolves around the table and the kitchen. The folk heroes of the nation, no matter who rules it, are often in some way or another connected with eating, drinking or making merry. In China today and in the homes of thirty million overseas Chinese scattered around the world, kitchen gods sit in family shrines staring amiably at housewives or chefs preparing the daily meals. Twice a year ancestral graves are swept and incense lit to pay homage to departed ancestors. Roast pork, rice wine and fruit are offered to the dead; food in Chinese culture is important even to those who have passed on.

A DIVERSE CUISINE

Any cuisine is limited by the raw ingredients that are available. In the case of China, the range is virtually boundless. The country is vast: twice as large as Europe excluding Russia, bigger than the United States including Alaska and Hawaii, a quarter as huge again as Australia. Into this gigantic land are crowded more than a billion people. They are unfairly distributed: packed into the rich flatlands along the east and southern coasts; jammed into the great valleys of the Yellow, Yangtze and Pearl rivers; stacked by the millions in the sprawling industrial conurbations; and crammed – no less than one hundred million of them – into the rice-bowl basin of inland Sichuan. But elsewhere they are scattered lightly. The steppes of Mongolia and Xinjiang are still thinly peopled by Kazakh, Uigur and Turkic tribesmen, and the descendants of Genghiz Khan. The ice plateau of Tibet, a land of soaring peaks, precipitous caverns and frigid highland plains, is bigger than Austria, Czechoslovakia, the Netherlands, Switzerland, Belgium, Italy, Portugal, Luxembourg and Hungary combined, and has fewer than two million people. In the jumbled mountains of the southwest, a chaos of races – minority tribes of dozens of nationalities – live in steep river valleys, unaware and uncaring about those who occupy the next ravine.

This huge landscape has dictated the scores of regional cuisines that have developed in China over the centuries. Although the country produces every delicacy under the sun, much of the grain, vegetables and live-

TIBETAN NOMADS ON HORSE AND YAK, SICHUAN PROVINCE LEO MEIER

A BAI WAITRESS AT A DALI CITY RESTAURANT, YUNNAN PROVINCE

stock is available only in the locality where it is produced. Even today, with vast improvements in communications and transport, what goes into the family pot tends to be that which is grown or raised nearby. The delectable camel hump of Mongolia is a rare and costly luxury in the south. Seafood is understandably scarce in Chengdu, 3000 kilometres (1,800 miles) upriver from the mouth of the Yangtze. Fresh vegetables are unknown in the frigid Manchurian winter, although the gardens blossom all year round in semi-tropical Guangdong.

From this immense geographical diversity have developed the manifold varieties of Chinese cuisine. In the past the climate dictated what people ate and to a lesser extent in the age of efficient artificial preservation, refrigeration and dehydration, so it still does today. This is partly because of the inherited and acquired love of the favourite dishes with which people grew up from childhood. While experimentation is encouraged in every Chinese kitchen, the family favourites of childhood tend to hold a tight gastronomic rein throughout life. For Chinese, as for every other people, this is probably because of the international love for the food that mother cooked.

But intertwined with the love of good food is also the ancient basic philosophy of China, the belief in harmony, of the balance of nature, of the duality of existence, of the blending of contrasts. Yin and yang, the two elements, are as significant in the Chinese kitchen as they are in the temple. Yin is soft, yielding, dark, feminine. Yang is hard, bright, masculine, vigorous. In the wok, the hotpot or the steamer, yin and yang combine and complement each other. Sweet contrasts with sour. The two basics of stir-frying – ginger and spring

onions – are yang and yin. Crunchy sea salt goes with Sichuan peppercorns. Steamed chicken goes with stir-fried fresh greens, the yang of fiery chillies goes with the gentle yin of sugar. The contrast of taste and texture, colours and cooking methods, which results in any balanced Chinese meal is a triumph of the philosophical theory of yin and yang, the world in a happy balance. A Chinese meal, ordered correctly, should be orchestrated like a Mozart symphony: hot and cold, sweet and sour, plain and spicy, meat and pickle, fish and greens, yin and yang.

THE NATIONAL DRINK

Tea is the drink of China and has been so since recorded history began. The preparation and sipping of tea are part of the education of a scholar and the daily life of a manual worker. Learned discussions about how best to make tea, with what implements, the source of the best water, the method of boiling it and the vital question of how long the leaves should be left to steep are matters which for thousands of years have preoccupied writers and artists, generals and merchants, mandarins and emperors. Throughout the land in almost every dialect it is called "cha". The exception is in Fujian where the word "deh" is used. Because the seafarers of Fujian exported the dried, chopped leaves of the tree, and because it was in the ports of the southeast coast that foreigners loaded it, the beverage is known in the Western world as "tea".

Tea has played a vital role in China throughout recorded history. It has been the reason for polite and learned academic discussions in teahouses; it caused social unrest and riots in China as it once did in Boston;

MARC BERNHEIM

PICKING THE FAMOUS DRAGON WELL TEA, HANGZHOU, ZHEJIANG PROVINCE

and it has been used as a national treasure, a state currency, a government fund-raising monopoly and, in the form of pressed bricks of leaves, as cash. It is also a relaxing, captivating, sacred drink.

There are thousands of varieties of tea. It grows on flat, fertile land but thrives equally well on steep hillsides up to 2000 metres (6,000 feet) amid eternal mist where other crops fail. In its untended state the tree sprouts to 10 metres (30 feet) or more, but when clipped and pruned for cultivation it is kept to 1.2 metres (4 feet) in height so the strength goes into the leaves. The three leaves on the tip of the bud are used in top-quality teas. There are three main types of tea: red, green and black. Among the most famous of the green varieties is the astringent, pale yellow Dragon Well tea from Hangzhou. The Keemun type grown all over east China, favourite of the British breakfast table, is among the best-known of the red teas. Oolong (Black Dragon) tea includes such leaves as the Iron Goddess of Mercy type from Jiangxi, which when pressed into bars is said to be as hard as metal.

Even the most learned scholar cannot say where tea originated. According to legend a forgotten emperor (or a thirsty deity, some versions hold) was sitting contemplatively in his garden sipping a bowl of hot water when a gust of autumn wind blew some leaves off a tree. They landed in the imperial bowl and coloured the water. The monarch sipped it and liked what he tasted. Tea was born.

Since then more legends have sprouted from the teacups of China than from almost any other source. Tea is said to soothe the excited and help the restless to sleep. On the other hand, it is held to awaken the senses and rouse the drowsy. It has been used as a medicine and a placebo, to quiet the restless young, relax the tensions of the mature, and to ease the discomfort of the old.

THE TEA CEREMONY

When Lu Yu wrote his scholarly but chatty "Classics of Tea" at the time of the early Tang Dynasty (618-907 AD), tea was more than just a drink, it was a symbol and a ceremony. He discoursed on types of water to use, the twenty-four different items of equipment needed to make a cup of tea and the way in which it should be prepared. The best tea leaves, he wrote, "should curl like the dewlap of a bullock, crease like the boot of a Tartar horseman, unfold like the mist rising from a ravine and soften gently like fine earth after it is swept by rain".

Lu Yu, along with similarly minded scholars, helped to inspire centuries of poetry, arts, porcelain manufacture and an enormous range of other academic and industrial activities all concentrating on the best way of making tea. This ostentatious, quasi-religious elevation of the tea ceremony rose to a pinnacle among the idle rich and the literati during the Song Dynasty (960-1279 AD) when fortunes would be paid for a perfectly glazed teacup, and officials would sit for hours discussing different brands. This came to an abrupt end with the arrival of the less sophisticated and more direct Mongols of the Yuan Dynasty (1260-1368 AD) for whom a cup of tea was a cup of tea. The tea ceremony still flourished in Japan where it had been exported to, but in China the ceremony was never again to reach such esoteric heights. However, in modern China the teahouse remains the favoured rendezvous.

ALCOHOLIC DRINKS

Loosely translated as wine, the Chinese expression "jiu" means any beverage containing alcohol, of which there are many in China. Like tea, wine is the fountainhead of a thousand legends, most of them affably eccentric. A chef of ancient times is said to have put some rice to soak in a covered jar, which he placed in a corner of his warm kitchen and promptly forgot. A few days later he raised the lid and was engulfed by a strong, unfamiliar aroma. He cautiously dipped in his serving spoon and tasted the contents; and again, and again. Other kitchen staff were attracted by his joyful mirth. They too tried the strange mixture. So was held the first cocktail party in China, and thus was born the Chinese tradition of drinking and making jolly.

The Chinese made a variety of jiu as far back as 2000 BC. Modern vintners would probably not award the ancient beverages any prizes, but ancient tipplers seemed partial to a glass with their meals, and for the past four thousand years Chinese imagination has run enthusiastically riot in distilling alcoholic drinks from almost anything that has come to hand. Today that tradition remains vibrantly alive with a staggering number of wines, beers, spirits and liqueurs being made in every corner of the land. Brewers, vignerons and distillers use as raw materials everything from transplanted French grapes and German hops, to rice, sorghum, wheat, maize, potatoes and fruit of all types. Beverages range from classic German-style wines, to foaming beers, to the explosive sorghum-based Mao Tai, with which Mao Zedong and Richard Nixon toasted pingpong diplomacy, to sweet but potent tipples such as the Panda brand liqueur made in Sichuan Province and based on the hirsute Chinese gooseberry.

Wine was carried into China in ancient times by Persian traders, and at least a century before Christ vines were growing around the imperial palace. The grape had a seesaw existence throughout history, often depending on the personal inclination of the emperor. If he drank, vines flourished. If he happened to frown on the pressed and fermented fruit of the vine, imperial decrees went out ordering farmers to rip up the vines and replant their land with food crops. A fillip to the vineyards came at the end of the last century when Europeans in north China, especially missionaries, planted extensive areas of grapes. Today they still exist in vast areas of Shandong and Hebei provinces, and new plantings by French and other joint-venture partners are renewing production of first-class wines in China. With the aid of foreign expertise and modern techniques used in Europe, America and Australia, Chinese wines have won international awards.

Beer also came from foreign influences, many of them unhappy. During the rush to grab parts of China in the last century, Europeans and Japanese brought with them a demand for their native drinks. This dismal episode in China's history had at least one auspicious result because there are thousands of ales and beers in the country today, many of them drawn from brewing techniques introduced into the Treaty Ports. The most famous is the magnificent Qingdao beer which originated in the port city of that name during German occupation of parts of Shandong Province in the late nineteenth, early twentieth century.

Most Chinese drinking is done along with eating; tradition abhors drinking alone or on an empty stomach,

and it is at banquets with family, friends or guests that most Chinese indulge in some of their huge range of drinks. Usually the glasses are filled with one of the countless varieties of rice wines, the most famous of which is Shaoxing wine from Zhejiang Province. This tends to be darkish in colour and is poured warm from a vessel like a teapot into small glasses and then drunk with flamboyant gusto. Also favoured at banquets, particularly during feasts or when foreigners are present, are some of the strong spirits of China. These include some truly fearsome distilled beverages like the fragrant but potent Mao Tai; the transparent Fen Chiew liquor which is used as a base for Zhu Ye Qing liqueur; and the ferocious Kaoliang of north China, designed to keep out the frigid cold of winter and which, to boot, numbs all other feelings with its 130 proof punch.

Much dinner-table drinking is associated with games. In one, the serving circle in the middle of the table is spun and the person who ends up staring into the head of the remains of a duck or chicken dish has to swallow his or her drink. Then the host toasts his guests, and the visitors toast the host, and the young raise their glasses to the old, and the aged drink to the more youthful, and everyone drinks to the person sitting next to them. As every glass is raised, everyone calls "kan pei", which in rough translation means good health.

Many of the stories associated with Chinese drinking deal with poets. Historically, poets were regarded as a rather bohemian, happy-go-lucky lot, a large number

SELLING MEDICINAL WINE IN A ZUNYI STREET MARKET, GUIZHOU PROVINCE

MICHAEL YAMASHITA

of them from wealthy or influential families, who spent their lives writing classical couplets, generally while deeply in their cups. Several of them often cited in classical tales came to bad ends because of overindulgence. One is said to have rolled to his death down a steep hill while staggering home from a wine shop. Another of these "drunken dragons", as poets were known, was Li Po who wrote with enthusiasm of "the rapture of drinking and wine's heady joy". He went everywhere accompanied by two servants whose job was to carry their literary master safely home. Li Po proclaimed during his bouts that he could not write without a drink. His end would seem to bear out this claim; he is said to have clambered into a sampan and pushed himself out on a lake on a still night to admire the reflection of the moon in the calm water. While enthusing about the view, he took another drink. Leaning over the side of the boat trying to embrace the vision of the glorious reflection, he fell into the water and drowned.

Even the stern Confucius liked a drop and noted that "there is no limit to wine drinking". One must not get drunk, he was swift to add, a lesson which was apparently not heeded by Li Po or hundreds of other poets who down the ages have sung the glories of jiu.

THE ART OF PRESERVATION

Entering a Chinese store that sells dried foods, herbs or medicines (and sometimes it is virtually impossible to draw a line between what you take for health and what is for sustenance) is akin to going into a museum of fauna and flora. There will be fungi of incredible sizes and bizarre shapes: tiny button mushrooms from the fields, large drooping fungi from the rainforests of the southern jungles, and the strange monkey brain fungi dug from the frozen soils of Manchuria. Some stores will also have birds' nests from the cliff-side caves of Kalimantan — foul-smelling balls of grass and excrement, but a vital ingredient for the soup of the same name. There will be countless varieties of pasta, fried chillies, a mysterious selection of hundreds of herbs adorning shelf upon shelf, and dangling from the roof will be the rustling skins and skeletal shapes of octopi, jellyfish, squid, fish intestines, seaweeds and other former inhabitants of the deep; just drop them into water for a few hours and they will return to an edible reincarnation. Deers' antlers, horns of rhinoceros, gall bladders of ox and buffalo, and the dried penis of whale are also to be found at awesome prices, because a pinch of the ground powder from such potent items is widely believed to hold aphrodisiac qualities.

Just how Chinese preserves are used is a secret which many chefs guard closely. And just as only a very fine line can be drawn between the ingredients used for medicine and those for food, so can the doctor's advice merge with the recipes used in a Chinese kitchen. The saying popular among Western food faddists, "You are what you eat", was probably expressed in a score of Chinese dialects several thousand years ago, and the raw material for many of the potions mixed then and commonly in use today can still be found on the shelves of any Chinese dried food store.

A MARKET STALL IN YONGXIN, JIANGXI PROVINCE

ENRICO FERORELLI

THE FIERY CHILLI, AN EXPLOSIVE COMPONENT OF SICHUAN CUISINE

MICHAEL YAMASHITA

SELLING MUSHROOMS AT SHIMIAN VILLAGE MARKET, SICHUAN PROVINCE

As with everything to do with the foods of China, preserving techniques were dictated by the climate. In the south, fresh foods were almost always available (just as well, because nothing keeps for long in the torrid, humid summer). In the north, for half the year nature provided natural refrigeration. And in both regions pickling has long been a favoured technique, for reasons of taste as well as for preservation.

The average cook in China uses an extensive range of preserves, spices and seasonings every day. Hot chilli paste, biting mustard, the inescapable soy sauce, preserved plums, pickled turnips, carrots or cabbage, mushrooms in endless species and black bean sauce are among the most common accompaniments for everyday dishes. And they are the merest tip of a gastronomic iceberg of formidable proportion. Perhaps the most visible preserves in China are the pressed flocks of ducks and the salted schools of fish which hang in the streets outside restaurants throughout the land. They are edible advertisements for what is on offer inside.

Nuts of all kinds are an important and often unseen and unsung part of the Chinese culinary art. They were prominently mentioned in the gourmet recipe book of Madame Wu, printed in the eleventh century. So were many other preserved foods which can still be found today in delicatessens or dried food stores in any self-respecting Chinatown.

To preserve meat Madame Wu advised rubbing dry salt into the flesh, putting it in a clay pot with a stone on top and pressing it overnight, then hanging it up to dry in a cool, airy room. The same technique is universally in use today. Fish were kept in times of abundance by grilling them, soaking them in oil and then packing them in

jars sealed with damp clay. Similar items, perhaps marketed in more modern containers, can still be bought to be eaten either as snacks or as a course in a feast with other out-of-season foods. Preserved meat and fish and pickled fruit and vegetables are never a meal on their own, but as side dishes and accompaniments to major courses, they are indispensable and valued parts of the culinary heritage.

A CULINARY HISTORY

Chinese culinary traditions have adapted freely and changed fluidly with time and circumstances. Five thousand years ago, at the time of the emerging Han tribes, the main crop in their arid, windblown homeland was probably a prehistoric form of millet. But archaeological digs in north China show that far before that time, Beijing Man had already developed a sophisticated caveman cuisine. Using stone weapons, he hunted down such prey as sabre-toothed tigers and roasted them over an open fire.

Steaming, that great basic kitchen technique still in very effective use today, was perfected long before the foundation of the first dynasty. Scientists testing remains outside Xian have ascertained that the inhabitants of a village named Banpo were cooking such delicacies as chicken, carp and elephant three thousand years before the birth of Christ.

Two millennia later the glorious Shang Dynasty flowered (sixteenth to eleventh century BC). In addition to art, commerce, culture and science, cuisine flourished in the rich atmosphere of the court and such delicacies as rhinoceros and elephant were consumed. Religion, closely linked with food, also developed, and as the cooking fires died down the shells of turtles and the thigh bones of oxen were thrown in the embers. From the shapes produced in the flames, soothsayers read omens and foretold the future.

There is no evidence that the prophets of Shang gave warning of the rise of Zhou (1122-256 BC), the dynasty that was to supplant them. The kings of Zhou claimed descent from a ruler of the northwestern plains named Hou Ji, which means Lord Millet, and by the time they imposed their rule over the embryonic northern kingdom that was to grow into the Chinese nation, they had learned how to grow rice, wheat, soy beans, melons, celery and squashes, and on feast days ate roast sheep and boar.

But early gastronomic development was not restricted to the north. As the Han people melded into a great and unified nation on the plains of the Yellow River, a political and culinary evolution was taking place along the fertile banks of the mighty Yangtze. Kingdoms and dukedoms rose and fell and flowered and wilted. But as armies marched, clashed, died and conquered, the peasants of China continued their eternal task of providing food for the ever-increasing population.

Thanks to modern scientific techniques, archaeologists and anthropologists can now fit together much fascinating historical evidence. The resulting jigsaw puzzles have many missing pieces, but enough have survived to tell us of a rich gastronomic feast in the vast Yangtze Valley during the ceaseless warring eras of the kingdoms of Wu, Yu and Chu. For three centuries, the warriors and lords battled for supremacy. Politically they were stalemated, but on the culinary front, seven hundred years before Christianity, chefs won magnificent victories with such outstanding dishes as noodles sautéed with honey, lamb stewed with sugarcane, braised ox tendons and bitter melon soup. The soldiers did not beat their swords into ploughshares, rather the farmers used the shoulder blades of their oxen to turn the deep, rich soils in which they grew such delicacies in the hot, damp summers as peaches and juicy melons. This gave rise to internal trade. Peaches went north to the sophisticated table of the emperor, and bear paws were dispatched south to the semi-barbarian kings of the warring states.

By the second century BC, the Yangtze Valley was the frontier of Chinese civilisation, an Oriental Wild West where the only law was the sword. But China was about to take the gastronomic and geographical shape of today, as the Qin Dynasty (221-206 BC) brought under imperial rule the blooming basin of Sichuan in the upper Yangtze and the broad plains of Guangdong. For the first time the four great branches that were to grow into modern Chinese cuisine – classical Beijing, rich Shanghai, delicate Guangzhou and hearty Sichuan – were all to come under one rule. That rule did not last long because on a tour of his new lands, the man who united China into one realm died. Legend says his body was carried back to the capital Xian amid a load of salted fish (even then a southern delicacy) which disguised the smell of death. He was buried with great honour, guarded by thousands of terracotta soldiers.

Next onto the imperial stage came a commoner from stout farming stock named Liu Bang. In blood and fire he forged the Han Dynasty (206 BC-220 AD), one of the greatest in China's history. Gastronomically the Han

ANCIENT CHINESE BANQUET MENUS

SHUFUNOTOMO

A STREETSIDE BREAKFAST, GUIZHOU PROVINCE

MICHAEL YAMASHITA

period was a vital one. There were staggering culinary achievements. Noodles were invented, so were flour mills. The ancient soy bean was made into tofu. Expeditionary forces went into central Asia (then green and fertile, now mostly arid) and brought back treasures like sesame, peas, grapes, coriander and garlic. The culinary delights of the New Territories added Sichuan peppercorn to the imperial banquets. From the tropical south horsemen galloped in relays to speed the exotic lychees of the Pearl River delta to Xian. Today the first lychees of autumn are still rushed north to gourmets, but now they go by express train or jet aircraft.

The Han had pacified, or at least kept at sword's length, the savage Hun horsemen. But when, in the third century AD the Han Dynasty toppled because of internal plots, the barbarians galloped into China and occupied the north. They brought gastronomic disaster with them as well as political terror: their favourite dishes were boiled sheep and smelly cheese. However, the culinary flame was kept burning brightly south of the Yangtze where the Wu Dynasty (222-280 AD) took what a bountiful climate, fertile soil and dedicated farmers and fishermen had to offer to raise cooking to an art. Oranges went into the cooking pots as did other southern crops such as lotus seeds and coconuts.

It took three centuries for the Huns to be thrown back from north China to their heartland on the steppes of central Asia, and then the Sui Dynasty was to rule for only four decades (581-618 AD). But what it accomplished in such a tiny span! The Grand Canal was frantically dug by armies of human bulldozers. It linked the two mighty rivers on which China's history had been written, and from Yangzhou on the Yangtze the grains of the south were towed by barge north to the Yellow River plains. Yangzhou became the capital and its chefs laboured mightily over charcoal stoves to bring forth miracles of culinary creation that are today some of the most famous manifestations of the Chinese kitchen. The fat, plump Wo noodles that make up rich winter soups came from the Sui Dynasty chefs. So did fried rice and immortal dim sum. It might not have long dominated the political throne of China, but the Sui Dynasty passed on a culinary heritage that today is still renowned.

TRAVELLERS' BOUNTIES

And then came the Tang (618-907 AD). Their legacy is both diverse and delectable. They bequeathed us the wok and therefore that most distinctive of Chinese cooking techniques, stir-frying. Distilled spirits came during their three-century rule, during which China was the dominant power on earth. Trade flowered and with the merchants from other lands came nutmeg, saffron, eggplants, spinach and dill. Travellers brought back ideas as well as herbs, and Buddhism, with its vegetarian cuisine, had an immense and lasting influence on Chinese cuisine.

The tides of history washed the Song Dynasty (960-1279 AD) into power, mostly on the shields of barbaric nomads. The Great Wall failed to keep out the savage horsemen, and wave after wave of invaders intent on plunder swarmed into the treasure house that was China. The Song emperors retreated before this storm of uncouth aliens, and once again it was in southern China that food and farming developed. Thwarted from spreading to the north, the Song reached for the sea and their traders brought home exotica from as far afield as India and Indonesia. More importantly, from what is now Vietnam came seeds for a rice that produced a crop much earlier in the year than existing strains. From these few sacks of seeds can be traced the vast rice-growing tradition of the humid southern provinces.

Most of the barbarians who invaded to plunder, loot and conquer soon fell under the awesome wonder of China's culture, including the cuisine. Over the centuries they were usually lulled into quiet good manners, generally after being liberally plied with gentle wine and strong spirits, soothed with tea and gorged with the incomparable delicacies of the Chinese table. This did not apply, however, to the rude Mongols of the Yuan Dynasty (1206-1368 AD). They gulped down fermented horse's milk and tore at chunks of meat, often raw, which they carried in their sheepskin jackets or stowed under the saddles where, legend has it, the meat was tenderised after being subjected to the pounding of a day's hard riding. Their contribution to culinary history is confined to the one dish that originated from the horseback-broken piece of meat, steak tartare, and an increased appetite for mutton in the north.

It was under the magnificent Ming (1368-1644 AD), the last truly Chinese imperial dynasty, that modern cuisine developed. Their traders roamed the seas to Madagascar and Arabia. Chinese culture was exported and in return foreign ingredients made their way to the kitchens — first in the court, then in the cities, and finally in the peasant homes of the nation. But once again, the

THE TERRACED HILL SIDES OF YUDU COUNTY, JIANGXI PROVINCE

GEORG GERSTER

glory and wealth of China proved a jewel too precious to be ignored by the hungry and fierce barbarians outside the Middle Kingdom. The Ming pleaded with their fearsome neighbours the Manchus for military aid, and they answered this invitation promptly by marching into China. The Manchus threw out the invaders and just as quickly decided that as they had saved China they might as well stay and rule it. Reigning as the Qing Dynasty, the Manchus set up a regime that was to last until the early twentieth century.

The Manchus, though not as crude as the Mongols, brought few gastronomic delights with them from the frozen plains of their homeland. Winter Fire Pot, designed to warm them during the frigid six months of winter, was their major legacy, and it is still enjoyed all over China today. After the initial savage repression of their new realm, designed successfully to terrorise the population into accepting their rule, the Manchus settled down to enjoy life in the graceful civilisation that suddenly was theirs. They became, it is said, more Chinese than the Chinese. A couple of generations removed from their horses, the Manchu rulers relaxed in a life of luxury and leisure and spent much of their time concentrating on concubines and the table, while Chinese scholars and civil servants administered the realm.

It was, for two centuries, a time of peace and prosperity. As the Manchus became decadent and feasted on elephants' trunks and larks' tongues in three-day imperial banquets, the food consumed every day by gourmets

was developing into the Chinese cuisine we know and love today. Portuguese traders brought chillies to Macau from where they travelled up the branches of the Pearl River and into Hunan and Sichuan, creating the basis of the modern spicy dishes of the southwest. Fujian was gaining fame for seafood cooked with imagination. Guangdong dishes were reaching the degree of subtlety and clarity they are now noted for.

Just as important perhaps, from the point of view of culinary history, was how Chinese cooking was being taken abroad. The Western powers who grasped parts of China during the nineteenth century had little impact on the cuisine. But out of China from the mid-nineteenth century onwards flowed a steady stream of labourers to work the tin mines of Malaya, to dig for gold in Australia, New Zealand and South Africa, to hack railways across the Rocky Mountains and to take their commercial skills to every corner of the Pacific and beyond. This exodus of people, the forebears of today's thirty million overseas Chinese, came mostly from the great southern provinces of Guangdong and Fujian and with them they took Chinese cooking to every country of the world.

But the greatest Chinese cuisine on earth is still found today in the land where it developed. A combination of many centuries of love of good food, a tradition of hospitality and endless experimentation with the fruits of the good earth has gone into making the rich and vibrant feast that is the culinary heritage of China the Beautiful.

DRYING MAIZE IN THE ERLANG MOUNTAINS, SICHUAN PROVINCE

HARALD SUND

THE SUMMER PALACE IN BEIJING

THOMAS HOPKER

北京
Beijing

北京

Beijing
CLASSICAL CUISINE

T HE cuisine of Beijing is a contradiction. It is a combination of two very different legacies, the magnificence
of classical court cooking being a splendid but thin ven-
eer over the honest, solid food prepared by farmers'
wives in the countless tiny hamlets that dot the dusty
plains of northern China.

What the world regards as Beijing food is very different from the daily diet of the peasants of Hebei, Shandong, Henan and Shanxi provinces. For this is poor country, infertile and often arid, a land where living has for
centuries been precarious, balanced delicately between
persuading the cruel land and bitter climate to provide
sufficient millet, wheat, lentils, maize and sweet
potatoes to feed the village, and all too often the threat of
famine. For the peasant farmers on their tiny plots nature
was as often an enemy as a friend. In November, almost
overnight it seems, a chill wind begins blowing from the
icy wastes of Manchuria and Siberia. The next morning
the village ponds are frozen. Over the next few weeks
the ground itself is gripped and for five solid months the
land is one vast block of unyielding ice.

Through this austere winter, grain, turnips and cabbage provide the basis for the peasant kitchen. Often in
the past there has been too little of even these basics.
Before the great irrigation works began three decades
ago, another unpredictable and savage enemy was that
sleeping dragon which curls in bizarre muddy loops
across the plains: the Huang Ho, the Yellow River,
China's Sorrow. The river that brought the water to give
life to the fields also brought floods that ruined crops and
signalled famine. So did the many other waterways that
meander over the flats towards the Gulf of Bohai or the
Yellow Sea.

After the thaw turns the roads to mud and the fields
suddenly awaken, the heat of summer comes like a blast
from hell itself. The heat sears the plains bringing a dry
wind that in autumn causes almost instant dehydration
to a million ducks hanging from every home to provide
the main ingredient in the most famous dish of the
north, Beijing duck. But if the heavy rains of summer

THE FORBIDDEN CITY IN BEIJING
THOMAS HOPKER

29

ONE OF BEIJING'S BUSY INDOOR MARKETS

have not come, the winds from the west bring dust clouds and add to the misery of drought. Little wonder that after a wet summer when the crops are in and the cold winds begin to blow, a time when the farmers of the northern plains have sufficient food to last themselves and their families through the icy months, they bring out the explosive Mao Tai spirits and celebrate in hearty feasts and banquets.

In Beijing the glittering banquets in the Great Hall of the People present the world with a glimpse of the pinnacle of modern Chinese feasts. The capital's business community, the diplomats, the foreign journalists, all have their favourite restaurants featuring gastronomic riches unknown to the millions of peasants of the plains. The capital has people from every province in China and, in addition to the northern dishes, offers a wide range of regional restaurants providing homely provincial favourites for those in the army, government or bureaucracy who serve in Beijing, as well as local gourmets and adventurous visitors to the capital.

Like every other region, the common food of north China, away from the state banquets, is a mixture of tradition, imported outside influences and restrictions imposed on agriculture by the savage climate. During the brief hot summer the cities of north China are almost choked with a flood of vegetables. Huge tomatoes, immense zucchini, giant cauliflowers, juicy melons, succulent marrows, plump eggplants and enormous pumpkins fill the markets. Alas, it is all too brief. Soon the summer vegetables are gone and the hardy dry staples of winter make for a long and dull gastronomic season until, weather permitting, the bounty of another

growing season is harvested. Despite the harsh environment the genius of Chinese chefs over the centuries has developed a cuisine out of necessity. A rich culinary stew takes a few local ingredients (millet or wheat), adds a dash of imported Muslim custom (mutton), a hardy staple that thrives in the summer and keeps well throughout the long winter (white turnip or that superb standby of the north, Tianjin cabbage), and from such simple components comes up with a succulent, filling meal like a delicious sliced lamb hotpot.

Muslim cooking has had a strong influence on northern cuisine. Horsemen who surged over the Great Wall into the flatlands were often Muslims. They came to conquer and stayed to settle, and today the countless millions of Chinese with the family name Ma (Horse) can often trace their ancestry to the Muslim raiders. Today, however, it is only in name and culinary tastes that their heritage shows. Mongol, Manchu, Muslim — all have merged in the common Chinese sea to bring influences to modern northern food.

The influence of the Mongols lingers still, although the Yuan Dynasty held sway for less than a century (1206-1368 AD) before the "Devil's Horsemen" retreated to their wide steppes. In no other area of China have the Mongols left any notable culinary legacy.

The Manchu influence, however, is pervasive in the north, particularly around Beijing itself. Over the three centuries of the Qing Dynasty (1644-1911 AD) intermarriage was so common that many residents of the capital today, knowingly or not, carry Manchu genes. After their initial conquest of China the Manchus sat back to enjoy three hundred years of the good life. They caroused with gusto, drank with enthusiasm, had large harems and armies of concubines, and although they may not have made much of a contribution as chefs, they certainly encouraged fine cooking by their conspicuous consumption of the better things of life.

There were up to two thousand chefs at any one time in the kitchens of the Forbidden City, cooking delicacies for the emperor and his court; officials such as the army of advisors, mandarins, and generals; foreign dignitaries seeking audiences with the occupant of the Dragon Throne; the hordes of concubines, eunuchs, members of the royal family, and the rest of the imperial court. The Manchus may have ruled the empire through their corps of fast-riding Bannermen, but in the kitchens of Beijing the Chinese reigned supreme. A standing joke was that the Manchus had invaded China to get a decent meal.

Hated and scorned though they were by many Chinese in the dying decades of their long dynasty, the Manchus enthusiastically assimilated Chinese culture. They became, it is said, more Chinese than the Chinese, and in no way was this more obvious than at the dining table. They had a lust for life. One reason for the strong Muslim influence in modern Beijing is often attributed to the Manchu Emperor Qian Long. Of all his hundreds of concubines recruited from throughout the empire he was obsessed above all with a Muslim girl he named the Fragrant One. To humour her the Emperor decreed that a town for her co-religionists be erected in the Forbidden City. From this love affair can be traced the large Muslim presence in Beijing today, and items on menus throughout the northern provinces such as lamb, kid and horse meat. Inland in Shanxi, donkey meat is also a legacy of the Muslim presence.

OUTSIDE A HOME IN SUBURBAN BEIJING   THOMAS HOPKER

EARLY MORNING BARGAINING AT A STREET MARKET

LEONG KA TAI

Despite the Yellow River slicing through the northern plain, freshwater fish does not play an important role in the diet. Some say the turgid, muddy waters that carry heavy loads of silt are too thick for a fish to breathe. In winter shallow ponds freeze solid, making fish farming a practical impossibility. Northern chefs hold that only when the Golden Carp was vigorous enough to fight the flow of the Yellow River and reach as far upstream as the town of Dragon Gate in Henan Province was it fit to eat. By reaching so far upriver the fish was held to have exhibited great courage and stamina. As such, it was classed as a dragon and therefore became worthy of the wok. Shandong is the exception in the north as far as seafood is concerned. It produces notable seafood from both coasts bordering the Gulf of Bohai and the Yellow Sea. The giant prawns of the gulf are sent by train and truck to Beijing where they have won fame in top gourmet kitchens and restaurants.

Shandong has other special claims to gastronomic fame. For thirty-five years until 1914 the area around the town of Qingdao was leased to Imperial Germany, and this brief spell gave a Teutonic flavour to the cuisine as well as to the architecture. One bequest was Qingdao beer, made to an old German recipe and now, very justifiably, the most famous beer in all of China.

CITY DWELLERS BICYCLE TO WORK   LEONG KA TAI

A CHINESE OPERA CHORUS

G. MONRO

Europeans planted large areas of grapes in Shandong, and these vines are now producing wine of international standing. Riesling, Chardonnay and other varieties are now helping Chinese vignerons and their partners from France, Germany, America and Australia to produce top quality table wines. The whites, in particular, have won awards in several international arenas. Many of the varieties of wine being produced from the grapes of Shandong are specially blended and balanced to accompany Chinese food.

Shandong food is a cuisine formed by combining a bountiful sea harvest with the richest agricultural production in northern China. The population has strong links with the outside world, and this has infused into their cuisine many culinary notions from other regions of China and overseas. It is the most vigorous of the cuisines of the north, but unfortunately is also one of the least known.

Just as wealth, power and influence flowed inexorably towards the seat of power during Beijing's years as capital of the nation, so too did many of the most talented chefs gravitate to the political centre of the Middle Kingdom. Here a young chef could make a name for himself, and with a lot of hard work and a bit of luck, catch the eye of a wealthy gourmet who would set him up in his own establishment – much the same as young

French chefs head for Paris today. From all over the nation such ambitious cooks took their knowledge of China's various regional cuisines with them to the kitchens of Beijing.

A wide variety of imported foods, like the sweet potatoes of Shandong, play a vital role in what are now regarded as purely local dishes. In the hard years of this century it was common for Shandong peasants, if they were fortunate, to have three meals a day of sweet potatoes: one potato per meal. This vegetable has become such an integral part of the northern cuisine that it is easily overlooked that sweet potatoes only reached coastal China, via the Philippines from America, in the sixteenth century, about the same time as the potato reached Europe. Today, as it has been for a couple of centuries, the sweet potato is to Shandong what the spud is to Ireland. And it has played just as vital a political role.

Within the sweep of the provinces of the northern plains there is variety upon variety in the way commonplace ingredients are prepared. From one village to the next a tiny but subtle change may be made to the staple kitchen fare so that the food at one side of a province may be very different to that at the other. But everywhere such delicacies as salty soy bean sauces, spring onions and strong garlic give a distinctive tang to the taste of the north.

A FAMILY OUTING

LEO MEIER

(following page)
SUBURBAN BEIJING
WELDON TRANNIES

Poultry

家禽及野味

YOUNG BOYS TEND THEIR FLOCK OF GEESE

ENRICO FERORELLI

家禽及野味

Poultry

"FIRST, steal a chicken" is the immortal first line of the recipe for Beggar's Chicken. Nobody knows the origin of the dish, but one version often repeated in ancient Chinese texts holds that a humble peasant was sitting by a cooking fire at the side of a lake in Anhui Province when a feudal lord approached. When the poor man saw the nobleman and his armed entourage, he quickly scooped out mud from the lake side, plastering it around a chicken he had just stolen and threw the bird onto the coals. The nobleman stopped and got off his horse to warm himself by the fire. By the time he remounted and rode on, the chicken was encased in a brick-hard ball of fired clay. Frustrated, the peasant hurled a stone at the clay which promptly broke, releasing the delicious aroma still enjoyed by modern diners who order this piquant dish.

POULTRY SELLERS AT A FARM MARKET, JIANGXI PROVINCE

YANG SHAOMING

Every regional kitchen has its own distinctive poultry favourite. Indeed, virtually every county town in China has a special way of cooking local birds. The visitor can go into a restaurant in any corner of the country and ask for chicken confident of getting a tasty, satisfying dish. Ask how it has been cooked and the answer is likely to be: "Our way". That way differs throughout the land. In Shandong, it could mean chicken legs steamed, seasoned and then fried. If the chef is from Yunnan, the chicken could have been double-steamed in a sealed container. The bird may have been cooked in oyster sauce in Guangdong; brushed with sweet honey in Hebei; smeared with hot red bean paste in Hunan; simmered with anise in Gansu: inflamed with hot chillies in Guangxi or barbecued with white pepper in Mongolia.

Poultry of every description was a favoured dish before the first recipe was ever written. Game was always popular at imperial courts and is still eagerly sought today by keen huntsmen. Eagles, owls and other rare creatures once shot for the pot are now totally protected under international agreements honoured by China; but ducks, swans, pheasants, quail, geese and a myriad of other birds are the targets of enthusiastic shooters and archers. A prized dish in certain specialty restaurants is made from tiny rice birds caught in nets strung above the ripening grain, salted or preserved in honey and eaten whole: bones, innards and all.

In the capital, of course, pride of place goes to the glory of Beijing Duck, dried in the arid northern winds then crisply roasted and served with classical grace. But the residents of Nanjing will by no means bow to the duck of the northern plains. Their award goes to the famed pressed duck of the central Yangtze. Further up the river, the proud chefs of the Sichuan kitchen haughtily concede nothing to any poultry dish other than their own smoked duck; while in Guangdong, the subtle delicacy of steamed chicken is the most honoured dish.

Then there is the magnificent goose of the Chiu Chow kitchen with its spectacular accompaniment of plum sauce; the Yellow Chicken of Hainan Island; the plump roasted pigeons of Fujian; the wild birds of prey shot by archers in the pine forests of the remote Black Dragon River in far northern Manchuria, and the young fowls cooked in coconut juice which are a specialty of the tribal people of the steamy tropical coasts of Guangxi. In Guizhou, a pepper-blasted diced chicken is named Guardian of the Palace after the title of the Ming Dynasty Mandarin who invented the dish.

Throughout the country, and even in Beijing where duck is the dish for celebrations, chicken is the daily king of every kitchen. The bird appears in thousands of guises. Sometimes, as in a famous Guangdong recipe, the chicken is not a bird at all. A fowl is skinned and the meat cooked. The chef or housewife puts away the skin for another day when it will be stuffed with glutinous rice, mushrooms, ham, bacon, sweet wine and seasonings. With the holes sewn, baked and put on the table, it looks like a plump bird. Only when the diners try to eat it is the joke discovered; but it still tastes magnificent.

The humble chicken eaten in China is usually a more mature fowl than that cooked in the Western kitchen. Most Chinese chefs prefer a bird of about 1½-2kg (3-4lb) because of the richer flavour. Important medicinal values are attributed to the fowl; it is said to keep the five vital internal organs – the heart, liver, kidneys, lungs and spleen – active, to stimulate the stomach, to strengthen muscles and bones and improve the circulation of the blood. The stock from a boiled bird is invariably kept to make one of a million varieties of chicken soup, held by Chinese grandmothers to be the cure-all for every ailment.

WHITE GEESE ON A VILLAGE POND

LEO MEIER

CHICKEN BALL AND PEA SOUP

Beijing 北京

CHICKEN BALL AND PEA SOUP

155 g (5 oz) chicken breast meat
1 egg white, lightly beaten
1 tablespoon cornflour (cornstarch)
iced water
½ teaspoon salt
2 cups (500 mL/16 fl oz) lard or oil for deep-frying
4 cups (1 L/32 fl oz) chicken stock (broth)
2 teaspoons rice wine or dry sherry
1 cup (155 g/5 oz) fresh peas, cooked
1 tablespoon rendered chicken fat, melted (optional)

Reduce the chicken meat to a paste with a cleaver or in a food processor. Add the egg white, cornflour and ½ cup (125 mL/ 4 fl oz) of iced water and season with the salt. Stir in one direction only. The mixture should be so smooth and moist that the chicken paste falls from a chopstick in large droplets.

※ Heat the lard or oil in a wok and reduce the heat. Pour the chicken paste into a funnel and allow it to drip into the hot fat in drops about the size of green peas. Fry until just white and cooked through, then lift out on a slotted spoon and drain.

※ Heat the chicken stock and add the rice wine. Then add the drained peas and the chicken balls and heat through. Season with salt to taste and thicken, if preferred, with 1½ tablespoons cornflour mixed with cold water. Add the chicken fat, if used, and serve.

Sichuan 四川

STEAMED WHOLE CHICKEN WITH GLUTINOUS RICE AND DELICACIES

Chicken prepared according to this recipe is one of the most delectable of the Sichuan traditional dishes. It requires skilful preparation, but the result is well worth the effort involved. The dried "eight delicacies" used are sold in packages and simply need to be soaked before adding the rice to make this unique stuffing.

1 x 1¼ kg (2½ lb) chicken
1 carrot (garnish)
1 small cucumber (garnish)
2 eggs (garnish)
1 tomato (garnish)

STUFFING

125 g (4 oz) glutinous rice
2 tablespoons barley
20 fresh or dried lotus seeds
¼ cup (30 g/1 oz) fox nuts or gingko nuts (white nuts)
1 tablespoon dried shrimp
4 dried black mushrooms, soaked for 25 minutes
75 g (2½ oz) salty ham or bacon
1 tablespoon fresh peas
1½ teaspoons salt
OR use one pack of "eight delicacies" and glutinous rice for the stuffing

SAUCE

½ cup (125 mL/4 fl oz) chicken stock (broth)
1 tablespoon arrowroot or cornflour (cornstarch)
½ teaspoon salt
few drops sesame oil
pinch of pepper

Clean the chicken and bone it, leaving the skin intact – use a sharp knife with a long narrow blade to work around the carcass until it can be completely removed. Sever the wing and leg bones from the carcass, leaving the skin and meat in place.

※ To prepare the stuffing, soak the rice in water for 1 hour, then place on a rack in a wok or steamer, cover and steam for about 25 minutes until almost cooked through.

※ Wash fresh lotus seeds or soak dried ones with the barley and fox nuts for 2-3 hours to soften. Shell gingko nuts and soak in hot water for about 25 minutes. Use a toothpick to push out the bitter core and discard. Soak the shrimp to soften, then chop coarsely. Squeeze water from the mushrooms, remove the stems and dice the caps. Dice the ham.

※ If using packaged "eight delicacies", soak for one hour and steam for 10 minutes.

※ Mix these ingredients with the peas, steamed rice and barley and stuff into the chicken, moulding it into its original shape. Sew up the opening, then place breast downwards in a heatproof dish on a rack in a wok or a steamer. Steam, covered, over gentle heat for 50-60 minutes until completely tender.

※ Prepare garnishes by carving the carrot and cucumber into attractive shapes. Beat the two egg whites and the yolks together separately. Pour into separate dishes and steam until firm. Slice and cut into diamond-shaped pieces. Drop the tomato into boiling water, remove and peel. Cut into wedges, trim away the pulp and seeds leaving petal shapes. Set the garnishes aside.

※ When the chicken is done, lift out and place breast upwards on a serving plate.

※ Pour about ½ cup (125 mL/4 fl oz) of the liquid from the steaming dish into a wok and add the sauce ingredients. Bring to the boil and simmer, stirring, until it thickens. Adjust seasoning.

※ Add the garnishes, simmer for a few moments, then pour over the chicken and serve.

STEAMED WHOLE CHICKEN WITH GLUTINOUS RICE AND DELICACIES

BRAISED CHICKEN WITH LEMON

CHICKEN AND GINGKO NUTS

Shanghai 上海

BRAISED CHICKEN WITH LEMON

1 x 1 kg (2 lb) chicken
2 tablespoons light soy sauce
1 tablespoon rice wine or dry sherry
2 tablespoons lemon juice
1 cup (250 mL/8 fl oz) peanut oil
1 lemon, sliced

SAUCE

2 cups (500 mL/16 fl oz) chicken stock (broth), or water
3 spring onions (shallots/scallions), chopped
6 slices young fresh (root) ginger, shredded
1 tablespoon tomato sauce (ketchup)
3 tablespoons lemon juice
1 tablespoon sugar
½ teaspoon salt

Clean the chicken and wash well. Dry with paper towels, then place in a dish. Mix the soy sauce, rice wine and lemon juice together and rub over the chicken, pouring the remainder inside the cavity. Cover and leave for 1 hour, turning once, then drain, reserving the marinade, and leave to dry on a rack.

🐾 Heat the peanut oil in a wok and fry the chicken over moderate heat on all sides until golden, then transfer to a casserole.

🐾 Pour the remaining marinade over the chicken and add the sauce ingredients. Cover and bring to the boil, then reduce heat and simmer very gently for about 1 hour until the chicken is completely tender.

🐾 Remove the chicken, drain and cut straight through the bones into serving portions. Arrange on a plate and place the sliced lemon in a line down the centre of the back.

🐾 Rapidly boil the sauce until well reduced, then pour over the chicken and serve.

Sichuan 四川

CHICKEN AND GINGKO NUTS

There are groves of gingko trees on Mount Ching Chen in Kuan Shian County. They are a popular tourist attraction, and many believe that the age-old trees will bless them with longevity.

In ancient China, people regarded the gingko as a fruit. Yang Wan Li, a famous poet in the Bei Song Dynasty (960-1127 AD) wrote: "Silver gingko might well keep the golden peach company".

The core of the gingko nut must be removed before the nut is used, as it is very bitter and is said to cause stomach pain.

375 g (12 oz) fresh peeled or canned gingko nuts
1 x 1¼ kg (2½ lb) chicken
3 spring onions (shallots/scallions)
6 slices fresh (root) ginger
2 tablespoons rice wine or dry sherry
1 teaspoon salt
pinch of white pepper

Soak fresh gingko nuts in boiling water, then drain and scrape off the skin. Pick off the two ends, push the bitter core through with a toothpick, then soak again.

🐾 Blanch the chicken in boiling water, then hold under cold running water to rinse. Drain and place breast upwards in a casserole.

🐾 Add the remaining ingredients, except the gingko nuts, cover with water, bring to the boil, reduce the heat and simmer for 15 minutes. Turn the chicken over, add the gingko nuts and continue to simmer until the chicken is completely tender.

🐾 Remove the chicken and cut in half lengthways. Then cut the meat diagonally from the centre into slices. Arrange in its original shape on a serving plate. Lift the gingko nuts from the stock with a slotted spoon, arrange around the chicken and serve at once.

Beijing 北京

CHICKEN IN A LANTERN

The presentation of this dish is impressive. Lightly cooked chicken pieces and selected vegetables are placed in a square of clear cellophane and tied with ribbon. The parcel is held over a wok of hot oil and the oil is quickly ladled over the bag. The heat causes the air inside the bag to expand, blowing it up like a lantern.

250 g (8 oz) chicken breast meat
2 teaspoons light soy sauce
1 egg white, lightly beaten
1 tablespoon cornflour (cornstarch)
1 spring onion (shallot/scallion)
2 slices fresh (root) ginger
1 clove garlic
3 dried black mushrooms, soaked for 25 minutes
4 canned water chestnuts, drained
2 tablespoons fresh peas
1 tablespoon blanched almonds
6 cups (1½ L/48 fl oz) oil for deep-frying
90 g (3 oz) rice vermicelli
1 tablespoon oil for stir-frying

SEASONING

1 tablespoon rice wine or dry sherry
1 tablespoon chilli sauce (or less, to taste)
2 teaspoons sugar
1 teaspoon salt

Cut the chicken into small cubes and place in a dish with the soy sauce, egg white and cornflour. Mix well and leave for 20 minutes.

Trim the spring onion and cut into short lengths. Shred the ginger and chop the garlic. Drain the mushrooms, squeezing out all the water, cut off the stems and dice the caps. Dice the water chestnuts. Parboil the peas and halve the almonds.

Heat the oil in a large wok over medium heat and deep-fry the chicken in a wire ladle or frying basket for about 2 minutes, shaking frequently to cook evenly. Lift out and drain well. Deep-fry the almonds briefly and set aside to drain.

Increase the heat under the oil, and when very hot deep-fry the vermicelli quickly. They will expand to several times their original volume and turn white. Lift out and drain – do not allow them to colour. Place on a serving plate.

In another wok heat about 1 tablespoon of oil and briefly stir-fry the spring onion, garlic, ginger and mushrooms. Add the seasoning ingredients and stir-fry briefly, then add the chicken, water chestnuts, peas and almonds. Mix together thoroughly.

Spoon the mixture into the centre of a square of clear cellophane, bring the corners together to enclose it and tie a ribbon round the centre. Reheat the oil, hold the parcel over the wok and quickly ladle oil over until it blows up. Drain and place in the centre of a serving dish. Untie the bag at the table and tip the contents over the vermicelli.

CHICKEN IN A LANTERN

PHOENIX BREAST WITH SOUR SAUCE

Sichuan 四川

PHOENIX BREAST WITH SOUR SAUCE

According to legend, the phoenix is the king of birds, symbolising nobility, respect and glory. The emperor's residence used to be called the phoenix residence, the emperor's carriage the phoenix carriage and the queen's head-dress the phoenix crown. Chicken breast, being the best part of the chicken, is known as phoenix breast in China, and in this dish is deliciously sour and tasty.

185 g (6 oz) chicken breast meat
1 tablespoon rice wine or dry sherry
½ teaspoon salt
1 egg white, well beaten
2 tablespoons soy bean powder or cornflour (cornstarch)
375 g (12 oz) lard or oil for frying

SAUCE

1½ tablespoons red vinegar
1 tablespoon sugar
1 tablespoon light soy sauce
2 slices fresh (root) ginger, finely chopped
2 cloves garlic, finely chopped
1 pickled red chilli, finely chopped
1 spring onion (shallot/scallion), minced (ground)
30 g (1 oz) fresh or canned bamboo shoots, very finely chopped

Cut the chicken into very small dice and place in a dish with the wine, salt, egg white and soy bean powder or cornflour. Mix well and leave for 20 minutes. Heat the lard or oil in a wok to smoking point, then lower the heat and fry the chicken, stirring with chopsticks to separate the pieces. When it turns white, lift out and drain well.

✿ Drain the wok and wipe out. Add 1 tablespoon of the lard or oil and stir-fry the chopped sauce ingredients for 1 minute, then add the remaining ingredients and return the chicken. Toss together over high heat until well mixed and the sugar dissolved, then serve.

Shanghai 上海

FRIED CHICKEN LEGS

8 chicken drumsticks, about 750 g (1½ lb)
2 pieces pork fat net (caul lining), cut into triangle shapes
1 egg, well beaten
1 cup (125 g/4 oz) dry breadcrumbs
oil for deep-frying
hot soy sauce
tomato or chilli sauce

SEASONING

1 tablespoon rice wine or dry sherry
2 tablespoons light soy sauce
3 tablespoons water
1 tablespoon finely chopped fresh coriander
1 tablespoon finely chopped spring onion (shallot/scallion)
¾ teaspoon finely chopped fresh (root) ginger
1 cinnamon stick
1 piece dried orange peel
1 teaspoon Sichuan peppercorns (Fagara or Sansho)
1 star anise
½ teaspoon salt
1 tablespoon sugar

Mix the seasoning ingredients together in a large, shallow heatproof dish and put in the chicken drumsticks. Cover with plastic wrap and leave for 3 hours, turning several times. Then uncover and place the dish on a rack in a wok or in a steamer, cover and steam over gently simmering water for about 30 minutes. Remove and leave to drain.

✿ Wrap each drumstick in a triangle of the pork fat net, then dip into beaten egg. Coat with dry breadcrumbs then refrigerate for about 30 minutes for the breadcrumbs to "set".

✿ Heat the oil in a wok to smoking point and deep-fry the drumsticks until crisp and golden on the surface. Drain and arrange on a serving place. Serve with small dips of hot soy sauce and tomato or chilli sauce.

✿ The drumsticks can also be served straight from the steamer, omitting the crisp-frying, and are excellent with a plain bowl of rice and a little of the sauce.

FRIED CHICKEN LEGS

Shanghai 上海

BRAISED CHICKEN LEGS IN A LOTUS SHAPE

12 chicken drumsticks
3 tomatoes
1 cup (250 mL/8 fl oz) fresh milk
1 egg
1 egg white
lard or vegetable oil
12 vegetable hearts (miniature Chinese white cabbage)
   or bok choy
pinch of salt
grated lemon rind (optional)

SEASONING/STOCK

2 cups (500 mL/16 fl oz) chicken stock (broth)
2 tablespoons dark soy sauce
1 tablespoon sugar
3 slices fresh (root) ginger
2 tablespoons vegetable oil

Use a sharp knife to cut around the chicken bones to where the meat begins to be fleshy. Scrape the skin completely away from the lower part of the bone, leaving it exposed.

❋ Arrange the chicken drumsticks in a wide flat saucepan. Mix the seasoning/stock ingredients together and pour over the drumsticks. Bring almost to the boil, then simmer gently for about 45 minutes until the drumsticks are very tender and the sauce reduced to a syrupy glaze.

❋ Blanch the tomatoes in boiling water, then skin. Cut each into large wedges and trim away the pulp and seeds to leave pointed petal shapes. Set aside.

❋ Lightly beat the milk and eggs together. Stir-fry in a wok in a little lard or vegetable oil over gentle heat until thickened. Set aside, keeping warm.

❋ In another wok, stir-fry the vegetable hearts in a little oil or lard, adding a pinch of salt. Pour in 1 tablespoon of water, cover and steam until tender. Lift out and arrange on a round serving plate, placing the drumsticks between each piece of vegetable.

❋ In the centre of the platter, mound the fried egg, and then place the tomato "petals" in a lotus flower shape in the egg and sprinkle the centre of the "flower" with a little grated lemon rind.

❋ Spoon any remaining sauce over the drumsticks and serve.

45

CHICKEN ROLLS WITH SESAME SEEDS

MANDARIN DICED CHICKEN

Beijing 北京

CHICKEN ROLLS WITH SESAME SEEDS

The best chicken for this dish is a special breed of Beijing chicken that is large and strong and said to have high nutritional value. The coating of sesame seeds gives it a delightfully nutty taste.

375 g (12 oz) chicken meat, cooked
1 spring onion (shallot/scallion)
2 slices fresh (root) ginger
125 g (4 oz) canned bamboo shoots, drained
1 tablespoon rice wine or dry sherry
1 teaspoon salt
4 eggs
oil for deep-frying
60 g (2 oz) white sesame seeds

GLAZE

1 egg, beaten
2 tablespoons flour

Finely chop the chicken, spring onion, ginger and bamboo shoots, add the rice wine and salt and mix well.

Beat the eggs with a pinch of salt. Rub out a wok with an oiled cloth and pour in one-sixth of the beaten eggs. Tilt and slowly move the pan so that the egg spreads out into a thin round omelet. Fry gently on both sides. Cook the remaining egg to give six omelets.

Divide the filling between the omelets, spreading one-sixth across the centre of each. Fold 3 sides over and roll up.

Coat each roll with the pre-mixed glaze, then roll in sesame seeds.

Heat the oil and fry the rolls over moderate heat until golden brown. Drain well and serve.

Sichuan 四川

MANDARIN DICED CHICKEN

This is one of the most famous traditional Sichuan dishes and its creation is connected with an interesting anecdote.

A few years before the downfall of the Qing Dynasty (1644-1911 AD), a new governor, Ting Pao Ts'en, was assigned to Sichuan. Upon his arrival a banquet was given in his honour. The cooks created a special dish for this old mandarin using spring chicken cut into tiny pieces and flavoured with local spices. They named it Kung Pao, or Mandarin Diced Chicken after him.

Kung Pao has since become a technical term in Sichuan cooking, referring to a dish containing dried chillies and Sichuan pepper (the seed of the prickly ash tree), with a tart, hot, slightly vinegary taste.

315 g (10 oz) chicken breasts
2-3 dried red chillies
1 teaspoon Sichuan peppercorns (Fagara or Sansho)
90 g (3 oz) raw peanuts
2 spring onions (shallots/scallions)
3-4 slices fresh (root) ginger
2 cloves garlic
2 cups (500 mL/16 fl oz) oil for deep-frying

MARINADE

1 tablespoon rice wine or dry sherry
1 tablespoon superior or other light soy sauce
1/2 teaspoon salt
1 1/2 teaspoons cornflour (cornstarch)

SEASONING/SAUCE

2/3 cup (150 mL/5 fl oz) chicken stock (broth)
1 tablespoon superior or other light soy sauce
1 teaspoon sugar
1 teaspoon brown vinegar
1 1/2 teaspoons cornflour (cornstarch)

Cut the chicken into small dice, place in a dish with the marinade ingredients, mix well and leave for 20 minutes.

Chop the chillies into short lengths and lightly crush the peppercorns. Drop the peanuts into boiling water, leave for a few minutes, then drain and peel off the skins. Cut the spring onion and ginger into shreds and thinly slice the garlic.

Heat the oil in a wok to smoking point. Deep-fry the chillies and peppercorns in a frying basket or wire strainer until crisp, remove and set aside. Add the chicken to the wok and fry until it turns white and firm. Remove, then fry the peanuts until lightly coloured, lift out and drain on paper towels.

Pour off all but about 2 1/2 tablespoons of the oil, then reheat and stir-fry the spring onions, ginger and garlic briefly. Return the chicken with the chillies and peppercorns and stir-fry together briefly over high heat. Add the pre-mixed seasoning/sauce ingredients and bring to the boil. Simmer, stirring, for about 1 minute, then stir in the peanuts and serve.

SLICED CHICKEN AND SEASONAL VEGETABLES

STEAMED WHOLE LANTERN-SHAPED CHICKEN

Sichuan 四川

SLICED CHICKEN AND SEASONAL VEGETABLES

This simple dish is typical of home-style Sichuan cooking, light and delicate ingredients contrasted by a hint of hot spice.

250 g (8 oz) chicken breasts
1-3 pickled red chillies
2 spring onions (shallots/scallions)
90 g (3 oz) marrow, choko (chayote) or winter melon
2½ tablespoons oil for frying
2 teaspoons brown vinegar

SEASONING/SAUCE

1 clove garlic, crushed
½ teaspoon grated fresh (root) ginger
1 tablespoon light soy sauce
2 teaspoons rice wine or dry sherry
1 teaspoon sugar
3 tablespoons chicken stock (broth)
pinch each of salt and Sichuan pepper (Fagara or Sansho)
1 teaspoon cornflour (cornstarch)

Skin and slice the chicken very thinly, then stack the slices and cut them into fine shreds. Shred the pickled chillies and spring onions. Peel the marrow, slice thinly, then cut into matchstick pieces and set aside.

※ Heat the oil in a wok and stir-fry the chicken until it turns white, then remove and set aside. Add the chilli, spring onions and marrow sticks and stir-fry over moderate heat for about 2 minutes. Add the garlic and ginger from the seasoning/sauce ingredients and stir-fry briefly, then return the chicken and add the vinegar. Stir-fry together for 1 minute over moderate heat, then add the remaining premixed seasoning/sauce ingredients, simmer until thickened and serve.

Sichuan 四川

STEAMED WHOLE LANTERN-SHAPED CHICKEN

Lanterns are used on many occasions to symbolise happiness. This particular dish is meant to bring that happiness to the table. The chicken is bright red and looks like an elegant lantern on the plate.

The red colour is obtained from chilli powder, so the chicken is quite hot, aromatic and very tasty. Only a tender young chicken will give good results.

1 x 1¼ kg (2½ lb) chicken
1 teaspoon chilli powder
carrot slices (garnish)
lemon peel (garnish)
steamed carrot (garnish)
salted cabbage (garnish)

MARINADE/SEASONING

2 tablespoons rice wine or dry sherry
1 tablespoon grated fresh (root) ginger
1 tablespoon minced (ground) spring onion (shallot/scallion)
1½ teaspoons salt
1 teaspoon Sichuan peppercorns (Fagara or Sansho)*

Clean and wash the chicken, then wipe dry inside and out.
※ Mix the marinade/seasoning ingredients together, rub on the chicken both inside and out, and pour any remaining liquid into the cavity. Place on a rack and leave for at least 12 hours.
※ Place the chicken in a pot and cover with cold water. Remove the chicken and bring the water to the boil, then return the chicken, reduce the heat, cover and simmer gently for about 30 minutes, turning once.
※ Lift out, drain, retain the stock and put the chicken on a rack to dry, then rub the chilli powder in the skin to make it bright red. Set the rack in a wok or steamer over simmering water, cover and steam for 30 minutes.
※ In the meantime briskly boil the retained stock until reduced to about 1 cup (250 mL/8 fl oz) and adjust the seasoning.
※ When the chicken is done, add the liquid from the cavity of the chicken to the stock and simmer briskly until well reduced. Spoon over the chicken and serve.
※ The simple but effective garnishing in the above photograph comprises carrot slices carved into Chinese characters and symbols. The two lanterns are carved from lemon peel with tassels of shredded steamed carrot, and the cord is made from shreds of salted cabbage.

Dry-fry the peppercorns to bring out their full flavour, then grind to a powder.

DICED TOMATO AMIDST CHICKEN SNOW

Sichuan 四川

DICED TOMATO AMIDST CHICKEN SNOW

The chicken paste cooked according to this recipe is white and soft as snow. The chef adds contrasting taste, colour and texture with diced tomato. A dish typical of Sichuan to serve in early spring.

1 large ripe tomato
250 g (8 oz) chicken breasts
¾ cup (175 mL/6 fl oz) chicken stock
2 egg whites
¾ teaspoon salt
1 tablespoon soy bean powder or cornflour (cornstarch)
pinch of white pepper
1½ tablespoons lard

Place the tomato in a pot of boiling water, leave for eight seconds, then remove on a slotted spoon and peel. Cut the flesh into dice, discarding the seeds.

Use either two cleavers simultaneously or a food processor to pound the chicken to a smooth paste. Pull away any tough tendons. Mix with one-third of the stock, the lightly beaten egg whites, salt, soy bean powder and pepper, and stir until the mixture is smooth and creamy.

Heat the lard in a wok and stir-fry the chicken gently over moderate heat until it turns white and is cooked through. Pour in the remaining stock and simmer for 1½ minutes.

Spoon onto a serving plate, carefully stir in the diced tomato, and serve at once.

Sichuan 四川

CHICKEN SHREDS AND GARLIC CHIVES

Bright green, tender and aromatic, garlic chives are one of the vegetables of early spring. They have a subtle flavour of onion and garlic, and are often cooked with pork and chicken.

12-18 garlic chives or small spring onions (shallots/scallions)
185 g (6 oz) chicken breasts
2 tablespoons oil for frying

SEASONING

1 egg white, lightly beaten
1 tablespoon cornflour (cornstarch)
½ teaspoon salt
pinch of white pepper

CHICKEN SHREDS AND GARLIC CHIVES

SAUCE

½ cup (125 mL/4 fl oz) chicken stock (broth)
2 tablespoons rice wine or dry sherry
pinch of salt
1½ teaspoons soy bean powder or cornflour (cornstarch)

Rinse the garlic chives in cold water, shake well, then cut into 5 cm (2 in) lengths and set aside.

Slice the chicken very thinly, discarding skin and any bone fragments. Stack the slices and cut into fine shreds. Place in a dish, add the pre-mixed seasoning ingredients and set aside for 20 minutes.

Heat the oil in a wok and stir-fry the chicken over moderate heat until white. Push to one side of the pan and add the chives. Stir-fry over higher heat for about 1 minute.

Pour in the pre-mixed sauce ingredients, mix with the chicken and chives and simmer until thickened and clear, stirring occasionally, then serve.

Shanghai 上海

CHRYSANTHEMUM FIRE POT

Chrysanthemum dishes are a speciality of Chinese cuisine. Over two thousand years ago poets wrote of the beauty and edibility of the chrysanthemum flower. The great medicinal expert Le She Zhen of the Ming Dynasty (1368-1644 AD) praised chrysanthemums for their ability to brighten the eyes and relieve internal heat, and today they are still used as a medicine and served as tea.

Chrysanthemum Fire Pot is a famous dish, served in autumn and winter. The uncooked ingredients are arranged in an attractive design on plates around a stove on the table and cooked by the diners.

24 prawns (shrimps)
1 x 315 g (10 oz) carp or other meaty white fish, filleted
2 duck gizzards or duck or chicken hearts
185 g (6 oz) chicken breasts
250 g (8 oz) spinach leaves
6 eggs
oil for deep-frying
125 g (4 oz) dried bean thread vermicelli
125 g (4 oz) dried egg noodles
assorted meat*

STOCK

6 cups (1½ L/48 fl oz) chicken stock (broth)
2-3 slices fresh (root) ginger
2 spring onions (shallots/scallions)
2 teaspoons salt
½ teaspoon white pepper
1 white chrysanthemum flower

DIP

1 cup (250 mL/8 fl oz) superior or other light soy sauce
½ cup (125 mL/4 fl oz) sesame oil
1-2 tablespoons toasted white sesame seeds (optional)

Peel and de-vein the prawns, leaving the tail section intact. Thinly slice the fish, duck gizzards and chicken breasts and arrange on small plates.

❋Wash the spinach under running cold water and trim, discarding stems. In a wok, heat the oil to smoking point, then reduce the heat slightly. Deep-fry the vermicelli for a few seconds. They will expand dramatically, but should not be allowed to colour. Drain on paper towels, then place on a large serving plate. Soak the egg noodles to soften, then drain and place in a dish.

❋Combine the dip ingredients and divide between six small bowls. Beat one egg in each of six rice or soup bowls.

❋Place all the stock ingredients except the flower petals in a hotpot or large saucepan over a portable cooker in the centre of the table, and bring to the boil. When gently bubbling, pull the chrysanthemum flower apart and scatter the petals over the stock.

❋Each diner can choose the ingredients he likes, hold them in the hot stock until lightly poached, and then dip into the beaten egg and the dip before eating. Take care to use wooden or bamboo chopsticks and not plastic ones.

❋The noodles and fried vermicelli are cooked after the other ingredients have been eaten, and consumed with the rich stock at the end of the meal.

Additional plates of very thinly sliced lean pork, ham, pork liver, beef, squid or tripe can be added to the above assortment.

CHRYSANTHEMUM FIRE POT

CHICKEN BRAISED IN SOY SAUCE WITH TWO KINDS OF MEATBALLS

Guangzhou 广州

CHICKEN BRAISED IN SOY SAUCE WITH TWO KINDS OF MEATBALLS

The soy sauce used in this recipe is a special product of Guangdong's Pu Ling county and has a distinctive flavour not found in other soy sauces. It is smooth, strong and golden coloured. The meatballs are optional additions to the basic recipe, which transform it into an elegant banquet dish.

1 x 1 kg (2 lb) spring chicken
2 teaspoons cornflour (cornstarch)

SEASONING

2 tablespoons Pu-Ling or other light soy sauce
2 tablespoons rice wine or dry sherry
1 teaspoon sesame oil
1 teaspoon sugar
1 tablespoon finely chopped spring onion (shallot/scallion)
1 teaspoon grated fresh (root) ginger
1 tablespoon chopped fresh coriander

Clean the chicken, rinse with cold water, dry thoroughly inside and out and place in a dish. Mix the seasoning ingredients together and rub over the chicken, pouring the remainder into the cavity. Leave for at least 2 hours to absorb the flavours.

✹ Prepare the meatballs as described in the following recipes.

✹ Place the chicken in a heatproof dish on a rack in a wok or steamer, cover and steam over rapidly boiling water for at least 30 minutes until tender. Remove and leave to cool.

✹ Chop the chicken into serving slices, cutting straight through the bones in the Chinese style and arrange on a serving plate.

✹ Pour the sauce from the dish in which the chicken was steamed into a wok and add the cornflour mixed with a little cold water. Bring to the boil and simmer, stirring, until thickened. Pour over the chicken, arrange the meatballs on the side and serve.

PRAWN BALLS

185 g (6 oz) fresh prawn (shrimp) meat
60 g (2 oz) finely minced (ground) pork fat
salt and pepper
1 egg, well beaten
1 cup (125 g/4 oz) flour, seasoned with salt and pepper
dry breadcrumbs
oil for deep-frying

Place the prawn meat on a board and bat with the side of the cleaver until reduced to a pulp, or use a food processor. Mix to a smooth paste with the pork fat, season with salt and pepper and roll into balls. Coat lightly with the seasoned flour, dip into the beaten egg, then coat with breadcrumbs.

✹ Heat the oil in a wok to smoking point, lower the heat slightly and deep-fry the balls for about 2 minutes until cooked through and golden brown. Remove, drain well and keep warm.

DUCK GIZZARD "FLOWERS"

3 duck gizzards or duck or chicken hearts
1 tablespoon Pu-Ling or other light soy sauce
1 teaspoon sugar
salt and pepper
oil for deep-frying

Score the duck gizzards very deeply from the inside, cutting almost through them in a criss-cross pattern so that the finished gizzard has the appearance of a chrysanthemum. Cut each into several pieces. Place in a dish with the soy sauce, sugar, salt and pepper and leave for 5-6 minutes.

✹ Heat the oil in a wok to smoking point and deep-fry the duck gizzards for about 45 seconds in a frying basket until they curl up and change colour. Drain well and serve.

Shanghai 上海

ASSORTED EARTHEN POT DISH

This recipe shows a delicious way to use leftover roast chicken and duck. Combined with the typical Chinese ingredients of simmered sea cucumber, fried pig's skin and fresh bamboo shoots it has a wonderfully rich flavour.

1 cooked dried or fresh sea cucumber*
185 g (6 oz) pig's skin (from the belly or leg)
oil for deep-frying
250 g (8 oz) cooked roast chicken
250 g (8 oz) cooked roast duck
125-250 g (4-8 oz) lean cooked ham
185 g (6 oz) cooked fresh or canned bamboo shoots
12 fresh or canned straw mushrooms
2 freshwater prawns (yabbies/crayfish)
2 tablespoons Shaoxing rice wine or dry sherry
6 cups (1½ L/48 fl oz) chicken or superior stock (*see page 124*)
1¾ teaspoons salt
2 tablespoons lard

Deep-fry the pig's skin in a wok in heated oil until bubbles appear on the surface, then place in water or stock and simmer for several hours until tender.

✹ Cut the sea cucumber, pig's skin, chicken, duck, ham, bamboo shoots and mushrooms into thin slices and arrange separately in a wide shallow casserole. Sprinkle with the wine and add the stock and salt.

✹ Set the pot on a rack in a wok or steamer, cover and steam over simmering water for at least 30 minutes until the flavours are well mingled and the stock full of flavour. Add the lard and place the prawns, still in their shells, on top. Return to the steamer for another 5-10 minutes. Serve in the pot.

*To cook the sea cucumber, soak in cold water until softened, then drain, cut open and clean. Simmer in water with spring onion, ginger, salt and wine for several hours until completely tender.

ASSORTED EARTHEN POT DISH

WENCHANG CHICKEN, GUANGZHOU STYLE

SLICED CHICKEN WITH SCALLION OIL

Guangzhou 广州

WENCHANG CHICKEN, GUANGZHOU STYLE

More than forty years ago, the chef of the Guangzhou Restaurant heard that chickens reared in Wenchang County on Hainan Island were particularly plump and tender. Journeying there to investigate, he found it was indeed true, the only setback being that the bones were rather hard, making it difficult to serve the chicken in the traditional ways. After much experimenting, he perfected this recipe.

1 x 1 kg (2 lb) tender young chicken
2 teaspoons salt
6 slices salted ham
4 chicken livers
1 angled luffa, or 10 stalks kale or broccoli
1 tablespoon vegetable oil
1 teaspoon sesame oil

SAUCE

1½ cups (375 mL/12 fl oz) chicken stock (broth)
1 tablespoon light soy sauce
½ teaspoon salt
pinch of white pepper
1½ tablespoons cornflour (cornstarch)

Clean the chicken, wipe dry and rub inside and out with the salt. Set aside for 30 minutes.
🦐 Cut the ham and chicken livers into pieces about 6 x 4 cm (2½ x 1½ in).
🦐 Using a sharp knife or vegetable peeler, remove the sharp ridges of the angled luffa, but do not peel the sections in between unless they are tough. Cut into pieces the same size as the ham. Plunge into boiling water with the vegetable oil and simmer until tender, then refresh under cold water. If using broccoli or kale, cut into short lengths and boil for 3-4 minutes in lightly salted water, refresh and drain.
🦐 Oil a large heatproof plate, cut the chicken in half down the centre back and spread out on the plate. Place on a rack in a wok or steamer, steam over briskly simmering water for about 25 minutes. Brush with sesame oil and leave to cool. Pour off the liquid to use in the sauce.
🦐 Bone the chicken and cut the meat into slices. Place a slice of chicken liver on each piece of chicken and top with a piece of ham. Arrange on a heatproof plate in a chicken shape with the head, wings and drumsticks. Return to the steamer and steam until the ham and chicken livers are tender and the dish hot and moist, for about 6 minutes. Surround with the vegetables and heat through briefly in the steam.
🦐 Pour the sauce ingredients into a wok and boil until the sauce clears. Pour over the dish and serve at once.

Guangzhou 广州

SLICED CHICKEN WITH SCALLION OIL

In Guangdong this dish features frequently in family meals and feasts. It is simple to prepare and has a pleasant, distinctive flavour.

1 x 1 kg (2 lb) spring chicken
1 tablespoon grated fresh (root) ginger
1 teaspoon salt
3 tablespoons peanut oil
4 spring onions (shallots/scallions)
cucumber slices (garnish)
carrot (garnish)

Wash the chicken, drain well and dry with a paper towel. Rub thoroughly inside and out with the ginger and salt and leave for 1 hour to absorb the flavours.
🦐 Heat the peanut oil in a wok and add the roughly chopped spring onions. Fry until light brown, then remove the onions with a slotted spoon and pour the scallion oil into a dish.
🦐 In a large saucepan, boil enough water to cover the chicken, adding a pinch of salt. Put in the chicken and then reduce the heat and simmer gently for about 25 minutes. Remove the chicken and cover with cold water. This shrinks the skin and gives it a better texture.
🦐 Return the chicken to the boiling water and simmer gently for another 10-15 minutes.
🦐 Lift out and drain well. Brush with the scallion oil and leave to cool. Cut into slices and arrange on a plate with a garnish of cucumber slices and carrot.

Guangzhou 广州

DONG JIANG SALT-BAKED CHICKEN

Historical records of the area of Dong Jiang in Guangdong state that cooked chickens wrapped in tissue paper were preserved in salt mounds in local salt fields. Their golden colour and moist, delicious taste were much appreciated by businessmen and bureaucrats of the area.

In the late Qing Dynasty (1644-1911 AD) the area became the collection and distribution centre for salt merchants who often served their guests the Dong Jiang style of salt-preserved chicken. Eventually they turned to baking fresh chickens in coarse salt for immediate consumption, thus retaining the unique salty flavour, while making the chickens even more tender and tasty.

DONG JIANG SALT-BAKED CHICKEN

BONED CHICKEN WINGS WITH CRAB ROE

1 x 1½ kg (3 lb) plump young chicken
1 teaspoon salt
¼ teaspoon ground star anise
6 slices fresh (root) ginger
2 spring onions (shallots/scallions)
3-4 large sheets tissue or greaseproof paper
4-5 kg (8-10 lb) rock or coarse salt
sesame oil (optional)

DIPPING SAUCE

1 tablespoon grated fresh (root) ginger or powdered galangal
1 tablespoon table salt
3 tablespoons melted lard or vegetable oil

Clean the chicken, rinse with boiling water and hang in an airy place for several hours to allow the skin to dry.

❈ Using a sharp knife or cleaver, slash through the skin on either side of the wings and legs to allow the flavours to penetrate the meat more thoroughly. Dust the cavity with the salt mixed with the star anise and place the ginger slices and spring onions inside. Brush the chicken skin sparingly with lard to prevent the paper sticking, then wrap the chicken with the paper.

❈ In a very large wok heat the rock salt until almost smoking. Stir with a ladle, then make a large well in the centre. Put in the chicken and mound the hot salt evenly over it.

❈ Maintain a steady moderate temperature under the wok and cook for about 25 minutes, then turn the chicken and cook the other side for about 30 minutes or until cooked through. It should be slightly pink around the bones but the juices should be clear when the bird is pierced near the thigh. Remove from the salt, unwrap carefully and discard the paper.

❈ Skin and bone the chicken, then cut the meat into strips. Place the head, wings and drumsticks in position on the serving plate and pile the bones in the centre. Mound the chicken over the bones to resemble its original shape. Brush sparingly with sesame oil if desired.

❈ Divide the ginger or galangal powder between three or four small dishes and add the table salt. Cover each dish with the melted lard, stir lightly and serve with the chicken.

Guangzhou 广州

BONED CHICKEN WINGS WITH CRAB ROE

This recipe is a good example of the Chinese approach to the balance of flavour, presentation and aroma in cooking.

Chicken wings are selected as the smoothest, most tender part of the chicken, especially when deep-fried. The bones are removed to enhance the diners' pleasure, and the chicken is complemented by a bright green vegetable, the coral red of crab roe with its unique flavour

and texture, and the fresh tang of ginger and spring onions. The result is a unique dish with the colours of jade, coral and pearl.

8 chicken wings, central sections only
2 tablespoons superior or other light soy sauce
500 g (1 lb) choy sum or other Chinese green vegetable
3 small dried black mushrooms, soaked for 25 minutes
2 cloves garlic
2 slices fresh (root) ginger
5 slices canned or cooked fresh bamboo shoots
1 spring onion (shallot/scallion)
90 g (3 oz) crab roe from a female crab
oil for deep-frying

SAUCE

¾ cup (175 mL/6 fl oz) chicken stock (broth)
1 tablespoon superior or other light soy sauce
¼ teaspoon dark soy sauce
¼ teaspoon sesame oil
¼ teaspoon salt
¼ teaspoon sugar

Using a sharp knife with a long thin blade, remove the bones from the wings. Place in a dish and add the soy sauce. Rub well into the chicken and leave for 20 minutes.

❈ Trim the choy sum, cutting off the thick ends of the stems, rinse and drain well. Squeeze water from the mushrooms. Finely chop the garlic and shred the ginger. Cut the bamboo shoot slices into decorative shapes and the spring onion into 2.5 cm (1 in) diagonal slices.

❈ Heat the oil to quite hot. Place the choy sum in a wire sieve and lower into the oil. As soon as it changes colour, remove and place under cold running water, then set aside.

❈ Reheat the oil and deep-fry the chicken wings until lightly coloured, then remove and drain on a paper towel.

❈ Drain off the oil, reserving about 3 tablespoons. Stir-fry the garlic briefly. Add the mushrooms, ginger and bamboo shoots and stir-fry for 1 minute, then pour in the sauce ingredients and bring to the boil, stirring continually.

❈ Push a stalk of choy sum into the cavity of each chicken wing. Place in the sauce and simmer gently until the wings and vegetables are tender.

❈ Place the crab roe on a plate over a saucepan or wok of gently simmering water and steam until bright red and firm.

❈ Arrange the wings and vegetables on a plate and top with the roe. Serve at once.

STEAMED CHICKEN WINGS WITH FILLING

Shanghai 上海

STEAMED CHICKEN WINGS WITH FILLING

12-15 chicken wings, central sections only
75 g (2½ oz) lean ham
75 g (2½ oz) fresh or canned bamboo shoots
3 dried black mushrooms, soaked for 25 minutes
2-3 fresh Chinese long-leaf lettuces
pinch of salt
1 tablespoon vegetable oil
1 egg
oil for frying
1 tablespoon chopped ham

SAUCE

1 cup (250 mL/8 fl oz) stock (broth)*
1 tablespoon Shaoxing rice wine or dry sherry
1 teaspoon dark soy sauce
2 teaspoons superior or other light soy sauce
2 teaspoons vegetable oil
½ teaspoon salt
2 teaspoons cornflour (cornstarch)

Use a long, thin-bladed knife to remove the bones from the chicken wings.

Cut the ham, bamboo shoots and drained mushrooms into matchstick lengths and insert several of each into the cavities in the chicken wings.

Lightly oil a heatproof plate and arrange the stuffed chicken wings on it. Set on a rack in a wok or steamer, and steam, covered, over simmering water for about 30 minutes.

Cut the lettuces in halves lengthways and drop into a saucepan of boiling water to which a pinch of salt and 1 tablespoon vegetable oil has been added. Blanch for 2 minutes, then remove and drain well. Arrange around the chicken wings.

Beat the egg lightly. Heat the frying oil in a wok and stir-fry the egg, breaking it up with a fork into fine drops (or fry the egg in a thin flat sheet without stirring, and cut into fine shreds). Arrange over the chicken.

In another wok, bring the pre-mixed sauce ingredients to the boil and stir until thickened. Pour over the dish and serve at once.

*An excellent stock can be made with the water in which the mushrooms were soaked and the wing tips, removed from the chicken wings. Simmer for 20 minutes.

Sichuan 四川

SHREDDED CHICKEN AND TENDER CELERY

Celery is said to strengthen vigour, calm the nerves and release summer heat. In this dish, tender stems of celery are cooked with shredded chicken. The contrasting greenish yellow of the celery, white of the chicken and the deep red of the pickled chilli complement each other perfectly.

250 g (8 oz) young celery stems
185 g (6 oz) chicken breasts
1 egg white
1 tablespoon cornflour (cornstarch)
125 g (4 oz) lard
2 spring onions (shallots/scallions), shredded
3 slices fresh (root) ginger, shredded
1 pickled red chilli, shredded

SEASONING

2 teaspoons rice wine or dry sherry
½ teaspoon sesame oil
3 tablespoons chicken stock (broth)
½ teaspoon salt

Cut the celery into 7.5 cm (3 in) lengths. Very thinly slice the chicken breast, cut into narrow strips, place in a dish and mix with the lightly beaten egg white and cornflour.

Heat the lard in a wok and stir-fry the chicken over moderate heat until it turns white, then remove. Drain off all but 1½ tablespoons of lard and stir-fry the celery over higher heat with the spring onions, ginger and chilli until the celery begins to soften.

Return the chicken and add the pre-mixed seasoning ingredients. Stir-fry together over high heat for 1 minute, then serve at once.

SHREDDED CHICKEN AND TENDER CELERY

STEWED CHICKEN, LI KOU FU STYLE

Guangzhou 广州

STEWED CHICKEN, LI KOU FU STYLE

During the 1930s, all restaurants in Guangzhou competed with each other in creating their own chicken specialities. When the Li Kou Fu Restaurant was newly established, the owner devised this chicken dish which he named after his restaurant, and only he and his wife knew the seasoning ingredients. The distinctive flavour is now known to come mainly from the Zhu Hou soy sauce and the mellow Mei Gui Lu wine. Both are famous for their exquisite fragrance.

1 x 750 g (1½ lb) spring chicken
4 spring onions (shallots/scallions)
fresh coriander

SEASONING

⅔ cup (150 mL/5 fl oz) Zhu Hou or other dark/mushroom soy sauce
⅓ cup (75 mL/2½ fl oz) Mei Gui Lu wine (rose-scented Chinese rice wine)
2 teaspoons sugar
2 teaspoons sesame oil
pinch of salt

Clean the chicken and wipe dry. Place the spring onions in the cavity and put into a deep, small casserole. Mix the seasoning ingredients together. Pour a little into the cavity, then pour the remainder over the chicken.

Cover the pot tightly and simmer the chicken very gently until tender, for about 1¼ hours, turning once or twice. Stand the casserole in a dish of boiling water to prevent the chicken coming into direct contact with the heat and burning.

Lift out the chicken, cut into serving pieces and arrange on a plate. Pour over the sauce and garnish with fresh coriander.

STEAMED SPRING CHICKEN WITH STRAW MUSHROOMS

DICED CHICKEN STIR-FRIED WITH SESAME SAUCE

Beijing 北京

STEAMED SPRING CHICKEN WITH STRAW MUSHROOMS

12-18 dried or canned small straw mushrooms
1 x 1 kg (2 lb) spring chicken
2 spring onions (shallots/scallions)
2 slices fresh (root) ginger
2 teaspoons cornflour (cornstarch)

SEASONING

2 teaspoons rice wine or dry sherry
2 tablespoons light soy sauce
¼ teaspoon salt
1 teaspoon sugar
2 tablespoons rendered chicken fat

Cover dried straw mushrooms with lukewarm water and soak for about 30 minutes. Drain, reserving the liquid, then trim the mushrooms removing the stems. Wash the caps thoroughly in clean cold water, squeeze out and set aside.

🔆 Cut the chicken into cubes, discarding all bones. Dice the spring onions and shred the ginger.

🔆 Arrange the chicken in a heatproof dish with the mushroom caps and place the spring onion and ginger on top. Pour on the reserved mushroom water (or use the liquid from the can if using canned mushrooms). Add pre-mixed seasoning ingredients and place on a rack in a wok or steamer. Cover and steam over gently simmering water for at least 15 minutes until the chicken is tender and the dish very aromatic.

🔆 Discard the spring onion and ginger, pour the liquid into a wok and thicken with cornflour mixed with a little cold water. Simmer, stirring until the sauce clears, then pour over the dish and serve at once.

Shanghai 上海

DICED CHICKEN STIR-FRIED WITH SESAME SAUCE

This style of cooking was originally the speciality of Sichuan Province, but the chef in the Green Willow Village Restaurant in Shanghai modified the original recipe and added a local speciality – wine-pickled egg yolk.

375 g (12 oz) chicken breasts
90 g (3 oz) raw peanuts
oil for frying
2 spring onions (shallots/scallions), chopped
½ cup (125 mL/4 fl oz) chicken stock (broth)

SEASONING/SAUCE

2 tablespoons sesame seed paste (tahini)
3 tablespoons light soy sauce
1 tablespoon brown vinegar
1-3 teaspoons chilli oil or chilli sauce
1 tablespoon sugar
½ teaspoon Sichuan peppercorns (Fagara or Sansho), ground
1 teaspoon grated fresh (root) ginger
1 teaspoon crushed garlic
1 wine-pickled egg yolk, mashed

Cut the chicken into small cubes, discarding any skin and slivers of bone. Drop the peanuts into boiling water to loosen the skins, then drain and peel.

🔆 Mix the seasoning/sauce ingredients together, mix with the chicken meat and leave for 20 minutes.

🔆 Heat about 2½ tablespoons of oil in a wok and stir-fry the peanuts for about 1 minute. Add the chicken and spring onions and stir-fry over fairly high heat until the chicken is done. Pour in the stock and simmer for about 1½ minutes until absorbed.

🔆 Spoon into a serving dish and serve at once.

Guangzhou 广州

SAUTÉED CHICKEN BREASTS WITH TOMATO SAUCE

375 g (12 oz) chicken breasts
1 tablespoon Shuang Huang or other light soy sauce
2 egg whites
½ cup (60 g/2 oz) cornflour (cornstarch)
12-18 dried prawn crackers
oil for deep-frying

SEASONING/SAUCE

1 tablespoon rice wine or dry sherry
2 tablespoons tomato sauce (ketchup)
1½ tablespoons vinegar
2 tablespoons sugar
½ teaspoon salt
½ teaspoon grated fresh (root) ginger

Skin the chicken breasts and cut into thin slices, cutting diagonally across the grain to improve tenderness. Place in a dish, add the soy sauce and leave for 20 minutes.

🔆 Beat the egg whites lightly and make into a thick batter with the cornflour. Heat the oil to quite hot and fry the prawn crackers until well puffed and crisp. Drain and set aside.

🔆 Dip the chicken pieces one by one into the batter, then place in the oil. Fry, turning twice, until cooked through and golden. Remove and drain well.

SAUTÉED CHICKEN BREASTS WITH TOMATO SAUCE

Pour off the oil, reserving about 1 tablespoon. Add the sauce ingredients and bring to the boil, stirring. Put in the chicken pieces and cook gently, stirring carefully from time to time until the liquid has been absorbed.

Arrange the chicken in the centre of a serving plate, pour a little of the hot frying oil over the chicken to give it a gloss and surround with the prawn crackers.

Beijing 北京

WHITE DEW CHICKEN

250 g (8 oz) chicken breast meat, steamed
185 g (6 oz) white fish fillets
5 egg whites
2 tablespoons rendered chicken fat, melted
red capsicum (bell pepper) or carrot shreds
fresh coriander

SEASONING

½ cup (125 mL/4 fl oz) milk
2 teaspoons rice wine or dry sherry
1 teaspoon ginger juice
¾ teaspoon salt
1½ tablespoons cornflour (cornstarch)

SAUCE

¾ cup (175 mL/6 fl oz) chicken stock (broth)
½ teaspoon salt
1 teaspoon rice wine or dry sherry
1 teaspoon ginger juice
1½ teaspoons cornflour (cornstarch)

Cut the chicken into thin slices and arrange evenly in the bottom of a shallow casserole. Sprinkle lightly with a little flour.

WHITE DEW CHICKEN

STEAMED CHICKEN WITH EGG WHITE

Finely mince (grind) the fish and mix with the pre-mixed seasoning ingredients. Beat the egg whites until fluffy but not stiff and fold in with the fish and chicken fat.

Spread over the chicken slices and garnish with the shredded capsicum or carrot and the fresh coriander.

Place on a rack in a wok or steamer, cover and steam for about 18 minutes until just firm.

Mix the sauce ingredients together and boil them in another wok, stirring until the sauce thickens and clears. Pour over the dish and serve.

Shanghai 上海

STEAMED CHICKEN WITH EGG WHITE

This is a meticulously prepared dish. The three layers of ingredients are subjected to three separate steaming procedures. The lower layer consists of very thinly sliced chicken breast; the central layer of minced prawn and pork fat mixed with wine; and the upper layer of whipped egg white. When the dish is completely assembled and cooked for the second time, it is cut into diamond-shaped sections and garnished with pea leaves and ham before its final steaming.

The elegant appearance of this dish enhances its delicious flavour.

125 g (4 oz) chicken breasts
250 g (8 oz) peeled fresh prawns (shrimps)
90 g (3 oz) pork fat
2 teaspoons rice wine or dry sherry
1 teaspoon salt
1 tablespoon cornflour (cornstarch)
4 egg whites, well beaten
fresh pea or young spinach leaves (garnish)
1 slice salted ham (garnish)
1 tablespoon rendered chicken fat, melted

Very thinly slice the chicken breasts, which should be skinless and without bones, and arrange in the bottom of an oiled, 20 cm (8 in) square baking tray.

Mince (grind) the prawns and pork fat and mix with the wine, salt and cornflour. Spread this over the chicken. Place on a rack in a wok or steamer and steam, covered, over high heat for about 20 minutes until cooked through.

While the tray is still hot, pour on the beaten egg whites, cover and steam gently until the egg is just set. Remove from the steamer and leave to cool.

Cut into diamond-shaped pieces and place a double pea leaf and a tiny piece of ham, cut into the shape of a flower, on each piece. Transfer them to a flat heatproof plate, then return to the steamer for about 5 minutes until heated through. Sprinkle over the chicken fat just before serving to give the dish a gloss.

QUICK-FRIED CHICKEN CUBES IN BROWN BEAN SAUCE

CHICKEN WING AND FROG LEG TAPESTRY

Beijing 北京

QUICK-FRIED CHICKEN CUBES IN BROWN BEAN SAUCE

Brown bean sauce is a special sauce from Beijing made from soy beans, flour and salt. It is light brown, and as fine and smooth as a paste, with a sweet and salty smell. It is used for quick-frying and to season stuffings.

This well-known Shandong dish is rated as one of the best quick-fried dishes seasoned with brown bean·sauce. The sauce should adhere to the chicken pieces when cooked, and not remain in the bottom of the wok.

315 g (10 oz) chicken breast meat
1 egg white, lightly beaten
2 tablespoons cornflour (cornstarch)
125 g (4 oz) lard
1 teaspoon sesame oil

SEASONING

1 tablespoon brown bean sauce
2 teaspoons sugar
2 teaspoons rice wine or dry sherry
1 teaspoon ginger juice

Cut the chicken breast into small cubes and dip into a mixture of beaten egg white and cornflour, coating evenly.

❊ Heat the lard in a wok and quick-fry the chicken until white and almost cooked through. Remove and pour off all but 1½ tablespoons of the lard. Add the sesame oil and heat well, then fry the brown bean sauce briefly before adding the remaining seasoning ingredients. Mix well, then return the chicken and stir-fry until the seasoning ingredients coat the chicken cubes. Transfer to a serving plate and serve immediately.

Guangzhou 广州

CHICKEN WING AND FROG LEG TAPESTRY

The wings are golden yellow, the frogs' legs are pale, the ham is pink and the vegetables green. This dish is as colourful as a tapestry, hence its name.

12 chicken wings, central joint only
3 slices lean ham
12 frogs' legs
6 stems choy sum or other Chinese green vegetable
oil for deep-frying
¾ cup (175 mL/6 fl oz) chicken stock (broth)
2 teaspoons cornflour (cornstarch)

SEASONING A

1 tablespoon rice wine or dry sherry
½ teaspoon sesame oil
¼ teaspoon salt
pinch of white pepper

SEASONING B

1 tablespoon rice wine or dry sherry
2 teaspoons cornflour (cornstarch)
½ teaspoon salt
pinch of white pepper

Cut the wings in halves and use a sharp knife to remove the small bones. Cut the ham into shreds the length of the chicken pieces, and place several ham shreds in the cavity of each chicken wing. Arrange side by side in a dish, add the seasoning A ingredients and set aside for 20 minutes.

❊ Bone the frogs' legs. Cut the vegetable stems in halves and place a portion in the cavity of each frog's leg. Arrange in a heatproof dish, add the seasoning B ingredients and set aside for 20 minutes.

❊ Set the dish of chicken wings on a rack in a wok, or in a steamer, over simmering water. Cover tightly and steam for about 35 minutes until tender.

❊ Heat the oil and deep-fry the frogs' legs until golden and cooked through. Drain well.

❊ Pour the liquid from the wings into a wok, add the stock mixed with the cornflour and bring to the boil. Simmer, stirring, until the sauce clears.

❊ Pile the chicken wings in the centre of a serving plate and surround with the frogs' legs. Pour over the sauce and serve.

Beijing 北京

VELVET CHICKEN WITH SHARKS' FINS

This classic dish is often served as the first course of an elaborate ten-course dinner banquet.

60 g (2 oz) dried shredded sharks' fins
5 cups (1¼ L/40 fl oz) superior stock (*see page 124*)
315 g (10 oz) chicken breasts
3 tablespoons ice cold water
4 egg whites, well beaten
1½ tablespoons cornflour (cornstarch)
¾ teaspoon salt
2 teaspoons rice wine or dry sherry
3 cups (750 mL/24 fl oz) chicken stock (broth)
½ cup (125 mL/4 fl oz) milk
2 spring onions (shallots/scallions)
3 slices fresh (root) ginger

Prepare the sharks' fins by soaking for one hour in cold water, then bring to the boil, simmer for 10 minutes and drain. Soak again in cold water for about 30 minutes, then bring to the boil and simmer for 30 minutes. Repeat the second soaking and boiling process, then drain well and cover with the superior stock. Simmer for about 1 hour until the fins are tender.

Very finely mince (grind) the chicken, mixing in the ice cold water. Add the egg whites and cornflour and season with salt and wine.

Set aside a small portion of the sharks' fins for decoration and stir the remainder into the chicken paste. Form this mixture into lotus flower petal shapes and arrange on a bamboo rack. Place the rack in a wok and pour in the chicken stock and milk. Add the whole spring onions and the sliced ginger. Cover and simmer over very low heat until most of the stock has evaporated or been absorbed. Lift out, transfer to a serving plate and garnish with the remaining sharks' fins shreds before serving.

VELVET CHICKEN WITH SHARKS' FINS

SWEET AND SOUR CHICKEN SHREDS

Shanghai 上海

SWEET AND SOUR CHICKEN SHREDS

This is the Shanghai version of a traditional Sichuan dish. Tender chicken breasts are cut into fine shreds, stir-fried and then flavoured with a spicy, sweet and sour mixture of condiments and seasonings.

250 g (8 oz) chicken breasts, skinned
1 tablespoon Shaoxing rice wine or dry sherry
1 small egg white, lightly beaten
1 teaspoon salt
2 teaspoons cornflour (cornstarch)
2 slices fresh (root) ginger
½ red capsicum (bell pepper)
1 spring onion (shallot/scallion)
250 g (8 oz) fresh spinach leaves
oil for frying

SEASONING

1 teaspoon black bean paste
2 teaspoons chilli oil or chilli sauce
1 teaspoon sugar

Very thinly slice the chicken breasts, then cut into shreds. Place in a dish and add the wine, egg white, salt and cornflour. Mix well and leave for 20 minutes to marinate.

Shred the ginger and the trimmed capsicum. Cut the spring onion into 4 cm (2 in) lengths, then lengthways into shreds. Rinse the spinach leaves thoroughly, remove stems and drain well.

Heat 2 tablespoons of the oil in a wok and stir-fry the spinach over high heat until wilted. Transfer to a serving plate.

Add about 2 tablespoons oil to the wok and stir-fry the ginger briefly, then add the capsicum and spring onion shreds and stir-fry for about 1 minute, adding the pre-mixed seasoning ingredients. Push to one side of the pan and add the chicken shreds. Stir-fry over high heat until cooked through and white, then mix thoroughly with the capsicum, spring onion and the sauce.

Lift onto the serving plate beside the spinach and serve.

DICED QUAIL STIR-FRIED IN CHICKEN FAT

Guangzhou 广州

DICED QUAIL STIR-FRIED IN CHICKEN FAT

Wild quails breed in northeast China and migrate to the southeast in winter. A type of turtledove, they eat grains and grass seeds which gives them a plump and tender breast. Nowadays they are bred commercially all over China for their delicious meat and tiny eggs, the latter a favourite in Guangdong.

4 quails, 185 g (6 oz) each
1 tablespoon light soy sauce
1 egg white, well beaten
3 tablespoons cornflour (cornstarch)
60 g (2 oz) fresh or canned winter bamboo shoots
3 dried black mushrooms, soaked for 25 minutes
peanut oil
3 tablespoons rendered chicken fat

SEASONING/SAUCE

1 clove garlic, finely chopped
2 slices fresh (root) ginger, finely chopped
2 spring onions (shallots/scallions), finely chopped
2 teaspoons rice wine or dry sherry
1 teaspoon sugar
½ teaspoon salt
pinch of white pepper
2 teaspoons oyster sauce

Cut the heads, necks, wings and legs off the quails. Reserve one lot for the presentation of the dish, place in a bowl and marinate with the soy sauce until required.

Remove the meat from the quail carcasses and cut into very fine dice. Mix with the egg white and 2 tablespoons cornflour.

Drop the fresh bamboo shoots into a saucepan of boiling water, simmer for 2 minutes, then drain well. Drain and trim the mushrooms, then dice them and the bamboo shoots finely.

Coat the marinated quail's head, neck, wings and legs thickly with cornflour. Heat the peanut oil in a wok and deep-fry these parts until crisp and golden, then arrange on a serving plate.

Drain the wok, reheat it with the chicken fat and stir-fry the mushrooms and bamboo shoots for 1½ minutes. Push to one side and add the diced quail meat. Stir-fry until just cooked, for about 2 minutes, then add the garlic, ginger and spring onions. Stir in the bamboo shoots and mushrooms and add the remaining seasoning/sauce ingredients, tossing together over high heat until well mixed. Place the mixture on the plate with the fried head, wings and legs, then serve.

Traditionally diced quail is served sandwich-style, wrapped in fresh lettuce leaves.

FRIED GOOSE LIVERS WRAPPED IN PORK FAT NET

Shanghai 上海

FRIED GOOSE LIVERS WRAPPED IN PORK FAT NET

This delicate dish is a speciality of the Ningbo area in Zhejiang Province, where the wrap and fry method of cooking is often used. Goose livers are said to be better than those of other poultry because they are large, soft and flavourful. Wrapping the livers in pork fat net, and then frying, preserves the tasty juices of the liver.

315 g (10 oz) fresh goose or duck livers
1 piece pork fat net (caul lining)
1 small egg
½ cup (60 g/2 oz) flour
salt and pepper
2 tablespoons cornflour (cornstarch)
oil for deep-frying

SEASONING

1 tablespoon Shaoxing rice wine or dry sherry
2½ tablespoons finely chopped spring onions
    (shallots/scallions)
pepper

HOT SOY SAUCE DIP

3 tablespoons dark soy sauce
1 fresh red chilli, finely chopped

SICHUAN PEPPER-SALT DIP

3 tablespoons fine table salt
1 tablespoon Sichuan peppercorns (Fagara or Sansho)

Trim the livers and cut into slices. Place in a dish and add the seasoning ingredients, mix well and leave for 30 minutes.

Rinse the caul fat and dry well, place on a dry paper towel.

Beat the egg and flour to make a smooth batter, adding salt and pepper. Cut the caul into long wide strips and brush with the batter. Place liver mixture in a thick line down the centre and roll up in a sausage shape, tucking the ends in. Repeat with the remaining caul fat and liver.

Grease a heatproof plate and place the liver rolls on it. Set on a rack in a wok or steamer, cover and steam for about 25 minutes until cooked, remove and leave to cool.

When cool, brush the outside with the remaining batter and coat lightly with cornflour. Heat the oil in a wok and deep-fry until golden and crisp on the surface. Drain well and arrange on a serving plate.

Mix the soy sauce dip ingredients and divide between several small dishes.

To prepare the pepper-salt dip, dry-fry the peppercorns in a wok for about 1 minute, then remove and grind finely. Heat the salt in the dry wok, stirring constantly, and remove from the heat just before it begins to colour.

DICED DUCK MEAT WITH GREEN CAPSICUMS

SMOKED DUCK WITH TENDER GINGER

Beijing 北京

DICED DUCK MEAT WITH GREEN CAPSICUMS

The large, dark green capsicums which grow in and around Beijing are characterised by their thick layers of pulp. Sweet and crisp, they are especially good for frying. In this recipe they are combined with very tender duck meat. For those who like it hot, some chilli oil can be added.

375 g (12 oz) boneless duck meat, preferably from the breast
1 egg white, well beaten
2 tablespoons cornflour (cornstarch)
¾ teaspoon salt
500 g (1 lb) lard, oil or rendered duck fat for frying
1 large green capsicum (bell pepper)
2 teaspoons cornflour (cornstarch)

SEASONING

2 tablespoons light soy sauce
2 teaspoons rice wine or dry sherry
1½ teaspoons sugar
½ cup (125 mL/4 fl oz) duck or chicken stock (broth)
1 teaspoon sesame oil
pinch of salt and pepper

Cut the duck meat into small cubes and place in a dish with the egg white, cornflour and salt. Mix well and leave for 15 minutes.
Cut the capsicum in half, trim away the seed core and inner white ribs and discard the stem. Cut into squares.
Heat the oil or fat in a wok until smoking, then reduce the heat to moderate. Fry the duck for about 3 minutes until cooked through, then remove and set aside. Add the capsicum and fry until slightly coloured, remove and drain. Pour off all but 2 tablespoons of the oil, add the seasoning ingredients and bring to the boil, stirring constantly.
Return the duck and capsicum and stir together for a few moments over high heat. Thicken slightly with a thin mixture of cornflour and cold water and then serve.

Sichuan 四川

SMOKED DUCK WITH TENDER GINGER

"Before going to bed, take some radish, after getting up take some ginger" is an old Chinese saying derived from the belief that the radish aids digestion, while ginger increases the appetite.

Ginger was first brought to China from Indonesia at least two thousand years ago. Poets and herbalists have written in praise of it, and chefs have created many delicious dishes using its fine flavour.

1 complete breast of a camphor and tea smoked duck*
12 slices fresh (root) ginger
1-2 fresh red chillies
2 spring onions (shallots/scallions) or garlic chives
3 cloves garlic
2 tablespoons oil for frying
1 teaspoon brown vinegar

SEASONING

2 tablespoons light soy sauce
2 teaspoons rice vinegar
1 tablespoon hot bean paste
2½ teaspoons sugar

Do not skin the duck, but cut through the breast into thin slices, then stack several slices on top of each other and cut into narrow shreds.
Cut the ginger, chillies and spring onions or garlic chives into shreds and slice the garlic.
Heat the oil in a wok to smoking point and stir-fry the duck until crisp on the edges, remove and set aside.
Stir-fry the vegetables and garlic together for about 1½ minutes, then add the seasoning ingredients and stir-fry together for another 30 seconds.
Return the duck meat and continue to stir-fry over high heat until the ingredients are all well mixed. Stir in the brown vinegar and serve.

Duck smoked over chips of camphor wood and Chinese black tea leaves to give a strong, smoky flavour and rich deep colour.

FRIED SESAME DUCK LIVER

Beijing 北京

FRIED SESAME DUCK LIVER

Duck livers offer a good source of protein and vitamins. They are said to be good for the liver and eyes, and able to cure night blindness and anaemia. Sesame seeds, a major source of rich cooking and flavouring oil, are said to replenish strength and help muscle and brain development. Thus the combination of duck livers and sesame in this recipe makes an extremely beneficial and nutritious dish.

10 duck or chicken livers
2 teaspoons rice wine or dry sherry
1/2 teaspoon salt
1 cup (125 g/4 oz) flour
2 egg whites
3/4 cup (90 g/3 oz) white sesame seeds
peanut oil for frying

Blanch the livers in boiling water, drain well, then cut open without cutting right through, and flatten out butterfly-style. Place in a dish, season with the rice wine and salt and leave for 20 minutes.

Pour the flour into a dish and break the eggs into another, beating until frothy. Spread sesame seeds on a plate.

Coat each piece of liver with flour, then dip into the beaten egg. Dip one side of each liver into the sesame seeds, coating thickly. Heat about 2.5 cm (1 in) of oil in a wide pan or wok and gently fry the livers for about 3 minutes until golden on the surface and tender inside. Serve immediately.

Beijing 北京

BEIJING DUCK

Records of the famed Beijing duck actually date back as far as the Song Dynasty (960-1279 AD) but the dish became a favourite of the imperial kitchen only during the Ming Dynasty (1368-1644 AD). The ducks used then were the small, black-feathered ducks from the Nanjing lakes, quite different to the plump-breasted white Beijing ducks used today.

At the beginning of the fifteenth century the capital of China was moved from Nanjing to Beijing, and rice had to be transported from Nanjing to Beijing to meet the extravagant demands of the imperial court. Canals were dug to transport the rice, but much was lost in the canals, and subsequently the ducks bred in this area became extremely well fed. A new breed of Beijing duck thus emerged, and duck breeding became a prosperous business.

Beijing ducks are now artificially fed, and sixty to seventy days after hatching their weight can be as much as 3 1/2 kilograms (7 pounds). Their distinctive features are white feathers, short wings, a long back and strong healthy body, with the thin skin that is best for roasting.

There are different ways of roasting the duck, although this is not usually done at home. At the famous Quan Ju De Restaurant in Beijing the ducks are hung inside a special brick oven suspended on steel rods over the fire. Just beyond the front opening is a small platform where aromatic fruit tree wood is burnt, and its specially fragrant smoke penetrates the ducks during the cooking process.

The method used by the equally famous Bian Yi Fang Beijing Duck Restaurant does not allow the flame to touch the ducks directly. The walls of the oven are first heated to the right temperature, then the oven door is tightly closed and the ducks roasted in the heat from glowing charcoal underneath. Gas and electric ovens used in other restaurants also give excellent results. The correct temperature results in minimal loss of oil and juice, a light crisp skin and the characteristic bright colour of Beijing duck.

Regardless of the roasting method, the ducks are always given a standard pre-roasting treatment. After the ducks have been killed and plucked, air is pumped beneath the skin to make it balloon. The internal organs are removed and the cavity is washed well. The ducks are then hung on a hook and scalded with boiling water. A syrupy mixture made from diluted malt sugar is poured over the skin and the ducks are left to dry. Finally, before hanging in the oven to roast, the bodies are filled with water which boils the meat from the inside as it roasts outside. This gives the duck its famed crisp dry skin and succulent tender meat.

Beijing Duck should be eaten immediately. The duck is taken to the table and the brightly coloured skin, resembling brilliantly lacquered wood (giving it the name of lacquered duck) is quickly sliced off in squares. While diners enjoy the slivers of skin dipped into sweet bean paste and eaten with thin, soft wheat-flour pancakes, sticks of cucumber and fresh spring onion, the meat is carved and arranged on a serving plate.

The meat is the second course of Beijing Duck, and it is sometimes served with lotus leaf cakes and sesame buns instead of pancakes. The leftover bones and fragments of meat are boiled with white cabbage and winter melon to make a soup which is brought to the table towards the end of the banquet.

BONED DUCK SIMMERED WITH LEMON JUICE

Guangzhou 广州

BONED DUCK SIMMERED WITH LEMON JUICE

375 g (12 oz) boned duck meat
2 eggs, well beaten
1 cup (125 g/4 oz) cornflour (cornstarch)
3 cups (750 mL/24 fl oz) oil for deep-frying
1 teaspoon sesame oil
1 tablespoon peanut oil (optional)
sliced tomatoes, fried

SEASONING

2 tablespoons water
1 tablespoon rice wine or dry sherry
1 teaspoon grated fresh (root) ginger
2 tablespoons finely chopped spring onion (shallot/scallion)
1 teaspoon salt
⅓ teaspoon bicarbonate of soda (baking soda)

SAUCE

1½ cups (375 mL/12 fl oz) chicken or duck stock (broth)
2 tablespoons rice wine or dry sherry
3 tablespoons lemon juice
1½ tablespoons sugar

Cut the duck meat into finger-sized pieces and place in a dish. Pour on the pre-mixed seasoning ingredients and mix well, cover and leave for 1-2 hours.

Drain and pat dry. Dip each piece into the beaten egg, then coat thickly with cornflour. Heat the deep-frying oil in a wok to smoking point, then reduce the heat slightly and deep-fry the duck pieces, several at a time, until golden on both sides. Lift out, drain well and place in a clay pot or casserole.

Add the sauce ingredients and bring just to the boil, then reduce the heat and simmer, partially covered, for about 40 minutes until the duck is very tender and the liquid almost absorbed.

Sprinkle on the sesame oil and peanut oil, if used, transfer to a serving plate and surround with fried sliced tomato.

Beijing 北京

SUNFLOWER DUCK

1 x 1½ kg (3 lb) duck
16 small dried black mushrooms, soaked for 25 minutes
12 small slices Yunnan or other salty ham
¾ cup (175 mL/6 fl oz) chicken stock (broth)
1 tablespoon rendered chicken fat
1 teaspoon sugar
1 tablespoon cornflour (cornstarch)
carrot sticks, parboiled (garnish)

SEASONING

2 teaspoons rice wine or dry sherry
1 tablespoon light soy sauce
2 tablespoons finely chopped spring onion (shallot/scallion)
½ teaspoon finely chopped fresh (root) ginger
pinch of salt

Clean and dry the duck inside and out and place in a dish. Mix the seasoning ingredients together, spoon into the cavity and marinate for 1 hour, turning the duck from time to time.

Set the duck on a rack in a wok or in a steamer, cover and steam over gently simmering water for about 1 hour until tender. Three-quarters of the way through cooking the duck add the mushrooms and ham to the steamer. Remove, allow to cool, then bone and cut off 16 slices of the most tender part of the duck, breast and upper thighs. Cut off the mushroom stems and arrange the caps, together with the ham and slices of duck, skin downwards, alternately in several rows on a heatproof plate.

Mix the chicken stock, chicken fat and sugar together and pour over the dish. Steam for a further 10-12 minutes. Drain the liquid into a wok, then place a plate over the dish and upturn so that the duck meat now has the skin facing upwards.

Add the cornflour mixed with a little cold water to the liquid in the wok. Bring to the boil and pour over the dish. Arrange the carrot sticks around the dish and serve at once.

SUNFLOWER DUCK

FLAMED DUCK HEARTS

Beijing 北京

FLAMED DUCK HEARTS

It takes just three seconds to cook this dish! The marinated duck hearts are tossed into a very hot wok where the moisture from the marinade, contacting the hot fat, bursts into flames. This dramatic spectacle illustrates the versatility of the Chinese wok and the creative genius of the Chinese chef.

185 g (6 oz) duck hearts
3 tablespoons rendered duck fat
4 spring onions (shallots/scallions), shredded
8 sprigs fresh coriander

SEASONING

1 tablespoon Mao Tai wine or dry sherry
2 tablespoons light soy sauce
1 teaspoon sesame oil
1 teaspoon sugar
1/3 teaspoon salt
pinch of pepper

Cut open each heart, place cut side upwards on a cutting board and bat several times with the side of the cleaver to flatten and tenderise. Make criss-cross scores across the cut side of each heart. Place in a dish, add the pre-mixed seasoning ingredients and leave for 20 minutes to marinate.

In a large wok heat the duck fat to smoking point. Quickly drop in the hearts and allow the fat to catch fire. Stir the hearts once and remove from the wok in a strainer.

Have the shredded spring onion and fresh coriander spread over a serving plate, pile the hearts onto the plate and serve immediately.

SHREDDED DUCK MEAT WITH BEAN SPROUTS

Beijing 北京

SHREDDED DUCK MEAT WITH BEAN SPROUTS

It is an old Chinese custom to eat spring rolls filled with fresh bean sprouts at the beginning of springtime every year. This dish of shredded duck with bean sprouts is quite similar to a traditional spring-roll filling and could be used as such.

315 g (10 oz) roast duck breast meat
125 g (4 oz) fresh mung or soy bean sprouts
1 spring onion (shallot/scallion), sliced
3 slices fresh (root) ginger, shredded
2½ tablespoons oil for frying
2 teaspoons Sichuan pepper (Fagara or Sansho) oil*

SEASONING/SAUCE

½ cup (125 mL/4 fl oz) chicken or duck stock (broth)
2 teaspoons rice wine or dry sherry
1½ teaspoons brown vinegar
3 cloves garlic, finely chopped

Cut the duck into thin slices, then into fine shreds. Blanch the sprouts in boiling water for a few seconds, then drain very well and leave to cool.

❁ Place the spring onion and ginger in a wok with the frying oil and heat to smoking point, then turn off the heat and leave to stand for 5 minutes. Remove and discard the onion and ginger and reheat the oil.

❁ Mix the seasoning/sauce ingredients together.

❁ When the oil is at smoking point, very quickly put the sprouts in and stir-fry for a few seconds, then add the duck meat and stir quickly. Pour in the sauce mixture and heat through very quickly. Transfer to a serving plate and sprinkle on the Sichuan pepper oil.

Heat 2-3 tablespoons of peanut or other vegetable oil in a wok to smoking point. Add 2 teaspoons of lightly crushed Sichuan peppercorns and fry for 1 minute, then turn off the heat and leave to stand in the oil until cool. Drain off the oil and store in a jar.

Beijing 北京

DUCK WING LANTERNS

Frills made from coloured cellophane are used to decorate the bones of these crisp-fried duck wings. If the lighting on the banquet table is correct, the brightly coloured paper causes a rainbow of coloured lights.

12 duck wings, central joint only
¾ cup (90 g/3 oz) cornflour (cornstarch)
oil or rendered duck fat for deep-frying
cellophane frills

SEASONING

1 tablespoon rice wine or dry sherry
1 tablespoon light soy sauce
2 teaspoons dark soy sauce
2 teaspoons sugar
¼ teaspoon salt
pinch of white pepper
2 tablespoons finely chopped spring onion (shallot/scallion)
1 teaspoon grated fresh (root) ginger

Use a small sharp knife to cut around one end of each wing bone and push the meat along to form a ball at one end. Leave only one bone in each wing. Place in a dish, add the pre-mixed seasoning and marinate for 1 hour, turning several times.

❁ Place the duck wings on a heatproof dish on a rack in a wok or steamer, cover and steam over gently simmering water for 20-25 minutes until the wings are very tender. Remove and drain well, leave to dry for a few minutes, then coat thickly with cornflour, shaking off the excess.

❁ Heat the oil in a wok and deep-fry the wings over high heat for about 1½ minutes until the surface is crisp and well coloured. Drain well, decorate the tips of the bones with cellophane frills and serve immediately.

DUCK WING LANTERNS

Shanghai 上海

STIR-FRIED PHEASANT MEAT WITH BEAN SPROUTS

Pheasant is sometimes called wild chicken. The texture of its meat is tight and fine-grained, as well as very tender and full of flavour, its breast meat being especially delicious and firm.

Bean sprouts, picked clean of their seed pods and tapering roots, are called silver sprouts. The colour of these two ingredients together is subtle and the texture smooth and crisp.

185 g (6 oz) pheasant breast meat, skinned
1 small egg white
2 tablespoons lard
250 g (8 oz) fresh silver sprouts
pinch of salt
2 tablespoons Shaoxing rice wine or dry sherry
¾ cup (175 mL/6 fl oz) stock (broth) made from the pheasant bones
1 tablespoon cornflour (cornstarch)

Very thinly slice the breast meat, then cut into fine, even shreds. Lightly beat the egg white, mix with the pheasant meat and set aside for 20 minutes.

❁ Heat the wok, add half the lard and stir-fry the silver sprouts until softened, adding a pinch of salt. Arrange around the edge of a serving dish.

❁ Add the remaining lard and stir-fry the pheasant meat over high heat for 2-3 minutes until it changes colour and is just cooked through.

❁ Add the wine and cook briefly, then add the stock and cornflour mixed together and boil until the sauce thickens. Check the seasoning and then pile the pheasant shreds in the centre of the dish and serve at once.

SHANGHAI'S LEGENDARY WATERFRONT, THE BUND

LEONG KA TAI

上海
Shanghai

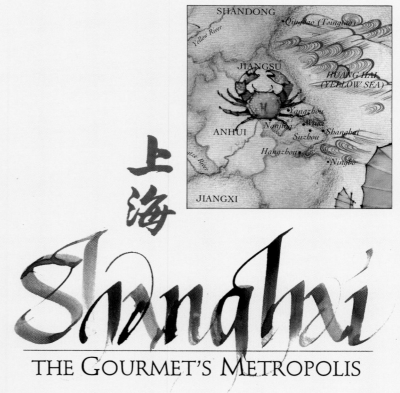

上海 Shanghai
THE GOURMET'S METROPOLIS

W HERE the mighty flood of the Yangtze River rushes 32 kilometres (20 miles) wide into the East China Sea, an astonishing maze of tributaries, creeks, rivers, lakes, ponds and marshlands twist, shimmering, between endless fields of rice and vegetables. On the river itself, and in the countless waterways stretching in all directions, nets are cast to harvest fish such as the Yangtze catfish, which grows up to 2 metres (6 feet) in length. A rich crop of freshwater carp and other table fish is raised to tender plumpness in a million ponds. At sea the sails of junks and sampans spread to the horizon as their crews await the flood tides to help carry them upriver to the biggest city in the world, where the twelve million inhabitants of Shanghai await their daily catch. To the north of the river lies the province of Jiangsu, now the richest in China, where more than sixty million people proudly refer to their lake-studded home as the Land of Fish and Rice. To the south, equally rich and proud of its culinary heritage, is Zhejiang Province which has made its own vital contribution to China's gastronomic heritage. As the Western world calls an area of bounteous plenty a Land of Milk and Honey, so to the Chinese a place where generous nature opens its heart and bestows all the good things of life is known as a Land of Fish and Rice. Hence the reason for joy in the bounteous harvest lands of the Yangtze delta.

And in the middle is the jewel, the immense industrial powerhouse of Shanghai. Sprawling around a river of its own, the Huangpu, with its endless wharves and berths and cranes and ferries, it is a city of superlatives. Shanghai works hard, and to keep its enormous workforce productive and churning out a third of China's industrial wealth, it supports a stunning range of restaurants. Shanghai is a working city and much of the eating is done on the run. The steaming hot buns stuffed with pork and vegetables are the Chinese equivalent of the American hamburger, the Australian meat pie or the British fish and chips. Crowds of thousands cram the hundreds of hot bun shops yelling orders.

THE GRAND CANAL IN WUXI, JIANGSU PROVINCE
TOM NEBBIA

But Shanghai is just one of the cities clustered in the fertile plain and studded on the waterways of the central coast of China. Historic and fabled places such as Suzhou, Wuxi, Hangzhou, Nanjing, Ningbo and a score of other cities all boast their own culinary traditions and local delicacies. And, above all, Yangzhou. Over the centuries this ancient city has given to the national table such dishes as the big, tender meatball known as Lion's Head, as well as fried rice, noodles and many others. In the gastronomic wealth of this region every city has a claim to culinary fame, every district has given some twist to the immense variety of dishes which originate in the Land of Fish and Rice. The busy port city of Ningbo bequeathed salted fish and other preserved foods designed to stock the galleys of its roaming fleet. Hangzhou gave a tradition of juicy carp from its West Lake, the famed Dragon Well tea, and of course its gentle but potent spiced rice wine. Little wonder Marco Polo called it the finest and most splendid city in the world, and for the rest of his life was to speak glowingly of its gastronomic glory. Some of Suzhou's specialities are so famous that gourmets from Shanghai will drive up for the day to sample the local crab, mandarin fish or eel. Spare ribs are said to have first been sizzled in Wuxi, and Nanjing claims the best pressed ducks in the land – producing a staggering fifty million birds every year. Zhejiang Province is proud of its vinegar, rightfully claimed to be the best in China and, therefore, the world.

The Shanghai region has one dish that is justifiably acclaimed as being supreme throughout the whole of China. No matter how ardent a culinary nationalist from another area of the country may be, he will concede that nothing can ever equal the freshwater delicacy known as Shanghai hairy crab. The very name of the creature that makes up this dish is misleading, because the most famous hairy crabs do not come from Shanghai but from Yangcheng Lake, halfway up the river to Nanjing. But it is as Shanghai hairy crab that they are known to the world, and the devotees who pay up to a hundred dollars for a 13 centimetre (5 inch) wide crab are certain that it is money well spent.

Those not familiar with the fame of this crustacean may look askance at such sums being paid for what appears to be an undistinguished creature which glares balefully out of two enraged tiny eyes and is covered with unsightly blackish fur. But come the autumn Yangcheng Lake delivers up its harvest, and gourmets flock from around the world to partake of the delicacy. Every day during the season two express trains leave Shanghai and rumble south to Hong Kong to deliver baskets of fresh crabs to specialist chefs in the city. The crabs are steamed alive and placed in front of eager diners. Those who throng to the tables to eat the delicacies are not only Chinese; in recent years Japanese gourmets have flown to Hong Kong by the hundreds merely to enjoy a meal of the small freshwater crabs.

The four-gilled carp is another freshwater delicacy. In all the world, the tiny fish, which averages about 15 centimetres (6 inches) in length, lives only in one small stretch of one river. The Chinese government permits only a limited number to be caught every year, and because the four-gilled carp is said to have numerous healthy benefits for those who eat it, the price paid for it is correspondingly high.

CHINA'S MAIN FILM-MAKING CENTRE, SHANGHAI HAS MANY CINEMAS   LEONG KA TAI

WATERWAYS DISSECT THE CENTRAL COAST OF CHINA

PAUL LAU

ONE OF SHANGHAI'S BUSY THOROUGHFARES

The lower Yangtze Valley is the area generally considered to be the centre of the Shanghai cuisine. Shanghai, however, became a city only in the nineteenth century when China was forced at gunpoint to open the series of coastal and river settlements known as Treaty Ports. So there is no such thing as a historical Shanghai cuisine. The city, as it swelled to its present immense size, first as an international settlement and then as China's premier port and industrial complex, borrowed the cuisines from the surrounding provinces. Into the conurbation on the banks of the Huangpu poured the genius of the people of Jiangsu, Zhejiang, Anhui and Hubei. They went to Shanghai to make their fortunes, and when they had made them they wanted to spend some of their money on eating their native foods. So up sprang thousands of provincial restaurants serving the countless delicacies of the central coast of China and the Yangtze Valley. Over the years these specialties merged into what is now known as the Shanghai kitchen.

What makes Shanghai food distinctive? Gourmets will tell you that it is more oily than that of other regions. Gentle, slow braising rather than vigorous stir-frying is a favoured cooking technique, making dishes more succulent and highly flavoured. To give balance a pinch of sugar is often added to meat recipes. Many dishes are spiced with the wine of Shaoxing, famous in all China and used so lavishly in dishes from this area that the gourmet will know immediately that he is being served Shanghai delicacies. China's favourite fish and seafood are found here in abundance, and the fish recipes from this eastern region are as good or better than those of any other part of the country. Meat and poultry are also excellent, the favourite choices being pork and chicken.

WELDON TRANNIES

73

The region is also famous for its beautifully arranged cold platters. The bountiful supplies of vegetables add colour and variety to the diet which, with its heavy reliance on fresh fish and fresh vegetables, is one of the healthiest and most balanced in the world.

The slower braising and stewing, and the natural delta ingredients, make for wonderful dishes in which the bounty of the canals, ponds and gardens combine their varying flavours with wine, soy and vinegar. The combination proved irresistible to one gourmet. The Manchu emperor who reigned under the name Chien Lung was noted for his love of art and literature as well as for his keen palate and enthusiastic eye for the ladies. But he was no idle dilettante. Dressing up in the clothes of a merchant, Chien Lung made it a practice to roam his realm to see for himself how people lived, to discover their problems, to uncover the mysteries of his vast domain. As a devoted student of fine food he took notes on what he ate. During one of these anonymous sojourns along the Yangtze he made lengthy notes on some of the dishes, and after his incognito trip was over he enthusiastically incorporated many of them into the menu of the imperial court.

The range is so extensive and its origins so diverse that it is impossible to generalise about the school of cooking now known as Shanghai cuisine. It has borrowed dishes, techniques, raw materials and traditions from an area as large as western Europe, with a similar population, and combined them all into the specialities of one vast metropolis. The cooking of the lower Yangtze Valley is the splendid result.

THE HUANGSHAN MOUNTAINS IN SOUTHERN ANHUI PROVINCE   PAUL LAU

THE PORT OF SHANGHAI   LEONG KA TAI

(following page) THE SERENITY OF THE HUANGSHAN MOUNTAINS, ANHUI PROVINCE

PAUL LAU

PINES CLING TO A DRAMATIC GRANITE PEAK IN
THE HUANGSHAN MOUNTAINS, ANHUI PROVINCE

PAUL LAU

海鮮
Seafood

CORMORANT FISHING, WUXI, JIANGSU PROVINCE

PAUL LAU

海鮮

Seafood

IN CHINESE the sound for fish is "yu". Pronounced with a slightly different inflexion, "yu" also means abundance. So a whole steamed or baked fish is the traditional final dish at a formal dinner banquet, signifying to the guests that although twelve courses of rich culinary delights have already been consumed, there is plenty more to eat if they are still hungry. Fish are abundant throughout China, in the enormous landlocked interior as well as along its jagged coastline. And in almost every provincial cuisine, fish, crabs, eels, frogs and other food from the rivers, streams, canals, ponds and swamps feature on the menu.

Nature has distributed seafood and freshwater fish generously but unevenly. The fishermen who ply their craft along the banks of the Black Dragon River in the frigid north of Manchuria have a life as harsh as the climate: most of the year the river is frozen. Much easier is the lot of those who sail the warm waters of the Gulf of Tonkin and the South China Sea. If they can avoid the great winds of the typhoons they can reap one of the richest marine harvests that any of the seven seas can offer. In the bitter winter the waters of the Gulf of Bohai freeze into an iceshelf reaching far out from shore. Huddled in their padded clothes, fishermen dangle hooks for their prey through holes cut in the thick ice. Life is much easier for the crab catchers of Suzhou who can sip tea on the banks of the Yangtze lakes as they await the hairy crabs – worth literally their weight in gold – to scamper up the mud to be trapped. And what an idyllic life for shore-based fishermen in the thousands of southern bays relaxing under a sunshade as they wait for their catch to swim into the big scoop nets dangling on long bamboo poles from a cliff face.

Chinese chefs have been conducting a love affair with fish for longer than history can record. It is a feeling

NETTING RED CARP   YANG SHAOMING

still ardently expressed in every province of the land. Over 3000 kilometres (2,000 miles) up the Yangtze fish is a daily feature on Yunnan menus, and fish, albeit salted, is a treasured item even in the remote Gobi. In southern coastal ports dwell the Hoklo people, bound to their junks and frail sampans with emotional ropes as strong as those that hold their nets. The Hoklo are born, grow up, marry, give birth and die on their boats. Some can trace their family back thirty generations on the water. Seldom, apart from selling their catch, do they venture ashore.

FISHING FOR CARP BY THE GIANT BUDDHA IN LESHAN, SICHUAN PROVINCE

SHUFUNOTOMO

When the catch is landed, from sea, river or pond, it must be cooked immediately. It is vital to catch the freshness of the fish in the wok – a maxim firmly held by chefs from every Chinese kitchen. A visit to a fishmarket anywhere in the country is a memorable experience: fish from sea and river swim and splash, tanks of eels squirm, live crabs, their nippers tied to safeguard the customers, crawl in huge rattan baskets, frogs hop, turtles crawl, toads squat, octopi and squid glare, and bucket after bucket holds different types of shellfish from tiny mussels to hulking whelks. If it swims, crawls, scrambles, has gills or lives in the water, it is guaranteed a pride of place on the Chinese menu. Even a creature as unattractive as the sea cucumber, difficult to define as animal or vegetable, is considered a delicacy; as indeed is seaweed, packed with vital minerals. Jellyfish is prized because it adds an unusual textural experience to a meal: chewy yet crunchy. The fin of a shark, tough as the horn of an elderly buffalo, and less attractive in appearance, is surely as indigestible an item as can be devised by nature, but it becomes the prime ingredient in one of the most famed dishes in Chinese cooking.

Shanghai 上海

PRAWNS BRAISED IN SAUCE

Prawns curl when they are cooked, but the chefs at the Dong Feng Restaurant in Shanghai wanted to create something different. The result is this dish, in which seven large prawns are aligned in swimming postures and bathed in a strong, sweet–sour sauce.

7 large fresh prawns (shrimps) in their shells, weighing
   about 750 g (1½ lb)
3 tablespoons peanut oil
1 spring onion (shallot/scallion), chopped
3 slices fresh (root) ginger, shredded

SAUCE

2 tablespoons tomato sauce (ketchup)
2 teaspoons Shaoxing rice wine or dry sherry
1 tablespoon light soy sauce
1½ teaspoons sugar
½ teaspoon brown vinegar
¼ teaspoon salt

Cut the legs and antennae from the prawns and devein. Make several cuts across and along the underside to prevent them curling during cooking.

✿ Heat the oil in a wok and stir-fry the prawns until they turn red-pink. Remove and drain off all but 1½ tablespoons of the oil.

✿ Add the spring onion and ginger and stir-fry briefly, then pour in the pre-mixed sauce ingredients. Bring to the boil and simmer for 1 minute, then return the prawns and simmer gently in the sauce until well glazed.

✿ Arrange on a serving plate with all the heads in the same direction, pour the rest of the sauce on and serve immediately.

Guangzhou 广州

FRIED PRAWN OMELET

Like all cuisines, Chinese cooking has evolved and expanded over the years until it is now among the most diverse in the world. This recipe has evolved from two traditional dishes: Smooth Fried Eggs and Oil-fried Fresh Prawns. The former is smooth and highlights the natural taste of egg; the latter is crisp yet tender, with the delicious aroma of fresh prawns.

250 g (8 oz) peeled fresh prawns (shrimps)
½ teaspoon salt
1 tablespoon cornflour (cornstarch)
2 spring onions (shallots/scallions)
6 eggs
¾ teaspoon salt
pinch of white pepper
⅓ teaspoon sesame oil
250 g (8 oz) lard

Devein the prawns and place in a dish with ½ teaspoon salt and the cornflour. Add a little cold water and rub the prawns gently to whiten them. Rinse thoroughly, then drain well.

✿ Finely chop the white parts of the spring onions. The green tops may be kept to use as a garnish. Beat the eggs with the salt, pepper and sesame oil.

✿ Heat the lard in a wok and fry the prawns quickly until they turn bright pink – about 2 minutes. Remove and drain. Pour off all but 2 tablespoons of the lard and fry the spring onions briefly, then add the eggs. Cook gently, stirring slowly, until the eggs begin to set. Add the prawns and continue to cook over gentle heat until the eggs are just firm.

✿ Transfer to a serving plate and serve at once.

SCALDED PRAWNS

Guangzhou 广州

SCALDED PRAWNS

Prawns scalded in their shells retain all their flavour and are easy to prepare. The prawns are eaten by hand, being first shelled and then dipped into an accompanying sauce of soy, chopped chillies and oil.

24 large fresh prawns (shrimps)
3-4 slices fresh (root) ginger
3 tablespoons Shuang Huang or other light soy sauce
1-2 green chillies, finely chopped
3 tablespoons oil for frying
spring onions (shallots/scallions), finely chopped

Rinse the prawns and drain. Boil a large wok or saucepan of lightly salted water and add the ginger. Place the prawns in a basket, lower into the water and simmer for about 5 minutes. When ready the shells will be bright pink and the prawns will feel firm. Test one by removing the segment of shell below the head – the meat should be white and firm, no longer transparent or gelatinous looking. Drain, pile onto a plate and garnish with spring onion.

Mix the soy sauce, chillies and oil together and pour into several dishes. Serve immediately.

Beijing 北京

TWO-COLOUR PRAWNS

8 large prawns (shrimps) in their shells
1½ tablespoons rice wine or dry sherry
1 teaspoon grated fresh (root) ginger
1 teaspoon sugar
½ teaspoon salt
oil for deep-frying
2½ tablespoons oil for frying
cornflour (cornstarch)
1 teaspoon black sesame seeds

FILLING

30 g (1 oz) pork fat, finely minced (ground)
2 water chestnuts, finely chopped
1 small egg white, lightly beaten
pinch of salt and pepper

Cut the prawns in halves, separating heads and tails. Peel the tail sections, leaving the tail shell in place. Cut deeply down the back without cutting through, then beat with the side of a cleaver to flatten. Pick out the vein. Sprinkle with ½ tablespoon of rice wine, and salt and pepper and set aside.

Cut through the head sections of the prawns just above the eyes. Cut down the centre back through the shell and pull away the vein. Place in a dish and marinate with the grated ginger, sugar, salt and 1 tablespoon of rice wine for 20 minutes.

Mix the filling ingredients together, working with your fingers until smooth and sticky. Place a portion of the filling on the cut part of each prawn tail, smoothing with a wet spoon. Sprinkle a few black sesame seeds over each, pressing in lightly, then coat lightly with cornflour.

Heat a wok with deep-frying oil and when almost at smoking-point heat another wok with about 2½ tablespoons of oil.

Place the prawn tails carefully in the deep-frying oil and leave to cook, while stir-frying the heads in the other wok. Turn the tails at least once to fry evenly. When the heads are bright red and cooked through, remove to the centre of a serving plate. Drain the fried tails and arrange around the edge of the dish then serve at once.

TWO-COLOUR PRAWNS

Beijing 北京

LANTERN PRAWNS

This dish is particularly well presented: the bright red prawns are piled in the centre of a platter with a tassle of yellow egg shreds, giving the appearance of a traditional red paper lantern trimmed with gold.

10-12 large fresh prawns (shrimps) in their shells, weighing about 1 kg (2 lb)
2½ tablespoons lard or vegetable oil
½ teaspoon sesame oil
2 eggs
1 strip dried beef (optional)
1 strip dried beancurd or carrot (optional)
1 medium cucumber (optional)

SEASONING/SAUCE

1½ tablespoons rice wine or dry sherry
2 tablespoons finely chopped spring onions (shallots/scallions)
1 teaspoon grated fresh (root) ginger
½ cup (125 mL/4 fl oz) chicken stock (broth)
½ teaspoon salt
1½ teaspoons sugar
pinch of white pepper

Cut off the tips of the prawn heads, then cut along the centre back through the shells and remove the intestinal vein. Rinse the prawns under cold running water, then dry well.

❋ Heat the lard in a wok and stir-fry the prawns for about 3 minutes, until they are pink and almost cooked through.

❋ Add the wine and cook for a few seconds before adding the remaining pre-mixed seasoning/sauce ingredients. Simmer until the prawns are coated with a rich red glaze, then pile them onto a serving plate with their heads pointing towards the top of the plate.

❋ Rinse the wok and oil it very lightly. Beat the eggs together and pour half of the batter into the wok. Tilt the pan until the egg spreads into a thin and very wide omelet. When firm on the underside, turn over and cook the other side, then remove from the pan. Cook the other omelet and cool before rolling them up and cutting into shreds to form the tassle of the lantern.

❋ Arrange the dried beef like the branches of a pine tree the lantern is hanging in, and very thinly slice and shape the cucumber to resemble its leaves. Form a handle for the lantern from the beancurd strip or carve a carrot in a chain shape. The decorations should be prepared before cooking the dish so that it can be served piping hot.

❋ Sprinkle the sesame oil over the prawns immediately before serving.

SCALDED PRAWN SLICES

Shanghai 上海

SCALDED PRAWN SLICES

500 g (1 lb) fresh prawns (shrimps) in their shells
½ teaspoon salt
2 tablespoons cornflour (cornstarch)
1 egg white, well beaten
1½ tablespoons lard
2 spring onions (shallots/scallions), white part only, chopped
2 slices fresh young (root) ginger, shredded
2 teaspoons rice wine or dry sherry
2 tablespoons chicken stock (broth)

Peel and devein the prawns. Cut in halves lengthways, then cut each prawn into several pieces. Rinse well in cold water, rubbing with a little cornflour and salt to whiten them and remove the fishy smell. Drain and place in a dish with the salt, cornflour and egg white, mixing well.

❀ Heat a wok, add the lard and stir-fry the spring onion and ginger until softened, then add the rice wine and stock and bring to the boil. Remove from the heat.

❀ Boil a saucepan of water, slide in the prawns to cook for about 40 seconds, just until they change colour. Lift out and drain well, stir in the wok with the spring onions and ginger, spoon onto a serving plate and serve immediately.

Shanghai 上海

PRAWNS SERVED IN TWO WAYS

1½ kg (3 lb) fresh prawns (shrimps) in their shells
4 cups (1 L/32 fl oz) oil for deep-frying
¾ cup (90 g/3 oz) cornflour (cornstarch)
2 spring onions (shallots/scallions), chopped
2 slices fresh (root) ginger, shredded
90 g (3 oz) thin rice noodles

SEASONING

1 tablespoon rice wine or dry sherry
1 teaspoon ginger juice
½ teaspoon salt
pinch of white pepper

SAUCE

2 teaspoons rice wine or dry sherry
2 teaspoons light soy sauce
2 teaspoons white vinegar
2 tablespoons tomato sauce (ketchup)
1 tablespoon sugar
pinch of salt
2 tablespoons chicken stock (broth)
2 teaspoons cornflour (cornstarch)

Peel and devein the prawns. Place two-thirds of the prawns in a dish and add the pre-mixed seasoning ingredients. Heat the oil in a wok. Coat the seasoned prawns with cornflour and deep-fry in the oil until pink and just cooked through. Remove, drain well and keep warm.

❀ Divide the noodles into six even portions and cook separately. Spread each in a small frying basket or perforated ladle, top with another basket or ladle and fry in the oil until crisp and golden. Remove the "nests" and set aside.

❀ Drain the wok, retaining about 1½ tablespoons of the oil and stir-fry the spring onions and ginger. Remove and mix with the stir-fried prawns.

❀ Add the uncooked prawns to the wok and stir-fry until they change colour, then add the pre-mixed sauce ingredients and simmer until the sauce thickens and clears.

❀ Pile the stir-fried prawns in the centre of a large serving platter and surround with the "nests". Fill each nest with a portion of the prawns in sauce and serve at once.

PRAWNS SERVED IN TWO WAYS

PRAWNS WITH RAPE HEARTS

Beijing 北京

PRAWNS WITH RAPE HEARTS

500 g (1 lb) fresh prawns (shrimps) in their shells
1 egg white, well beaten
2 tablespoons cornflour (cornstarch)
¼ teaspoon bicarbonate of soda (baking soda)
¾ teaspoon salt
pinch of white pepper
2 spring onions (shallots/scallions), white parts only
8-10 young rape hearts or other fresh Chinese vegetable
2 tablespoons lard
2 thin slices fresh (root) ginger, shredded

SAUCE

½ cup (125 mL/4 fl oz) chicken stock (broth)
1 teaspoon rice wine or dry sherry
¾ teaspoon sugar
pinch of salt and pepper
¼ teaspoon sesame oil
1½ teaspoons cornflour (cornstarch)

Peel and devein the prawns, rinse thoroughly in cold water and drain well. Place in a dish with the egg white, cornflour, bicarbonate of soda, salt and pepper. Mix well and leave for 20 minutes.

Shred the spring onion and set aside. Trim and rinse the vegetables. Heat half the lard in a wok and put in the drained vegetables to stir-fry for 2 minutes over moderate heat. Splash in 2 tablespoons of cold water, cover and cook until the vegetables are tender and the liquid absorbed. Remove and set aside.

Heat the remaining lard in the wok and stir-fry the prawns over high heat, stirring briskly until they turn white. Push to one side of the pan, add the spring onion and ginger and fry for a few moments, then pour in the pre-mixed sauce ingredients and bring to the boil until the sauce thickens. Add the vegetables, heat through, then transfer to a serving plate.

Beijing 北京

ZHUA CHAO YU
FRIED PRAWNS

375 g (12 oz) fresh prawns (shrimps) in their shells
¾ cup (90 g/3 oz) cornflour (cornstarch)
oil, preferably peanut oil, for deep-frying

SAUCE

1 spring onion (shallot/scallion), white part only
3 slices fresh (root) ginger
2 tablespoons lard
1 tablespoon light soy sauce
1 teaspoon rice wine or dry sherry
1 teaspoon sugar
2 teaspoons brown vinegar
pinch each of salt and pepper

Peel and devein the prawns. Rinse thoroughly and dry on paper towels. Mix the cornflour with water to make a thin paste. Coat the prawns with the paste, then deep-fry in a wok with the hot peanut oil for about 1½ minutes until cooked through and golden on the surface. Drain well.

Finely chop the spring onion and ginger and stir-fry in the lard in another wok for about 45 seconds. Add the pre-mixed remaining sauce ingredients and bring to the boil. Add the prawns, turn carefully in the sauce until it has been completely absorbed and serve.

ZHUA CHAO YU FRIED PRAWNS

YUNLUO PRAWNS

Beijing 北京

YUNLUO PRAWNS

This dish of large golden prawns with their prominent red tails "swimming" through a cloud of white vermicelli makes an attractive appetiser or main course.

375 g (12 oz) fresh prawns (shrimps)
4 egg whites
1¼ tablespoons flour
2 tablespoons cornflour (cornstarch)
oil for deep-frying
45 g (1½ oz) rice vermicelli
fresh coriander or parsley (garnish)
slivers of coloured pickled radish (garnish)

SEASONING

2 teaspoons rice wine or dry sherry
½ teaspoon salt
large pinch of white pepper

Peel and devein the prawns, then rinse under running cold water and drain well. Dry on paper towels, then mix in a dish with the seasoning ingredients and leave for 10 minutes.
❋ Beat the egg whites until frothy, mix in the flour and cornflour. Do not overstir, but leave the batter slightly lumpy.
❋ Heat the oil in a wok to smoking point, then reduce the heat slightly and put in the vermicelli. They will immediately expand and turn white. Turn and cook the other side briefly without allowing to colour. Lift out and drain well, then place on a serving plate and break up lightly.
❋ Dip the prawns into the batter and deep-fry them in a wok for about 1¼ minutes until the surface is golden. Remove from the oil and leave for 5 minutes, then reheat the oil to very hot and deep-fry the prawns briefly for a second time to make the batter very crisp. Drain and arrange over the vermicelli, adding fresh coriander or parsley and slivers of coloured pickled radish to garnish.

Beijing 北京

PHOENIX-TAILED PRAWNS

In Chinese legend the phoenix is portrayed as a five-coloured creature with the head of a chicken, neck of a snake, chin of a swallow, back of a turtle and the tail of a fish. It signifies dignity and good luck.

The following dish received its name because the tails of the prawns bear some resemblance to the flared tail of the phoenix.

8 large fresh prawns (shrimps)
½ teaspoon salt
2 egg whites
½ cup (60 g/2 oz) cornflour (cornstarch)
oil for deep-frying

SAUCE

4 tomatoes
1 teaspoon sugar
1 teaspoon sesame oil
½ teaspoon salt

Peel and devein the prawns, leaving the tails in place. Rinse in cold water and dry well. Place the cut side down on a cutting board and beat with the side of a cleaver to flatten. Sprinkle with the salt.
❋ Beat the egg whites until stiff and fold in the cornflour to make a batter. Add a few drops of water if necessary.
❋ Heat the deep-frying oil in a wok to smoking point, then lower the heat slightly. Coat each prawn thickly with the batter and deep-fry, in batches of four, for about 1½ minutes each, then remove and drain well.
❋ Drop the tomatoes into boiling water, remove after about 8 seconds and peel, discarding the soft centres and seeds. Finely dice the flesh and stir-fry in another wok with the sugar, sesame oil and salt until tender.
❋ Reheat the deep-frying oil and return all of the prawns to fry briefly for a second time to make the batter very crisp. Drain and arrange in a circle on a serving plate with the tomato sauce placed in the centre.

PHOENIX-TAILED PRAWNS

STIR-FRIED PRAWNS WITH LONGJING TEA

Shanghai 上海

STIR-FRIED PRAWNS WITH LONGJING TEA

Longjing tea is named after the Dragon Well, China's famous tea growing region. After picking, the leaves are processed until they are neat and smooth, flat as a sparrow's tongue and as green as an orchid's stem. The tea's four famous qualities are its green colour, fragrant lingering aroma, sweet taste and pleasant appearance.

Prawns of the highest grade must be used for this dish. They are first stir-fried and then covered with the green tea leaves taken from a pot of freshly brewed Longjing tea before serving.

2 tablespoons Longjing or other green tea leaves
1 kg (2 lb) fresh prawns (shrimps) in their shells
1 tablespoon Shaoxing rice wine or dry sherry
¾ teaspoon salt
1 egg white, well beaten
1 tablespoon cornflour (cornstarch)
2 tablespoons lard

Brew the tea leaves with 1½ cups (375 mL/12 fl oz) of boiling water, cover and set aside.

Peel and devein the prawns, rinse under cold running water and rub with a little salt and cornflour to make them very white and remove the fishy smell.

Place in a dish and season with the wine and salt, then mix in the egg white and cornflour and set aside for a few minutes.

Heat the wok over high heat and add the lard. Stir-fry the prawns quickly until cooked through and lightly pink in colour, then remove and set aside.

Rinse the wok and return to the heat. Return the prawns and pour in half a cup (125 mL/4 fl oz) of the tea, plus a spoonful of the brewed leaves. Heat through briefly, mix well and serve.

TOMATO PRAWN CAKES

Beijing 北京

TOMATO PRAWN CAKES

500 g (1 lb) fresh prawns (shrimps)
2 egg whites
1 tablespoon cornflour (cornstarch)
1 teaspoon ginger juice
oil for deep-frying

SWEET AND SOUR SAUCE

½ cup (125 mL/4 fl oz) chicken stock (broth)
3 tablespoons tomato sauce (ketchup)
4 tablespoons vinegar
2 tablespoons rice wine or dry sherry
½ cup (125 g/4 oz) sugar
¾ teaspoon salt
1 tablespoon cornflour (cornstarch)

Peel and devein the prawns. Rinse in cold water, drain and pat dry with paper towels. Beat to a pulp with the side of a cleaver or use a food processor.

❄ Beat the egg whites until frothy and add the cornflour and ginger juice. Mix with the prawns and stir the mixture in one direction only until thoroughly amalgamated.

❄ Heat the oil in a wok, form spoonfuls of the prawn mixture into coin-shaped pieces and deep-fry over moderate heat until golden. Remove, place in a strainer and drain well.

❄ In another wok or a saucepan, mix the sauce ingredients and bring to the boil, stirring constantly until it thickens, then simmer for another minute.

❄ Arrange the prawn cakes on a plate and pour the sauce over them before serving.

Guangzhou 广州

DEEP-FRIED SNOW-WHITE PRAWNS

250 g (8 oz) peeled fresh prawns (shrimps)
2 tablespoons cornflour (cornstarch)
½ teaspoon salt
2 cups (500 mL/16 fl oz) milk
6 egg whites
1 slice lean ham, very finely diced
2 tablespoons lard
vegetable flowers and cucumber fans (garnish)

SEASONING

½ teaspoon sesame oil
1 teaspoon salt
pinch of white pepper

DEEP-FRIED SNOW-WHITE PRAWNS

Devein the prawns and rub with half the cornflour and the salt, then rinse under cold running water. This helps to whiten the prawns and remove any fishy taste.

❄ Pour the milk into a mixing bowl, add the lightly beaten egg whites and the ham. Add the seasoning ingredients and mix well.

❄ Heat the lard in a wok over moderate heat. Fry the prawns gently until they just colour, then remove with a slotted spoon and set aside.

❄ Pour the milk batter into the wok and cook gently, stirring until it begins to firm up. Return the prawns and continue to cook, stirring gently, until the milk batter is cooked through and the prawns are tender.

❄ Transfer to a serving plate and garnish with brightly dyed vegetable flowers and cucumber fans. The finished dish is said to resemble "treasures buried beneath the snow".

Guangzhou 广州

STRAW MUSHROOMS WITH PRAWN FILLING TOPPED WITH CRAB ROE

15 fresh or canned straw mushrooms
90 g (3 oz) fresh prawn (shrimp) meat
90 g (3 oz) white fish fillets
½ egg white
2 teaspoons rice wine or dry sherry
½ teaspoon salt
pinch of pepper
4 fresh crab pincers*

SAUCE

125 g (4 oz) fresh crab roe
vegetable oil
½ cup (125 mL/4 fl oz) fish stock (broth)
2 teaspoons cornflour (cornstarch)
salt and white pepper
sesame oil

Rinse the fresh mushrooms after trimming the bases off, leaving only the darker rounded tops. Pound the prawn meat and fish on a board with the flat side of a cleaver until thick and pastelike, then add the egg white, wine, salt and pepper, mixing well with the fingers.

❄ Use a wet spoon to mound a portion of the filling over the cut side of each mushroom, smoothing the top. Stand the mushrooms on a heatproof plate and set on a rack in a wok, or in a steamer, over simmering water. Cover and steam for about 7 minutes if using canned mushrooms, 8-10 minutes if the mushrooms are fresh. (Canned mushrooms may be smaller than the fresh variety. If so, simply cut from the top almost through to the bottom, spread open and stuff the slit with the filling.)

※ In a wok, sauté the crab roe in very little vegetable oil for 20-30 seconds, then add the remaining sauce ingredients, mixed together. Simmer, stirring, until the sauce thickens and the roe is brightly coloured and firm.

※ Simmer the crab pincers in boiling, lightly salted water for about 5 minutes, then remove, crack the shells and extract the meat.

※ Transfer the mushrooms to a serving plate, arrange the crab pincer meat around the edge and pour over the sauce.

Fresh crab meat can be substituted, or the pincers may be omitted.

STRAW MUSHROOMS WITH PRAWN FILLING TOPPED WITH CRAB ROE

Sichuan 四川

JADEITE PRAWNS

This delicately textured and subtly flavoured dish is often served at banquets. The jadeite refers to the bright green peas dotted amongst the pearl white of the prawns.

250 g (8 oz) fresh peeled prawns (shrimps)
2 egg whites, lightly beaten
1 tablespoon soy bean powder or cornflour (cornstarch)
pinch of salt
3 tablespoons oil for frying
½ cup (60 g/2 oz) frozen peas, or parboiled fresh peas
1 spring onion (shallot/scallion), finely chopped
1 pickled red chilli, finely chopped

SAUCE

1 cup (250 mL/8 fl oz) chicken or fish stock (broth)
1 teaspoon rice wine or dry sherry
¾ teaspoon salt
pinch of white pepper
1 tablespoon cornflour (cornstarch)

Devein the prawns. Rinse in cold running water after rubbing with a little cornflour and salt. Dry on paper towels and place in a dish, adding the egg whites, soy bean powder or cornflour and the pinch of salt. Mix well and leave for 20 minutes.

※ Heat the oil in a wok and stir-fry the prawns over high heat until cooked through, then remove. Add the peas, spring onion and chilli to the wok and stir-fry for 1 minute, then add the sauce ingredients, except the cornflour and a little of the stock. Cover and simmer until the peas are tender, then return the prawns.

※ Mix the cornflour with the retained stock, pour into the sauce and simmer, stirring, until thickened and clear, then serve at once.

JADEITE PRAWNS

Guangzhou 广州

CRISPY CRAB PINCERS

River crabs are caught throughout the year, but in greatest quantity during autumn, the season of orange fragrance and blooming chrysanthemums. Some are found in the rivers flowing towards the sea, but they lay their eggs only in shallow water near the river mouths. Fu Zuan of the Song Dynasty (960-1127 AD) described their reproductive pattern and noted that during the change of seasons from autumn to winter, the crabs follow the river currents and swim to the sea. Hence if a net is cast during this period, you are sure of a catch.

The chef of the Ban Xi Restaurant removes the hard shell from the foremost section of the crab pincer, extracts the meat in one piece and supplements it with prawn and pork meat before returning it to the shell to be steamed. Alternatively, the tip of the pincer can be covered with a ball of prawn and pork meat, as in this recipe. The mock crab claw is then coated with a light crisp batter and deep-fried.

The very large oysters gathered along the coast of this region are also cooked in this way.

12 crab pincers
315 g (10 oz) fresh prawn (shrimp) meat
75 g (2½ oz) fatty pork
1 teaspoon salt
pinch of white pepper
pinch of sugar
cornflour (cornstarch)
oil for deep-frying
light soy sauce or spiced salt dip

CRISP BATTER

1 cup (125 g/4 oz) flour
1 teaspoon baking powder
⅓ cup (45 g/1½ oz) cornflour (cornstarch)
2 large egg whites

Break away the main part of the crab pincer shell, leaving just the points attached to the meat.

✱ Place the prawns on a cutting board and crush to a smooth paste with the flat side of a cleaver, or in a food processor. Finely mince (grind) the pork until smooth and sticky and mix with the prawn, adding the salt, pepper and sugar.

✱ Divide the mixture into 12 equal portions. Dust the crab claws lightly with cornflour and mould a portion of the prawn and pork mixture around each, forming a ball shape. Coat lightly with cornflour and set aside.

✱ Sift the flour and baking powder together and add the cornflour. Beat the egg whites lightly and fold into the batter, adding enough cold water to give a coating consistency.

✱ Heat the oil in a large wok. Dip the crab claws into the batter, holding onto the pincers so that they remain uncoated. Deep-fry over moderate to high heat, turning several times, until golden and crisp – about 5 minutes.

✱ Remove, drain well and arrange on a napkin on a serving plate. Serve with soy sauce or spiced salt dip (a mixture of ground Sichuan pepper, or Chinese five spices, and salt).

Beijing 北京

SUANSHAZI CRABS

6 female hairy river crabs, or small mud crabs
½ cup (125 mL/4 fl oz) rice wine or dry sherry
¼ small green capsicum (bell pepper)
¼ small red capsicum (bell pepper)
5 cm (2 in) piece giant white radish
6-8 slices young fresh (root) ginger

SAUCE

½ cup (125 mL/4 fl oz) chicken stock (broth)
2 tablespoons rendered chicken fat
½ teaspoon salt
2-3 teaspoons red vinegar
1 tablespoon sugar
2 teaspoons cornflour (cornstarch)

Rinse the crabs well in cold water and remove the undershell. Discard the inedible parts, cut the bodies in halves then put the halves back together, placing them in a wide, heatproof dish. Sprinkle on the rice wine and set the dish on a rack in a wok or in a steamer, cover and steam for 15 minutes. Transfer to a serving plate.

✱ Cut the capsicum, radish and ginger into fine shreds. Simmer the radish briefly in the stock for the sauce, then arrange the shredded vegetables in groups over the crabs.

✱ Bring the stock and remaining pre-mixed sauce ingredients to the boil, stirring until it thickens and clears. Pour over the crabs and serve hot.

CRISPY CRAB PINCERS

STIR-FRIED CRABS AND EGG

Shanghai 上海

STIR-FRIED CRABS AND EGG

The green crab differs in shape and taste from other common crabs found in clear water, their shell being rhombus shaped and their meat very tender. The green crabs from Xiangshan, Zhejiang Province, are known for their full, rich meat.

This dish, combining green crabs with beaten egg, is a traditional meal from Xiangshan and was introduced to Shanghai by the cooks in the Ningbo Restaurant.

4 medium-sized green crabs, or sand crabs
1 cup (125 g/4 oz) cornflour (cornstarch)
1/3 cup (75 mL/2 1/2 fl oz) oil for frying
3 spring onions (shallots/scallions), sliced
5 slices fresh (root) ginger
1 tablespoon Shaoxing rice wine or dry sherry
1 teaspoon salt
3 large eggs, well beaten
1 tablespoon lard, melted

Kill the crabs by piercing them through the head and into the stomach with a sharpened chopstick or bamboo stick. Wash well in cold water, cut off the tips of the claws and discard. Remove the pincers and crack the shells with the back of a cleaver. Pull the crab shells away from the bodies, remove the inedible parts and chop each body into quarters. Then coat with cornflour.

✹ Heat the wok over high heat and put in the oil. Stir-fry the crab for about 2 minutes, add the spring onion and ginger and continue stir-frying for another 2-3 minutes until the crabs are bright red and cooked through.

✹ Pour off most of the oil and add the rice wine and salt, then pour in the beaten egg and cook gently, stirring only occasionally until the egg is just set. Pour on the lard and serve.

Shanghai 上海

STEAMED HAIRY CRABS

Freshwater crab is a highly regarded delicacy in China. In all the coastal areas, from Liaoning Province in the north to Guangdong Province in the south, the rivers and lakes yield freshwater crabs, although the best by far come from the Shanghai region. Because the Shanghai lakes are inhabited by millions of minute organisms, the crabs harvested in them are fat and delicious.

The female crab is considered to be at its best during the ninth lunar month when it is full of roe; the male's peak season is during the tenth lunar month. The most delicate part of the crab is the roe, and the most tender part is the flesh inside the two front claws. Crab tastes best when steamed alive. The Chinese of ancient times loved to nibble on chrysanthemum flowers while eating crabs.

As it is cold in nature, crab is said to be bad for the health if too much is eaten. People with weak stomachs should be particularly careful not to overindulge themselves.

The Shanghai hairy crab is an expensive delicacy which should be served with shreds of young tender ginger, a dip of red vinegar and a glass of wine.

6 Shanghai freshwater hairy crabs, or small mud crabs
2 spring onions (shallots/scallions)
fresh (root) ginger
red vinegar

Wash the crabs thoroughly, then tie the claws and legs together with string before steaming. This prevents them struggling during cooking, releasing their roe and juices and making them dry and tasteless. Place the crabs upside down on a bamboo rack in a wok or in a steamer and put the spring onion and several slices of ginger on top. Cover and steam for about 8 minutes until the crabs are cooked through. Untie before serving.

STEAMED HAIRY CRABS

Beijing 北京

CRABS WITH CHRYSANTHEMUM

6-8 fresh Shanghai river crabs, or small mud crabs
1 large chrysanthemum blossom (garnish)

SEASONING

1 tablespoon finely chopped spring onion (shallot/scallion)
1/2 teaspoon finely chopped fresh (root) ginger
1 teaspoon rice wine or dry sherry
1 1/2 teaspoons red vinegar
1 teaspoon sugar
3/4 teaspoon salt

Wash the crabs, open them from the underside and remove the inedible parts. Take out as much meat as possible without breaking the shell. Mix the meat with the seasoning ingredients, fill the shells with the mixture and tie with string to prevent the filling escaping during cooking.

✹ Set on a rack in a wok or in a steamer, cover and steam for about 15 minutes, then arrange in a circle on a serving plate and garnish with a single large chrysanthemum blossom.

Shanghai 上海

FRIED AND BRAISED RIVER CRABS

River crabs captured in June are full of roe which is therefore called June gold. The shell is bright red after cooking and the sauce prepared according to this recipe is thick and golden, while the crabmeat remains tender and tasty. Only the choicest live crabs should be used for this dish.

3-4 x 250 g (8 oz) freshwater crabs
3 tablespoons tapioca flour or cornflour (cornstarch)
250 g (8 oz) lard
1 tablespoon finely chopped spring onion (shallot/scallion)
2 teaspoons grated fresh (root) ginger

SEASONING/SAUCE

1 tablespoon rice wine or dry sherry
2 tablespoons superior or other light soy sauce
½ cup (125 mL/4 fl oz) chicken or fish stock (broth)
¼ teaspoon salt
1½ teaspoons sugar
1 teaspoon cornflour (cornstarch)

Clean the crabs thoroughly to remove mud and sand, then halve each crab, cutting straight through the centre of the shell from head to rear. Remove part of the soft undershell and scrape out the inedible parts. Use a cleaver to cut off the tips of the claws.

🦀 Dip the cut edges of the crab into the tapioca flour, coating thickly.

🦀 Heat the lard in a large wok and stir-fry the crabs until they turn bright red. Add the spring onion and ginger and stir-fry briefly, then pour in the pre-mixed seasoning/sauce ingredients, except the cornflour. Cover and braise over moderate heat for about 8 minutes until the crabs are completely tender. The pan should be tightly covered during braising so that the crab is steamed and braised at the same time and the cooking liquid is not reduced. If it begins to dry up, add a little extra stock or water.

🦀 Mix the cornflour with a little cold water, stir into the sauce and boil gently until the sauce clears, then serve at once.

Beijing 北京

ABALONE SLICES WITH DUCK MEAT

Connoisseurs of Chinese cooking are traditionally rather partial to abalone, an expensive mollusc. In this recipe the duck meat is used as a filling between two slices of abalone, and the sandwich is topped with green peas. It is then steamed to perfection.

1 x 425 g (13½ oz) can of abalone
250 g (8 oz) duck breast meat
8 water chestnuts
2 spring onions (shallots/scallions), white parts only
2 slices fresh (root) ginger
1½ teaspoons rice wine or dry sherry
½ teaspoon salt
½ teaspoon sesame oil
1 tablespoon green peas

SAUCE

¾ cup (175 mL/6 fl oz) duck stock (broth)
1½ tablespoons rendered duck fat
2 teaspoons rice wine or dry sherry
¾ teaspoon salt
1 tablespoon cornflour (cornstarch)

Drain the abalone and cut each piece into thin horizontal slices, discarding the frilly outer edges.

Very finely mince (grind) the duck meat with the water chestnuts, spring onions and ginger. Add the rice wine, salt and sesame oil and mix to a smooth paste.

Spread half of the abalone slices with the duck paste and top with the remaining abalone slices, pressing them gently together. Arrange on a wide, heatproof plate and place on a rack in a wok or in a steamer, cover and steam for about 20 minutes over gently simmering water.

Bring the sauce ingredients to the boil, omitting the cornflour, add the peas and simmer until tender. Mix the cornflour with a little cold water and stir into the sauce. Simmer until thickened, then remove the abalone slices from the steamer and drain the plate.

Pour on the sauce and serve at once.

RAZOR CLAMS BOILED WITH SALT

Shanghai 上海

RAZOR CLAMS BOILED WITH SALT

20 razor clams in their shells
1 cup (250 mL/8 fl oz) water
1 teaspoon salt
1 spring onion (shallot/scallion), roughly chopped
2 slices fresh (root) ginger, chopped
1 tablespoon rice wine or dry sherry
2 tablespoons vinegar
curls of spring onion or sprigs of fresh coriander (garnish)

Wash the clams thoroughly with cold water, then put them in a pot of lightly salted water for several hours so they will empty the contents of their intestines. Wash thoroughly in cold water again and cut loose the black tendon on the back of each clam.

In a wok, bring the water to boil, adding salt, onion, ginger and wine. Put in the clams, cover and shake the pan over high heat until the shells open, then remove immediately from the heat. Do not overcook or they will become tough. Use a slotted spoon to transfer them to a serving plate.

Boil up the cooking liquid, add the vinegar and spoon over the clams. Decorate the dish with curls of spring onion or fresh coriander and serve.

ABALONE SLICES WITH DUCK MEAT

BOILED CLAMS WITH SOY SAUCE AND SESAME OIL

Shanghai 上海

BOILED CLAMS WITH SOY SAUCE AND SESAME OIL

625 g (1¼ lb) clams in their shells
1 teaspoon salt
2 tablespoons finely chopped fresh (root) ginger
2 tablespoons finely chopped chives or spring onions (shallots/scallions)

DIP

3 tablespoons dark soy sauce
2 tablespoons sesame oil

Wash the clams thoroughly, brushing off all the grit and mud. Soak for 20 minutes in cold salted water, then drain.
❀ Boil a large pot of water and put in the clams, stirring for about 2 minutes until the clams open.
❀ Drain and remove the top shells. Arrange clams in a serving dish and sprinkle on the chopped ginger and chives.
❀ Mix the soy sauce and sesame oil together and divide between several small dishes. Serve as dips with the clams.

Beijing 北京

STEAMED DRIED SCALLOPS

Scallops are an expensive seafood found right along the coast of China, although the best come from Shandong Province. The scallops used in the following recipe are sun-dried, which preserves them as well as intensifying their flavour. Good quality dried scallops are large, reddish yellow, fine grained and aromatic.

10-12 large dried scallops
½ cup (125 mL/4 fl oz) chicken stock (broth)
1-2 teaspoons chilli oil or chilli sauce
1 tablespoon cornflour (cornstarch)

SEASONING

1 cup (250 mL/8 fl oz) chicken stock (broth)
2 tablespoons rice wine or dry sherry
1 teaspoon ginger juice

Rinse the scallops and soak in cold water for about 1 hour until they swell up and become pliable.
❀ Place in a heatproof dish and add the seasoning ingredients. Set the dish on a rack in a wok or in a steamer and steam, covered, over gently simmering water for about 1 hour.
❀ Strain, retaining the seasoning liquid, and arrange on a serving plate. Set aside to keep warm. Mix about ½ cup (125 mL/4 fl oz) of the retained liquid with the chicken stock, chilli oil and cornflour. Simmer for 1 minute, stirring until thickened, adjust the seasoning and pour over the scallops before serving.

STEAMED DRIED SCALLOPS

Beijing 北京

STIR-FRIED DRIED SCALLOPS WITH CELERY

There are many ways to cook dried scallops, but when combined with crisp young celery the result is outstanding.

In ancient China there are detailed records about the medicinal and dietary values of celery. In particular it is suggested that celery may help to reduce high blood pressure.

This dish must be eaten hot or its subtle flavours will be lost.

12 dried scallops, soaked for 25 minutes
¾ cup (175 mL/6 fl oz) chicken stock (broth)
250 g (8 oz) fresh young celery stems
2 tablespoons oil for frying
1 spring onion (shallot/scallion), sliced
2 slices fresh (root) ginger
2 teaspoons rice wine or dry sherry
½ teaspoon salt

Rinse the celery, drain well and cut into 7.5 cm (3 in) lengths.
❀ Place the scallops in a wok or saucepan with the stock and bring to the boil. Cover and steam for about 40 minutes over moderately high heat until the scallops are tender and the stock full of their flavour. Set aside.
❀ Heat the oil in a wok and stir-fry the celery, spring onions and ginger for about 3 minutes until tender. Add the scallops in their liquid, the rice wine and salt, simmer together very briefly and serve immediately.

STIR-FRIED DRIED SCALLOPS WITH CELERY

HERO'S THREE-IN-ONE FISH

Beijing 北京

HERO'S THREE-IN-ONE FISH

This innovative Chinese dish is spectacular enough to impress a returning hero. One large fish is cut across into three pieces which are prepared in three different ways, and then arranged on a serving platter with the head and tail to resemble two fish side-by-side. Fresh carp is the fish favoured for this dish, but pearl perch (sea bass) gives excellent results.

1 x 1½ kg (3 lb) fresh carp or pearl perch (sea bass)
60 g (2 oz) Yunnan or other salty ham, finely shredded
5-6 slices white radish, finely shredded
1 tablespoon rice wine or dry sherry
1 spring onion (shallot/scallion)
3 slices fresh (root) ginger
1 tablespoon lard

2 tablespoons peanut oil
1 tablespoon lard
1 spring onion (shallot/scallion), chopped
2 slices fresh (root) ginger, chopped
1 clove garlic, chopped
1 tablespoon hot bean paste
2 teaspoons rice wine or dry sherry
1 tablespoon brown vinegar
2 teaspoons dark soy sauce
1 tablespoon sugar
½ cup (125 mL/4 fl oz) fish or chicken stock (broth)
oil for deep-frying
2 tablespoons rice wine or dry sherry
¾ cup (90 g/3 oz) cornflour (cornstarch)
1 egg white, well beaten

Clean and scale the fish, rinse in cold water and dry well. Cut off the head, slice in half and set aside. Cut the body of the fish across into three portions, leaving the tail on the lower part.
※ Make shallow cuts across the central section on both sides, place on a lightly oiled, heatproof plate and top with the ham and radish. Add the rice wine and place the spring onion and ginger on top. Melt the lard and pour over, then set the plate on a rack in a wok or steamer, cover and steam for about 20 minutes until completely tender. Keep warm.
※ Score diagonally across the upper part of the fish on both sides. Heat the wok and add the peanut oil and lard. Fry on both sides until cooked through and lightly coloured on the surface, then set aside. Add the spring onion, ginger, garlic and bean paste to the wok and stir-fry for 2 minutes, then add the wine, vinegar, soy sauce, sugar and stock and bring to the boil. Reduce heat, return the fish and simmer until the flavours have been absorbed. Remove and set aside, keeping warm.
※ In a clean wok, heat the deep-frying oil of the third part of the ingredients list. Cut the tail end of the fish in half lengthways, sprinkle with the rice wine, coat with cornflour then dip into the beaten egg and coat thickly with the cornflour again, shaking off excess. Slide into the oil and deep-fry until cooked through and golden. Lift out and drain well.
※ Coat the head halves with cornflour and deep-fry in the hot oil until crisp and well-coloured. Place the heads at one end of a large platter and tails at the other, and the braised and steamed parts side-by-side between the heads and tails. Serve a dish of spiced salt (1 tablespoon of warmed salt mixed with 1½ teaspoons of five-spice powder) to accompany the crisp fried section of the fish.

STIR-FRIED FISH AND PINE NUTS

Shanghai 上海

STIR-FRIED FISH AND PINE NUTS

250 g (8 oz) fillet of rock carp or other meaty white fish
3 tablespoons peanut or vegetable oil
½ cup (60 g/2 oz) pine nuts
1 tablespoon finely chopped red capsicum (bell pepper)
1 tablespoon finely chopped green capsicum (bell pepper)
1 tablespoon finely chopped spring onion (shallot/scallion)

SEASONING

2 teaspoons Shaoxing rice wine or dry sherry
1 teaspoon ginger juice
½ teaspoon salt
1 tablespoon cornflour (cornstarch)

Skin the fish and cut it into very small dice. Place in a dish with the pre-mixed seasoning ingredients and mix well. Leave for about 10 minutes.

Heat the oil in a wok and fry the pine nuts until lightly golden, then lift out and drain well.

Stir-fry the capsicums and onion in the wok over high heat until just softened, then remove from the oil with a slotted spoon.

Add the fish to the wok and stir-fry for about 2 minutes until white and cooked through. Return the capsicum and onion, mix well, then pile into the centre of a serving plate, arranging the fried pine nuts in a circle around the fish.

Guangzhou 广州

STEAMED TENCH FISH

Only the very best and freshest fish should be steamed, and only the merest hint of seasoning or other added ingredients is needed to high-light the freshness and flavour. At the peak of summer, when the thought of oily food dulls the taste buds, steamed tench fish is very popular, both in restaurants and at home.

1 x 375 g (12 oz) fresh tench fish (catfish or bream)
2 dried black mushrooms, soaked for 25 minutes
6 slices young fresh (root) ginger
60 g (2 oz) lean pork fillet
2 spring onions (shallots/scallions)
2 tablespoons superior stock (*see page 124*)

SEASONING

2 tablespoons superior or other light soy sauce
½ teaspoon sesame oil
pinch of white pepper

STEAMED TENCH FISH

Clean and scale the fish and slash along the top of the back bone on either side. Place in the centre of an oval heatproof dish which will fit inside a wok or steamer.

Drain the mushrooms, squeeze out excess water and shred finely. Shred the ginger, pork fillet and the white parts only of the spring onions. Arrange these ingredients along the top of the fish, set the dish on a rack in a wok or in a steamer, cover and cook the fish over gently simmering water for about 15 minutes, or until very tender.

Bring the stock and the seasoning ingredients to the boil separately, pour over the fish and serve at once.

Sichuan 四川

CRUCIAN CARP WITH BEAN JELLY

Jelly is a popular snack in Sichuan Province and is sold throughout the year in cities and in the country at hawkers' stands or in restaurants. The jelly can be made from powdered rice, beans or buckwheat, and is usually eaten cold.

*   This particular combination of crucian carp with cubes of mung bean jelly is unique to Sichuan cooking.*

2 x 315 g (10 oz) crucian carp or other meaty white fish
1 tablespoon rice wine or dry sherry
1 teaspoon salt
1 sheet pork fat net (caul lining)
3 spring onions (shallots/scallions), finely chopped
1 teaspoon grated fresh (root) ginger
¾ teaspoon ground Sichuan peppercorns (Fagara or Sansho)
185 g (6 oz) green mung bean jelly

SEASONING

1½ tablespoons fermented black beans, chopped
1 teaspoon chopped garlic
2 tablespoons finely chopped bean sprouts or celery
2 tablespoons light soy sauce
1 teaspoon chilli oil or chilli sauce
¾ teaspoon sesame oil

Clean the carp and score diagonally across each side. Place in a heatproof dish and sprinkle with the wine and salt. Leave for 5 minutes, then wrap each fish in a piece of the pork fat net and return to the dish. Cover with the spring onions, ginger and Sichuan pepper. Place on a rack in a wok or in a steamer, cover and steam for about 20 minutes until cooked.

Dice the jelly and simmer in boiling water for 2-3 minutes, then drain. Mix with the seasoning ingredients in the wok and heat through. Remove the fish from the steamer and remove the pork fat. Slide the fish into the wok and simmer gently for 2-3 minutes with the jelly and seasonings.

Lift onto a serving plate and serve.

SILVER CARP AND TURNIP IN BROTH

Sichuan 四川

SILVER CARP AND TURNIP IN BROTH

Fish simmered in broth is a great favourite throughout China. As far back as the Tang Dynasty (618-907 AD) chefs cooked fish supplemented with mutton, rabbit and deer meat to make delicious pot meals. This dish was devised fifty years ago by the well-known chef Liao Chin-tin, who adapted the following recipe from an ancient one.

500 g (1 lb) silver carp steaks or other meaty white fish
4 tablespoons lard
1 fresh turnip
4 cups (1 L/32 fl oz) superior stock (*see page 124*)

SEASONING

4 spring onions (shallots/scallions)
3 slices fresh (root) ginger
2 pickled red chillies
½ cup (125 mL/4 fl oz) rice wine or dry sherry
1 teaspoon salt

DIPPING SAUCE

3 tablespoons superior or other light soy sauce
1 tablespoon red or brown vinegar
1 teaspoon grated fresh (root) ginger
1 teaspoon sesame oil

Wipe the fish steaks dry with paper towels. Heat the lard in a wok and fry the steaks on both sides until lightly browned. Drain and transfer to a casserole with a tight-fitting lid.

Peel and shred the turnip. Stir-fry it in the remaining lard for 2 minutes, then add the stock and bring to the boil. Pour into the casserole.

Shred or dice the spring onions, ginger and chillies and add all the seasoning ingredients to the casserole.

Cover and simmer for 20 minutes or until the fish is tender. Do not overcook or the fish will begin to dry out.

Mix the dipping sauce ingredients together and serve it in several small dishes with the pot of broth.

Sichuan 四川

SPECIAL BRAISED ROCK CARP

Sichuan is a vast territory laced with rivers. The warm climate and fine water favour the reproduction of many different varieties of fish; rock or black carp in particular grow abundantly. Rock carp is characterised by its small head, thick body, small bones and rich meat. It is regarded as one of the most delicious freshwater fish in China.

1 x 500 g (1 lb) rock carp or other meaty white freshwater fish
185 g (6 oz) yam
3 spring onions (shallots/scallions)
3 slices fresh (root) ginger
3 cloves garlic
2 tablespoons lard

SPECIAL BRAISED ROCK CARP

SAUCE

2 cups (500 mL/16 fl oz) water
1 tablespoon rice wine or dry sherry
1 tablespoon hot bean paste
1 tablespoon sugar
1 tablespoon brown vinegar
1 tablespoon red fermented rice (wine lees)
1 tablespoon light soy sauce
pinch of salt

Clean the fish and make several diagonal slashes across each side. Peel and finely dice the yam. Chop the spring onions, ginger and garlic finely.

※ In a wok, sauté the yam in the lard for about 2 minutes until lightly coloured, then place in the bottom of a casserole. Add the fish to the wok, sauté on both sides until lightly coloured and place on top of the yam. Lightly fry the spring onions, ginger and garlic in the lard and add to the casserole with the pre-mixed sauce ingredients.

※ Bring to the boil, skim any froth and residue from the surface and reduce the heat. Simmer very gently, partially covered, until the fish is tender and the stock reduced to a thick clear layer over the fish.

※ Chinese chefs call this method "gaining wonder from fire".

103

CARP WITH SICHUAN HOT BEAN SAUCE

Sichuan 四川

CARP WITH SICHUAN HOT BEAN SAUCE

4-6 crucian carp or other meaty white fish,
    150-200 g (5-7 oz) each
¾ cup (175 mL/6 fl oz) oil for frying
3 cloves garlic, chopped
1½ tablespoons hot bean sauce (chilli bean sauce)
1 spring onion (shallot/scallion), chopped (garnish)

SEASONING/SAUCE

¾ cup (175 mL/6 fl oz) water or fish stock (broth)
1 tablespoon brown vinegar
1 tablespoon rice wine or dry sherry
1 pickled red chilli, chopped
2-3 slices fresh (root) ginger, chopped
1 tablespoon dark soy sauce
1 tablespoon sugar
½ teaspoon salt
1½ teaspoons cornflour (cornstarch)

Clean the fish and rinse in cold water, then drain and dry thoroughly. Heat a wok with half the oil to smoking point and fry half of the fish until lightly browned on both sides. Remove to a plate and keep warm.

Add the remaining oil and fry the other fish until browned, then place with the first batch. Cover and keep warm.

Pour the oil out, rinse the wok, then return about 2 tablespoons of the oil. Stir-fry the garlic briefly, then add the bean sauce and stir-fry for about 40 seconds. Add the pre-mixed sauce ingredients and bring to the boil, stirring constantly. Slide the fish into the sauce, reduce heat, cover and simmer gently for about 20 minutes. Splash in a little more water from time to time if it begins to dry up during cooking.

Use a wide spatula to transfer the fish onto a serving plate, stacking them together in the same direction. Scatter the spring onion over the fish and pour on the sauce.

WHOLE GRASS CARP BARBECUED IN A BAMBOO TUBE

The fish cooked in the following typical country fashion is insulated by green bamboo and a net of pork fat to keep it tender and moist with no risk of burning. During cooking the marinade ingredients slowly permeate the fish, which loses its usual fishy smell and takes on some of the unusual fragrance of the fresh bamboo.

1 x 750 g (1½ lb) whole grass carp or other meaty white fish
1 sheet pork fat net (caul lining)
a thick tube of green bamboo, or several layers of bamboo
    leaves and aluminium foil
thin wire to fasten

SEASONING

1 teaspoon salt
1 tablespoon ginger juice
1 tablespoon rice wine or dry sherry
pinch of white pepper

SAUCE

juice of 2 oranges
½ cup (125 mL/4 fl oz) water
1 tablespoon sugar
½ teaspoon sesame oil
1½ teaspoons cornflour (cornstarch)

Scale, gut and thoroughly wash the fish. Place the pork fat on a board and lay the fish in the centre. Rub the seasonings over the fish, inside and out, and wrap it in the pork fat net.

❈ Split the bamboo in half lengthways and place the wrapped carp in the hollow. Cover with the other piece of bamboo and tie the bundle securely with wire. Have ready a quantity of glowing charcoal. Place the bamboo in the charcoal to roast slowly until the fish is cooked, 30-40 minutes. If using bamboo leaves and aluminium foil the dried leaves must be soaked first to soften. Wrap the fish in at least 8 leaves and a double layer of aluminium foil. Roast for about 30 minutes only.

❈ Mix the sauce ingredients together and stir in a wok or saucepan over gentle heat until thickened. Pour into a jug or small bowl. Unwrap the fish and serve with the sauce.

WHOLE GRASS CARP BARBECUED IN A BAMBOO TUBE

Sichuan 四川

CRUCIAN CARP WITH LOTUS EGG

In Sichuan Province, the word lotus has several meanings and chefs have got into the habit of calling steamed egg white "lotus egg". This very popular steamed dish uses crucian carp and lotus egg as its main ingredients. The result is very light and delicious.

3 x 200 g (6½ oz) small crucian carp or other meaty white fish
4 egg whites
⅓ cup (75 mL/2½ fl oz) fish stock (broth)
1 tablespoon cornflour (cornstarch)
½ teaspoon salt
¼ red capsicum (bell pepper) (garnish)
lemon rind or grated hard-boiled egg yolk (garnish)
fresh coriander (garnish)

SEASONING

1 tablespoon rice wine or dry sherry
½ teaspoon grated fresh (root) ginger
1 tablespoon finely chopped spring onion (shallot/scallion)
pinch of white pepper
dash of chilli oil or chilli sauce

CRUCIAN CARP WITH LOTUS EGG

SAUCE

½ cup (125 mL/4 fl oz) fish or chicken stock (broth)
salt and pepper
1 teaspoon rice wine or dry sherry
1 teaspoon cornflour (cornstarch)

DIP

1 tablespoon finely minced (ground), young fresh (root) ginger
1 tablespoon sesame oil

Clean the carp and place in a saucepan of boiling water to cook briefly. Lift out, drain well and scrape off the skin. Arrange them side by side in a heatproof dish and add the pre-mixed seasoning ingredients. Place on a rack in a wok or in a steamer, cover and steam for about 15 minutes until tender.

✻ Beat the egg whites, fish stock, cornflour and salt together and pour into a flat, heatproof dish. Steam for about 6 minutes until set, then cut into lotus petal shapes.

✻ Finely shred the capsicum and blanch in boiling water.

✻ Mix the sauce ingredients, except the cornflour, together, pour into a wok and bring to the boil. Mix the cornflour with a little cold water, stir in and simmer until thickened. Add any liquid from the dish in which the fish were steamed and simmer again briefly.

✻ Arrange the lotus egg around the fish and pour on the sauce. Add the garnish of capsicum, lemon rind or grated egg and fresh coriander. Serve at once with the minced ginger and sesame oil in a separate dish to use as a dip.

CARP WITH TRI-HOT FLAVOURS

Sichuan 四川

CARP WITH TRI-HOT FLAVOURS

1 x 440 g (14 oz) carp or other meaty white fish
oil for deep-frying
2-3 dried red chillies
1 teaspoon Sichuan peppercorns (Fagara or Sansho)

SEASONING

2 teaspoons fermented black beans
1 cup (250 mL/8 fl oz) water
1¼ teaspoons sugar
1 teaspoon rice wine or dry sherry
1 teaspoon vinegar
pinch of salt

Clean and scale the carp, rinse under running cold water, then dry well inside and out. Make several diagonal slashes across each side.

❈ Heat the oil in a wok to smoking point, lower the heat and deep-fry the fish on both sides until golden. Lift out and drain well.

❈ Pour off all but 2 tablespoons of the oil and stir-fry the whole chillies and peppercorns for about 1 minute or until crisp and dry. Remove from the oil, drain well, then chop or grind coarsely.

❈ Chop the fermented beans finely, place in the oil and stir-fry for 30-40 seconds. Add the remaining seasoning ingredients and bring to the boil. Skim off any froth, then place the fish in the pan, cover and simmer gently for about 3 minutes on each side. If the pan is tightly covered the liquid will not evaporate; if it does, add a little more water during cooking.

❈ Lift the fish onto a serving plate, pour on the sauce, sprinkle with the ground pepper and chilli and serve.

Shanghai 上海

CRUCIAN CARP STEAMED WITH EGG

1 x 375 g (12 oz) crucian carp or other meaty white fish
3 large eggs
¾ cup (175 mL/6 fl oz) chicken stock (broth)
½ teaspoon salt
1 slice cooked salted ham

Clean and scale the carp and make several deep diagonal slashes across each side.

❈ Lightly beat the eggs, add the chicken stock and salt and pour into an oval heatproof dish. Place the fish on top, then set the dish on a rack in a wok or in a steamer, cover and steam for about 12 minutes over simmering water until the fish is cooked through and the egg firm. When the dish is removed from the steamer the fish will have sunk halfway into the egg.

❈ Finely chop the ham and sprinkle over the top of the fish and serve at once.

❈ For extra flavour, add the ham halfway through cooking, when the egg has firmed up enough to prevent it from sinking through to the bottom.

CRUCIAN CARP STEAMED WITH EGG

FRIED BLACK CARP IN A GRAPE-BUNCH SHAPE

Shanghai 上海

FRIED BLACK CARP IN A GRAPE-BUNCH SHAPE

This unusual traditional dish from Anhui Province is made from a big fillet of fish cut from a large black carp, scored and coated so that when crisply fried it takes on the appearance of a bunch of grapes. Grape juice in the sauce adds to the flavour.

375-440 g (12-14 oz) thick central piece of white fish fillet
1 teaspoon grated fresh (root) ginger
1 tablespoon finely chopped spring onion (shallot/scallion)
1 teaspoon salt
1½ cups (185 g/6 oz) cornflour (cornstarch)
oil for deep-frying
grapevine leaves and stem (garnish)

SAUCE

3 tablespoons chicken stock (broth)
1 cup (250 mL/8 fl oz) dark grape juice
1½ tablespoons red vinegar
2 tablespoons light soy sauce
1 teaspoon sugar
1 teaspoon lard
½ teaspoon salt
1 tablespoon cornflour (cornstarch)

Place the piece of fish, skin side downwards on a cutting board and cut a criss-cross pattern diagonally across it, cutting down to the skin but not through it. Place in a dish and scatter on the ginger, onion and salt. Leave for 15 minutes, then coat thickly with cornflour.

In a small wok or saucepan, boil the pre-mixed sauce ingredients for about 3 minutes, stirring constantly. Check the seasoning and keep warm.

Heat the oil in a large wok to smoking point, then reduce the heat slightly. Slide in the fish, skin side upwards, and deep-fry for about 5 minutes until golden and cooked through. As it cooks, the skin will curl up, giving the fish the appearance of a bunch of grapes.

Drain, place on a dish and arrange the vine leaves and stem at the top of the "bunch". Pour on the sauce and serve.

GOLDEN CRISP FISH WITH SWEET AND SOUR SAUCE

Sichuan 四川

GOLDEN CRISP FISH WITH SWEET AND SOUR SAUCE

In a small town near a river, many many years ago, there was a popular snack called "Aromatic Fried Fish". The fish, probably a carp from the river, was cleaned and marinated, then coated thickly with a paste of soy bean powder and water before frying. This dish has been developed from the original by skilful Sichuan chefs.

1 x 1 kg (2 lb) carp or other meaty white fish
3/4 cup (90 g/3 oz) soya bean powder or cornflour (cornstarch)
oil for deep-frying
3 spring onions (shallots/scallions), shredded
2-3 fresh red chillies, shredded
fresh coriander leaves

MARINADE

2 tablespoons light soy sauce
1 tablespoon rice wine or dry sherry
1/2 teaspoon salt
2 teaspoons ginger juice (optional)

SAUCE

2 tablespoons vegetable oil
2 cloves garlic, crushed
1 teaspoon grated fresh (root) ginger
1-2 fresh red chillies, chopped
2 tablespoons vinegar
1 1/2 tablespoons sugar
3/4 teaspoon sesame oil
1 1/2 teaspoons cornflour (cornstarch)
3/4 cup (175 mL/6 fl oz) fish or chicken stock (broth)
pinch of salt and white pepper

Clean and scale the carp, rinse well, then dry thoroughly inside and out. Place in a dish, rub on the pre-mixed marinade ingredients and leave for 15 minutes. Mix the soy bean powder or cornflour with enough water to make a batter of coating consistency.

Use a sharp knife or cleaver to cut deep scores across each side of the fish, cutting at an angle so that each segment of fish stands out like a large fish scale. Coat the fish lightly with additional soy bean powder or cornflour, then dip into the batter, holding the fish by the tail so that the "scales" open and all the meat is covered evenly with the batter.

In a large wok heat the oil to smoking point, put in the fish, then lower the heat slightly and deep-fry for about 10 minutes, turning once. Lift out and drain well.

In another wok heat the oil for the sauce and then fry the garlic, ginger and chillies over moderate heat for about 1 1/2 minutes. Add the vinegar, sugar and sesame oil and increase the heat slightly, then stir the cornflour into the stock and pour the mixture in the wok. Boil briefly, adding salt and pepper.

Reheat the deep-frying oil and fry the fish again for about 2 minutes to make the surface very crisp. Drain and place on a serving plate. Pour the sauce into a jug.

Scatter the spring onions, chillies and coriander leaves over the fish and pour the sauce on immediately before serving.

Shanghai 上海

SMOKED POMFRET

1 x 750 g (1 1/2 lb) pomfret or John Dory
1/2 cup (60 g/2 oz) black Chinese tea leaves
1 1/2 tablespoons sugar
mayonnaise or salad dressing
cucumber fans (garnish)
pickles or tomato slices (garnish)

SEASONING/MARINADE

1 tablespoon Shaoxing rice wine or dry sherry
1 teaspoon salt
3 teaspoons sugar
1 1/2 tablespoons finely chopped spring onion
  (shallot/scallion)
1 tablespoon grated fresh (root) ginger

Clean the fish and cut through the body diagonally in three places. Place in a dish. Mix the seasoning/marinade ingredients together and rub thoroughly over the fish, then leave for at least one hour to absorb the flavours.

Line the bottom of a heavy duty wok, preferably an old iron one, with aluminium foil and put the tea leaves and sugar on this. Place over high heat until they begin to smoke. Set the fish on a metal rack over it, cover and smoke the fish over slightly reduced heat for about 25 minutes. The fish will take on a rich deep colour, and the heat within the wok should be sufficient to cook the fish through.

Transfer to a serving plate, garnish attractively with fans of cucumber, a little brightly coloured pickled vegetable or tomato slices and serve with the mayonnaise.

SMOKED POMFRET

MANDARIN FISH COOKED IN CHILLI BEAN SAUCE

Shanghai 上海

MANDARIN FISH COOKED IN CHILLI BEAN SAUCE

1 x 500 g (1 lb) mandarin fish (perch/sea bass)
125 g (4 oz) lard
2 spring onions (shallots/scallions)
6 slices young fresh (root) ginger
¾ cup (175 mL/6 fl oz) water

SEASONING

1 tablespoon chilli bean paste
1-2 pickled red chillies
1 tablespoon rice wine or dry sherry
1 tablespoon sugar
½ teaspoon red vinegar

Select a live fish if possible, kill and clean it. Heat the lard in a wok and fry the fish on both sides until golden. Lift out and set aside.

✿ Cut the spring onions into 2.5 cm (1 in) lengths and fry with the ginger in the wok for about 30 seconds. Add the seasoning ingredients except the vinegar, and simmer for 1 minute, stirring constantly. Add about ¾ cup (175 mL/6 fl oz) water and bring to the boil. Return the fish and simmer, covered, for about 3 minutes, then remove the lid and continue simmering the fish until tender and the sauce well reduced. A little cornflour (cornstarch) can be used to thicken the sauce, if necessary.

✿ Transfer to a serving plate and sprinkle on the vinegar before serving.

BRAISED CHUB'S HEAD IN AN EARTHENWARE POT

Shanghai 上海

BRAISED CHUB'S HEAD IN AN EARTHENWARE POT

Chub is variegated carp, a delicious freshwater fish. All four kinds of carp – rock, silver, grass and variegated – are eaten and cooked in many different ways throughout China.

Chub's head is especially large, accounting for about one-third of the body size. The flesh near the gills and jaw, especially the walnut-shaped flesh inside the mouth is fatty, tender and full of flavour.

The clay pot used to cook the fish heads allows them to simmer slowly, thus retaining their shape and producing a richly flavoured clear sauce. This famous dish is served in the autumn and winter.

1 x 1¼ kg (2½ lb) variegated carp (chub) head or several large meaty fish heads, supplemented with extra fish meat, if necessary
125 g (4 oz) lard
2 bean sheets, soaked to soften*

SEASONING

3 tablespoons superior or other light soy sauce
1 tablespoon Shaoxing rice wine or dry sherry
1½-2 teaspoons salt
½ teaspoon white pepper
1 teaspoon sugar
1½ tablespoons soybean oil (optional)

Rinse the fish head and wipe dry. Heat the lard in a large wok and stir-fry the fish head until it takes on a light colour, then transfer to an earthenware pot or casserole.

Cut the bean sheets into squares and place in the pot, adding the seasoning ingredients. Add enough water to just cover the fish, then cover the pot and bring almost to the boil. Simmer gently for about 1½ hours until the fish is completely tender and the stock has become rich, whitish in colour and well reduced. Serve in the pot.

Transparent edible sheets made from a paste of ground mung beans and water. If unavailable, substitute mung bean vermicelli, or use strips of beancurd skin, cubes of fried beancurd or soaked dried "wood ear" fungus.

Beijing 北京

PAN'S FISH

This dish was created by the chef of a high-ranking official in the Qing Dynasty (1644-1911 AD). This official, whose name was Pan, loved fish but abhorred the grease that normally results from frying. So Pan's chef steamed the fish and named the dish after him.

1 x 410 g (13 oz) fresh carp or other meaty white fish
4 dried black mushrooms, soaked for 25 minutes
6-8 dried shrimps, soaked for 25 minutes
1 spring onion (shallot/scallion), chopped
3 slices fresh (root) ginger

SEASONING

¾ cup (175 mL/6 fl oz) chicken or fish stock (broth)
2 tablespoons rice wine or dry sherry
2 tablespoons light soy sauce
⅓ teaspoon salt

Scale and clean the fish, wash in cold water, then dip into a pot of boiling water for a few seconds and drain well. Make several slashes diagonally across each side and place in a heatproof bowl.

Drain the mushrooms and remove the stems. Then drain the shrimps and arrange both over the fish, adding the spring onion and ginger. Pour on the pre-mixed seasoning ingredients, place on a rack in a wok or in a steamer, cover and steam for about 20 minutes. The fish is ready when the thick flesh adjoining the head is tender and flakes easily.

Serve at once in the same bowl.

PAN'S FISH

STEAMED TRI-SHREDS ROLLED IN FISH

Shanghai 上海

STEAMED TRI-SHREDS ROLLED IN FISH

A variety of foods can be used as filling for these slender fish rolls. Although this dish is called tri-shreds, the number of ingredients can vary and include ham, winter bamboo shoots, black mushrooms, chicken meat, spring onions and ginger.

By cooking them in a steamer, the original textures of the different ingredients are preserved, while the various flavours are able to permeate each other. In one tiny roll, you can experience the tender smoothness of fish, the salty flavour of ham, the crispness of bamboo shoots, and the tasty, somewhat chewy consistency of mushroom, complemented by the pungency of onion and ginger.

625 g (1¼ lb) thick central piece of fresh rock carp or other white fish fillet
60 g (2 oz) salted ham
60 g (2 oz) fresh or canned winter bamboo shoots
2-3 dried black mushrooms, soaked for 25 minutes
2-3 spring onions (shallots/scallions)
12 slices fresh (root) ginger

SAUCE

1 tablespoon rice wine or dry sherry
2 teaspoons light soy sauce
1 teaspoon rendered chicken fat, melted
½ teaspoon salt
1 teaspoon cornflour (cornstarch)

Holding the knife at a sharp angle, slice the fillet into very thin slices.

▨ Drain the mushrooms, remove the stems and finely shred the caps, together with the ham, bamboo shoots, spring onions and ginger, keeping the slices about 5 cm (2 in) long.

▨ Place a few pieces of each ingredient in the centre of each slice of fish and roll it around the filling, squeezing firmly into a smooth roll – the ingredients may be allowed to protrude slightly past the ends of the roll. Arrange on an oiled heatproof plate, place on a rack in a wok or in a steamer, cover and steam over gently simmering water for about 20 minutes until cooked and tender. Remove, retaining the cooking liquid and keep warm.

▨ Mix the sauce ingredients together, adding the liquid from the steamed fish, and simmer, stirring, until thickened. Check the seasoning, then pour over the fish rolls and serve at once.

ZHUA CHAO YU FRIED FISH SLICES

Beijing 北京

ZHUA CHAO YU FRIED FISH SLICES

The story is told of the time the Empress Dowager Cixi picked out one dish of smooth, shining and tender fish slices from the many dishes on a table. When asked for the name of the dish the cook, caught unawares, called it Zhua Chao Yu, which means "grasping and frying".

The distinctive feature of the dish is that the fish is first deep-fried and then stir-fried. Its flavour is slightly sweet and sour, with a touch of saltiness.

315 g (10 oz) fresh white fish fillets
1 cup (125 g/4 oz) cornflour (cornstarch)
oil, preferably peanut oil, for deep-frying

SAUCE

2 spring onions (shallots/scallions), white parts only
2 slices fresh (root) ginger
2 tablespoons lard
1 tablespoon light soy sauce
1 tablespoon brown vinegar
2 teaspoons sugar
1 teaspoon rice wine or dry sherry
pinch each of salt and pepper
½ teaspoon cornflour (cornstarch)

Cut the fish into long thin slices. Mix the cornflour with enough cold water to make a thin paste.

▨ Heat the oil in a wok to smoking point then reduce the heat. Dip the fish slices into the cornflour paste and deep-fry 8 pieces at a time for about 1½ minutes until golden and crisp on the surface and cooked through. Lift out, drain well and keep warm while the sauce is prepared.

▨ Very finely chop the spring onions and ginger. Heat a wok with the lard and stir-fry the spring onion and ginger for about 45 seconds, add the remaining pre-mixed sauce ingredients and heat through. When the sauce begins to thicken, slide in the fried fish and stir-fry, turning the fish carefully until coated with all the sauce. Serve at once.

STEAMED THREE-LAYER FISH

BRAISED FISH WITH MINCED MEAT

Beijing 北京

STEAMED THREE-LAYER FISH

1 x 625 g (1¼ lb) garoupa or other meaty white fish (coral cod or grouper)
9 dried black mushrooms, soaked for 25 minutes
185 g (6 oz) fresh or canned winter bamboo shoots
6 slices Yunnan or other salty ham
3 tablespoons fish or chicken stock (broth)
1 tablespoon rice wine or dry sherry
1 teaspoon melted lard
pinch of salt and pepper
4 slices fresh (root) ginger
3 spring onions (shallots/scallions)
250 g (8 oz) choy sum or other Chinese green vegetable
6-8 slices young fresh (root) ginger

SAUCE

½ cup (125 mL/4 fl oz) chicken or fish stock (broth)
1 teaspoon melted lard
½ teaspoon salt
pinch of white pepper
½ teaspoon cornflour (cornstarch)

Clean and wash the fish, then scald with boiling water and drain. Cut off the head and tail and set aside. Use a sharp knife to remove the fillets from each side, then place skin-side down on a board and carefully detatch the skin from the fillet by holding firmly at the tail end and running the knife between skin and meat. Hold the knife at a sharp angle to the fillet and cut across it into slices. There should be 18 slices of fish, 9 from each fillet.

❈ Drain the mushrooms, remove the stems and cut each cap in half. Cut the bamboo shoots and ham into pieces the approximate size of the fish slices.

❈ Arrange the fish, mushrooms, bamboo and ham alternately in two rows along an oval heatproof plate, then position the head and tail at either end. The head can be halved so that it will remain flat on the plate.

❈ Mix the stock, wine, melted lard, salt and pepper together and pour over the fish, then place the ginger and spring onion on top. Place on a rack in a wok or in a steamer, cover and steam over simmering water for about 20 minutes, until done. Discard the spring onions, ginger and the liquid.

❈ Trim the choy sum and drop into a saucepan of boiling water with a tablespoon of oil. Simmer until tender, then drain well and arrange around the edge of the plate and along the centre between the two rows of ingredients.

❈ Cut the ginger for the garnish into butterfly or other decorative shapes and use to decorate the dish.

❈ Boil the sauce ingredients in a small pan until thickened and pour over the fish immediately before serving.

Sichuan 四川

BRAISED FISH WITH MINCED MEAT

Braised Fish with Minced Meat is one of the many famous fish dishes of the Sichuan cuisine, and very popular at banquets. The fish is supplemented by special Shiu Fu pickled potherb mustard and pickled red chillies, and is cooked using a special braising technique. The dish is known for its bright red colour, fragrant aroma and slightly spicy, yet delicate taste.

2 x 250 g (8 oz) crucian carp or other meaty white fish
2 cups (500 mL/16 fl oz) lard or oil for frying
90 g (3 oz) belly pork (fresh bacon)
30 g (1 oz) pickled potherb mustard
2 spring onions (shallots/scallions)
1½ pickled red chillies
2 slices fresh (root) ginger

SAUCE

2 cups (500 mL/16 fl oz) fish stock (broth)
1 tablespoon rice wine or dry sherry
1 tablespoon dark soy sauce
1 teaspoon light soy sauce
1 teaspoon salt
1 teaspoon sesame oil
1 teaspoon sugar

Clean and scale the fish, make several deep scores diagonally across each side and dry well with paper towels. Heat the lard or oil in a wok and slide in the fish. Fry gently on both sides until crisp and partially cooked, then lift out carefully and drain well.

❈ Finely chop (coarsely grind) the pork, mustard, spring onions, chillies and ginger.

❈ Drain the wok, wipe out and return about 2 tablespoons of the oil. Sauté the pork until lightly coloured, then add the mustard, spring onions, chillies and ginger and stir-fry briefly. Pour in the pre-mixed sauce ingredients and bring to the boil.

❈ Place the fish in the sauce, cover and simmer over gentle heat for about 45 minutes until the fish is completely tender and the sauce well flavoured.

❈ Serve the fish with the sauce in a deep serving dish.

SANDWICHED PERCH

LIGHT-FRIED AND SIMMERED MANDARIN FISH

Guangzhou 广州

SANDWICHED PERCH

155 g (5 oz) perch fillets, skinned
125 g (4 oz) fresh chicken livers
90 g (3 oz) fat pork
2 teaspoons rice wine or dry sherry
½ teaspoon sesame oil
⅓ teaspoon salt
½ cup (60 g/2 oz) cornflour (cornstarch)
2 eggs
oil for deep-frying
12 stalks young choy sum or other Chinese green vegetable

Cut the perch and pork into pieces about 4 x 3 cm (1½ x 1¼ in) and slice the livers thinly. Place the fish in a dish and add the rice wine, sesame oil and salt and leave for 20 minutes.
※ Sandwich the ingredients together, layering fish, chicken liver and fat pork, and coat each sandwich thickly with cornflour. Beat the eggs thoroughly.
※ Heat 4-5 cups (1-1¼ L/32-40 fl oz) of oil in a wok to moderately hot. Dip the fish into the egg, coating evenly, then deep-fry (preferably in two batches) until cooked through and golden – about 6 minutes. Drain well and arrange on a serving plate.
※ Drop the vegetables into a pan of boiling water and simmer briefly. They should remain crisp and brightly coloured. Drain and arrange around the fish.

Beijing 北京

LIGHT-FRIED AND SIMMERED MANDARIN FISH

The rivers and lakes to the south of the Yangtze River are teeming with mandarin fish. The method of preparing this dish, called "ta" in Chinese, allows time for the seasoning to penetrate the meat and means that the sauce will be well reduced and concentrated.

1 x 250 g (8 oz) piece of mandarin fish (perch/sea bass) fillet
1 tablespoon light soy sauce
½ cup (60 g/2 oz) flour
185 g (6 oz) lard
2 eggs, well beaten
2 tablespoons onion oil*

SAUCE

1½ cups (375 mL/12 fl oz) chicken stock (broth)
1 tablespoon light soy sauce
1½ tablespoons rice wine or dry sherry
2 teaspoons ginger juice
½ teaspoon salt

Made by heating peanut or vegetable oil with sliced spring onions or red onions until the onions are well coloured. Strain and store the oil in a jar.

Cut the fish into a fish shape and pound with the side of a cleaver to tenderise, sprinkle on the soy sauce and then coat with the flour. Heat the lard in a wok, dip the fish into the beaten egg, coating it thickly and fry on both sides until golden. Lift out and place in a casserole.
※ Add the pre-mixed sauce ingredients and bring just to the boil. Cover and simmer very gently for about 20 minutes. Pour on the onion oil and serve in the casserole.

Sichuan 四川

STIR-FRIED SQUID SHREDS

Squid can be dry and tough, unless it is gently cooked or soup is added. However, the chefs in Sichuan do not follow these common rules but cook squid using the stir-fry method. By cleverly handling the duration and degree of heat, they turn the dryness into crispness and toughness into puffiness, the result being tasty and aromatic.

1 x 60 g (2 oz) piece dried squid
125 g (4 oz) pork belly (fresh bacon)
250 g (8 oz) lard
2 teaspoons rice wine or dry sherry
90 g (3 oz) fresh silver sprouts*
1 tablespoon light soy sauce
1 teaspoon sesame oil
salt

Use a sharp cleaver to cut the dried squid and the pork into very fine shreds and set aside.
※ Heat the wok and add the lard. Stir-fry the squid shreds for about 2 minutes until they are crisp and red-brown. Drain off the excess lard and add the pork and the rice wine. Stir-fry together until the pork is done, then add the beansprouts and the remaining ingredients. Stir-fry together over high heat for 45 seconds, then serve.

Fresh mung beansprouts from which the yellow seed pods and long tapering roots have been removed, leaving a slender, silver-coloured sprout.

STIR-FRIED SQUID SHREDS

Sichuan 四川

FRIED WHOLE FISH WITH DUMPLINGS

1 x 500 g (1 lb) fresh carp or other meaty white fish
185 g (6 oz) semi-fat pork
1 egg white
1 cup (125 g/4 oz) cornflour (cornstarch)
oil for deep-frying
five-spice salt*

SEASONING

1 tablespoon rice wine or dry sherry
2 tablespoons finely chopped spring onions
   (shallots/scallions)
1 teaspoon grated fresh (root) ginger
1/2 teaspoon salt
pinch of white pepper

STUFFING

30 g (1 oz) pickled pot-herb mustard
2 spring onions (shallots/scallions)
2 slices fresh (root) ginger
1 teaspoon rice wine or dry sherry
2 teaspoons light soy sauce
1 teaspoon sugar
1/4 teaspoon sesame oil
lard or oil for frying

DUMPLINGS

60 g (2 oz) flour
250 g (8 oz) spinach
2 cabbage leaves
1/3 teaspoon sesame oil

Clean the carp and make several slashes diagonally across each side. Place in a dish and add the pre-mixed seasoning ingredients, rub in well and set aside for 1 hour.

❊ Very finely mince (grind) a third of the pork and cut the remainder into fine shreds.

❊ To prepare the stuffing, finely shred the pot-herb mustard, spring onions and ginger and mix with the remaining stuffing ingredients. Heat a little lard or frying oil in a wok and sauté the stuffing mixture and the shredded pork briefly until the pork turns white, then set aside to cool.

❊ For the dumplings, sift the flour into a mixing bowl. Very finely chop the spinach and cook without water for about 7 minutes, then transfer to a colander and allow the liquid to drip onto the flour. Knead into the flour to make a soft dough.

❊ Finely chop the cabbage leaves, mix with the minced pork and season with the sesame oil.

❊ Roll the dough out into a long sausage shape and divide into 18 pieces. Roll or pull each piece into a thin round dumpling wrapper and fill with a portion of the pork and cabbage filling. Fold over and pinch the edges together to enclose the filling. Arrange the dumplings on an oiled, heatproof plate and set on a rack in a wok or in a steamer, cover and steam for about 14 minutes until tender.

❊ Stuff the prepared stuffing into the cavity of the fish. Make a paste with the egg white and a little cornflour to seal the opening, then brush the remaining paste over the fish and coat thickly with cornflour.

❊ Heat the oil in a wok to smoking point, put in the fish, then lower the heat. Deep-fry for about 5 minutes, turning once, until cooked through and golden brown on the surface.

❊ Lift out and drain well. Place in the centre of a large serving plate and surround with the steamed dumplings. Pour the five spice salt into a small dish and serve separately as a dip for both the dumplings and the fish.

*To make the five-spice salt, heat 1 1/2 tablespoons of fine table salt in a wok until it begins to crackle, add 1 teaspoon of Chinese five-spice powder, remove from the heat, stir and cool.

CRISP FISH WITH SPRING ONION SAUCE

Guangzhou 广州

CRISP FISH WITH SPRING ONION SAUCE

1 x 1¼ kg (2½ lb) whole fresh fish
1 teaspoon salt
2 egg whites
1 cup (125 g/4 oz) cornflour (cornstarch)
oil for deep-frying

SAUCE

3 tablespoons peanut oil
¼ red capsicum (bell pepper), finely diced
¼ green capsicum (bell pepper), finely diced
3 spring onions (shallots/scallions), finely chopped
1 clove garlic, crushed
1 teaspoon grated fresh (root) ginger
2 dried black mushrooms, soaked then diced
60 g (2 oz) cha siew (Chinese roast pork), diced
2 tablespoons light soy sauce
½ teaspoon sesame oil
½ teaspoon salt
1 cup (250 mL/8 fl oz) fish or chicken stock (broth)
1 tablespoon cornflour (cornstarch)

Clean, scale and wash the fish, then drain and dry thoroughly inside and out. Make several deep diagonal slashes across each side, then cut in the other direction to create a diamond-shaped pattern on each side, and sprinkle on the salt.
※ Beat the egg whites until frothy and brush all over the fish. Coat thickly with the cornflour and set aside.
※ To prepare the sauce, heat the peanut oil in a wok and stir-fry the capsicums, onion, garlic and ginger for 2 minutes. Add the mushrooms and pork and stir-fry for another minute, then add the soy sauce, sesame oil and salt and toss together. Mix the cornflour with the stock and pour into the pan. Simmer gently, stirring until thickened and set aside.
※ Heat the deep-frying oil in a very large wok to smoking point, slide in the fish and deep-fry for about 7 minutes, turning once or twice, until the fish is cooked through and crisp and golden on the surface.
※ Reheat the sauce to boiling point and pour into a jug.
※ Carefully lift the fish onto a wide serving plate and take to the table with the hot sauce, which should be poured over the fish in front of the diners.

Guangzhou 广州

BRAISED FISH HEAD, COUNTRY-STYLE

Dishes offered by the teahouses in the Guangdong countryside generally use local ingredients, skilfully prepared in ways unfamiliar to town dwellers. Some even have their own small vegetable plots and fish ponds from which customers can select the ingredients for their meals.

Carp can grow to a massive size, and the heads, although bony, have deliciously sweet pockets of meat and give a unique gelatinous texture to a dish.

1 kg (2 lb) variegated carp (chub) head or several other meaty
    fish heads, supplemented with extra fish meat, if necessary
oil for deep-frying
12 cloves garlic
90 g (3 oz) lean pork
8 small cubes dried beancurd, soaked for 10 minutes
4-6 slices fresh (root) ginger
6 dried black mushrooms, soaked for 25 minutes
12 small, fresh (or canned) straw mushrooms, trimmed
12 stalks choy sum or other Chinese green vegetable

SEASONING/STOCK

3 tablespoons superior or other light soy sauce
1 teaspoon sesame oil
½ teaspoon salt
1 teaspoon sugar
¼ teaspoon ground white pepper
3 cups (750 mL/24 fl oz) superior stock (*see page 124*)

Rinse the fish head, drain and wipe dry. Heat the oil and fry the head for several minutes until it takes on a good colour. Drain and transfer to a casserole.
※ Peel the garlic, shred the pork, drain the beancurd and squeeze out all the water. Place in a frying basket or large perforated ladle and deep-fry in hot oil for about 2 minutes, drain and arrange over the fish. Add the ginger, mushrooms and the seasoning/stock ingredients. Bring just to the boil, then braise gently, half covered, until the fish is completely tender and the sauce well reduced.
※ The green vegetable can be boiled or stir-fried separately then arranged around the dish to serve.

BRAISED FISH HEAD, COUNTRY-STYLE

SHREDS OF FISH, GINGER AND PICKLED CUCUMBER

Shanghai 上海

Shreds of Fish, Ginger and Pickled Cucumber

The following recipe describes a seasonal dish prepared at the end of summer and the beginning of autumn. Each ingredient complements the other to make this a sweet, tasty, tender, yet crisp and delightfully light dish.

375 g (³⁄₄ lb) mandarin fish fillets or other meaty fish
1 egg white
pinch of salt
8 slices young fresh (root) ginger
2 tablespoons lard
¹⁄₂ teaspoon sesame oil

SEASONING

1 teaspoon Shaoxing rice wine or dry sherry
¹⁄₃ cup (75 mL/2¹⁄₂ fl oz) chicken or fish stock (broth)
¹⁄₂ teaspoon sugar
¹⁄₂ teaspoon salt
¹⁄₂ teaspoon cornflour (cornstarch)

PICKLED CUCUMBER

2 small cucumbers
1 cup (250 mL/8 fl oz) boiling water
1 tablespoon sugar
2 tablespoons white vinegar
2 teaspoons salt

Make the pickled cucumber first as it should be allowed to marinate for several hours before use. Peel the cucumbers thinly, cut into matchstick strips, discarding the ends and seed cores and place in a bowl. Mix the remaining ingredients together, pour over the cucumber and leave to stand. Drain very thoroughly before use.

※ Cut the fish into shreds, place in a dish with the lightly beaten egg white and the salt and set aside.

※ Shred the ginger slices.

※ Heat a wok and add the lard. Stir-fry the fish shreds until white and firm, then remove to a strainer to drain.

※ Stir-fry the drained cucumber and the ginger together, adding the wine after about 30 seconds. Pour the remaining pre-mixed seasoning ingredients into the pan, and when the sauce begins to thicken, return the fish and stir-fry all together over high heat for a few moments.

※ Transfer to a serving plate and sprinkle on the sesame oil before serving.

FISH SLIVERS WITH LOTUS FLOWER

Beijing 北京

Fish Slivers with Lotus Flower

The lotus flower with its light and pure fragrance and exquisitely shaped petals found its way into the hearts of the Chinese people long ago, as a symbol of beauty and perfection. The eating of lotus seeds is recorded in ancient Chinese writings, but the flower is bitter, and is only used for its colour and fragrance.

125 g (4 oz) white fish fillets
90 g (3 oz) canned bamboo shoots, drained
1 lotus flower
1 egg white, lightly beaten
1 tablespoon cornflour (cornstarch)
1 teaspoon rice wine or dry sherry
1¹⁄₂ cups (375 mL/12 fl oz) oil for frying

SEASONING

2 slices fresh (root) ginger, shredded
1 teaspoon rice wine or dry sherry
¹⁄₂ teaspoon salt
¹⁄₃ teaspoon sesame oil

Hold the knife at a 45° angle to cut each fish fillet into thin slices and then into shreds. Shred the bamboo shoots and rinse the petals of the lotus flower.

※ Arrange the lotus petals on a serving plate, preferably jade green, in a lotus leaf shape.

※ Place the sliced fish in a dish. Add the egg white, cornflour and rice wine and stir together lightly.

※ Heat the oil in a wok and deep-fry the fish in several batches over moderate heat until cooked through but not coloured on the surface. Lift out and drain well.

※ Pour off all but 2 tablespoons of the oil. Stir-fry the bamboo shoots for 1 minute, then add the seasoning ingredients and stir-fry together briefly. Add the fish and cook slowly, mixing lightly so as not to break up the fish.

※ Transfer to the serving platter, placing the fish in the centre of the "flower" and serve.

SAUTÉED FISH SLICES

Beijing 北京

SAUTÉED FISH SLICES

This dish is said to have appeared at every birthday banquet held for the Empress Dowager Cixi. It is especially suitable for the elderly because the fish has been deboned and the meat is extremely tender.

375 g (12 oz) white fish fillets
5-6 slices carrot, parboiled
2 tablespoons oil for frying
3 tablespoons fish or chicken stock (broth)
cucumber slices (garnish)
fresh coriander or watercress (garnish)

SEASONING

1 tablespoon rice wine or dry sherry
1 teaspoon melted lard
1 egg white, well beaten
1/2 teaspoon sugar
1/2 teaspoon salt
1 tablespoon cornflour (cornstarch)

Skin the fish and pat dry with a paper towel. Holding the knife at a sharp angle to the cutting board, cut each fillet into thin slices. Place in a dish with the pre-mixed seasoning ingredients and leave for 20 minutes.

❋ Cut the carrots into decorative shapes.

❋ Heat the oil in the wok and quickly stir-fry the fish for about 2 minutes over high heat. Add the carrot slices and stir-fry for another minute, then pour in the stock and simmer briefly. Check the seasoning, transfer to a serving plate and garnish with cucumber slices and a sprig of watercress or fresh coriander. Serve immediately.

Beijing 北京

FIVE WILLOW FISH

Mandarin fish is a freshwater fish found in China's large rivers and lakes. They live in the Yihou Imperial Garden Lake in Beijing, where legend has it that every spring they feast on the peach blossoms that fall into the lake. As a result the meat of the mandarin fish is supposed to be especially fragrant. In reality, however, these fish are quite aggressive and their diet consists of prawns and smaller fish.

This recipe, with the fish garnished with five different ingredients, was inspired by the Five Willow Hermit, so called because he dwelt near a lake surrounded by five willow trees. He loved to sit under one of these trees to write and recite poetry and essays. At times he would just scoop up a big fat fish, cook it on the spot and eat it all by himself.

1 x 440 g (14 oz) mandarin fish (perch/sea bass)
1 small carrot
2 slices pickled cabbage, soaked for 10 minutes
2 dried black mushrooms, soaked for 25 minutes
1/2 green capsicum (bell pepper)
5 slices young fresh (root) ginger
2 tablespoons oil for frying

SEASONING/SAUCE

1/2 cup (125 mL/4 fl oz) fish or chicken stock (broth)
2 teaspoons rice wine or dry sherry
1 tablespoon rendered chicken fat, melted
1/2 teaspoon salt
1/2 teaspoon sugar
small pinch of ground star anise
1 teaspoon cornflour (cornstarch)

Clean and scale the fish and make several diagonal cuts across each side. Set the fish in a heatproof dish and place on a rack in a wok, or in a steamer, cover and steam over simmering water until almost cooked through, then remove and place on a rack to drain.

❋ Shred the carrot, drained cabbage and mushrooms, the capsicum and ginger.

❋ Heat the oil in a wok and slide in the fish. Carefully fry over moderate heat until cooked and lightly crisp on both sides, then lift onto a serving plate and keep warm.

❋ Add the shredded vegetables in separate piles to the wok and pour in the pre-mixed seasoning/sauce ingredients except the cornflour. Simmer gently, occasionally stirring carefully so as not to disorganise the groups of ingredients. Lift out separately and arrange across the top of the fish. Mix the cornflour with a little cold water and stir into the sauce, boiling until the sauce thickens and clears. Pour over the fish and serve at once.

FIVE WILLOW FISH

STEAMED PORGY

Beijing 北京

STEAMED PORGY

This fish is commonly found in the East China Sea. Its flesh is snow white and very finely textured; it is full of nutritional value, and is said to have properties that keep it fresh longer than other fish.

There is a legendary figure in Japan that carries such a fish under his arm. It is said to bring blessings of peace and prosperity to the country and its people.

1 x 500 g (1 lb) bream (sea bass/porgy)
3 slices Yunnan or other salted ham
1 fresh bamboo shoot, parboiled or canned
3 dried black mushrooms, soaked for 25 minutes
2 tablespoons melted lard
2 spring onions
3-4 slices fresh (root) ginger
2 teaspoons cornflour (cornstarch)

SEASONING

2 teaspoons rice wine or dry sherry
½ teaspoon salt
¼ teaspoon white pepper

Clean and scale the fish. Make diagonal slashes across each side then hold it by the tail and dip briefly into a pot of boiling water. Lift out and dry thoroughly.

Rub with the seasoning ingredients and place in a heatproof shallow dish. Cut the ham into decorative oval shapes and insert a piece into each of the cuts on the top side of the fish. Thinly slice the bamboo shoot, cut it decoratively, and arrange along the fish. Drain the mushrooms well, remove the stems and halve the caps. Use the point of a sharp knife to shred the caps, leaving them connected in the centre to give a chrysanthemum-like appearance. Place along the fish. Sprinkle on the lard, arrange the spring onions and ginger along the fish and pour the seasoning ingredients over it. Leave for about 10 minutes to absorb the flavours, then place on a rack in a wok or in a steamer, cover and steam for 20 minutes until tender.

Discard the spring onion and ginger, remove the fish to a serving plate and pour the liquid from the steaming dish into a wok. Bring to the boil and add the cornflour mixed with a little cold water, stirring until the sauce is clear and thick. Pour over the fish before serving.

FRIED PERCH AND PORK WITH CRAB SAUCE

Guangzhou 广州

FRIED PERCH AND PORK WITH CRAB SAUCE

185 g (6 oz) perch fillets, skinned
125 g (4 oz) pork fat*
1 tablespoon rice wine or dry sherry
1 cup (125 g/4 oz) cornflour (cornstarch)
3 egg whites
salt and white pepper
oil for deep-frying

CRAB SAUCE

90 g (3 oz) fresh crabmeat
60-90 g (2-3 oz) fresh crab roe
2/3 cup (150 mL/5 fl oz) fish stock (broth)
2 egg whites
1/2 teaspoon salt
pinch of white pepper
1 1/2 teaspoons cornflour (cornstarch)
3/4 teaspoon sesame oil

Cut the fish and the pork fat into pieces about 3 x 2 cm (1 1/4 x 3/4 in). Place in a dish and sprinkle with the wine. Leave for 20 minutes, then sandwich pieces of pork and fish together. Coat each parcel thickly with cornflour.

Lightly beat 3 egg whites, adding a pinch of salt and pepper.

Heat the oil to smoking point, then reduce heat to moderate. Dip the meat parcels into the egg and fry gently in two or three batches, turning once or twice, until golden and cooked through – about 6 minutes. Lift out and drain well.

Pour the oil from the wok, rinse out and return about 1 tablespoon of oil. Add the crabmeat and roe and stir-fry briefly. Pour in the stock and bring just to the boil. Lightly beat 2 egg whites and pour into the hot stock in a slow stream. Do not stir for about 40 seconds while the egg cooks. Add salt and pepper. Mix the cornflour with a little cold water and stir into the sauce.

Arrange the perch and pork sandwiches on a serving platter. Cover with the crab sauce and sprinkle with sesame oil.

The fat just beneath the skin of a pork leg roast (fresh ham) is ideal.

FISH BALLS WITH STRAW MUSHROOMS

Guangzhou 广州

FISH BALLS WITH STRAW MUSHROOMS

In many Guangdong dishes a starch dressing (sauce thickened with cornflour or pea starch) is used to enhance the appearance of the food. This also increases the density of the dish, so it lingers on the taste buds, and keeps it moist.

250 g (8 oz) white fish fillets
1 egg white
3/4 teaspoon salt
2 tablespoons flour
12 fresh or canned straw mushrooms
1 spring onion (shallot/scallion)
3 slices fresh (root) ginger
2 teaspoons rice wine or dry sherry
oil for deep-frying
2 teaspoons cornflour (cornstarch)
1 teaspoon sesame oil
fresh coriander and carrot slices (garnish)

SIMMERING SAUCE

1/2 cup (125 mL/4 fl oz) fish stock (broth)
1/2 teaspoon sugar
pinch each of salt and white pepper

STARCH DRESSING

1/3 cup (75 mL/2 1/2 fl oz) water
1 teaspoon mushroom soy sauce
1 teaspoon cornflour (cornstarch)

Check the fish for bones, cut into small pieces and pound to a paste using the flat side of a cleaver or a food processor. Add the egg white, salt and flour and mix with your fingers to a smooth and sticky paste. Form into about 12 balls.

Trim the straw mushrooms, removing the straw and dirt fragments from the bases. Place in a wok with the spring onion, ginger and wine and add 1 cup (250 mL/8 fl oz) of water. Cover and bring to the boil, remove the lid and simmer for about 10 minutes.

Meanwhile, heat the oil in another wok and deep-fry the fish balls until golden, stirring with chopsticks to turn and colour evenly. Remove and drain. Drain the oil from the wok and add the simmering sauce ingredients. Simmer for 5-6 minutes, turning from time to time.

Add 2 teaspoons of cornflour mixed with a little cold water to the simmering mushrooms and stir until thickened, then transfer the mushrooms and sauce to a serving plate. Place the fish balls on top of the mushrooms.

Boil the starch dressing separately, stirring until thickened. Pour over the dish and sprinkle the sesame oil on top. Garnish with carrot slices and fresh coriander.

FISH CAKES AS MANDARIN DUCKS

Beijing 北京

Fish Cakes as Mandarin Ducks

Mandarin ducks live in lifelong couples, and the Chinese often compare them to husbands and wives. Guangdong people like to refer to things that are matching yet not completely alike as "mandarin ducks". A pair of chopsticks of different colours, for example, is called "yuan yang kuai zi" (mandarin duck chopsticks).

This dish is called "Fish Cakes as Mandarin Ducks" because the fish cakes have been coloured and flavoured in two different ways. One batch is simmered in a milky soup and the other in a clear soup coloured with molasses.

250 g (8 oz) dace or whiting
½ cup (125 mL/4 fl oz) water
pinch of salt
3 egg whites
½ teaspoon salt
2 tablespoons rendered chicken fat, melted
1 spring onion (shallot/scallion), shredded
2 slices fresh (root) ginger, shredded
1½ teaspoons Shaoxing rice wine or dry sherry
1 teaspoon molasses
1 cup (250 mL/8 fl oz) chicken stock (broth)
½ cup (125 mL/4 fl oz) milk
½ cup (125 mL/4 fl oz) water

Finely chop the fish, then beat to a smooth paste with the side of a cleaver or use a food processor. Mix in ½ cup (125 mL/4 fl oz) of cold water, stirring in one direction only, and add a large pinch of salt. Beat the egg whites until stiff, then fold in the fish mixture and add half of the chicken fat.

❀ Heat a large pan with water and add ½ teaspoon of salt. When simmering, form the fish batter into ovals by moulding between two wet tablespoons. Slide them into the water and simmer for about 5 minutes in gently bubbling water, until they are cooked through but retain their shape. Lift out with a slotted spoon and drain.

❀ Heat the remaining chicken fat in a wok and gently stir-fry the spring onion and ginger for 40 seconds. Add the rice wine and boil briefly, then add the molasses and chicken stock and stir until dissolved. Add half the fish cakes and simmer gently, turning carefully when the underside is well coloured. Continue to cook until there is little sauce left.

❀ In another pan, bring the milk and ½ cup (125 mL/4 fl oz) of water to a slow boil and add the remaining fish cakes. Simmer uncovered until the liquid is well reduced, then thicken with a little cornflour mixed with cold water. Turn the fish cakes in the thickened sauce until well coated.

❀ Arrange the fish cakes on a platter in pairs of gold and white.

FRIED FLAT FISH

Beijing 北京

Fried Flat Fish

1 x 375 g (12 oz) flat fish (sole, flounder or turbot)
2 teaspoons rice wine or dry sherry
½ teaspoon salt
1 teaspoon sesame oil
2 tablespoons cornflour (cornstarch)
1 egg white, well beaten
oil for frying
carrot slices (garnish)
sprigs of fresh coriander (garnish)

SAUCE

2 slices fresh (root) ginger
2 spring onions (shallots/scallions), roughly chopped
2 tablespoons rice wine or dry sherry
1 teaspoon sugar

With slightly diagonal cuts, separate the head and tail of the fish and discard. Use a knife with a flexible blade to carefully trim off the skin of the remaining central section, scrape out the gut, then rinse the fish and dry well. Place in a dish, add the wine, salt and sesame oil and leave for 1 hour, turning once.

❀ Coat the fish with cornflour, then dip into the beaten egg white and coat with cornflour again.

❀ Heat the oil in a wok and fry on both sides until golden and cooked through. Transfer to a serving plate.

❀ Pour off the oil, rinse out the wok, then return to the heat and add about 2 tablespoons of the oil. Stir-fry the ginger slices and spring onions until lightly browned, then discard. Add the rice wine and sugar with a pinch of salt and bring to the boil.

❀ Spoon the sauce over the fish, then garnish with attractively cut carrot slices and sprigs of fresh coriander and serve.

SQUID SLICES WITH JASMINE TEA

Shanghai 上海

SQUID SLICES WITH JASMINE TEA

Artistically cut, curled slivers of pearly white squid, presented in a sauce flavoured with fragrant jasmine tea and strewn with jasmine flowers, is an unforgettable dish.

500 g (1 lb) fresh squid
2 teaspoons jasmine tea leaves
2 teaspoons rice wine or dry sherry
2/3 teaspoon salt
2½ teaspoons cornflour (cornstarch)
1 tablespoon vegetable oil
3 cloves garlic, finely chopped
4 slices fresh (root) ginger
1 spring onion (shallot/scallion), roughly chopped
jasmine flowers (garnish)

Pull away the head, tentacles and stomach of the squid and dislodge the transparent cuttle. Cut the squid open and pull off the fins and skin. Rinse well under cold water and drain.

Place outerside downwards on a cutting board and score the inside very lightly lengthways, then turn over. Holding the knife at a 45° angle to the board, make deep diagonal scores across the surface, then score from the other direction so that the surface has been dissected into points giving the appearance of the spines of a pine cone.

Drop the squid into a bowl of boiling water, leave for about 20 seconds, then drain. The squid should curl attractively and the points rise up.

Place the tea leaves in a pot or jug and add 1 cup (250 mL/8 fl oz) of boiling water, leave for 2-3 minutes, then pour the water off. Add another cup (250 mL/8 fl oz) of boiling water, cover and leave for 2 minutes.

Pour the tea into a wok, add the rice wine and salt, bring to the boil, then drop in the squid and poach for 1 minute. Mix the cornflour with a little cold water and stir into the sauce, simmering briefly.

In another wok heat the vegetable oil and add garlic, ginger and spring onion. Stir-fry for 1 minute until the garlic is lightly coloured, then pour in the squid with its tea sauce and simmer briefly. Pick out the ginger and spring onion and transfer the dish to a serving plate.

Strew with fresh jasmine flowers, and serve at once.

COUNTRY-STYLE FRIED STUFFED DACE

FRIED MELON DATES

Guangzhou 广州

COUNTRY-STYLE FRIED STUFFED DACE

The people of Guangdong are particularly fond of the smooth flesh, delicate flavour and rich protein of the dace. Its fine bones do, however, make it less enjoyable, but prepared the following way, the fish is boneless, tender and more flavourful. The meat is minced and mixed with diced sausage, dried mushrooms and shrimps to make a stuffing which is filled into the skin and served in the original shape of the fish. Although it is difficult to skin fish, nearly every housewife in Shundeh County is an expert in preparing dace in this way. Whiting will give equally good results.

2 x 375 g (12 oz) dace or whiting
2 dried Chinese sausages, or 30 g (1 oz) Yunnan or
    salted ham
2 tablespoons dried shrimps, soaked for 25 minutes
3 dried black mushrooms, soaked for 25 minutes
1-2 cloves garlic, crushed
½ cup (60 g/2 oz) cornflour (cornstarch)
2 cups (500 mL/16 fl oz) oil for frying
1 tablespoon superior or other light soy sauce
2 teaspoons rice wine or dry sherry
⅔ cup (150 mL/5 fl oz) fish or chicken stock (broth)
fresh coriander (garnish)

SEASONING

⅓ teaspoon sesame oil
½ teaspoon sugar
⅓ teaspoon salt
pinch of white pepper
2 teaspoons cornflour (cornstarch)

Clean and rinse the fish. Use a sharp knife to slit each fish closely along the backbone, severing it completely. Lift out the backbone completely and discard. Place the fish skin side down and carefully cut the meat from the skin, then do the same with the other side so that the skin remains attached to the head and tail while the meat has been completely detached. Pick or cut away the line of fine bones which runs down the centre of each fillet. Chop the fish meat roughly, then beat vigorously with a side of a cleaver until reduced to a smooth paste.

🦐 Steam the sausages on a rack in a wok or in a steamer for 5-6 minutes until softened. Drain the shrimps and mushrooms. Finely dice all three ingredients and mix with the fish, adding the seasoning ingredients and the garlic.

🦐 Dust the inside of each fish skin lightly with cornflour. Divide the mixture into two parts and spread half along the centre of each fish skin, moulding the stuffed fish into their original shape.

🦐 Coat the fish evenly with more cornflour, brushing off the excess. Heat the oil in a wok and when quite hot fry the two stuffed fish until well coloured on both sides. Carefully lift onto a serving plate.

🦐 Drain the wok, return about 1 tablespoon of the oil and add the soy sauce, wine and stock. Boil briskly, then thicken with about 1½ teaspoons of cornflour mixed with a little cold water. Pour over the fish and garnish with fresh coriander.

Guangzhou 广州

FRIED MELON DATES

This is a well-known Fujian dish, but the ingredients include neither melon nor dates. Its name comes from the yellow melon fish which is plentiful along the coast of Fujian Province. This is sliced and rolled into date shapes, which are coated and fried and served on a bed of crisply fried salted vegetable leaves.

315 g (10 oz) melon fish or other white fish fillets
2 teaspoons rice wine or dry sherry
1 teaspoon ginger juice
½ teaspoon salt
lard or oil for frying
6-8 leaves dried salted cabbage or rape, shredded
oil for deep-frying
five-spice salt*

BATTER

3 egg whites, well beaten
3 tablespoons cornflour (cornstarch)
3 tablespoons flour

Cut the fish into strips and place in a dish, adding the wine, ginger juice and salt. Mix well and leave for 1 hour.

🦐 Mix the batter ingredients, adding just enough cold water to make a thick batter.

🦐 Heat the lard or oil in a wok to smoking point, then lower the heat slightly. Dip the fish into the batter and slide into the oil to fry for about 1¼ minutes until golden, then drain and keep warm.

🦐 Heat another wok with the oil for deep-frying to smoking point, place the shredded vegetable leaves in a frying basket, deep-fry for a few seconds until bright green and crisp, remove and arrange on a serving platter. Place the fish on top of the vegetables and serve with the five-spice salt as a dip.

To make the five-spice salt, heat 1½ tablespoons of fine table salt in a wok until it begins to crackle, add 1 teaspoon of Chinese five spice powder, remove from the heat, stir and cool.

JADE WHITE SLICED FISH

Sichuan 四川

JADE WHITE SLICED FISH

220 g (7 oz) white fish fillets
1 egg white, well beaten
3 tablespoons soy bean powder or cornflour (cornstarch)
2 cups (500 mL/16 fl oz) oil for frying

SAUCE

6 thin slices fresh young (root) ginger
1 pickled red chilli
2 spring onions (shallots/scallions), white parts only
1 clove garlic
12 sprigs fresh pea leaves or 2-3 lettuce leaves
½ cup (125 mL/4 fl oz) fish stock
1 teaspoon rice wine or dry sherry
1 teaspoon sugar
pinch each of salt and white pepper
2 teaspoons cornflour (cornstarch)

Cut the fish into thin slices and place in a dish with the egg white. Mix well, then coat each slice of fish lightly on both sides with the soy bean powder or cornflour.

Heat the oil in a wok to smoking point, then reduce the heat and fry the fish, about 8 pieces at a time, over moderate heat until just cooked through and still white. Lift out and drain well.

To prepare the sauce, cut the ginger into decorative shapes, slice the chilli and onions diagonally and chop the garlic. Chop the lettuce leaves into squares, if used.

Drain off the oil and wipe out the wok. Return about 2 tablespoons of the oil and stir-fry the ginger, chilli, onions and garlic for 1 minute over moderate heat. Add the remaining pre-mixed sauce ingredients and bring to the boil. Add the pea leaves or lettuce squares and the fish and simmer very gently, stirring to mix evenly. Transfer to a serving dish and serve at once.

Guangzhou 广州

SHARKS' FINS BRAISED IN BROWN SAUCE

Shark's fin is a delicacy that featured at most Imperial banquets of the Qing Dynasty (1644-1911 AD). Its esteem in the Chinese cuisine comes from the use of the best ingredients, the culinary skills required to prepare it, and its high nutritional value. Shark's fin cooked in the method described here is golden and translucent with a smooth texture and luscious aroma. A dish of this calibre is rarely made at home, but can be enjoyed in most fine restaurants.

280 g (9 oz) prepared dried sharks' fins
4 slices fresh (root) ginger
2 spring onions (shallots/scallions)
2 tablespoons rice wine or dry sherry
1 tablespoon cornflour (cornstarch)
125 g (4 oz) silver sprouts*
2 red chillies
2-3 slices cooked ham
black or red vinegar

SUPERIOR STOCK

½ chicken
6 chicken feet
½ pig's trotter (knuckle)
155 g (5 oz) lean pork
1 tablespoon dark soy sauce
½ teaspoon salt
pinch of white pepper
4 cups (1 L/32 fl oz) water

Soak the sharks' fins in cold water for 2 hours, bring to the boil and simmer gently for 30 minutes. Drain and cover with more cold water, soak for a further 2 hours, bring to the boil and simmer 30 minutes again. Repeat this twice more, then rinse the fins well in cold water and drain.

In the meantime, place the stock ingredients in a separate saucepan, bring to the boil and skim. Continue boiling gently, covered, for 3 hours, until the liquid has been well reduced.

Place the sharks' fins on a closely woven bamboo rack and arrange the ginger and spring onions on top, then sprinkle with the wine. Place the rack in a casserole and strain over the stock. Set the pot on a rack in a wok or in a steamer, cover and steam over simmering water for about 1½ hours. Top up the water in the steamer from time to time. Remove the sharks' fins from the rack and place on a serving plate.

Bring the stock to the boil, thicken with the cornflour mixed with a little cold water and simmer until the sauce becomes transparent. Adjust seasoning to taste and pour the sauce over the fins.

Blanch the sprouts, finely shred the chillies and ham, and arrange the three ingredients on several small dishes. Serve with the sharks' fins, together with dishes of black or red vinegar.

*Fresh mung beansprouts from which the yellow seed pods and tapered roots have been removed, leaving the silver-coloured sprouts.

SHARKS' FINS BRAISED IN BROWN SAUCE

BRAISED SHARKS' FINS, TAN FAMILY STYLE

Beijing 北京

BRAISED SHARKS' FINS, TAN FAMILY STYLE

The famous Tan family, who started their first restaurant during the Qing Dynasty (1644-1911 AD) apparently had twenty ways of cooking sharks' fins. This one has been handed down for generations and is considered one of their best.

75 g (2½ oz) dried sharks' fins
1 x 1¼ kg (2½ lb) chicken
½ x 1¾ kg (3½ lb) duck
5 dried scallops, soaked for 1 hour
125 g (4 oz) Yunnan or other salted ham, chopped
8 cups (2 L/64 fl oz) water
1 tablespoon rice wine or dry sherry
1 teaspoon sugar
2 tablespoons superior or other light soy sauce
salt and pepper
2-3 teaspoons dried prawn (shrimp) roe (optional)
red vinegar (dip)

Place the sharks' fins in a saucepan, cover with water and bring to the boil. Simmer for 20 minutes, then drain and cover with cold water again. Bring to the boil and simmer gently for about 2 hours. Leave to cool in the water, then pour the water off. Scrape away any tough pieces of skin, then rinse the fins, cover with cold water and bring to the boil. Reduce the heat and simmer gently for another hour. Leave to cool in the water.

❀ Drain and place the sharks' fins on a closely woven bamboo rack in a wok and cover with another bamboo rack. Chop the chicken and duck into pieces and arrange on the top rack. Add the scallops, ham and the water. Cover, bring to the boil and simmer gently for 3 hours, or until the sharks' fins are soft and tender and the stock richly flavoured.

❀ Remove the chicken, duck, scallops and ham to use in another dish, or discard.

❀ Bring the sharks' fins and their stock to the boil, season with the wine, sugar and soy sauce, and add salt and pepper to taste. Sprinkle with the fish roe, if used, and simmer, uncovered, for about 15 minutes until the liquid has reduced to just cover the fins.

❀ If shrimp roe has not been used, very finely dice a little of the ham and use this to garnish the dish.

❀ Serve with small dishes of red vinegar dip.

Shanghai 上海

EEL SHREDS WITH SESAME OIL

Eel is delicious and highly nutritious. Traditional Chinese folk medicine holds that eel gives one energy and helps in the treatment of rheumatism.

Eel has different distinctive features during each of the four seasons. It is tender and delicately flavoured in spring, most delicious during the rice transplanting time from the end of spring to early summer, tough in autumn and fat in winter.

Eels should be killed just before cooking as the meat deteriorates quickly and then acquires a muddy and strong fishy flavour.

1 kg (2 lb) freshwater eels
3 tablespoons lard
6 slices young fresh (root) ginger
1 tablespoon sesame oil
½ teaspoon white pepper

SEASONING/SAUCE

¾ cup (175 mL/6 fl oz) chicken or fish stock (broth)
2½ tablespoons superior or other light soy sauce
1 tablespoon rice wine or dry sherry
1½ teaspoons sugar
⅓ teaspoon powdered ginger
1 teaspoon cornflour (cornstarch)

EEL SHREDS WITH SESAME OIL

Drop the eels into boiling water to kill, then remove. Cut off the heads and then use a sharp knife to remove the meat in long fillets from the backbone and cut into shreds. Eels do not need to be skinned if they are young and small.

⚘ Rub out a wok with an oiled cloth, add the lard and heat to smoking point. Drop in the eel meat and stir-fry over very high heat until it changes colour and is cooked through. Remove to a plate. Add the pre-mixed seasoning ingredients, except the cornflour, to the wok, and stir until boiling. Return the eel, cover and simmer gently for 2-3 minutes.

⚘ Mix the cornflour with a little cold water and pour into the sauce, stirring until thickened. Transfer the eel and sauce to a serving dish.

⚘ In another pan heat the sesame oil until very hot. Make a small well in the centre of the eel meat and pour in the oil, then sprinkle on the pepper. The hot oil will sizzle and make the dish very fragrant. Serve at once.

Guangzhou 广州

EEL STEWED IN A CLAY POT

"When the north wind blows, the wind eel is plump" is an old Chinese saying. The wind eel is a highly nutritious seafood delicacy. Every winter the eels swim out from the Zhu Jiang River into the ocean where spawning takes place on the sea bed some 400 metres (1,300 feet) deep. The young fry later swim back to the mouth of the river where they continue to grow buried in the silt, emerging between the end of autumn and early winter when the north winds blow and the temperature falls. Thus they have become known as "feng shan", or wind eel.

Apart from pot roasting and stewing, wind eels are also eaten sliced and poached, steamboat-style, or made into a porridge with glutinous rice – a milk-coloured, rich, warming dish.

1 x 750 g (1½ lb) feng shan eel or other meaty eel
1 tablespoon mushroom soy sauce
oil for deep-frying
155 g (5 oz) roasted or boiled belly pork (fresh bacon)
10 cloves garlic
6-8 dried black mushrooms, soaked for 25 minutes
6 slices fresh (root) ginger
2 pieces dried orange peel, soaked for 10 minutes
1 tablespoon cornflour (cornstarch)
1 tablespoon vegetable oil (optional)
fresh coriander (garnish)

SEASONING/STOCK

1 tablespoon rice wine or dry sherry
2 tablespoons superior or other light soy sauce
¼ teaspoon salt
¼ teaspoon white pepper
2 cups (500 mL/16 fl oz) hot fish stock (broth) or
    superior stock (*see page 124*)

Kill the eel by severing the head. Place in a strainer and pour on boiling water, then rinse thoroughly. Cut into 5 cm (2 in) pieces, rub with the mushroom soy sauce and leave for 10 minutes.

⚘ Slice the pork, peel the garlic and leave whole, drain and shred the mushrooms.

⚘ Heat the oil in a wok and fry the eel until well coloured. Using a slotted spoon, transfer the eel to a clay pot or casserole. Fry the pork and garlic in the oil until lightly coloured.

⚘ Arrange the pork, garlic, mushrooms, ginger and orange peel over the eel. Add the seasoning/stock ingredients, cover tightly and simmer for about 20 minutes until the eel is tender. Thicken with the cornflour mixed with a little cold water and add the vegetable oil, if used. Garnish with fresh coriander.

EEL STEWED IN A CLAY POT

广州

Guangzhou

HUNAN

FUJIAN

Guilin

GUANGDONG

Xi River

Dong River

Foshan *Guangzhou*

NAN HAI (SOUTH CHINA SEA)

Guangzhou
THE JAGGED COAST

Between China's two major islands, Taiwan and Hainan, 1600 kilometres (1,000 miles) of jagged coastline curves in a gigantic arc. Taiwan, with its snowy peaks, rich rainforests and sandy beaches, straddles the straits off the province of Fujian. The island of Hainan, a tropical paradise where coconut palms wave above plantations of exotic fruit, guards the Gulf of Tonkin from the full fury of the Dai Fung, the typhoons that sweep in over the South China Sea. These two islands, and thousands of other less significant outcrops that speckle the coast, rim the southern flank of China. This indented coastline provides the rich bounty that forms the basis of China's best-known cuisine: Cantonese food, in all its diverse and splendid variety.

The coastline between the islands has everything that generous nature can bestow. Narrow river valleys broaden into fertile plains, and the sprawling estuary of the Pearl River delta provides a wonderland of twisting waterways where fish and fowl luxuriate. Countless coves and bays glow at night with the flaring twinkle of sampan lamps guiding juicy tiger prawns into the nets. On steep cliffs above azure waters fishermen tend long snap nets drooping from bamboo poles, ready to hoist ashore any school of fish unwary enough to venture past.

Out from land, on the expanse of the South China Sea, the sails of junks flap in the monsoon breeze as their nets haul taut behind. Most junks today have engines, but the romance of the sailing junk is inseparable from the legends of the China coast. Closer inshore, under the craggy rocks, tiny sampans bob in the surf as their occupants dangerously pluck shellfish from cliffs pounded by the waves. Seaweed, disdained and discarded in the West, is a profitable crop on the China coast. Jellyfish also grace the table along with sea urchins and slugs that crawl along the ocean bed.

More than half the area of the beautiful island of Hainan is an autonomous prefecture for the Li and Miao peoples. The market in their mountain capital of Tongshi offers a rewarding glimpse of their varied

A FISHING FLEET OFF HAINAN ISLAND
PAUL LAU

(previous page) SUNRISE OVER HAINAN ISLAND   PAUL LAU

THE YUSHAN MOUNTAINS, A MISTY BACKDROP TO THE MEI JIANG RIVER, JIANGXI PROVINCE   LEO MEIER

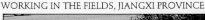

WORKING IN THE FIELDS, JIANGXI PROVINCE

cuisine. Rice is the staple in this fertile paradise, but it is often accompanied by jungle delicacies such as stewed freshwater turtle or baked civet cat. Almost every Li household has a shotgun, and hunting is a passion. Even today, when much of the farmland grows rubber, sisal, peppers, cocoa, coffee and other tropical cash crops, the traditional hunting parties go out into the hills after game. The catch is still distributed in the ancient manner: the man who fired the successful shot gets a quarter and the rest of the quarry is divided between members of the hunting party, and any strangers they meet on the way home.

The southern coast, and more specifically the vast steamy delta of the Pearl River have given the Western world the flavour of Chinese food. This is not surprising, as most of the original American–Chinese came from this region: three hundred and fifty thousand Californians can trace their roots back to the county of Toishan, a former pirate haven and bandit den. The men from the delta left in a wave of despair to dig the gold mines of the sierras and hack the railroads across the Rocky Mountains. Foshan men went to the gold diggings in Australia, Hakka hill villagers left to grow pineapples in Hawaii and pan gold in New Zealand, and the Guangzhou city dwellers went to every port in the world. With them they took not only commercial cunning and a staggering ability to work, but also a gastronomic legacy that has enriched every land they reached.

The Cantonese cuisine found outside China is, however, unlike that of Guangdong Province. The dishes have been adapted to cater for local tastes: steamed chicken with bamboo shoots, for example, has a flavour in Sydney different to the dish of the same name served in San Francisco or Liverpool. It is no coincidence that all three of these great cities with their big Chinatowns are major ports, because it was by ship that the Guangdong

LEO MEIER

132

exodus reached the Western world, and it was by ship, when they had enough money to buy a tiny plot of the good earth of China, that they planned to come home. Very few left the delta with the intention of settling overseas. Their aim was to work to buy a wife and a plot of land back in their native village. But as the presence of thirty million overseas Chinese vividly testifies today, the dream of returning to the Middle Kingdom was for many of them a forlorn hope.

The land they left behind is very different these days from the piratical coast of the mid-nineteenth century. Nowhere in the entire country do climate and geography play a more vital role in shaping cuisine than along the jagged southern coastal rim. Food is fresh and bursting with vigour, juice and goodness. The astonishing bounty of the seas is rushed alive to market. In even the most humble of restaurants, live fish, crabs, prawns, lobsters and eels swim in large tanks before the eyes of appreciative diners. Seafood in the Cantonese kitchen has been elevated to an art. It is the supreme food of the southern school of cooking, the preparation of which calls for great skill. The love of fish is coupled with a compulsion for fresh food, so the main item on a menu is likely to be swimming in a fish tank one minute and the next served steaming on a platter with a whisper of spring onions and a hint of ginger.

To the adoration of seafood add a great desire for vegetables. Once again the gentle southern climate, hot and steamy for most of the year like some gigantic glass-

VIBRANT COSTUMES AT FOSHAN FESTIVAL, GUANGDONG PROVINCE   JACKY YIP

BOAT RACES AT FOSHAN FESTIVAL, GUANGDONG PROVINCE   JACKY YIP

HAINAN ISLAND

PAUL LAU

house given by the gods, provides the best that nature can offer. From lowland fields, which produce six crops of prime vegetables every year, farmers come to market bringing the splendid results of their labour. It is said that the Chinese agriculturalist is more a gardener than a farmer – perhaps, but the men and women who stoop endlessly over their patches of fertile earth are more lovers of the soil than simple gardeners. The earth is their passion as well as their pride. The summer rains soak deeply into the fertilised soil, the sun blazes, the tiller of the soil walks between the rows of glowing vegetables giving each plant its own private dousing from a bamboo watering can. The steam rises, the fruit hangs heavy in the summer noon, the very air reeks of fertility. The coastal rim and its inland valleys produce a range of vegetables probably unequalled on earth, and they are picked every day to be carried or trucked to markets in Fujian, Guangdong, Taiwan and Guangxi, where the housewives are unbending in their insistence on the freshest of foods, and refuse to contemplate cooking something not picked that very day.

The pride and the passion of the farmers is matched by the fanaticism to be found among the chefs in any southern kitchen. Cantonese cooks are the best in the world. Chefs in other provinces agree with this, and there is no higher praise than that. Cooking and eating the best that nature has to offer is a vital part of southern life. Much of that life is spent in the pursuit of excellent

A COLOURFUL DISH FROM GUANGXI PROVINCE   PAUL LAU

A FINE EXAMPLE OF CHINESE INTERIOR ART IN A GUANGZHOU DINING ROOM

MICHAEL COOK

134

food. Day begins in many a city of the south with old men walking with their caged birds to special restaurants where their pets can twitter at each other as their owners eat. At the most famous teahouse on earth, the Panxi in Guangzhou, every morning long before public transport starts, regular breakfast customers walk great distances to stand in line to be first at the tables when the doors open at 6 am. The Panxi is noted for its invention of thousands of new varieties of dim sum and, of course, everyone wants to be first to try the newest version of the ancient titbits.

Devotees of the southern kitchen like to announce to visitors that they will eat anything. The newcomer to their ways should not doubt it, or he might find himself feasting on owl, anteater or cobra, all firmly favoured by Cantonese gourmets. Wild cats and plump, black-tongued Chow dogs are also bred for the pot. "We eat anything whose backbone does not point to heaven" goes one old saying. True, but that was before men of the delta emigrated to South America and found the sloth that hangs upside down in trees, and discovered that this also provided the basis of a dainty treat.

"Be born in Suzhou" urges a traditional poem much quoted in the Pearl River delta. Suzhou, near Shanghai, is said to produce the most beautiful women in China. Be born in Suzhou; live in Hangzhou where the nation's finest silk comes from; die in Luzhou where the wood best suited for noble coffins grows; and eat where the best food in the world can be found – in the kitchens of Guangzhou, naturally.

The people of Guangzhou like to point out the predominant position they have held in the kitchens of China and the world over the centuries. Cantonese cuisine is, however, a varied mixture. Within the province of Guangdong alone there are major variations. The Hakka people, the gypsies of China who settled on the southern rim after fleeing from barbarian invaders in the north, have their own style of cooking. The gastronomic delights of Chiu Chow cuisine are in a class of their very own. Fujian Province rivals even Guangdong in its pursuit of treasures from the sea, and the aboriginal tribes on the east coast of Taiwan make a seafood soup that is more ambitious than the heartiest bouillabaisse to be found on the waterfront of Marseille.

The strength that underlies the region is provided by nature. From the sea, the land and the ponds that harbour fat carp and contented duck, the stress is on natural, fresh goodness. It is on this basis of fresh food that Cantonese cuisine is built. Along the entire coast nature's abundance has provided raw materials that make life easy for master chef and imaginative housewife alike. Few additional flavourings are needed: a hint of ginger, a small dash of salt, a gentle sprinkling of spring onions. The natural goodness and sweet taste of food straight from the garden or the water is the trademark of the famous Cantonese kitchen.

SUNSET OVER HAINAN ISLAND   PAUL LAU

(following page)
TERRACED HILL SIDES IN GUANGXI PROVINCE
PAUL LAU

NOMADS TEND THEIR SHEEP ON THE GRASSLANDS OF NORTHERN SICHUAN

LEONG KA TAI

肉類
Meat

Meat 肉類

WHEN a Chinese chef talks of meat, it is almost certain that the animal to which he refers is the pig. In every corner of the land pork is the most common and preferred meat. The only exceptions are the Muslim areas of the northwest, and even there the increasing settlement of Han Chinese has led to pork becoming commonly available. It is no coincidence that in Chinese script the character for "home" consists of the ideogram for a "pig" under a "roof". For centuries the home was where the pig lived, often sharing a modest hut in a tiny village with its owner. Pigs are still common throughout China, although they are now raised by agronomists using more scientific methods as well as by farmers' wives in the barnyard.

Chefs use pork in at least seven out of every ten meat dishes. The reasons are historic, culinary and economic. Pigs are easy to raise and can live virtually anywhere there are people. They are cheap to feed, simple to care for and adaptable. They grow quickly and produce meat of high quality that can be sliced, shredded or cubed for any style of cooking. Pork has no strong flavour of its own, making it ideal to use as a base on which to build a combination dish with virtually any vegetable. It can be covered with honey and roasted whole, or ground to make the ideal raw ingredient for the beloved meatball. Indeed, if the pig did not exist a Chinese cook would have to invent it.

Pork in one guise or another appears prominently in every regional cuisine. A thousand years ago recipe books contained instructions for the dutiful housewife on how to prepare pork for sacrifices to ancestors and family deities. Today there is keen provincial rivalry about which area produces the best ham in China; but the most famous, with much justification, comes from Yunnan. The bacons of Hunan, laid out to dry in the winter sun, are renowned. Winter sausages, strongly akin to the spicy sausages of Hungary, are a speciality of Shanxi. Shanghai chefs use ground pork in soup and inside pastries; and heavy hearty dumplings – each large enough to feed three hungry people in the northern winter – are famous in Liaoning. Guangdong prides itself on whole suckling pigs suspended from a chain in a special kiln which bakes them crisply to produce the incomparable roast pork of Guangzhou. As the pig cooks,

A PIG SELLER, SICHUAN PROVINCE PAUL LAU

the fat drains off to sizzle in a pan of water at the bottom of the huge upright oven which then fills with steam so the meat stays sweetly succulent as it roasts.

Pork may be predominant, but every other sort of meat has at one time or another, somewhere in the country, been enjoyed. Historically, beef has been rare in China. For the past two thousand years there simply has not been sufficient land to raise grazing herds. The only cattle generally seen by the average Chinese is the dignified old water buffalo, more a friend and a tool to the peasant farmer with whom the creature grows up and works the fields for most of its life. Only when old and useless, after years of toil which have developed muscles instead of meat, does the buffalo ever find its way into the pot, by which time it is disdainfully rejected by the gourmet.

A strongly held article of faith of many southerners is that they simply cannot abide the strong smell of sheep or goat. No such prejudices prevent the northerner from enjoying lamb, kid, sheep or goat. A dish that is a delight to a Beijing gourmet, like lamb fried with coriander, will be eaten swiftly and without pleasure by someone from Guangzhou who is taking it as a medicine instead of a meal. But although repelled by the thought of eating sheep, the southerner will go to considerable trouble and spend as much as necessary to enjoy a bowl of dog stew. This delicacy is not only believed to warm the blood and help the circulation during the chilly winter months, but is also a gastronome's joy.

Although they are the proud inheritors of the oldest agrarian tradition on earth, the Chinese have always been keen hunters. The hunt, strictly for the pot, is an interest that continues today all over the country except in the most densely populated areas. Even in provinces with huge populations there still remain large areas of mountain and forest where game is abundant. There is now no necessity for peasants to hunt to eat; starvation is no longer the spur, but the sport is enjoyed and rare creatures that are not grown domestically sometimes add spice to the family table. Venison, rabbit, bear, tiger, snake, boar, pangolin, mountain goat, hare and other game are prized species which feature prominently in ancient recipe books. Alas for the modern gourmet, they are now more difficult to find.

YAKS, A SOURCE OF MILK AND MEAT FOR NOMADIC TIBETAN TRIBES — LEO MEIER

GOATS AND OXEN GRAZE IN MOUNTAINOUS NORTHERN YUNNAN

GREGORY HEISLER

Sichuan 四川

APPETISERS IN A LACQUER BOX

A banquet in Sichuan will often begin with an assortment of cold appetisers served in a multi-sectioned box made of lacquered wood. This classical and elegant presentation displays the efforts of the chef and the host, together with the traditional craft of lacquer work.

The contents of these boxes vary according to season, but each item must have a different taste and cooking method. Some may be salted, others quick-fried, others mixed. The cutting methods too must differ – slices, chunks, dice, strips, curls, rolls.

The colours must present attractive patterns and contrast. Flavours must complement – some mild, others strong.

THIS SELECTION COMPRISES

Steamed, thinly sliced Yunnan ham
Salt-simmered duck with peeled broad beans
"Thousand-year" eggs
Cabbage rolls with dried chillies
Thinly sliced Chinese sausage
Sliced poached winter bamboo shoots
Dry-fried beef with Sichuan pepper and chillies
Diamonds of boiled winter melon interlaced with
    dried shrimp
Curls of spring onion centred with slivers of red chilli,
    served on a bed of edible black moss and dried shrimp

Guangzhou 广州

SKEWERED PORK DIPPED IN MALT SUGAR

Slightly fatty pork should be used in this dish, otherwise it will burn and dry out during the cooking process. The malt sugar, brushed over the pork during roasting, gives a rich, red-brown glaze and adds a crisp texture and salty sweet taste.

500 g (1 lb) pork leg with a little fat
3 tablespoons malt sugar
½ cup (125 mL/4 fl oz) boiling water

SEASONING

1½ tablespoons light soy sauce
1 tablespoon dark or mushroom soy sauce
1 tablespoon Fen liquor, rice wine or dry sherry
2 tablespoons soy bean oil
¼ teaspoon salt
1 tablespoon sugar
1 teaspoon sesame oil

Cut the meat into strips and place in a dish with the pre-mixed seasoning ingredients. Mix well and marinate for 2-3 hours, turning frequently.

✻ Thread the strips of pork on a thick metal skewer and suspend them in a pre-heated hot oven (200°C/400°F) over a drip-tray to roast for 10 minutes.

✻ Mix the malt sugar and boiling water together, stirring until the sugar has melted. Remove the pork from the oven and brush liberally with the syrup, then return to the oven to roast for a further 5 minutes. Brush again with syrup, roast again very briefly, then remove from the oven and brush with a final coating of syrup.

✻ Cut into slices and arrange on a serving plate. Can be served warm or cold.

(inset) APPETISERS IN A LACQUER BOX

SKEWERED PORK DIPPED IN MALT SUGAR

LOTUS EGGS WITH BARBECUED PORK

Guangzhou 广州

LOTUS EGGS WITH BARBECUED PORK

The lotus "grows out of the mud but is not stained. It stands firmly against the wind, elegantly beautiful and mildly scented." Many famous people praised the lotus and even compared it to the beauty of women. In Guangdong cuisine, when egg is an important ingredient in a dish, the name of the dish often incorporates the word lotus (fuyong). This alludes to the resemblance of the egg's delicate texture and pale colour to the beauty of the lotus.

2 eggs
4 egg whites
125 g (4 oz) barbecued pork
45 g (1½ oz) fresh or canned bamboo shoots
2 spring onions (shallots/scallions), white parts only
2-3 tablespoons lard or oil for frying
¾ teaspoon salt
pinch of pepper

Beat the eggs and egg whites together thoroughly and set aside.
❊ Cut the barbecued pork, bamboo shoots and spring onions into fine shreds. Heat the lard or oil in a wok and sauté the shredded ingredients briefly.
❊ Season the egg with salt and pepper, pour over the shredded ingredients and cook over moderate heat, stirring only occasionally, until golden brown underneath. Turn the whole omelet without cutting and gently cook the other side until the egg is just firm, then slide onto a serving dish.

Beijing 北京

DEEP-FRIED SHREDDED PORK

315 g (10 oz) pork fillet
½ cup (60 g/2 oz) cornflour (cornstarch)
2½ cups (625 mL/20 fl oz) peanut oil
¼ small red capsicum (bell pepper), shredded
¼ small green capsicum (bell pepper), shredded
2 spring onions (shallots/scallions), white parts only, shredded
1 teaspoon chilli oil or chilli sauce

SEASONING

1 tablespoon light soy sauce
2 teaspoons ginger juice
2 teaspoons rice wine or dry sherry
2 teaspoons brown vinegar
½ teaspoon salt

DEEP-FRIED SHREDDED PORK

Cut the pork fillet into paper-thin slices, then into shreds, finer than matchsticks. Mix the cornflour with enough cold water to make a thin paste. Add the pork and mix well until each shred is thinly coated with the paste.
❊ Heat the peanut oil in a wok to smoking point and deep-fry the pork shreds until crisp, using wooden chopsticks to separate the shreds. The pork will turn a light golden brown and rustle slightly when drained, as soon as it is done. Remove and set aside.
❊ Drain the oil, leaving about 1 tablespoon, add the pre-mixed seasoning ingredients and bring to the boil. Return the fried pork and stir-fry in the sauce until evenly coated, add the capsicums and onions and toss all together, then sprinkle on the chilli oil, toss well and transfer to a serving plate.

Sichuan 四川

PORK WITH SICHUAN PRESERVED CABBAGE

Chinese preserved cabbage, and especially that from Fulin in Sichuan, is famous for its unique flavour and has been exported all over the world. In the preparation it is seasoned with a great variety of condiments, in particular fennel, pepper, licorice root, Chinese cassia, chilli, salt and spirits.

185 g (6 oz) Sichuan preserved cabbage
375 g (12 oz) pork fillet (tenderloin)
1 leek or 2-3 spring onions (shallots/scallions)
3 slices fresh (root) ginger
1-2 fresh red chillies
3 tablespoons lard or vegetable oil

SEASONING

1 tablespoon light soy sauce
2 tablespoons rice wine or dry sherry
1 tablespoon cornflour (cornstarch)
½ teaspoon sugar

Soak the salted cabbage in cold water for 1 hour. Drain and squeeze out as much water as possible, then cut into strips of about 5 x 1 cm (2 x ½ in) and set aside.
❊ Very thinly slice the pork, cutting across the grain, then stack the slices and cut them into fine shreds. Place in a dish with the pre-mixed seasoning ingredients, mix well and leave for 20 minutes.
❊ Cut the leek, ginger and chillies into fine shreds.
❊ Heat the lard in a wok to smoking point. Stir-fry the pork and cabbage together until the pork changes colour. Push to one side of the pan and add the remaining ingredients, stir-frying for 1 minute. Mix with the pork and cabbage, add 1 tablespoon of water, check the seasoning and serve.

STIR-FRIED DICED PORK WITH CASHEW NUTS

Guangzhou 广州

STIR-FRIED DICED PORK WITH CASHEW NUTS

The cashew nut grows abundantly in sub-tropical climates. Its strange looking fruit consists of two parts: the upper part called the "pear" or "false fruit" is soft and juicy with the flavour of musk, and is eaten as a fruit; the lower part comprises the shell and crescent-shaped kernel of the cashew.

Deep-fried cashew nuts are extremely crisp, with a flavour surpassing peanuts which are often used in Chinese cooking.

315 g (10 oz) lean pork
2 spring onions (shallots/scallions)
1/3 red capsicum (bell pepper)
1/3 green capsicum (bell pepper)
2 cloves garlic
2 dried black mushrooms, soaked for 25 minutes
oil for deep-frying
90-125 g (3-4 oz) raw cashew nuts

SEASONING

1 teaspoon rice wine or dry sherry
1/2 teaspoon salt
3/4 teaspoon sugar
2 teaspoons cornflour (cornstarch)

SAUCE

1/3 cup (75 mL/2 1/2 fl oz) chicken stock (broth) or water
1 teaspoon dark soy sauce
1/2 teaspoon salt
1/2 teaspoon sugar
pinch of white pepper
1 teaspoon cornflour (cornstarch)

Dice the pork finely, add the seasoning ingredients, mix well and leave for 20 minutes.

⚒ Cut the spring onions into short lengths, dice the capsicums, finely chop the garlic and squeeze the water from the mushrooms before cutting into small dice.

⚒ Heat the oil in a large wok and deep-fry the pork in a frying basket or large perforated ladle for about 3 minutes until cooked through. Remove and drain well. Deep-fry the cashew nuts until they begin to colour and remove quickly. Do not overcook or they will be bitter. Set aside.

⚒ Drain the wok, reserving about 1 tablespoon of the oil, and stir-fry the vegetables and garlic for 2-3 minutes. Mix the sauce ingredients together and pour into the wok, stirring to thicken. Add the pork and toss together until well coated with the sauce and mixed with the vegetables.

⚒ Transfer to a serving plate and arrange the cashews on top. Serve at once.

SWEET AND SOUR PORK

Guangzhou 广州

SWEET AND SOUR PORK

280 g (9 oz) pork belly (fresh bacon)
1/2 teaspoon salt
2 teaspoons rice wine or dry sherry
1 egg, well beaten
1 medium green capsicum (bell pepper)
60 g (2 oz) fresh or canned bamboo shoots
2-3 spring onions (shallots/scallions)
3 cloves garlic
1 cup (125 g/4 oz) cornflour (cornstarch)
oil for deep-frying
1/2 teaspoon sesame oil (optional)

SWEET AND SOUR SAUCE

2 tablespoons sugar
1 tablespoon oil for frying
3 tablespoons brown vinegar
1/2 cup (125 mL/4 fl oz) stock (broth)
salt and pepper
1 teaspoon cornflour (cornstarch)

Use a sharp knife to closely crosshatch the pork skin, then cut the meat into cubes, each with a piece of skin attached. Place in a dish with the salt, rice wine and egg, mix well and set aside.

⚒ Cut the capsicum in half, remove the seeds, stem and inner ribs and cut into squares. Thinly slice the bamboo shoots and the spring onions and finely chop the garlic.

⚒ Place the cornflour in a plastic bag, add the pork and shake vigorously to coat thickly and evenly, transfer to a colander and shake off the excess.

⚒ Heat the oil in a wok to smoking point and deep-fry the pork for 1 minute, then lower the heat slightly and continue to fry for about 3 minutes until well cooked and crisp on the surface. Remove and drain well.

⚒ Drain off the oil and wipe out the wok. Return 2 tablespoons of the oil and stir-fry the capsicum, bamboo shoots, spring onions and garlic for about 1 1/2 minutes. Add the pork and mix well, then remove to a plate.

⚒ Pour the sugar and oil of the sauce ingredients into the wok and cook until it turns a light caramel colour, stirring minimally. Add the vinegar and remaining sauce ingredients and bring to the boil, stirring.

⚒ Return the pork and vegetables, stir in the sauce until evenly coated, sprinkle on the sesame oil and serve.

FRIED PORK FLAVOURED WITH LAUREL

Shanghai 上海

FRIED PORK FLAVOURED WITH LAUREL

Flowering laurel is a treasured aromatic plant in China, being used for ornamental and medicinal purposes. Chefs often use the flowers in cooking to enhance the colour, taste and aroma of the food. The pork in this dish is golden, light and tender, with the added fragrance of laurel flowers. Served with a sweet and sour sauce and peppercorn salt it is especially delicious, and is a traditional speciality of the Shanghai area.

280 g (9 oz) lean pork
2 eggs
¾ cup (90 g/3 oz) cornflour (cornstarch)
oil or lard for deep-frying
2 spring onions (shallots/scallions), white parts only
1 teaspoon sesame oil
silver laurel flowers
peppercorn salt*

SEASONING

1 tablespoon light soy sauce
1 tablespoon rice wine or dry sherry
1 tablespoon finely chopped spring onion (shallot/scallion)
¼ teaspoon salt

SAUCE

1 tablespoon light soy sauce
2 teaspoons rice wine or dry sherry
1 teaspoon sugar

Cut the pork into thin slices and pound with the side of a cleaver or a rolling pin to flatten and tenderise, then cut into strips. Place in a dish and add the pre-mixed seasoning ingredients, mix well and leave for 20 minutes.

Beat the eggs and mix into a batter, adding the cornflour.

Heat the oil in a wok over moderate heat. Dip the pork into the batter, then deep-fry in the oil for about 1 minute. Remove and drain well. Increase the heat and fry the pork again for about 20 seconds. Remove, drain and fry again, cooking until the surface is crisp and the pork cooked through. Remove and drain well.

Finely chop the spring onions.

Heat a clean wok and add a little oil. Stir-fry the spring onions with the pork, adding the sesame oil. Add the pre-mixed sauce ingredients and toss the pork over high heat until the sauce is absorbed. Sprinkle on the laurel flowers, stir in and serve with the peppercorn salt as a dip.

---

*To make peppercorn salt, dry-fry 1 teaspoon of Sichuan peppercorns (Fagara or Sansho) in a wok until fragrant, then grind finely. Heat 1 tablespoon of fine table salt in the wok, add the pepper, mix together and cool before using.

PORK "COINS" WITH HONEY

Beijing 北京

PORK "COINS" WITH HONEY

The name of this dish derives from the way the meat is skewered for cooking. When removed from the skewer each piece of meat has a hole in the centre similar to an old Chinese coin.

Although the meat is barbecued over an open fire, the interlayered pork fat prevents the normally dry fillet from becoming parched and tough.

500 g (1 lb) pork fillet (tenderloin)
250 g (8 oz) duck livers or fresh ham
750 g (1½ lb) pork fat
½ cup (155 g/5 oz) clear honey
½ cup (125 mL/4 fl oz) peanut oil

PORK MARINADE

1 egg white, lightly beaten
1 tablespoon dark soy sauce
1 tablespoon rice wine or dry sherry
1½ tablespoons sugar
1 teaspoon five-spice powder
pinch of salt

PORK FAT MARINADE

2 teaspoons rice wine or dry sherry
2 teaspoons sugar
1 teaspoon salt

Cut the pork, livers and fat into thin slices, then shape into rounds of approximately 4 cm (1¾ in) diameter. Place the pork fillet and the pork fat in separate dishes and add their respective pre-mixed marinade ingredients, mix well and leave for 20 minutes.

Use thick metal skewers or wooden butchers' rods soaked for one hour in water to prevent them burning during barbecueing and rub them with oil. Thread the pork, liver and fat in alternate layers along the rods.

Cook over a moderately hot charcoal fire, brushing alternately with honey and oil to keep them moist. Or roast in a preheated oven at 180°C (350°F) for about 30 minutes, turning several times during cooking. Serve at once.

Guangzhou 广州

BARBECUED PORK

Skewered and barbecued meat, usually lamb, is a speciality of the wandering tribes of the north-western regions of China. The southern Chinese have devised a similar recipe using pork, which they prefer to lamb. The ingredients used to flavour the meat impart a sweetish taste, a bright red-brown colour and a crispness to the surface. Cooked over charcoal, the meat gets a mouthwateringly delicious smoky taste. It can be served as a main course or as a starter with drinks.

1 kg (2 lb) lean pork (loin or hand/picnic shoulder)
fresh pineapple (garnish)
cucumber (garnish)

SEASONING/GLAZE

⅔ cup (125 g/4 oz) malt sugar
3 tablespoons boiling water
1 tablespoon light soy sauce
1 tablespoon oyster sauce
2 tablespoons rice wine or dry sherry
1 teaspoon sesame oil
½ teaspoon salt
½ teaspoon orange or red food colouring (optional)

Cut the pork into long strips about 4 cm (2 in) wide, and place in a dish. Mix the seasoning/glaze ingredients together, first mixing the malt sugar and boiling water until dissolved. Pour over the pork and leave for at least 5 hours, turning from time to time.

※ Prepare a charcoal fire or pre-heat an oven to 240°C (460°F). Hang the strips of meat on metal butchers' hooks and suspend over the fire, or hang from a rack in the oven, placing a drip-tray underneath.

※ Roast for about 15 minutes, then remove and brush thickly with the remaining marinade. Return to the oven to complete roasting until just cooked through and very crisp on the surface.

※ Cut into thick slices and pile onto a serving plate. Surround with pineapple and cucumber. Serve warm or cold.

BARBECUED PORK

PORK IN WINE LEES

KIDNEY SLICES WITH SESAME PASTE DRESSING

Guangzhou 广州

PORK IN WINE LEES

In Chinese cooking, the chef pays careful attention to the choice and use of seasoning ingredients, the red fermented rice used in this recipe being one such speciality. This is polished glutinous rice prepared through a process of steaming, fermenting and filtration, and is a local product of Fujian Province. It is bright red and has the fragrant smell of wine, and is often known as wine lees. Fujian dishes are characterised by their frequent use of this ingredient.

315 g (10 oz) pork fillet
1 medium-sized cucumber
2 egg whites, lightly beaten
3 tablespoons cornflour (cornstarch)
3 tablespoons red fermented rice (wine lees)
250 g (8 oz) lard

SEASONING/SAUCE

¾ cup (175 mL/6 fl oz) chicken stock (broth)
2 tablespoons rice wine or dry sherry
1½ teaspoons sugar
¾ teaspoon salt
2 teaspoons cornflour (cornstarch)

Cut the pork fillet and unpeeled cucumber into small cubes, discarding any tendons and sinews from the meat and the seeds from the cucumber.

❈ Mix the pork with the egg whites, then place in a plastic bag and add the cornflour. Shake briskly until the meat is well coated with the flour, then transfer to a plate and add the red fermented rice, mixing in well.

❈ Heat the lard in a wok and stir-fry the pork over high heat until bright red, separating pieces that stick together. Add the cucumber and stir-fry briefly, then remove the pork and cucumber and drain off the fat.

❈ Return the pork and cucumber and add the pre-mixed seasoning/sauce ingredients, stirring over high heat for about 45 seconds before serving.

Beijing 北京

KIDNEY SLICES WITH SESAME PASTE DRESSING

The cooking method described in the following recipe is unusual. The thin slices of kidney are scalded several times in boiling water, dipped in the sesame paste dressing and then served. The scalding removes the strong taste and aroma of the kidneys while cooking it just enough to preserve its delicate texture.

2 pork kidneys
salt
1 teaspoon rice wine or dry sherry
cucumber slices

DRESSING

½ teaspoon sesame oil
2 teaspoons dark soy sauce
2 tablespoons sesame paste (tahini)
1 tablespoon sugar
pinch of salt

Cut the kidneys in halves horizontally to expose the inner core of white fat. Remove this and the connected veins, and place the kidneys in a dish of cold water to soak for several hours. Change the water 3-4 times. Drain well, then slice the kidneys very thinly.

❈ Bring a saucepan of water to the boil. Scald the kidneys for just a few seconds, then remove and drain. Boil a second pot of water and scald again, just long enough for them to lose their pink colour. Drain well and sprinkle with a little salt and rice wine.

❈ Mix the dressing ingredients together, adding cold water if the paste is very thick – depending on the brand of sesame paste used.

❈ Arrange slices of cucumber on a serving plate and pile the kidney slices on top, pour on the sesame paste and serve.

PORK SHREDS AND CAPSICUM

BALSAM PEAR WITH PORK AND PRAWN FILLING

Sichuan 四川

Guangzhou 广州

PORK SHREDS AND CAPSICUM

Capsicum, also called "lantern" or "bell" pepper, has a sweet, yet slightly hot taste. Pickled red capsicum is served with many Sichuan meals as a side dish, as it is said to stimulate the appetite. Being a good source of Vitamin C, and growing and bearing fruit readily, it has been an essential part of the Sichuan cuisine for many centuries.

250 g (8 oz) pork fillet (tenderloin)
1 large or 2 small red capsicums (bell peppers)
90 g (3 oz) canned or cooked fresh bamboo shoots
6 garlic chives
4 slices young fresh (root) ginger
2 tablespoons cornflour (cornstarch)
3 tablespoons lard, vegetable or rapeseed oil

SEASONING/SAUCE

⅔ cup (150 mL/5 fl oz) chicken or veal stock (broth)
1 tablespoon light soy sauce
2 teaspoons rice wine or dry sherry
½ teaspoon salt
pinch of white pepper
1 teaspoon cornflour (cornstarch)

Slice the pork into paper thin slices, cutting across the grain, then stack the slices into piles of five or six, cut into matchstick shreds and set aside.

Cut the capsicums in halves, trim and cut lengthways into narrow shreds. Cut the bamboo shoots, garlic chives and ginger into similar-sized pieces.

Stir the cornflour into the pork shreds, coating them evenly.

Heat the wok over moderate heat and stir-fry the capsicum shreds without oil until browned on the edges and half tender. Add a large pinch of salt, stir, then remove.

Add the lard and stir-fry the pork over high heat until white. Add the bamboo, garlic chives and ginger and stir-fry for another minute, then add the pre-mixed seasoning/sauce ingredients and return the capsicum. Simmer, stirring, until the sauce thickens and clears, then serve.

BALSAM PEAR WITH PORK AND PRAWN FILLING

Balsam pears are said to be able to lighten the heart and brighten eyesight, promote respiration and reduce fever. There is a folk song in Guangdong which goes: "They say the balsam pear is bitter/But I take it to be sweet/Sweet or bitter to your choice/How can there be sweetness without bitterness?" This implies that the bitter balsam pear (commonly referred to as Chinese bitter melon) can be made sweet. The bitter taste of the balsam pear is not, however, passed on to other ingredients cooked with it. Hence it is said to possess a "gentleman's behaviour".

3-4 balsam pears (Chinese bitter melons)
pinch of bicarbonate of soda (baking soda)
185 g (6 oz) fatty pork
90 g (3 oz) fresh prawn (shrimp) meat
½ teaspoon salt
cornflour (cornstarch)
oil for frying

SAUCE

1 tablespoon fermented black beans
3 cloves garlic
1 teaspoon finely chopped fresh (root) ginger
2 teaspoons rice wine or dry sherry
2 teaspoons mushroom soy sauce
1 teaspoon sugar
pinch of white pepper
½ cup (125 mL/4 fl oz) chicken stock (broth)
1 teaspoon cornflour (cornstarch)

Cut the balsam pears into 1.5 cm (½ in) slices, scoop out the seeds and fibrous centres, then place in a saucepan with cold water to cover. Add the bicarbonate of soda and bring to the boil. Simmer until the pears are beginning to soften, then drain.

Very finely mince (grind) the pork and prawn meat to a smooth paste, using two cleavers simultaneously, or a food processor. Add the salt and mix well. Dust the inside of the pear rings with cornflour and fill with the pork and prawn paste, smoothing the tops. Coat lightly with cornflour.

Heat about 1.5 cm (½ in) of oil in a flat pan and fry the pears gently on both sides, until the filling is crisp on the surface and the pear rings are bright green and tender. Remove from the pan, drain and arrange on a serving plate.

Drain the pan, reserving about 2 tablespoons of the oil. Finely chop the black beans and garlic and fry briefly in the hot oil, add the ginger and fry briefly again. Add the wine and soy sauce, then after a few seconds add the sugar, pepper and the stock mixed with the cornflour. Bring to the boil, stirring, then pour over the prepared dish and serve at once.

Guangzhou 广州

ROAST SUCKLING PIG

Roast suckling pig is a renowned traditional Chinese delicacy. During the fifth century, it was considered by the common people to be "Yao Shu" (important art). In the Qing Dynasty (1644-1911 AD), it was one of the dishes featured in banquets held at the Qing Palace, and even today, roast suckling pig appears only at grand banquets and is always considered one of the highlights of the meal.

The pig has a characteristic bright red colouring, a sweetish flavour and skin that is smooth as glass, yet crisp and feather light. Special large iron forks are used to hold the prepared pig over glowing charcoal, and it is slowly rotated – usually by hand – until cooked to perfection. In a quality restaurant one of the masterchefs will often tend the roasting over a tub of charcoal on the verandah or footpath outside the restaurant.

1 x 6-8 kg (12-16 lb) suckling pig (to serve about 24)
1 cup (185 g/6 oz) malt sugar
½ cup (125 mL/4 fl oz) red vinegar
boiling water

SEASONING

1 tablespoon crushed garlic
½ cup (155 g/5 oz) bean paste
½ cup (155 g/5 oz) sesame paste (tahini)
½ cup (125 mL/4 fl oz) sweet vinegar
3 tablespoons Fed liquor, rice wine or dry sherry
3 tablespoons peanut oil
½ cup (125 mL/4 fl oz) soy bean milk
1 tablespoon mushroom soy sauce
½ cup (125 g/4 oz) sugar

Have the butcher slit the pig down the centre underneath, cutting through the head as well so that the whole pig can be pressed out as flat as possible. Pierce with a large iron fork which will hold the pig open, or devise a cooking method which suits your equipment or circumstances. Have ready a large quantity of charcoal for roasting.

※ Hold the pig over the sink and pour over plenty of boiling water. This will contract the skin and help make it crisp. Mix the malt sugar and red vinegar with enough boiling water to make a thick syrup and paint this over the skin of the pig. Hang in an airy place for several hours until the skin feels dryish to the touch.

※ Mix the seasoning ingredients together, stirring until the sugar has dissolved and all ingredients are well blended. Coat the pig thickly on the underside with some of the seasoning mixture and rub the remainder over the skin.

※ Roast slowly over glowing charcoal until no pink liquid runs off when the pig is pierced through the thickest part of the thigh. This will take several hours. During cooking, pierce any bubbles which appear on the skin with a large needle or skewer to ensure the skin remains flat and smooth.

※ There is a traditional way to serve this delicious dish. First, slice the crisp red skin from the back of the pig, place the whole pig on a large platter and put the skin back in place. At the first serving, only the skin will be eaten. Return the pig to the kitchen where the choicest pieces of meat will be cut into serving portions and reassembled on the carcass. This is presented as the second course.

※ The first and second courses are usually accompanied by multi-layered white buns or thin pancakes and dips of sweetened soy sauce or sweet bean paste. Spring onion (shallot/scallion) bulbs or curls, and crisp sweet-sour pickled vegetables, such as beetroot, cucumber, turnip or radish, are also served. The meat is dipped into the sauce, then eaten with the bread or pancake and a piece each of vegetable and onion. This combination of ingredients counteracts the richness of the pork and provides an interesting contrast of tastes and textures.

※ Finally, the bones may be simmered and made into a rich broth, or the remaining pieces of meat stir-fried – usually with ginger and onions – to make a third course.

ROAST SUCKLING PIG

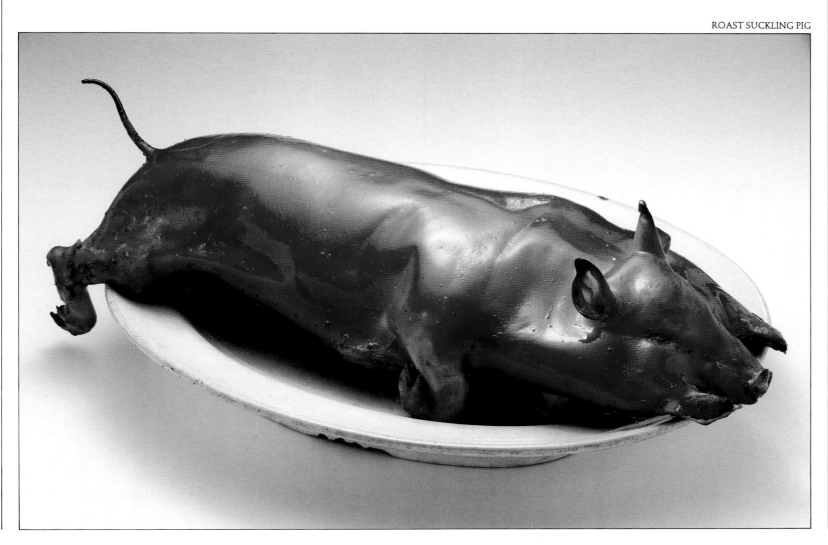

BRAISED RUMP OF PORK

Guangzhou 广州

BRAISED RUMP OF PORK

1 kg (2 lb) pork rump (upper leg/fresh ham)
8 cups (2 L/64 fl oz) oil for deep-frying
8 slices fresh (root) ginger
4-5 spring onions (shallots/scallions)
12 dried black mushrooms, soaked for 25 minutes
250 g (8 oz) choy sum or other Chinese green vegetable
vegetable oil

SEASONING/SAUCE

3 tablespoons light soy sauce
1 tablespoon dark soy sauce
1 tablespoon rice wine or dry sherry
1½ teaspoons salt
1 tablespoon sugar
1 teaspoon sesame oil

Wipe the skin of the pork with kitchen paper. Heat the oil in a large wok and when quite hot, deep-fry the pork, skin side downwards, until it turns a light golden colour and bubbles have appeared on the skin. Take care at this stage, as the frying pork is inclined to spatter. Lift out and place immediately in a casserole half filled with cold water. This causes the skin to ripple and it will be very tender when braised.

※ Add the ginger, whole spring onions, drained mushrooms and the seasoning ingredients. Cover and bring to the boil, then simmer gently for about 2 hours until the meat is very tender.

※ Trim the choy sum or other vegetables and stir-fry in a hot wok with a little vegetable oil. Add 2-3 tablespoons of water, cover and cook until almost tender.

※ Arrange around the edge of a serving dish. Place the pork in the centre, and slice. Arrange the mushrooms over the meat and pour over a generous serving of sauce.

152

Shanghai 上海

MEATBALLS IN MYRICA BERRY SHAPES

Including the juice of the myrica berry in the preparation of meatballs is a speciality of Anhui Province. They are both sweet and sour, invigorating and useful for treating hangovers.

The Chinese have an expression, "looking at the berry quenches one's thirst", which derives from the late Han Dynasty, around the year 200 AD, when General Cao Cao was leading his exhausted soldiers on a long march. To revitalise them he told them of a forest of berry trees ahead, their spirits picked up and they marched swiftly towards their imaginary goal.

410 g (13 oz) pork belly (fresh bacon)
3 tablespoons myrica berry juice, tamarind water
    or a tart mixture of fruit and lemon juice
1 cup (125 g/4 oz) dry breadcrumbs
4 cups (1 L/32 fl oz) oil for deep-frying

SAUCE

¾ cup (175 mL/6 fl oz) water
2 tablespoons sugar
2 tablespoons vinegar
pinch of salt
2 teaspoons light soy sauce
2 teaspoons cornflour (cornstarch)
1 tablespoon lard

Finely mince (grind) the pork and mix with the fruit juice. Form into small balls and coat with the breadcrumbs.

✤ Heat the oil in a wok to smoking point and put in one-third of the meatballs. Deep-fry until cooked through and golden brown, for about 3 minutes, then cook the remainder in two batches.

✤ Insert a small twig or toothpick into the top of each meatball so that they resemble myrica berries or small plums, and pile on a serving plate.

✤ Boil the sauce ingredients in another wok, stirring until thickened. Pour over the meatballs and serve.

MEATBALLS IN MYRICA BERRY SHAPES

PORK TWICE-COOKED

Sichuan 四川

PORK TWICE-COOKED

Sichuan cooking makes much use of pork. Records show that even six thousand years ago the inhabitants of Ba and Shu (the ancient names of the east and west parts of Sichuan) kept domesticated pigs.

The following recipe, incorporating two separate cooking processes, is especially good with pork. It eliminates some of the fat, making it easier to digest and very tender.

375 g (12 oz) belly pork (fresh bacon)
1 medium-sized red capsicum (bell pepper)
60 g (2 oz) canned or cooked fresh bamboo shoots
2 spring onions (shallots/scallions) or garlic chives
4 slices fresh (root) ginger
2 tablespoons lard

SEASONING

1 tablespoon sweet bean paste
2 teaspoons hot bean paste
1 tablespoon light soy sauce
1 teaspoon mushroom soy sauce
1½ teaspoons sugar
2 teaspoons rice wine or dry sherry
2 tablespoons water

Place the pork, skin upwards, on a rack in a wok or in a steamer over simmering water. Cover and steam gently for about 25 minutes until the pork is soft, but not completely cooked through.

✤ Cut the capsicum and bamboo shoots into squares, the spring onions or garlic chives into 2.5 cm (1 in) lengths, and shred the ginger.

✤ Remove the pork from the steamer and leave for about 20 minutes to cool and firm up.

✤ Use a very sharp knife to cut the pork into thin slices, then into pieces about 5 cm (2 in) long. The slices should curl up like rose petals during frying.

✤ Heat the lard in a wok and stir-fry the capsicum and bamboo shoots until softened, then add the spring onions or garlic chives and ginger and stir-fry briefly. Push to one side of the pan or remove, and stir-fry the pork slices until cooked through and crisp on the edges. The fat should turn translucent, like bacon fat. Mix in the pre-mixed seasoning ingredients and stir-fry with the capsicum and other vegetables over high heat for about 1½ minutes, then serve.

CANDIED FRIED PORK

Beijing 北京

CANDIED FRIED PORK

375 g (12 oz) belly pork (fresh bacon)
6 cups (1½ L/48 fl oz) chicken stock (broth)
125 g (4 oz) Chinese rock candy or caramelised white sugar
1 teaspoon finely chopped fresh red chilli
1 tablespoon finely chopped spring onion (shallot/scallion)
oil for deep-frying

BATTER

2 egg whites, well beaten
½ cup (60 g/2 oz) flour
½ cup (60 g/2 oz) cornflour (cornstarch)

Cover the belly pork with stock and simmer gently for about 1 hour until very tender. Cool in the stock, drain and remove the fat. Cut the meat into slices approximately 5 x 2 cm (2 x 1 in).
Crush the rock candy finely and set aside.
Mix the egg whites, flour and cornflour to make a batter of coating consistency (add a little cold water if needed). Dip the pork into the batter and deep-fry several pieces at a time until golden and crisp on the surface. Drain and keep warm.
Heat the rock sugar in a heavy wok or saucepan until it caramelises. Add the chilli and spring onion, turn off the heat and turn each piece of meat in the caramel until coated.
Arrange on a lightly oiled plate and serve at once.

Guangzhou 广州

PORK WITH FRUIT SAUCE

280 g (9 oz) boneless lean pork
1 egg, well beaten
1 cup (125 g/4 oz) cornflour (cornstarch)
oil for deep-frying
12 prawn crackers (krupuk)
1 cup (250 mL/8 fl oz) pineapple or apricot juice
½ teaspoon sesame oil

SEASONING

2 teaspoons rice wine or dry sherry
½ teaspoon salt
1 teaspoon grated fresh (root) ginger
1 tablespoon finely chopped spring onion (shallot/scallion)

Cut the pork into slices and place on a board. Pound with the side of a cleaver or a rolling pin to tenderise. Place in a dish, add the pre-mixed seasoning ingredients, mix well and leave for 20 minutes.
Add the egg to the above ingredients, mix well and then coat each slice thickly with cornflour.

PORK WITH FRUIT SAUCE

Heat the oil in a large wok to smoking point. Deep-fry the pork slices for about 3 minutes, until crisp and well coloured on the surface, stirring constantly to prevent them from sticking together. Lift out and drain well.
Fry the prawn crackers in the oil until puffed up and lightly coloured, lift out and drain. Arrange in the centre of a serving plate.
Pour off the oil and return the meat, adding the fruit juice. Simmer until the juice has been absorbed, then transfer to a plate. Sprinkle with the sesame oil and serve at once.

Beijing 北京

PLAIN BOILED PORK SLICES

This dish was introduced with the Manchurians who conquered and ruled the country as the Qing Dynasty (1644-1911 AD). It was a custom during that era for the king to bestow his favour on the subjects who came to wish him happiness during New Year by treating them to this simple, but delicious dish. Similarly Manchurian nobility offered this speciality at weddings and other festive occasions. Each person would cut meat for himself from a large piece of pork and guests were invited to eat as much as they could. The more one ate of this dish, the more delighted the host would be.

1 kg (2 lb) meatier portion of pork hand (picnic shoulder)
1 teaspoon salt

BROWN BEAN SAUCE DIP

1 tablespoon brown bean sauce
1 teaspoon sugar
1 teaspoon sesame oil

GARLIC SAUCE DIP

3 cloves garlic, crushed
1 teaspoon salt
1 tablespoon vegetable oil

CHILLI SAUCE DIP

1 fresh red chilli, finely chopped
2 tablespoons light soy sauce

Place the pork in a wok with the skin downwards, add the salt and cover with water. Bring to the boil, cover and simmer for at least 2 hours until the pork is very tender. A chopstick will easily penetrate the skin when the pork is cooked through. Remove from the heat but leave in the stock to cool.
Cut off the skin and part of the fat before cutting the pork into paper-thin slices. Arrange in overlapping rows on a serving plate.
Mix the sauce ingredients together and serve as cold dips in small dishes.

DICED PORK, STIR-FRIED WITH SOY BEAN PASTE AND CAPSICUM

Shanghai 上海

DICED PORK, STIR-FRIED WITH SOY BEAN PASTE AND CAPSICUM

375 g (12 oz) belly pork (fresh bacon)
2 tablespoons dried shrimps, soaked for 25 minutes
½ green capsicum (bell pepper)
½ red capsicum (bell pepper)
1-2 dried red chillies
2 tablespoons soy bean paste
3 tablespoons vegetable oil

SEASONING/SAUCE

1 tablespoon rice wine or dry sherry
1½ tablespoons light soy sauce
¼ teaspoon salt
1 teaspoon sugar
⅓ cup (75 mL/2½ fl oz) chicken stock (broth)
1 teaspoon cornflour (cornstarch)

Cut the pork into very small dice, discarding any skin and fragments of bone. Drain the shrimps. Cut the capsicums into small squares, removing the stems, seeds and inner ribs. Finely chop the chillies.

Heat the vegetable oil in a wok to smoking point. Stir-fry the capsicums for about 1½ minutes, then remove and set aside. Stir-fry the pork until it changes colour. Add the chilli and soy bean paste and continue to cook over high heat for 3-4 minutes until the meat is cooked through, stirring continually.

Add the capsicums and the seasoning ingredients except the chicken stock and cornflour, and stir-fry briefly. Mix the stock and cornflour together and stir into the dish. Simmer until thickened, then serve.

DRAGON AND PHOENIX HAM

Sichuan 四川

DRAGON AND PHOENIX HAM

There are many legends about the dragon and the phoenix in China. In ancient times, people thought of the dragon as the embodiment of a king and the phoenix as that of a queen. Sometimes the dragon and phoenix are combined into one symbol of glory, honour, riches and good luck. At wedding or birthday celebration banquets people always like to have dishes using dragon and phoenix names.

375 g (12 oz) boneless duck meat
250 g (8 oz) pork
90 g (3 oz) water chestnuts
10 chicken wing bones
2 pieces pork fat net (caul fat)
5 slices salted ham
5 slices white bread
oil for deep-frying

SEASONING

2 tablespoons water
2 teaspoons rice wine or dry sherry
2 tablespoons light soy sauce
¾ teaspoon salt
¼ teaspoon white pepper
1 egg yolk
3 tablespoons cornflour (cornstarch)

Very finely mince (grind) the duck meat and pork together with the water chestnuts until reduced to a smooth, sticky paste. Add the pre-mixed seasoning ingredients and stir briskly with a wooden spoon until completely amalgamated, then form into 10 oblong shapes resembling drumsticks. Cut each pork fat net into 5, giving 10 similar-sized pieces. Insert one chicken bone into the narrow end of each drumstick, wrap them in pieces of the pork fat net and set aside.

Cut the ham and bread slices in halves and trim them into rectangular shapes of equal size. Place the ham on a rack in a wok or in a steamer, cover and steam until tender. In the meantime lightly toast the bread.

Heat the oil in a wok to smoking point and slide in the drumsticks, several at a time. Deep-fry for about 3 minutes until cooked through, then drain well.

Place a piece of ham on top of each slice of toast, arrange the drumsticks and ham sandwiches alternately around a large platter and serve.

Sichuan 四川

YUNNAN HAM SHAPED AS PLUM FLOWERS

The Chinese love plum flowers as much as the Japanese revere the cherry blossom. For three thousand years they have cultivated plum trees and praised the characteristics of the plum. It can bloom in snow, is very resistant to bitter cold and hardship, and it is the first to greet the spring. The poet Chen Liang of the Song Dynasty (960-1279AD) said: "One plum flower blooms first, hundreds of flowers follow; they spread the news of spring, even while it is behind the snow".

5 slices Yunnan ham or other well-salted ham
185 g (6 oz) white fish fillets
1 spring onion (shallot/scallion), minced (ground)
⅓ teaspoon grated fresh (root) ginger
⅓ teaspoon salt
pinch of white pepper
1 egg white
125 g (4 oz) pork fat
lard
lemon peel (rind), optional

Use a sharp knife or vegetable cutter to cut or stamp out plum flower designs from the ham. Make a hole in the centre of each, then cut small pieces of the lemon rind, if used, to fill these holes, to create the centre of the blossoms.

※ Cut the fish into small pieces and bat with the flat side of a cleaver, or use a food processor, to make a smooth paste. Add the spring onion, ginger, salt, pepper and egg white and mix with your fingers until smooth.

※ Spread the fish over a large sheet of very thinly sliced pork fat, then cut into diamond shapes, large enough for the ham blossoms to fit in the centre (*see photograph above*). Place the ham in position.

※ Heat a wide flat pan and wipe out with a little melted lard. Gently fry the fish cakes until the pork fat is crisp and melting. Cover halfway through cooking so that the top is cooked by steam.

※ Lift onto a serving plate, arrange attractively and garnish with a carved vegetable rose.

BRAISED PORK WITH DRIED VEGETABLE

Guangzhou 广州

BRAISED PORK WITH DRIED VEGETABLE

The meat used for this dish is pork belly (fresh bacon) which consists of alternating layers of fat and meat with a thin skin. The dried vegetable is a salted and sun-dried leaf mustard, the best of which is the "Huizhou" dried vegetable which is exported around the world. This has a thick heart and well flavoured leaves and is frequently used in vegetarian cooking.

750 g (1½ lb) pork belly (fresh bacon)
1 heart of Huizhou dried vegetable (mui-choy)
2 tablespoons peanut oil
2 tablespoons mushroom soy sauce
2 tablespoons sugar
½ teaspoon sesame oil

Scald the pork in boiling water, then leave to drain. Soak the vegetable in cold water for 30 minutes, rinse well and squeeze dry; repeat several times.

Heat a wok or large saucepan and add the peanut oil. Fry the pork over high heat until brown on both sides. Add the mushroom soy sauce and sugar, then reduce the heat. Turn the pork several times until it is coated with the sauce. Add the whole piece of vegetable, cover the meat with boiling water and bring back to the boil.

Reduce heat to very low and simmer for at least 2 hours until the pork is very tender and has a smooth, almost gelatinous texture. Add the sesame oil.

Lift out the vegetable, cut into pieces and arrange on a serving plate.

Carefully lift out the pork and cut into slices. Arrange in its original shape on top of the vegetable.

Reduce the sauce further, if it is not yet thick and syrupy, or add a little extra water if it has become too concentrated. Spoon over the pork and serve.

Shanghai 上海

BOILED AND FRIED PORK LEG IN BROWN SAUCE

Boil and fry is a cooking method particularly suitable for the cooking of large joints of meat such as pork leg. It reduces the fat content while tenderising the meat and enhancing the flavour.

In ancient times, the village people in the Shanghai area often cooked large fish or massive joints of meat for wedding banquets, funeral gatherings, and other celebrations.

BOILED AND FRIED PORK LEG IN BROWN SAUCE

750 g (1½ lb) pork leg/butt (boneless)
1½ teaspoons salt
1 tablespoon dark soy sauce
3 cups (750 mL/24 fl oz) lard or vegetable oil
12 stalks Chinese kale (gai larn) or spinach
2 tablespoons superior or other light soy sauce
1½ tablespoons rice wine or dry sherry
1 teaspoon sugar
salt and pepper

Place the pork in a saucepan, cover with water and add the salt. Bring to the boil, then reduce heat and simmer for about 30 minutes. Drain, then wipe the skin and meat as dry as possible with kitchen paper, piercing any bubbles in the skin, as these can expand during frying and splatter.

Rub the pork with the dark soy sauce, leave for 1 hour.

Heat the lard or vegetable oil in a wok, put in the pork, skin side downwards, and deep-fry over moderate heat for about 3 minutes. Turn and cook the other side for 1-3 minutes, then lift out, drain and place in a clean casserole.

Cover with cold water and set aside for 10 minutes, then add the remaining ingredients and simmer gently until the meat is very tender with a texture similar to beancurd.

Shanghai 上海

FRIED AND BRAISED SPARE RIBS

Spare ribs are an inexpensive ingredient, being quite bony with little meat. However, when cooked in the following way the result is lustrous, with finger-licking succulence.

750 g (1½ lb) pork spare ribs
¾ cup (90 g/3 oz) waterchestnut powder or cornflour (cornstarch)
prawn crackers (krupuk)
oil for deep-frying

SEASONING

2 tablespoons Jizhi or other ketchup
2 tablespoons tomato juice
2 tablespoons sweet vinegar
2 tablespoons sugar
¾ cup (175 mL/6 fl oz) superior stock (*see page 124*)

Cut the ribs into short lengths and toss in the waterchestnut powder or cornflour to coat thickly. Shake off the excess.

Heat the oil in a wok to moderately hot and deep-fry the prawn crackers until well expanded and crisp. Do not allow to colour. Remove, drain well, then place around the edge of a serving dish and set aside.

Place the ribs in the oil and deep-fry for about 6 minutes until well coloured, crisp on the surface and almost cooked through. Remove with a slotted spoon and set aside.

FRIED AND BRAISED SPARE RIBS

SHREDDED PORK WITH SPECIAL SAUCE

※ Drain off the oil and add the pre-mixed seasoning ingredients to the wok. Bring to the boil and boil for 2-3 minutes, then add the ribs, cover and braise for about 10 minutes until the ribs are very tender and the sauce has reduced to a thick glaze on the meat.

※ Spoon into the centre of the dish and serve.

Beijing 北京

MEATBALLS WITH SESAME SEEDS

500 g (1 lb) belly pork (fresh bacon)
½ cup (125 mL/4 fl oz) water
2 tablespoons cornflour (cornstarch)
3 cups (750 mL/24 fl oz) peanut oil
¾ cup (90 g/3 oz) white sesame seeds
1 cup (220 g/7 oz) sugar

Mince (grind) the pork finely, adding first the water, then the cornflour. The mixture should be very smooth.

※ Heat the peanut oil in a wok to smoking point, then reduce the heat slightly.

※ Form the meat into small balls about the size of a walnut and drop into the oil. Fry in several batches for about 3 minutes until cooked through and well coloured on the surface. Lift out and drain well.

※ Spread the sesame seeds on a plate.

※ Pour the sugar into a clean wok adding 2 tablespoons of the hot oil. Cook gently without stirring until it turns to a pale caramel colour, then turn off the heat and quickly roll each meatball through the caramel to coat evenly. Roll in the sesame seeds and place on a lightly oiled serving plate.

Sichuan 四川

SHREDDED PORK WITH SPECIAL SAUCE

220 g (7 oz) lean pork, preferably fillet (tenderloin)
½ teaspoon salt
pinch of white pepper
1½ tablespoons cornflour (cornstarch)
1-2 pickled red chillies
2 slices fresh (root) ginger
2 cloves garlic
2 spring onions (shallots/scallions)
2 tablespoons lard or oil for frying

SAUCE

3 tablespoons stock (broth)
1 tablespoon light soy sauce
1 teaspoon brown vinegar
2 teaspoons sugar
¾ teaspoon sesame oil
½ teaspoon cornflour (cornstarch)

Very thinly slice the pork across the grain, then cut into fine shreds and place in a dish. Add the salt, pepper and cornflour, mix well and set aside.

※ Finely chop the chillies, ginger, garlic and spring onions. Mix the sauce ingredients.

※ Heat the wok and stir-fry the pork shreds in the lard or oil until white. Push to one side of the pan and add the chopped chillies, ginger, garlic and spring onions and stir-fry quickly, then mix in with the pork.

※ Add the sauce ingredients and heat quickly over high heat, stirring into the pork, and serve.

MEATBALLS WITH SESAME SEEDS

STIR-FRIED PORK TENDERLOIN

Beijing 北京

STIR-FRIED PORK TENDERLOIN

375 g (12 oz) pork fillet (tenderloin)
3 tablespoons peanut oil
1 tablespoon finely chopped spring onion (shallot/scallion)
½ teaspoon finely chopped fresh (root) ginger
1 tablespoon brown vinegar
2 teaspoons sugar

SEASONING

1 tablespoon rice wine or dry sherry
1 tablespoon dark soy sauce
1 tablespoon cornflour (cornstarch)
½ teaspoon salt
pinch of pepper

Cut the pork into thin slices and place in a dish with the pre-mixed seasoning ingredients, mix well and leave for 20 minutes.

※ Heat the wok and add the peanut oil. Stir-fry the pork for about 2 minutes over high heat until lightly coloured and cooked through. Remove and set aside.

※ Add the spring onions and ginger and stir-fry briefly, then add the vinegar and sugar and toss together for a few seconds. Return the meat and stir-fry together until the meat is well coated with the ingredients. Serve immediately.

Beijing 北京

FRIED MEAT-FILLED EGG ROLLS

315 g (10 oz) fat pork, finely minced (ground)
4 eggs
2 tablespoons peanut oil
½ cup (60 g/2 oz) flour
oil for deep-frying

SEASONING

1 tablespoon finely chopped spring onion (shallot/scallion)
½ teaspoon grated fresh (root) ginger
1 teaspoon cornflour (cornstarch)
1 teaspoon sesame oil
½ teaspoon salt
pinch of white pepper

Mix the pork with the seasoning ingredients, squeezing the mixture through your fingers until it is smooth and sticky and set aside.

※ Add enough water to the flour to make a sticky paste.

※ Beat the eggs with 2 teaspoons of the peanut oil. Heat a wok or omelet pan over moderate heat and wipe out with a cloth dipped in the peanut oil. Pour in half of the egg batter and tilt

FRIED MEAT-FILLED EGG ROLLS

the pan so that the egg spreads out as much as possible, and is very thin. Cook evenly, moving the pan constantly until lightly-coloured underneath, then cook the other side briefly. Cook the other omelet and leave them both on a work top to cool.

※ Spread the flour paste over the omelets, then spread on a layer of the pork filling, leaving a border all around. Roll up, tucking the sides in securely. Heat the deep-frying oil to smoking point, then reduce heat slightly. Cut the rolls into 4 cm (2½ in) lengths and deep-fry in several batches until golden. Lift out and drain well, then serve at once.

Beijing 北京

STIR-FRIED KIDNEYS

4 pork or lamb kidneys
2 tablespoons lard
1 teaspoon finely chopped fresh (root) ginger
1 tablespoon sugar

SAUCE

1 tablespoon water or chicken stock (broth)
1 tablespoon rice wine or dry sherry
1 tablespoon dark soy sauce
1 tablespoon finely chopped spring onion (shallot/scallion)
½ teaspoon salt
1 teaspoon cornflour (cornstarch)

Soak the kidneys in cold water for 1 hour, then drain. Cut in halves, remove the fatty core then turn the cut sides downwards and score deeply with diagonal cuts.

※ Soak in cold water for 20 minutes, then drain very thoroughly and cut each kidney into several pieces.

※ Heat a wok and add the lard. Stir-fry the ginger briefly, then add the kidneys and stir-fry over high heat until just cooked through. They should remain pink inside but no blood should run out when pierced. Do not overcook or they will become tough. Stir the sugar in and place on a serving plate.

※ Add the pre-mixed sauce ingredients to the wok and bring to the boil. Simmer, stirring, until slightly thickened. Return the kidneys and toss in the sauce until thoroughly coated and the sauce reduced to a glaze, then serve immediately.

Shanghai 上海

STEWED LARGE MEATBALLS

The Chinese call these meatballs "lion heads". Stewed large meatballs have long been a traditional speciality in the Yangzhou area and are prepared principally with minced (ground) pork, although they may consist of a combination of meats and sometimes contain a delicious filling, such as crabmeat. The delicate colours of the dish – the light pink of the meatballs and the bright green of the tender cabbage – plus the rich aroma and flavour create a meal to delight the senses.

750 g (1½ lb) lean pork (preferably fillet/tenderloin)
2½ tablespoons finely chopped spring onion
   (shallot/scallion)
1 teaspoon grated fresh (root) ginger
1½ teaspoons salt
1 tablespoon Shaoxing rice wine or dry sherry
500-750 g (1-1½ lb) Chinese cabbage
lard or vegetable oil for frying
chicken stock (broth) or superior stock (*see page 124*)

Cut the pork into small pieces, then mince (grind) it finely, using two cleavers simultaneously or a food processor.
Mix in the spring onion, ginger, salt and wine and work the meat with your fingers until smooth and sticky. Form into 3-4 large meatballs.
Wash the cabbage and cut lengthways into quarters. Stir-fry it briefly in a wok, in lard or vegetable oil, adding a generous pinch of salt.
Spread half of the cabbage across the bottom of a casserole and place the meatballs on top, then cover with the remaining cabbage.
Add enough boiling stock to just cover the meatballs. Cover the casserole tightly and simmer over low heat for about 1½ hours until the meatballs are melt-in-the-mouth tender.
Serve in the casserole, pushing the vegetables to one side to expose the meatballs.

MANDARIN DICED KIDNEY

FRIED BEEF AND WATER SPINACH WITH SHRIMP PASTE

Sichuan 四川

MANDARIN DICED KIDNEY

250 g (8 oz) pork kidneys
1½ tablespoons cornflour (cornstarch)
2 cloves garlic
3 slices fresh (root) ginger
2 spring onions (shallots/scallions)
2 dried red chillies
3 tablespoons lard or oil for frying
1 teaspoon ground Sichuan peppercorns (Fagara or Sansho)
1 teaspoon rice wine or dry sherry
large pinch of red chilli powder or chilli oil (optional)

SEASONING/SAUCE

½ cup (125 mL/4 fl oz) chicken stock (broth)
2 tablespoons light soy sauce
2 teaspoons red vinegar
2 teaspoons sugar
pinch of salt
2 teaspoons cornflour (cornstarch)

Cut the kidneys in halves horizontally, remove the skin and cut away the fatty inner section. Use a sharp knife to deeply score each piece in crosshatch fashion. Place in a dish and sprinkle on the cornflour, mixed to a thin paste with water. Stir until the kidney pieces are evenly coated, then set aside.

✳ Finely chop the garlic, ginger, spring onions and chillies.

✳ Heat the lard or oil in a wok to smoking point. Stir-fry the chopped chillies and Sichuan peppercorns for 20-30 seconds, then add the kidneys and the garlic, ginger and onions and stir-fry together over high heat until the kidneys are partially cooked. Add the wine and chilli powder, if used, reduce heat and continue cooking until the kidneys are tender. Then add the pre-mixed seasoning/sauce ingredients and simmer, stirring, until the sauce thickens and serve.

Guangzhou 广州

FRIED BEEF AND WATER SPINACH WITH SHRIMP PASTE

Water spinach is one of the main green vegetables available in Guangdong during the hot summer. It is cultivated on floating rafts made of reeds with small holes, through which the water spinach grows. The jade-like vegetable must be cooked with care. If underdone, it will be astringent; if overdone, yellow, dull and with little flavour.

185 g (6 oz) beef fillet (tenderloin)
250 g (8 oz) water spinach, or young English spinach
1 spring onion (shallot/scallion)
2 cloves garlic
½ cup (125 mL/4 fl oz) vegetable oil
salt
½ teaspoon fresh (root) ginger
2 teaspoons shrimp paste
1 teaspoon rice wine or dry sherry
3 tablespoons chicken stock (broth)
½ teaspoon cornflour (cornstarch)
⅓ teaspoon sesame oil

SEASONING

1 teaspoon dark soy sauce
1 teaspoon fish sauce or anchovy essence
1 tablespoon vegetable oil
1 tablespoon water
1 teaspoon cornflour (cornstarch)
½ teaspoon bicarbonate of soda (baking soda)

Very thinly slice the beef, cutting across the grain, then cut into narrow, short strips. Place in a dish and add the pre-mixed seasoning ingredients. Mix well and leave for 20 minutes.

✳ Thoroughly wash the spinach and drain well. Chop the spring onion into 2½ cm (1 in) lengths. Finely chop the garlic.

✳ Heat the vegetable oil in a wok and stir-fry the spinach over high heat for about 2 minutes until the leaves wilt and the stems soften but retain crispness. Add a sprinkling of salt, then use chopsticks to lift onto a serving plate.

✳ Reheat the wok, add the beef and stir-fry over very high heat until it changes colour. Remove from the pan. Stir-fry the ginger, garlic and spring onion until tender, then return the beef. Add the shrimp paste and wine and toss all ingredients together until well mixed. Stir the cornflour into the stock and pour over the beef, stirring until the sauce thickens.

✳ Arrange the beef on or near the vegetables, sprinkle over the sesame oil and serve.

Sichuan 四川

BOILED BEEF WITH CHILLI

This is a traditional dish famed for its characteristically heavy, hot and spicy, yet tender and delicious flavour. It originated in the salt mining area of Sichuan, where people usually cooked beef by boiling it in a soup heavily seasoned with chilli, bean paste and pepper. This old recipe was very popular for its heavy flavour which banishes cold and whets the appetite. Over the years many improvements have been made to the dish and it is now a local speciality.

315 g (10 oz) beef steak (rump/sirloin/loin)
6-8 lettuce leaves
1 tablespoon hot oil
½ teaspoon fried Sichuan peppercorns (Fagara or Sansho), ground
1 teaspoon finely chopped garlic (optional)

SAUCE

2 tablespoons lard or oil for frying
6 dried chillies
1 teaspoon Sichuan peppercorns (Fagara or Sansho), ground
1 tablespoon fermented black beans, finely chopped
3 cloves garlic, finely chopped
3-4 slices fresh (root) ginger, finely chopped
6-8 garlic chives or 3 spring onions (shallots/scallions), chopped
1 tablespoon hot bean paste
½ cup (125 mL/4 fl oz) water

Cut the meat across the grain into paper thin slices and set aside. Rinse the lettuce and tear into small pieces.

✿ To make the sauce, heat the lard or oil in a wok and fry the dried chillies and Sichuan peppercorns for about 30 seconds, then remove and chop the chillies finely. Add the black beans to the wok and fry for about 30 seconds, then add the garlic, ginger, garlic chives or spring onions and the bean paste and fry together until aromatic. Return the chillies and pepper, add the water and bring to the boil, then set aside.

✿ Heat a large saucepan of water to boiling point. Add the beef and cook just long enough for the meat to change colour, then drain well.

✿ Add the meat to the wok with the sauce, reheat and stir-fry together until all the sauce has adhered to the meat slices, then stir in the lettuce.

✿ Transfer to a serving plate and splash on the hot oil. Sprinkle on the ground Sichuan pepper and the chopped garlic, if used, and serve at once.

STEWED BEEF WITH TENDER GARLIC CHIVES

Sichuan 四川

STEWED BEEF WITH TENDER GARLIC CHIVES

500 g (1 lb) stewing/braising beef
2 tablespoons lard or vegetable oil
1 tablespoon soy bean paste or mashed fermented black beans
3 cups (750 mL/24 fl oz) beef stock (broth)
10 slices fresh (root) ginger
2 spring onions (shallots/scallions), halved
1 tablespoon soy bean powder or cornflour (cornstarch)

SEASONING

1 tablespoon rice wine or dry sherry
½ teaspoon Sichuan peppercorns (Fagara or Sansho)
1 teaspoon salt
2 teaspoons sugar

GARNISH

2 fresh red chillies
20 garlic chives or spring onions (shallots/scallions)
1 tablespoon oil for frying

Cut the beef into slices about 1 cm (½ in) thick, then into sticks about 8 x 2 cm (3 x 1 in).

Heat a wok over moderate heat and add the lard. Stir-fry the bean paste or mashed black beans for about 40 seconds until fragrant, then add the beef and stir-fry over high heat until lightly coloured and well sealed on all surfaces.

Pour in the stock, heat through briefly over high heat, then reduce the heat and simmer for about 1 hour, covered, until the beef is tender and the liquid reduced to about 1 cup (250 mL/8 fl oz).

Halfway through cooking, add the ginger and spring onions and the pre-mixed seasoning ingredients.

Meanwhile prepare the garnish. Cut the chillies into long thin shreds, discarding the seeds. Use only about 5 cm (2 in) of the white end of the chives or spring onions. Use a toothpick or bamboo skewer to make a hole in one end of each piece of onion and insert a sliver of chilli to resemble the wick of a candle or firecracker. Heat another wok or pan and add the oil. Stir-fry the onions quickly and carefully. Sprinkle with 1 tablespoon of water to help them to soften, simmer until evaporated, then set the garnish aside.

Mix the soy bean powder with a little cold water and stir into the sauce with the beef. Simmer, stirring, until it thickens and the oil floats on the surface.

Spoon into the centre of a serving plate and arrange the onions around the edge of the plate.

Shanghai 上海

STEAMED THREE SHREDDED MEATS

This much revered dish, incorporating pork, ham and chicken meat with cooked bamboo shoots is a traditional food in Shanghai homes. Locals often serve it during festival times and family get-togethers. The three kinds of shredded meats packed closely together imply a reunion.

250 g (8 oz) ham
250 g (8 oz) lean pork
250 g (8 oz) chicken breast
2 dried black mushrooms, soaked for 25 minutes
185 g (6 oz) canned or cooked fresh bamboo shoots, thinly sliced
1 cup (250 mL/8 fl oz) clear chicken stock (broth)

Place the ham, pork and chicken in a saucepan, cover with water, bring to the boil, then simmer gently for one hour. Remove, drain and cut the meat into fine shreds.

Select one or two heatproof bowls large enough to contain all of the ingredients. Place a black mushroom, cap downwards, in the bottom of the bowl. Arrange the shredded meats and the bamboo shoots in the bowl and set on a rack in a wok or in a steamer with simmering water. Cover and steam for about 10 minutes until the meat is compact.

Turn the bowl upside down into a serving dish and remove the bowl so that the meat retains its shape. Boil the stock up, pour over the meat and serve.

This is delicious either as a main course or is enough for 12 guests as an appetiser.

STEAMED THREE SHREDDED MEATS

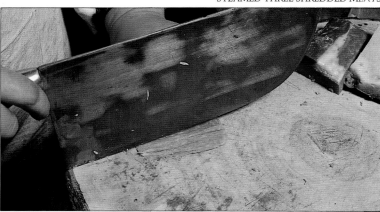

DEEP-FRIED BEEF ROLLS FILLED WITH QUAIL EGGS

Guangzhou 广州

DEEP-FRIED BEEF ROLLS FILLED WITH QUAIL EGGS

250 g (8 oz) lean beef steak
1 small carrot
2 teaspoons cornflour (cornstarch)
½ teaspoon bicarbonate of soda (baking soda)
10 quail eggs, fresh or canned
¼ teaspoon powdered cloves (optional)
oil for frying

SEASONING

2 teaspoons superior or other light soy sauce
1 teaspoon rice wine or dry sherry
½ teaspoon sesame oil
½ teaspoon salt
1 teaspoon sugar
pinch of ground star anise
pinch of white pepper

Using two cleavers, one in each hand, mince (grind) the meat very finely, or process to a smooth pulp in a food processor. Grate the carrot finely and add to the beef with the cornflour, bicarbonate of soda and the seasoning ingredients. Mix with your fingers until a smooth paste. On a piece of greaseproof paper or thick plastic wrap spread the meat in a rectangle about 30 cm (12 in) long and 12 cm (5 in) wide.

❈ Boil the fresh quail eggs for 5 minutes, place under cold running water to cool and remove the shells. Dry the eggs and arrange end to end along the centre of the meat. Use the paper or plastic to lift the meat up around the eggs, so that they are completely encased within a long sausage of meat. Pinch the ends together. Coat the roll thickly with cornflour, brushing off the excess.

❈ Heat about 2.5 cm (1 in) of oil in a wide flat frying pan or large wok and fry the beef roll over moderate heat until well and evenly coloured all over. Roll it gently in the pan, using two wide spatulas to ensure it does not break during cooking. Lift out, drain and sprinkle over the powdered cloves, if used. Slice to serve.

Beijing 北京

TWICE-COOKED BEEF

1 kg (2 lb) beef top rump (bottom round)
3 tablespoons peanut oil
3 pieces star anise
2 pieces dried mandarine/tangerine peel
3 spring onions (shallots/scallions)
6 slices fresh (root) ginger
4 cloves garlic
2 teaspoons Sichuan peppercorns (Fagara or Sansho)
3 tablespoons rice wine or dry sherry
½ cup (125 mL/4 fl oz) light soy sauce
3 tablespoons dark soy sauce
2 tablespoons brown bean sauce
1 tablespoon sugar
salt and pepper
2 teaspoons cornflour (cornstarch)
1 teaspoon sesame oil

Cut the beef into thick slices, then into square pieces. In a wok, heat the oil to smoking point and fry the beef in several batches until well coloured. Lift out and set aside.

❈ Drain off most of the oil. Stir-fry the star anise, peel, whole onions, ginger, garlic and peppercorns for 2 minutes until fragrant. Add the wine and soy sauces and simmer for 4 minutes. Discard the star anise, spring onion, ginger and garlic, then add the beef slices, bean paste and sugar and cover with water.

❈ Bring to the boil, then reduce heat to very low and simmer, covered, for about 3 hours until the beef is very tender.

❈ Season the sauce with salt and pepper and thicken with cornflour mixed with cold water. Sprinkle on the sesame oil and serve at once.

TWICE-COOKED BEEF

DEEP-FRIED BEEF CROQUETTES

KASAYA BEEF

Beijing 北京

DEEP-FRIED BEEF CROQUETTES

This dish is also called "Tien Dan Regains Chi", a name which can be traced back to 279 BC. Tien Dan, the great general of the Kingdom of Chi, was suffering from the onslaught of the warring Kingdom of Yen, which had captured some seventy Chi cities. In desperation he devised a remarkable plan.

His men gathered together a thousand cows, tied swords and knives to their horns and hay soaked with oil to their tails. In the dead of night they set fire to the hay and sent the cows charging into the enemy camp, followed by five thousand soldiers.

Victory was theirs, the cities were recovered and great honours were bestowed on Tien Dan.

The red beef fillet in this dish represents the fire-cows of Tien Dan, hence its name.

375 g (12 oz) beef fillet
4 water chestnuts, finely shredded
155 g (5 oz) ham, finely shredded
1 stem Chinese kale (gai larn) or spinach, shredded
1 tablespoon rice wine or dry sherry
1 teaspoon salt
375 g (12 oz) chicken meat
½ egg
1 tablespoon cornflour
pinch of salt
deep-fried, dried vegetable leaves or fresh sprigs
    of coriander (garnish)

COATING

½ cup (60 g/2 oz) flour
1 egg, beaten
1 cup (125 g/4 oz) dry breadcrumbs
oil for deep-frying

Cut the beef into long thin slices, then beat gently with the side of a cleaver to flatten.

☗ Season the shredded ingredients with the rice wine and salt.

☗ Mince (grind) the chicken meat finely and mix with the egg and cornflour, adding a pinch of salt.

☗ Place a few strands of shredded ingredients in the centre of each strip of beef and roll up into cylinders. Cover each roll with a thin coating of chicken paste, then dust with flour, dip into beaten egg and coat with breadcrumbs.

☗ Heat the oil in a large wok and deep-fry the croquettes in batches until cooked through and golden brown. Lift out and drain well.

☗ Arrange the croquettes on a bed of deep-fried vegetable leaves or surround them with sprigs of fresh coriander and serve at once.

Beijing 北京

KASAYA BEEF

China raises a great number of cattle of many varieties, including Mongolian cattle and the pien niu – the offspring of a bull and a female yak. The pien niu can withstand hardship better than cattle, it produces more milk than a yak and is easy to tame.

Beef used in Beijing cooking usually comes from Inner Mongolia, being rich and tender with a delicious aroma. It is said to strengthen bones and muscles and to reduce water retention.

In this recipe the fillet is pounded to a paste and spread between two layers of omelet before being crisp-fried.

250 g (8 oz) beef fillet
2 egg whites, lightly beaten
2 tablespoons cornflour (cornstarch)
2 teaspoons rice wine or dry sherry
2 tablespoons finely chopped spring onion (shallot/scallion)
1 teaspoon finely grated fresh (root) ginger
2 cloves garlic, finely chopped
¾ teaspoon salt
2 eggs
2½ cups (625 mL/20 fl oz) peanut oil
½ teaspoon sesame oil
3 tablespoons cornflour (cornstarch)

Very finely mince (grind) the beef, removing any sinews. Add the beaten egg white, cornflour and rice wine and mix well, then add the spring onion, ginger, garlic and salt and beat with a wooden spoon until the mixture is very smooth and slightly sticky.

☗ Beat the eggs well. Heat a wok and rub with a piece of kitchen paper, dipped in sesame and peanut oil. Pour in half of the egg mixture and tilt the pan until it spreads into a thin, wide sheet of about 33 cm (13 in) in diameter. When firm and lightly coloured on the underside, turn and lightly cook the other side. Repeat with the remaining egg.

☗ Lay out one omelet and spread the beef paste over it. Cover with the other omelet, pressing it firmly into place. Cut into diamond shapes and dip the cut edges into the cornflour. Heat the peanut oil and add the sesame oil. Fry the "sandwiches" in batches over moderate heat until crisp and golden. Ensure that the meat filling is cooked through before removing from the oil. Drain well and stack on a serving plate. Serve at once.

BEEF SLICES STIR-FRIED IN OYSTER SAUCE

Guangzhou 广州

BEEF SLICES STIR-FRIED IN OYSTER SAUCE

250 g (8 oz) fillet of beef (tenderloin)
1 egg white, well beaten
3 tablespoons oil for frying
1 spring onion (shallot/scallion), chopped
2 slices fresh (root) ginger, shredded
2 teaspoons cornflour (cornstarch)
2 tablespoons water

SEASONING

2 tablespoons oyster sauce
1 tablespoon rice wine or dry sherry
1 tablespoon light soy sauce
1 teaspoon mushroom soy sauce
1 teaspoon sugar
pinch of salt and white pepper
2 tablespoons beef stock (broth)

Cut the beef across the grain into very thin slices, then cut into small squares. Place in a dish with the egg white and mix well. Add the pre-mixed seasoning ingredients and leave to marinate for 20 minutes.

🦚 Drain the beef, reserving the marinade. Heat the wok with the oil and stir-fry the beef over high heat until it changes colour. Remove immediately.

🦚 Add the spring onions and ginger to the wok and stir-fry for 45 seconds, then return the beef, the marinade ingredients and the cornflour mixed with water. Stir over very high heat until thickened, then serve at once.

Beijing 北京

STIR-FRIED FILLET OF LAMB

185 g (6 oz) lamb fillet (tenderloin)
1 egg white
1½ tablespoons cornflour (cornstarch)
½ teaspoon salt
pinch of pepper
60 g (2 oz) canned bamboo shoots, drained
5 cm (2 in) piece cucumber
1 small red capsicum (bell pepper)
2 spring onions (shallots/scallions)
3 slices fresh (root) ginger
2½ cups (625 mL/20 fl oz) peanut oil
2 teaspoons rice wine or dry sherry

Use a sharp knife to cut across the fillet into thin slices. Stack the slices together and cut into narrow shreds. Place in a dish.

STIR-FRIED FILLET OF LAMB

🦚 Lightly beat the egg white, adding the cornflour, salt and pepper and pour over the lamb. Mix in well and leave for 20 minutes.

🦚 Shred the bamboo shoots, the skin and flesh of the cucumber, the capsicum, onions and ginger.

🦚 Heat the oil in a wok and deep-fry the lamb strips for 1½ minutes over moderate heat, using chopsticks to separate the shreds. Lift out and drain well.

🦚 Pour off all but 2 tablespoons of the oil and stir-fry the bamboo shoots, cucumber and capsicum for 2 minutes, then add the onions and ginger and stir-fry together briefly.

🦚 Return the lamb and toss the ingredients together over very high heat. Add the rice wine and toss again, then serve.

Beijing 北京

DEEP-FRIED LAMB SLICES

280 g (9 oz) lamb fillet (tenderloin)
¾ cup (90 g/3 oz) cornflour (cornstarch)
oil for deep-frying

SAUCE

½ cup (125 mL/4 fl oz) water
2 tablespoons light soy sauce
1 teaspoon ginger juice
1½ teaspoons rice wine or dry sherry
1½ teaspoons vinegar
2 teaspoons sugar
1 teaspoon cornflour (cornstarch)

Cut across the fillet into thin slices, then thin strips.

🦚 Mix the cornflour with water to a very thin batter.

🦚 Heat a wok with the oil to smoking point. Coat with the batter and deep-fry the meat in several batches, stirring with chopsticks to separate the strips. The meat will take about one minute to be cooked through and well coloured on the surface. Remove and drain well.

🦚 In another wok bring the pre-mixed sauce ingredients to the boil, add the meat slices and simmer, stirring carefully, until the sauce glazes the meat. Spoon onto a serving plate and serve at once.

DEEP-FRIED LAMB SLICES

Beijing 北京

IT'S LIKE HONEY!

A story is told about a special lamb dish cooked for the Empress Dowager Cixi. Being very pleased with it, she asked the chef for the name of the dish. He did not dare to venture an answer and instead asked her to name it. She said casually, "It's like honey!" and that has been the name of this dish ever since.

The lamb pieces in this recipe are brownish red in colour, and soft and tender. It really tastes like honey with a slightly sour aftertaste.

220 g (7 oz) lamb fillet
1 tablespoon Hoisin sauce
2 tablespoons cornflour (cornstarch)
3 tablespoons peanut or other oil for frying
1/3 teaspoon sesame oil

SEASONING

1 tablespoon light soy sauce
1 teaspoon brown vinegar
1 teaspoon rice wine or dry sherry
1 teaspoon ginger juice
1/4 teaspoon molasses or 1/2 teaspoon golden syrup/treacle
2 teaspoons sugar
1/2 teaspoon cornflour (cornstarch)

Very thinly slice the lamb across the grain into slices. Place in a dish and add the Hoisin sauce, mixing well, then sprinkle with the cornflour and mix until coated evenly.

※ Mix the seasoning ingredients together and set aside.

※ Heat the oil in a wok and stir-fry the lamb over moderate heat until reddish-brown and just cooked, stirring constantly with chopsticks to separate the slices. Remove and drain well.

※ Pour off most of the oil and add the seasoning ingredients. Bring to the boil and add the sesame oil. Return the lamb and stir quickly over high heat until the seasoning ingredients coat the lamb. Serve at once.

MONGOLIAN FIRE POT

Beijing 北京

MONGOLIAN FIRE POT

The traditional Mongolian Fire Pot, or Hotpot as it is also known, is positioned in the centre of a large round table over a charcoal fire. The pot is filled with simmering broth and everybody cooks their own meal by using wooden chopsticks or small wire baskets to suspend pieces of meat and vegetables in the hot stock. Plates with paper-thin slices of lamb, bean thread vermicelli and different sorts of vegetables are arranged around the fire pot. The meat, or other cooking ingredients, is dipped into one or more of the seasonings, served separately in small bowls on the table. At the end of the meal all the remaining vegetables and side dishes are added to the broth and the banquet is finished off with bowls of the resulting rich soup.

10 cups (2½ L/80 fl oz) chicken stock (broth)
2 tablespoons dried shrimp
6 dried black mushrooms, soaked for 25 minutes
1 kg (2 lb) lean lamb loin
500 g (1 lb) Chinese cabbage
90 g (3 oz) dry bean thread vermicelli
90 g (3 oz) canned pickled garlic
large bunch fresh coriander

SEASONINGS/DIPS

3 tablespoons sesame paste (tahini)
½ cup (125 mL/4 fl oz) rice wine or dry sherry
⅓ cup (125 g/4 oz) preserved beancurd
2 tablespoons chilli oil
½ cup (125 mL/4 fl oz) dark soy sauce
2 tablespoons shrimp paste
½ cup (125 mL/4 fl oz) light soy sauce

Fill the fire pot or other vessel suitable for table-top cooking with the stock and add the dried shrimp. Drain the mushrooms, remove the stems, dice the caps and add to the stock. ❈ Slice the lamb very thinly (made easy by partially freezing it beforehand) and arrange on plates. Rinse the cabbage, cut into squares and place in a dish. Pour boiling water over the vermicelli to soften, drain and arrange on a plate. Place the garlic and coriander on plates. Arrange all the plates around the fire pot on the dining table. Serve at least 2 small bowls of each seasoning/dip and place these on the table with spoons. ❈ Give each guest one bowl to eat from, one or two small bowls for mixing the sauce, and a pair of wooden chopsticks.

LAMB TENDERLOIN WITH FRESH CORIANDER

Beijing 北京

LAMB TENDERLOIN WITH FRESH CORIANDER

375 g (12 oz) lamb fillet (tenderloin)
1 tablespoon rendered chicken fat
125 g (4 oz) broccoli or other green vegetable
2 dried black mushrooms, soaked for 25 minutes
4 stalks fresh coriander
1 spring onion (shallot/scallion)
2 teaspoons rice wine or dry sherry
1 tablespoon dark soy sauce
½ teaspoon salt

SEASONING

2 teaspoons sugar
1 teaspoon sesame oil
2 teaspoons cornflour (cornstarch)

Cut the lamb into thin slices, then into strips and rinse with cold water. Drain and dry thoroughly. Place in a dish and add the pre-mixed seasoning, mix well and leave for 15 minutes.
※ Heat the chicken fat in a wok and stir-fry the shredded lamb until just cooked, then remove and set aside.
※ Trim and slice the broccoli. Drain the mushrooms, remove the stems and shred the caps. Rinse the spring onion, dry well and cut into 5 cm (2 in) lengths. Trim and chop the coriander.
※ Add the vegetables to the wok and stir-fry together until the broccoli is tender, then add the wine, soy sauce and salt, return the meat and toss together over high heat for 1 minute. Add the coriander and serve immediately.

Beijing 北京

ROAST LAMB ON SKEWERS

Muslims along the north-western borders of China have a high regard for this delicious dish of cubed, seasoned lamb, tossed in sesame seed and roasted on skewers over charcoal.

The dish was introduced into Beijing some 20 years ago and now a number of restaurants include it in their menu.

1 kg (2 lb) lamb fillet (tenderloin)*
3 eggs
¾ cup (90 g/3 oz) flour
1 tablespoon salt
1½ teaspoons pepper
1½ teaspoons ground Sichuan peppercorns (Fagara or Sansho)
¾ cup (125 g/4 oz) minced (ground) spring onions (shallots/scallions)
2 large tomatoes, finely chopped, seeds discarded
3 tablespoons white sesame seeds

ROAST LAMB ON SKEWERS

Cut all the white sinews and membrane covering off the meat, then cut into small, uniform cubes.
※ Beat the eggs lightly and mix with the remaining ingredients except the sesame seeds. Pour the marinade over the meat cubes and stir in evenly. Cover with plastic wrap and leave for at least 3 hours.
※ Toss the meat cubes in sesame seed and thread onto metal skewers which have been rubbed with an oiled cloth to make the removal of the cooked meat easier. Take 6-7 pieces of meat for each skewer.
※ For best results roast over a charcoal burner with gently glowing coals. Turn skewers over once to ensure even cooking. When the meat turns reddish brown, after 3-4 minutes, it is done. Tender lamb should be crisp and coloured on the surface, but still pink inside, as it dries out with prolonged cooking.
※ Serve on the skewers.

Less expensive cuts, such as boneless leg meat, can be used, but the result will be a tougher textured meat with a stronger flavour.

Beijing 北京

HAND-GRASPED LAMB

Hand-grasped lamb is a traditional dish of the nomadic desert dwellers of north-western China. At the end of a journey they prepare a fire, slaughter a lamb, cook it simply and enjoy the hearty meal. The name of this dish comes from their practice of grasping the rib bones while eating the meat.

2 kg (4 lb) lamb ribs (approximately 20 ribs)
1 spring onion (shallot/scallion), finely chopped
3 fresh red chillies, finely chopped
1 tablespoon grated fresh (root) ginger
2 tablespoons finely chopped fresh coriander

SEASONING

2 tablespoons rice wine or dry sherry
1 fresh red chilli, sliced
2 spring onions (shallots/scallions), roughly chopped
4 slices fresh (root) ginger
1 teaspoon salt
2 star anise
2 cloves garlic, crushed
1 x 5 cm (2 in) stick cinnamon

Cut the meat into sections of two ribs each, then trim away the meat and fat at the end of the bones.
※ Place the ribs in a large saucepan and cover with water. Add the seasoning ingredients and bring to the boil. Cover and simmer gently for about 1½ hours until the meat is very tender. Leave to cool in the stock, then drain well.
※ Arrange on a serving plate. Serve with small dishes of raw spring onion, chilli, ginger and coriander.

BARBECUED MUTTON

Beijing 北京

BARBECUED MUTTON

When night falls on the northern seafront of China, all is peaceful and quiet except for the brightly lit small restaurants along the shore, filled with the laughter of happy diners. The aroma of barbecued mutton fills the air.

The meat chosen for this traditional dish comes from the hind leg of a certain type of sheep. The crescent-shaped knife used to slice the meat, and even the grid on which the mutton is cooked, are especially made for this purpose. In the past even a special pose was adopted as one cooked and feasted on the barbecued meat. With one foot on the ground and the other on top of a stool, the cooking, chatting and feasting might have brought to mind stories handed down by nomadic ancestors.

The following recipe shows an improved version of the traditional dish, consisting of richly marinated shreds of mutton, quickly barbecued with shredded leeks. It is stuffed into sesame-covered pocket bread and eaten sandwich-style, often with pickled garlic.

500 g (1 lb) lean mutton or lamb
3 tablespoons light soy sauce
1½ tablespoons rice wine or dry sherry
2 teaspoons ginger juice
1½ tablespoons sugar
2 teaspoons sesame oil
pinch of salt
2 fresh leeks
fresh coriander
pickled garlic

Cut the meat across the grain into very thin slices, then stack several slices together and cut into shreds. Place in a dish and add the soy sauce, wine, ginger juice, sugar, sesame oil and salt and mix well. Leave for at least 30 minutes.

✳ Rinse the leeks thoroughly, cut into 5 cm (2 in) lengths and shred lengthways.

✳ Heat a ribbed barbecue plate over a charcoal fire. Rub with oil and spread the leeks over it. Place the meat in a single layer on top of the leeks, then use a pair of long-handled chopsticks to turn the leeks and meat over and over until the leeks are soft and the meat cooked through and tender.

✳ Stuff the pocket bread with the meat and fresh coriander leaves, and serve the pickled garlic separately.

SESAME POCKET BREAD

3 tablespoons vegetable oil
3½ cups (440 g/14 oz) flour
¾ cup (175 mL/6 fl oz) boiling water
3 tablespoons cold water
2 teaspoons salt
2-3 tablespoons white sesame seeds
oil for frying

Heat the oil in a wok, add ½ cup (60 g/2 oz) flour and cook over low heat until the mixture is smooth and golden, stirring constantly. Set aside to cool.

✳ Pour the remaining flour into a bowl, reserving 1 tablespoon. Pour in the boiling water and stir quickly, using the handle of a wooden spoon, to a smooth dough, adding the cold water to make it soft and pliable. Knead for about 7 minutes on a lightly oiled board. Roll out into a long sausage shape and divide into 10-12 pieces. Cover with a damp cloth.

✳ Roll each piece out separately into a square-shaped cake about 12 cm (5 in) wide. Spread on a coating of the flour-and-oil dough and sprinkle with salt and some of the reserved flour. Fold in two sides to overlap in the centre, seal the edges by pinching the two ends, then fold the other two sides in to just overlap in the centre. Roll in the direction of the folds into a rectangular shape. Dip the smooth side into sesame seeds, pressing on lightly.

✳ Bake on an oiled and floured baking tray in a pre-heated oven at 220°C (425°F) or fry on both sides until puffed and golden. Cut in halves to fill.

SICHUAN RABBIT CAKE

STUFFED OXTAIL

Sichuan 四川

SICHUAN RABBIT CAKE

Confucius taught the Chinese to be meticulous about fine food and in particular minced meat. Food should be savoured rather than devoured: it is the quality not the quantity of the food that counts. As for minced meat, the finer the mince the better, as it should be easily digested and easily absorbed.

In this dish, the rabbit meat is minced, seasoned, steamed into cakes and then deep-fried until crisp. A rich Sichuan sauce containing minced ginger, spring onion and garlic is poured over before serving. The meat is tender and salty, sweet and sour, and pepper hot.

1 x 625-750 g (1¼-1½ lb) rabbit
2 egg whites, well beaten
½ cup (125 mL/4 fl oz) water
1½ tablespoons cornflour (cornstarch)
¾ teaspoon salt
cornflour (cornstarch)
oil for deep-frying

SAUCE

2 pickled red chillies
3 cloves garlic
3 spring onions (shallots/scallions)
3 slices fresh (root) ginger
½ cup (125 mL/4 fl oz) chicken or rabbit stock (broth)
1 tablespoon sugar
1½ tablespoons brown vinegar
1 tablespoon light soy sauce
1½ teaspoons cornflour (cornstarch)
pinch of salt and Sichuan pepper (Fagara or Sansho)

Remove the rabbit meat from the bones and mince (grind) very finely. Add the egg whites, water, cornflour and salt and mix thoroughly until the paste is smooth, picking out all the fine sinews. Spread the mixture in a lightly oiled, heatproof dish and place on a rack in a wok or in a steamer, cover and steam for about 14 minutes until the cake is firm. Remove and leave to cool. Cut into thick slices, about 5 cm (2 in) long and coat thickly with cornflour.

For the sauce, finely mince (grind) the chillies, garlic, spring onions and ginger. Mix the remaining sauce ingredients together and set aside.

Heat the oil in a wok to smoking point and deep-fry the slices of rabbit cake, several at a time, until golden brown, then drain well.

In a clean wok, sauté the chillies, garlic, spring onions and ginger in a little oil until fragrant. Add the rabbit cake, mix in evenly, then pour in the other pre-mixed sauce ingredients and bring to the boil, stirring carefully, and serve.

Beijing 北京

STUFFED OXTAIL

Oxtail meat is different from the meat of all other parts of the ox. It is bright red, finely textured and contains a sticky substance which is specially pleasing to some palates. In this recipe the star-shaped central bone is removed and the cavity filled with a mixture of minced (ground) fish and chicken.

1 x 1 kg (2 lb) oxtail
5 cups (1¼ L/40 fl oz) beef stock (broth)
2 spring onions (shallots/scallions)
2 slices fresh (root) ginger
1 teaspoon salt
1 tablespoon rice wine or dry sherry

STUFFING

125 g (4 oz) white fish
125 g (4 oz) chicken meat
1 egg white
2 teaspoons rice wine or dry sherry
½ teaspoon salt

SAUCE

2 spring onions (shallots/scallions), chopped
2 slices fresh (root) ginger, chopped
2 tablespoons lard or oil for frying
¾ cup (175 mL/6 fl oz) chicken or beef stock (broth)
2 teaspoons rice wine or dry sherry
1 tablespoon cornflour (cornstarch)

Have the butcher cut the oxtail through between the joints. Place the meat in a large saucepan and add the stock, onions, ginger, salt and rice wine. Cover and bring to the boil. Skim off the froth, then reduce the heat and simmer gently for about 2 hours.

Allow to cool slightly, then remove the meat from the stock and drain well. Use a knife with a narrow sharp blade to remove the central bone from each piece of meat.

Finely mince (grind) the fish and chicken together adding the egg white, rice wine and salt. Knead to a smooth paste, then fill into the holes in the pieces of oxtail. Arrange them on a lightly oiled, heatproof plate and set on a rack in a wok or in a steamer, cover and steam for about 15 minutes until the filling is cooked through.

For the sauce, stir-fry the spring onions and ginger in the lard or oil until softened, then add the remaining sauce ingredients and bring to the boil, stirring constantly.

Stir the liquid from the dish in which the oxtail was steamed into the sauce, pour sauce over the meat and serve.

Shanghai 上海

COLD DISHES

On the lower reaches of the Yangtze River, there is a shop that specialises in selling cold dishes and game. The story goes that when this shop was over a hundred years old, business was slack because of poor management.

One day a beggar came into the shop and asked to stay overnight. Seeing that he was tired and hungry, the owner gave him a meal. During the night the beggar spread out his mat to sleep, and before leaving the next morning the beggar left his mat in grateful repayment. The shop owner thought it useless and burnt it in his cooking fire. But the pork cooked over the fire that day was delicious, and business soon picked up. The beggar was said to have been an incarnation of the deity Lu Dongbing, and as the story spread, the owner changed the shop's name to Lu Gaojian to honour the god, selling pork stewed in soy sauce in the spring, goose pickled in grain in the summer, duck in autumn, and mutton, roast fish, roast eggs, duck stewed in soy sauce, prawns, pigs' trotters, game and more in the winter.

COLD DISHES ON A SINGLE PLATE

Cold, cooked food is often served as the first course at a dinner and cold dishes in Shanghai have undergone several stages of development. Over a hundred years ago, each item of food was served on a separate plate. At a banquet, there would be dried and fresh fruit, cold and hot plates, beverages and so on. Even at the simplest dinner there were at least four cold dishes, and usually there were six or eight.

The food was finely cut and served neatly on plates. For instance, ham was cut into thin slices of equal size and thickness. Pai ham was cut into squares and Qiao ham was cut into thin pieces and placed on a plate in the shape of an arched bridge.

ASSORTED COLD DISHES OF TWO OR THREE INGREDIENTS

Forty or fifty years ago, cold dishes developed into assorted cold dishes. Usually one assorted dish was made up of two or three ingredients, and four to six such dishes were served at dinner. There were also assorted cold dishes of five or six ingredients, but these were only served at informal dinners.

Assorted cold dishes vary according to the different ingredients, shapes, colours and cuisines. Particular care is taken in selecting and arranging the ingredients so as to match the colours well.

LARGE ASSORTED COLD PLATTERS

About thirty years ago large assorted cold dishes became popular. A large round or oval plate would contain 10 or 12 ingredients. All the ingredients were carefully prepared, boned and well presented. Preparation involved skill in slicing, matching colours and arrangement.

The photograph below shows a typical assorted cold platter of beautifully arranged cold cooked meat including ham, beef, chicken, luncheon meat, vegetarian "chicken" and bamboo shoots, with poached prawns and shredded marinated cabbage in the centre.

Beijing 北京

FRIED RED AND WHITE MEATS

This is a traditional Shanxi speciality found on the menus of many of the restaurants in northern China. There are two kinds of meat in this dish, white chicken meat and red pork fillet. They complement each other and are both tender. Black wood ear fungus and green vegetable strips give additional colour.

RED MEAT

250 g (8 oz) pork fillet
½ egg, well beaten
3 tablespoons cornflour (cornstarch)
½ cup (125 mL/4 fl oz) peanut oil
1 tablespoon brown vinegar
1 spring onion (shallot/scallion), sliced
2 cloves garlic, sliced
3 pieces dried wood ear fungus, soaked for 20 minutes
1 stalk Chinese kale (gai larn) or spinach, sliced diagonally

SAUCE

2 teaspoons rice wine or dry sherry
2 teaspoons dark soy sauce
½ cup (125 mL/4 fl oz) chicken stock (broth)
large pinch of five spice powder

WHITE MEAT

250 g (8 oz) chicken breast meat
1 egg white, well beaten
3 tablespoons cornflour (cornstarch)
2 tablespoons lard
½ cup (125 mL/4 fl oz) chicken stock (broth)
¾ teaspoon salt
1 tablespoon rice wine or dry sherry
1 spring onion (shallot/scallion), sliced
3-4 slices fresh (root) ginger, shredded
3-4 slices cucumber, seeds removed
1 tablespoon rendered chicken fat, melted

Slice the pork fillet thinly, then cut into smaller pieces. Place in a dish and add the egg and cornflour, coating the pork evenly.
❀ Heat the peanut oil in a wok and fry the pork until cooked through, stirring constantly to separate the slices. Remove and set aside.
❀ Add the vinegar, spring onion, garlic, drained fungus and vegetable slices and stir-fry for 2 minutes, then return the pork and stir-fry briefly before adding the pre-mixed sauce ingredients. Cook, stirring, until the sauce coats the ingredients, then spoon onto one side of a serving dish and keep warm.
❀ Slice the chicken and place in a dish with the egg white and cornflour, mixing until each piece is well coated.
❀ Heat a wok and add the lard. Stir-fry the chicken over high heat, adding the chicken stock, salt and rice wine. Then add the spring onions, ginger and cucumber and simmer gently until the chicken is tender, and the sauce reduced to a glaze.
❀ Arrange beside the pork meat on the serving plate and serve.

THE WILD RUSH OF THE DADU RIVER, WESTERN SICHUAN

LEO MEIER

四川
Sichuan

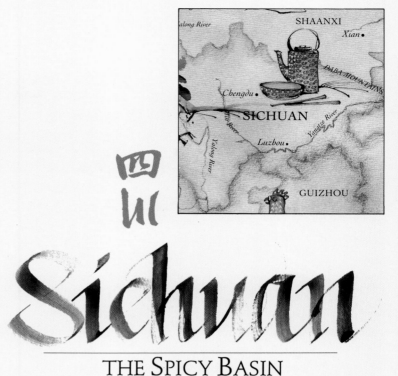

Sichuan

THE SPICY BASIN

IN THE geographical heartland of China is the huge natural bowl of Sichuan. Surrounded by range after range of mountains, slashed by the gathering flood of the Yangtze, the plains of the Red Basin are one of the most fertile areas in all China. Into these lowlands the Yangtze comes bursting with the ice-melt from the high ranges of remote Qinghai. When it leaves the red earth of Sichuan to carve its way through the Daba mountains to the east China plains, the Yangtze is mightier still – swollen by the waters of four substantial tributaries. These four rivers, the Min, Jialing, Yalong and To, give the province its name: Sichuan means Four Streams. They also give the area much of the agricultural muscle that has helped shape its gastronomic heritage and which today feeds a hundred million people with one of the best balanced and most spectacular cuisines on earth.

Three centuries before Christianity began, and sixteen centuries before Sichuan became a province of China, the flow of the mighty Min river was harnessed to water the thirsty land. A huge barrage built by human might diverted the river away from its natural channel into the surrounding plains. The flow was halved again and again, until countless irrigation streams trickled through the fields covering the plains on which the present provincial capital of Chengdu now stands. From these fields peasants harvested rich crops. They still do, and their produce gives the province its proud and spicy culinary legacy, which in recent years has swept the dinner tables of the world.

Sichuan cuisine today is a happy medley of many traditions and influences. The tangy tastes of India are blended into Sichuan cooking. Travellers brought Buddhism into the province more than two thousand years ago. The traders and missionaries carried Indian spices, herbs and cooking techniques with them as well as Buddhist teachings, and the strong vegetarian legacy is still very much alive in such family dishes as peppery hot beancurd and Sichuan pickled vegetables, items which sometimes take pride of place at a meatless table. The

A WARM WELCOME FROM TIBETAN VILLAGERS IN WESTERN SICHUAN

LEO MEIER

181

AT SHIMIAN VILLAGE MARKET, SICHUAN PROVINCE

HARALD SUND

SPRING ONIONS, AN ESSENTIAL INGREDIENT OF CHINESE COOKING

LEO MEIER

provincial cooking also has links with the cuisines of Indochina to the south. The Thai people trace their beginnings back through the mists of time to the shrouded mountains that surround the Sichuan basin, and many aspects of the cooking of Thailand bear a close similarity to Sichuan cooking. Thai-speaking tribes still live in the mountains, as do Miao, Li and other hill peoples whose racial relatives are scattered over the highlands of Vietnam, Laos and Kampuchea.

Vegetarian dishes flourish in Sichuan in staggering variety. For two thousand years Buddhist customs dictated a meatless diet for a large minority of the population, and imaginative chefs created an exhaustive repertoire of dishes from the abundant produce of the land. As the huge population grew, grazing space for animals dwindled as every available piece of land went under the plough. The animal that pulled the plough, the faithful, plodding water buffalo, the eternal tractor of China, was more often than not the only source of meat.

Many vegetarian dishes are garnished with the memorable and delicious, but wrongly named, Fish Flavoured Sauce. This splendid example of culinary ingenuity tastes like fish, but its unforgettable flavour comes from a careful mixing of vinegar, garlic, ginger, spring onions and hot bean paste. There is an old saying in Sichuan that a cook could pour the searingly spicy Fish Flavoured Sauce over rocks washed up on the banks of the Min River and hungry diners would devour them with enthusiasm.

Another old saying concerns the seven flavours used in the cooking of provincial specialities. This is the first lesson given to a novice cook and it stays with him throughout his career: *sweet* (tien) comes from honey or sugar; *sour* (suan) from vinegar; *salty* (tien) from salt or soy; *fragrant* (xiang) from garlic and ginger; *bitter* (ku) from spring onions or leeks; *nutty* (ma) from sesame seeds or oil; and, most importantly for Sichuan, *hot* (la) from the red chilli.

Beans and beancurd, together with flavoursome ingredients like spring onions, garlic, peppercorns and ginger, combine with sesame oil, vinegar and the ubiquitous chilli to form memorable dishes. To these are added carefully tended crops from the deep rich soil, the products of the wild mountains and steep valleys that make up ninety per cent of the 540 000 square kilometres (210,000 square miles) of the province. In these mountains, covered in semi-tropical forests rising to cool growths of pine, are gathered some of the most highly praised mushrooms and fungi in China. Here, too, in magnificent towering stands, grow the imposing bamboos for which Sichuan is famous. The bamboo provides a delicacy not only for human gourmets but for the nation's most famous animal, the giant panda. The bamboo forests are home and refuge for these bulky black and white animals, and the people of Sichuan are as proud of the pandas as they are of their distinctive cuisine. The animals are totally protected, and on cold winter nights often venture down from their mountain strongholds to seek shelter, which is given willingly, in highland farmyards. Peasants in the mountains go to the aid of the pandas during periods of drought or flood when their delicate staple diet is threatened. Like the human inhabitants of Sichuan, the pandas are connoisseurs of the food of the province, and their preferred diet

TASTY AND COLOURFUL SPICES ADD FLAVOUR TO REGIONAL DISHES   LEO MEIER

NOMADIC TIBETAN SHEPHERDS IN THE GRASSLANDS OF NORTHERN SICHUAN

LEO MEIER

is fresh bamboo shoots which grow in plenty only in their remote and misty mountains. When the supply is threatened, local farmers carry loads of bamboo on their backs up steep tracks to feed the animals that are the symbol of Sichuan.

Although Chengdu is 2900 kilometres (1,800 miles) up the Yangtze from the East China Sea, fish figures prominently in the diet. Until railways were forged through the mountains earlier this century, the great waterway provided the only reliable form of communication with the outside world. Today the waters of the Yangtze yield a good catch, but a good deal of the fish, freshwater crabs, eels and other water-dwellers consumed in the province are raised for the wok in fishponds, canals and irrigation ditches. A bonus of plump frogs, juicy turtles and tender snakes is also harvested by farmers going to their fields and children tending their flocks of wandering ducks. But despite its location, seawater fish also appear on Sichuan menus, and for many hundreds of years junks loaded with dried or salted fish and seaweed have been towed by armies of toiling coolies through the narrow Yangtze gorges.

If the cuisine of Sichuan Province is built on a solid foundation of red-hot, mouth-pursing chillies, then that tradition is even more apparent over the border in neighbouring Hunan. This landlocked province has a hot, humid summer and a winter that brings bracing chills. To open the pores and keep cool in the summer and to heat the blood in the cold months are two reasons that Hunan people give for flavouring almost every dish with chillies. As in Sichuan, there is an awesome variety of chillies and capsicums. They range from the familiar, harmless large green capsicum to the tiny red pepper known as the delayed action bomb. Why the name? Any innocent visitor can tell you that. Just ask the question five minutes after they have eaten one and, if they can

splutter out an answer while trying to quaff buckets of cold water, they will explain that the peppers take a little while to take effect. When the fire is lit, however, it is hard to put out – perhaps one reason why the people of Sichuan and Hunan are also known for their ample consumption of prime beers which wash down the hearty, spiced meals.

Not all Sichuan food is hot, either in temperature or in flavour. Especially in summer, a meal will start with a selection of cold dishes or a platter holding a selection of cold meats. And the famed peppercorn of the province, used in moderation, tends to be tasty rather than hot. But let the visitor beware the small scarlet peppers that are used as the raw ingredient of pungent red oil and to add the fire to fermented hot bean paste. When they grow, and they are harvested on every patch of earth in Sichuan, the chillies lift themselves upright on the branches. That is why they are called "reach for the sun" chillies – belief has it that they are striving to get closer to the warmth of the sun to take in more of its fire.

CARD PLAYERS IN A TRADITIONAL TEAHOUSE

HARALD SUND

THE TIBETAN VILLAGE OF ANLANG, SICHUAN PROVINCE

HARALD SUND

TIBETAN MOUNTAIN VILLAGERS

LEO MEIER

(following page) TIBETAN HOUSES CLIMB
THE QIONGLAISHAN MOUNTAINS, WESTERN SICHUAN

LEO MEIER

糧食豆品

Grains
& Curd

Grains & Curd

NORTH of the Yangtze, wheat; south of the river, rice; all over China, beancurd. Like most schoolboy maxims, this one is too simplified to be completely true, but it is basically correct. While one of the seven thousand varieties of long-grained rice is the staple staff of life for people of the south and centre of China, northerners build their sturdy diet on a foundation of steamed buns or noodles. People don't say "Hullo" in Cantononese, the polite phrase is "Have you eaten rice yet?" In Shanghai, holding a secure job in the government is said to be like having an iron rice bowl – the bowl can't be broken and the public servant can't be sacked. While rice-eating has been ingrained for centuries in the south where benevolent nature provides ample rain and sunshine to harvest up to three bumper crops a year, the cold, dry plains of the north support mainly wheat, barley and millet. In Manchuria the farmers have to move quickly to harvest their crops before the freezing winter snaps down after the all too brief summer.

Throughout the southern provinces life revolves around the paddy field. Landscapes are painted in different shades of green, from the brilliant emerald of the newly transplanted rice to the deep luxuriant greens of the mature plants. Thousands of years of experience has laid down immutable laws for peasant farmers to follow as they bring in the white gold of the rice crop. The rice plant provides a greater yield in the flooded fields than any other crop, and it brings to the table a much-loved staple that plays a vital role in the daily diet of most Chinese. Eaten three times a day, it is an integral part of every meal – much more so than bread and potatoes in a Western kitchen. Rice to many Chinese is not just part of a meal, but the body on which the delicacies of meat, fish and vegetables are the gorgeous clothes: "A meal without rice is like a beautiful girl with one eye" says an old proverb.

The situation is quite different in the northern provinces, where the people feel deprived if they cannot enjoy the buns and noodles they were weaned on. The basic dough used reflects the no-nonsense approach to food of a busy farmwife who has crops, a home and children to attend to as well as a family to cook for. One part of water and two parts of flour are the simple ingredients of the pancake of northern China. Add a thousand choices of different stuffings or accompaniments and you have the start of many northern meals. Plain steamed buns or thin fried pancakes can be eaten with the filling stews of Hebei and Shandong or to mop up the remains of a bubbling Mongolian Fire Pot.

Whether from rice flour or wheat, a staggering variety of pasta is made in China. Fat or thin, flat or round, pasta comes in sheets, strings, strands and nodules. Noodles can be cooked by themselves or as a steaming bed on which to serve a regional delicacy. They can be fried, stewed, boiled or baked, and eaten for breakfast, lunch, dinner, as an in-between meal or a midnight snack.

While rice and bread give Chinese cuisine much of its carbohydrates, a lot of the protein comes from the miraculous soy bean. Cultivated since the beginning of China's recorded history, over five thousand years ago, there are more than two thousand five hundred varieties of the soy bean. They grow easily in the harsh climate of the north, even in frigid Manchuria; they produce an immense yield, are easy to grow, simple to harvest and are processed into a vast range of healthy and edible products. Dieticians say the beans in one form or

COOKING NOODLES IN A STREETSIDE RESTAURANT   WELDON TRANNIES

another provide almost everything needed by the human body. Certainly, in the form of beancurd, the soy bean provides a high-protein meat substitute healthier than the original animal product it so flatteringly copies.

Beancurd has for a long time provided protein for those who could not afford meat, and today, in a more health-conscious world, beancurd is often used in place of meat by the more prosperous societies. Over the centuries chefs have invented tens of thousands of recipes using beancurd. The Buddhist influence which seeped gently through many eras of China and spread the gospel of a meatless diet did much to take the humble bean and elevate it to be a gourmet's delight. Stir-fried with vegetables, stewed with seafood, braised along with meat, boiled to add body and potency to soups, beancurd is a versatile addition to the diet.

Another well-known by-product of the bean is soy sauce; indispensable in Chinese cooking, it adds a unique flavour to any dish. With sugar added the soy bean becomes a health drink or a dessert sweet. The bland bean picks up the flavour of whatever it shares a pot with. In the hard years that have come so often to China, countless lives of poor peasants have been saved by this modest culinary chameleon.

MAKING DIM SUM, A FAMILY AFFAIR

Sichuan 四川

PEPPERY HOT BEANCURD

This deliciously hot and aromatic dish was created by pockmarked grandmother Ch'eng who operated a small beancurd stall on a street corner in Chengdu, centuries ago. Using a few cakes of beancurd, a little ground meat and local seasonings, she produced one of the tastiest and most nutritious of the Chinese dishes, yet one of the least expensive. Today the dish is still called after her "Ma Po Dofu" (pockmarked mother's beancurd).

4 x 140g (4½oz) squares soft beancurd
185g (6oz) lean beef, preferably fillet (tenderloin)
3 spring onions (shallots/scallions)
2-3 tablespoons vegetable or rapeseed oil
3 cloves garlic, crushed

SEASONING/SAUCE

1 teaspoon grated, fresh (root) ginger
1 tablespoon fermented black beans, chopped
2 pickled red chillies, chopped
2 tablespoons light soy sauce
1-2 teaspoons hot bean paste
½ teaspoon salt
1½ teaspoons sugar
½ teaspoon Sichuan peppercorns (Fagara or Sansho), ground
1 cup (250mL/8floz) chicken stock (broth)
1 tablespoon cornflour (cornstarch)

Cut the beancurd into small cubes and set aside. Very finely mince (grind) the beef, and finely chop the spring onion.
❋ Heat the oil in a wok, and stir-fry the beef, spring onions and garlic until half cooked.
❋ Add the ginger, black beans, chillies, soy sauce and hot bean paste and stir-fry together for about 1½ minutes, then add the remaining seasoning/sauce ingredients, except the cornflour, and bring to the boil. Slide in the beancurd and simmer for about 5 minutes over gentle heat, carefully stir in the cornflour mixed with a little cold water, simmering gently until thickened.
❋ For extra flavour, sprinkle on some flaked red chilli and a little crushed Sichuan pepper just before serving.

Sichuan 四川

BEANCURD IN CONSOMMÉ

6 x 140g (4½oz) squares soft beancurd
3 egg whites
1 tablespoon softened lard
1½ tablespoons cornflour (cornstarch)
7 cups (1¾L/56floz) clear chicken or vegetable stock (broth)
salt to taste
white pepper
500g (1lb) fresh lettuce, Chinese cabbage or other leafy
    Chinese green vegetable

Place the beancurd in a dish and mash smoothly. Beat the egg whites well and stir into the beancurd. Add the lard and the cornflour, mixed with a little cold water, and beat the whole mixture together until thoroughly amalgamated. Pour into a lightly oiled square tin and place on a rack in a wok or in a steamer. Cover and steam for about 14 minutes until firm, then remove and leave to cool.
❋ Cut the beancurd mixture into rectangular-shaped pieces.
❋ Boil the stock up and season with salt and pepper.
❋ Rinse the vegetables thoroughly and separate the leaves, place them in the bottom of a serving bowl and arrange the beancurd on top. Upturn the sliced beancurd onto the vegetables, cover with the boiling stock and serve at once.

PEPPERY HOT BEANCURD

BEANCURD IN CONSOMMÉ

STUFFED CALTROP-SHAPED BEANCURD

Sichuan 四川

STUFFED CALTROP-SHAPED BEANCURD

4 x 140 g (4½ oz) squares beancurd
1 cup (250 mL/8 fl oz) rapeseed or peanut oil
2 x 45 g (1½ oz) slices ham
8 water chestnuts
125 g (4 oz) fatty pork
2 tablespoons finely chopped bamboo shoots
1 egg white, lightly beaten
½ cup (60 g/2 oz) cornflour (cornstarch)
4 slices fresh (root) ginger
2 spring onions (shallots/scallions), sliced
4 cloves garlic, chopped

SAUCE

¾ cup (175 mL/6 fl oz) chicken stock (broth)
1 tablespoon light soy sauce
2 teaspoons rice wine or dry sherry
½ teaspoon salt
½ teaspoon sugar
2 teaspoons cornflour (cornstarch)

Hold each square of beancurd in the palm of your hand and carefully cut into four triangular-shaped pieces. Heat the oil in a wok and fry the beancurd until the surface is crisp and slightly bubbly. Lift out and drain well. Make a slit in one side of each piece of beancurd.

※ Finely mince (grind) the ham, water chestnuts, pork and bamboo shoots, mix together and stuff into the beancurd triangles. Dip the cut edges in the egg white, then into cornflour, and fry gently in the oil for about 2½ minutes until the beancurd has become very crisp and the stuffing has cooked through. Remove, drain well and arrange on a serving plate.

※ Sauté the ginger, spring onion, and garlic in the oil for about 45 seconds, then add the pre-mixed sauce ingredients and simmer, stirring, until the sauce thickens. Pour over the beancurd and serve at once.

Sichuan 四川

BRAISED CRUCIAN CARP WITH BEANCURD

1 x 625 g (1¼ lb) fresh carp or other meaty white fish
4 x 140 g (4½ oz) squares beancurd
1 cup (250 mL/8 fl oz) peanut oil
1½ tablespoons red fermented rice (wine lees)
1½ tablespoons sweet bean paste

SEASONING/SAUCE

1½ tablespoons fermented black beans
1 teaspoon finely grated fresh (root) ginger
3 tablespoons finely chopped spring onions (shallots/scallions)
1 teaspoon finely chopped garlic
2 tablespoons dark soy sauce
½ teaspoon ground Sichuan peppercorns (Fagara or Sansho)
1 tablespoon rice wine or dry sherry
½ cup (125 mL/4 fl oz) chicken stock (broth)

Clean the fish, dip into boiling water, drain and dry well. Make several deep scores diagonally across each side. Cut the beancurd into cubes and slide into a pot of simmering water. Boil gently for 2 minutes, then drain well.

※ Heat the oil in a wok and fry the fish on both sides until well coloured. Pour off most of the oil, then add the pre-mixed seasoning/sauce ingredients, except the stock, and fry for 1 minute. Add the stock and beancurd, cover the dish and simmer gently until the flavours are well absorbed. Add the fermented rice and sweet bean paste, simmer briefly and transfer to a serving dish. Serve at once.

BRAISED CRUCIAN CARP WITH BEANCURD

BEANCURD IN AN EARTHENWARE POT

Beijing 北京

BEANCURD IN AN EARTHENWARE POT

3-4 dried black mushrooms, soaked for 25 minutes
1 dried scallop, soaked for 25 minutes
1 tablespoon dried shrimp, soaked for 20 minutes
60 g (2 oz) chicken breasts, finely minced (ground)
60 g (2 oz) lean pork, finely minced (ground)
30 g (1 oz) prawn (shrimp) meat, minced (ground)
4 x 140 g (4½ oz) squares beancurd
4 spring onions (shallots/scallions)
3 slices fresh (root) ginger
1 teaspoon salt
3 cups (750 mL/24 fl oz) superior stock (*see page 124*) or
  chicken stock (broth)
sesame oil

Place the mushrooms, scallops and shrimps in the heatproof dishes they have been soaked in on a rack in a wok or steamer. Cover and steam for about 15 minutes over high heat until softened, then drain well.

Cut the stalks from the mushrooms and finely dice half of the tops. Mix the minced chicken, pork and prawn meat together and season lightly with salt.

Cut each square of beancurd into four and make a slit through the centre of each quarter. Fill one end of each slit with the minced filling and the other with the diced mushrooms, and place in an earthenware pot.

Slice the spring onions diagonally and add to the pot with the ginger, remaining mushrooms, shredded scallop and the shrimp meat, then add the salt, a dash of pepper, sesame oil and the stock.

Bring to the boil and simmer gently for about 30 minutes. Serve in the pot.

195

SAN XIAN STUFFED BEANCURD

"SILVER FISH" WRAPPED IN SNOW

Beijing 北京

SAN XIAN STUFFED BEANCURD

Beancurd was first made some two thousand years ago by an emperor of the Han Dynasty (206 BC-220 AD). An accomplished scholar, well versed in medicine and astrology, he assembled a group of researchers to look for new medicines, and in the course of their research they produced beancurd. They found it both cheap and very nutritious. Since that time beancurd has remained one of the most highly regarded Chinese foods, and many different ways of preparing and cooking it have been devised.

2 x 140 g (4½ oz) squares of firm-textured beancurd
90 g (3 oz) chicken breasts, finely minced (ground)
60 g (2 oz) fresh prawn (shrimp) meat
2 tablespoons finely chopped, soaked and prepared sea
    cucumber (optional)
1½ tablespoons finely chopped spring onion
    (shallot/scallion)
¼ teaspoon grated, fresh (root) ginger
1 egg white, well beaten
1 tablespoon rice wine or dry sherry
½ teaspoon sesame oil
½ teaspoon salt
oil for frying

BATTER

1 cup (125 g/4 oz) flour
1 egg

SAUCE

1 cup (250 mL/8 fl oz) chicken stock (broth)
1½ teaspoons rice wine or dry sherry
½ teaspoon salt
1 teaspoon cornflour (cornstarch)

ONION OIL

1 small red onion, very thinly sliced
3 tablespoons peanut oil

Cut the beancurd squares in halves and slice each piece thinly to give about 28 square slices in all.
※ Make a reasonably smooth filling by mixing the chicken breasts, prawn meat, sea cucumber if used, spring onion, ginger, egg white, rice wine, sesame oil and the salt. Squeeze the mixture through your fingers until thoroughly amalgamated and sticky. Divide into 14 portions and roll each into a ball, then press flat to about the size of the beancurd slices.
※ Place one piece of filling between two squares of beancurd to make sandwiches and coat lightly with flour. Use the remaining flour and some cold water to make a fairly thick batter for coating.
※ Heat enough oil in a wok to gently fry the beancurd, turning once, until lightly browned on both sides. Lift out and place on a serving plate.

※ Drain the wok, retaining about 2 tablespoons of the oil. Mix the sauce ingredients together and pour into the wok. Simmer, stirring, until the sauce thickens, then pour over the beancurd.
※ In a clean wok or saucepan heat the peanut oil until smoking. Add the sliced red onion and cook until lightly browned. Use a slotted spoon to remove the onion, drain well and reserve as a garnish for another dish. Pour a portion of the onion oil over the finished dish and serve at once.

Beijing 北京

"SILVER FISH" WRAPPED IN SNOW

This unusual and economical vegetarian dish goes well with wine. It is simply cooked macaroni dipped into an egg-white batter and fried. The long whitish pieces look like whitebait or silver fish dipped into snow. Silver fish come from the northern coast of China.

45 g (1½ oz) dry macaroni
1 teaspoon salt
2 egg whites
½ cup (60 g/2 oz) cornflour (cornstarch)
2 tablespoons flour
oil for deep-frying
1 tablespoon five-spice salt*

Place the macaroni in a saucepan and add half the salt. Cover with plenty of boiling water, stir up well and cook until the macaroni is tender, then drain well and leave to cool.
※ Whip the egg whites until firm and fluffy, fold in the cornflour, the remaining salt and the flour and add just enough cold water to make a thick batter.
※ Heat the oil in a wok to smoking point, then lower the heat slightly. Dip the macaroni into the batter and deep-fry until crisp and puffy, but without turning golden. Remove and drain well.
※ Arrange the fried "silver fish" on a serving plate and serve with the five-spice salt in a small dish.

To make the five-spice salt, heat 1½ tablespoons of fine table salt in a wok until it begins to crackle, add 1 teaspoon of Chinese five-spice powder, remove from the heat, stir and cool.

Guangzhou 广州

SILVER NEEDLE NOODLES WITH ASSORTED MEAT SHREDS

Guangdong has a long history of making noodles from dried rice; in one of the oldest methods, cooked rice is dried in the sun, ground to a powder, mixed with boiling water and rubbed into short noodles, sharp at both ends like needles. A better result is, however, achieved by making the noodles from wheat starch.

90 g (3 oz) lean pork
90 g (3 oz) boneless chicken meat
90 g (3 oz) cleaned squid
90 g (3 oz) fresh prawn (shrimp) meat
3-4 dried black mushrooms, soaked for 25 minutes
1 egg
30 g (1 oz) fresh bean sprouts
1 small fresh leek, white part only
1 small slice salted ham
fresh coriander
lard or oil for frying

SEASONING

1 tablespoon light soy sauce
2 teaspoons rice wine or dry sherry
1 teaspoon salt
1½ teaspoons sugar
1 teaspoon sesame oil

SILVER NEEDLE NOODLES

1 cup (125 g/4 oz) wheat starch (gluten-free wheat flour)
½-⅔ cup (125-150 mL/4-5 fl oz) boiling water
1 teaspoon lard
2 tablespoons cornflour

Prepare the noodles first. Sift the flour and cornflour into a mixing bowl, make a well in the centre, pour the boiling water in and add the lard. Mix in quickly, working with a wooden spoon, then cover and leave for 5-6 minutes for the flour to soften. Working with oiled hands on a lightly oiled worktop, break off small pieces of the dough and roll into a ball, then rub across the worktop with the palm of your hand to form thin noodles, pointed at each end. Use up all the dough and set the noodles aside.

❀ Finely shred the pork, chicken and squid, cut the prawns into small pieces, drain the mushrooms, remove the stems and cut the caps into shreds. Beat the egg lightly and set aside. Rinse the bean sprouts and drain well. Shred the leek and ham, rinse the coriander and drain.

❀ Heat a wok, wipe out with an oiled cloth and pour in the egg, tilting and turning the wok so that the egg flows into a wide omelet. Cook until set, then turn and cook the other side. Lift out and spread on a cloth to cool.

❀ Add 2-3 tablespoons of lard or oil to the wok and stir-fry the noodles over high heat for 1 minute, then reduce the heat and continue to stir-fry for another 2 minutes. Remove to a serving plate and set aside.

❀ Add the shredded meats, except the ham, to the wok and stir-fry together until cooked, then add the mushrooms, bean sprouts and leek and stir-fry briefly.

❀ Add the seasoning/sauce ingredients and toss together thoroughly over high heat. Spoon the cooked ingredients over the noodles.

❀ Cut the egg into fine shreds and use together with the ham and coriander to garnish the dish. Or alternatively, stir these in with the noodles and other ingredients.

SILVER NEEDLE NOODLES WITH ASSORTED MEAT SHREDS

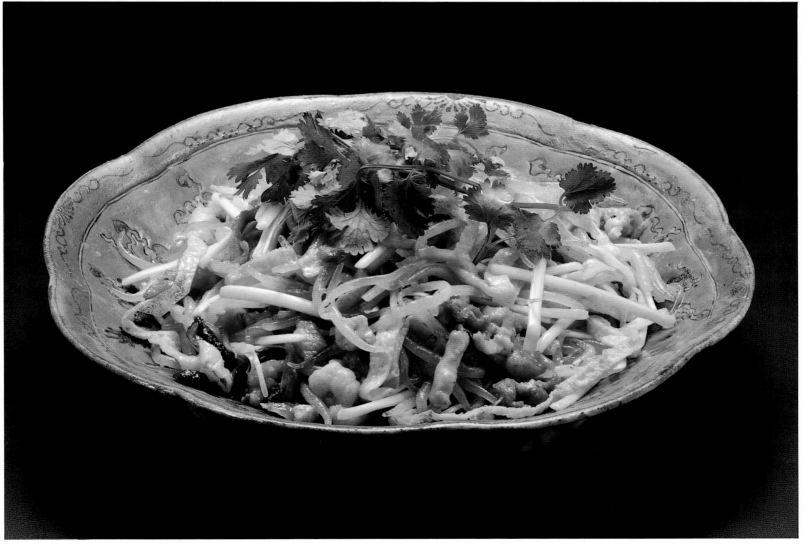

SHA HE NOODLES WITH LEEKS AND SHREDDED PORK

Guangzhou 广州

SHA HE NOODLES WITH LEEKS AND SHREDDED PORK

The Sha He Restaurant in Guangzhou is well known both at home and abroad for the special flavour of its sha he noodles. More than thirty dishes are offered featuring these tender noodles made from rice flour and water from the Nine Dragon Spring, which gives them their unique flavour.

315 g (10 oz) fresh rice ribbon noodles (sha he noodles)
salt
lard or vegetable oil
125 g (4 oz) lean pork, shredded
90 g (3 oz) silver sprouts*
2 young leeks, shredded

SAUCE

⅔ cup (150 mL/5 fl oz) superior stock (*see page 124*) or
   chicken stock (broth)
1½ tablespoons Shuang Huang or other light soy sauce
1 teaspoon rice wine or dry sherry
⅓ teaspoon salt
½ teaspoon sugar
pinch of white pepper
½ teaspoon sesame oil
1½ teaspoons cornflour (cornstarch)

Stir-fry the noodles with the lard until soft and very slightly crisp on the edges. Lift onto a serving plate, sprinkle with salt and set aside.

※ Wipe out the wok, add a little more lard and stir-fry the pork until it changes colour. Remove, then stir-fry the silver sprouts and leeks until the leeks are tender and wilted. Add the pre-mixed sauce ingredients, return the pork and simmer, stirring, until the sauce thickens. Pour over the noodles and serve at once.

Fresh mung beansprouts from which the yellow seed pods and long tapering roots have been removed, leaving a slender silver-coloured sprout.

Sichuan 四川

STEAMED DRAGON'S EYE ROLLS

375 g (12 oz) pork belly (fresh bacon)*
1 tablespoon white sugar
½ cup (185 g/6 oz) sweetened red bean paste, available canned
18 glacé cherries
1 cup (155 g/5 oz) glutinous long-grain rice
1 teaspoon salt
2 tablespoons brown sugar

STEAMED DRAGON'S EYE ROLLS

Place the pork on a rack, skin side upwards, and pour several cups of boiling water over it. Drain, then wipe dry. Melt the white sugar in a wok and rub over the pork skin, then use a very sharp knife to cut the pork into long, thin strips like bacon. Roll each strip of pork around a small portion of the sweetened red bean paste and top each with half a cherry. Place cherry downwards in a heatproof bowl and set aside.

※ Steam or boil the glutinous rice with plenty of salt until just cooked, mix with the brown sugar and pile on top of the pork rolls. Place on a rack in a wok or in a steamer, cover and steam for about 40 minutes. Invert onto a serving plate. The dragon's eyes form a beautiful pattern.

Choose the best quality pork meat near the ribs, which should be in one piece.

Beijing 北京

RICE AND DUCK MEAT IN LOTUS LEAVES

315 g (10 oz) duck breast meat
3 fresh or dried lotus or 12 bamboo leaves
oil for brushing leaves
¾ cup (125 g/4 oz) glutinous rice
¾ cup (125 g/4 oz) long-grain white rice
1 whole star anise
1 teaspoon Sichuan peppercorns (Fagara or Sansho)
2 teaspoons sesame oil

SEASONING

1 tablespoon light soy sauce
2½ teaspoons rice wine or dry sherry
¾ teaspoon salt
2 tablespoons finely chopped spring onion (shallot/scallion)
1 teaspoon grated fresh (root) ginger

Blanch the fresh leaves or soak the dried ones until softened, then squeeze out the water and brush the underside with oil.

※ Cut the duck into small strips, place in a dish with the seasoning ingredients, mix well and set aside.

※ Finely grind the glutinous and the long-grain rice together with the star anise and Sichuan peppercorns. Mix with the duck meat and sesame oil, adding just a little water to moisten.

※ Divide the lotus leaves into quarters, place a portion of the rice mixture onto each and fold the leaves, ribbed side inwards, around the rice to make little loose parcels.

※ Arrange side by side on a heatproof plate, set on a rack in a wok or in a steamer, cover and steam over gently simmering water for about 1 hour. Serve immediately.

RICE AND DUCK MEAT IN LOTUS LEAVES

COCONUT BUNS

Guangzhou 广州

COCONUT BUNS

2½ cups (315g/10oz) flour
1¾ teaspoons baking powder
3 tablespoons sugar
2 egg yolks
½ cup (125mL/4floz) lukewarm milk
3 tablespoons lard or butter
1 egg, beaten

FILLING

45g (1½oz) fat bacon
1 tablespoon sugar
1½ tablespoons pine nuts
½ cup (125mL/4floz) peanut oil
¾ cup (45g/1½oz) shredded coconut
2 tablespoons sugar
1 small egg, well beaten

Sift the flour and baking powder into a mixing bowl, make a well in the centre and put in the sugar, egg yolks and milk, then cut the lard or butter into small cubes, add to the mixture and work in well. Transfer to a lightly floured board and knead lightly until the dough is smooth and soft. Cover and set aside.

To prepare the filling, finely chop the bacon and fry gently with the 1 tablespoon sugar until the fat is almost transparent, then set aside. Deep-fry the pine nuts in the peanut oil until lightly coloured, mix with the bacon, shredded coconut, sugar and the well beaten egg and set aside.

Divide the dough into about 12 portions and flatten each into a round shape. Place a portion of the filling in the centre of each, pull the dough up around the filling and pinch the edges together to completely enclose the filling.

Place the buns, joined edges downwards, on a lightly oiled baking sheet, brush the tops with beaten egg and set aside until it feels dry, then brush a second time.

Bake in a pre-heated hot oven, 220°C (425°F), for 20 minutes, or until crisp and golden on the surface.

Beijing 北京

SESAME CAKES WITH MINCED PORK

Sesame cakes can be eaten with sweet or savoury fillings. They were a speciality of the chefs of the Qing Dynasty (1644-1911 AD), and a story is told about the Empress Dowager Cixi having a dream in which she was eating some sesame cakes. To her astonishment the next morning she was served sesame cakes for breakfast. She rewarded the chef of the imperial kitchen with peacock feathers and twenty pieces of silver. Thus the dish became famous.

SESAME CAKES – MAKES 18

½ cup (125mL/4floz) vegetable oil
7 cups (875g/1¾lb) flour
1½ cups (375mL/12floz) boiling water
½ cup (125mL/4floz) cold water
3 teaspoons salt
extra water or sugar-water for brushing cakes
½ cup (60g/2oz) white sesame seeds
oil for deep-frying (optional)

FILLING

375g (12oz) lean pork
oil for frying
1 tablespoon dark soy sauce
pinch of salt and pepper
2 teaspoons sugar
1 tablespoon rice wine or dry sherry
chopped fresh coriander or diced pickled vegetables

Gently heat the vegetable oil in a wok and add 1½ cups (185g/6oz) of the flour. Mix into a thick paste and continue to cook very gently, stirring continually until it is a light, golden, smooth, soft ball. Remove and leave to cool.

Sift the remaining flour into a bowl and make a well in the centre. Pour in the boiling water and quickly work into the flour, then add the cold water and 1 teaspoon of the salt and work in thoroughly. Transfer to a board and knead until smooth and elastic.

Divide into 36 portions, rolling each into a ball, then roll or press them out flat. Spread a portion of the flour-and-oil dough over half of them and sprinkle generously with the remaining salt. Press the remaining single pieces of dough on top and pinch the edges together to seal tightly.

Brush one side of each cake with water or a mixture of sugar and water and coat thickly with sesame seeds.

Bake in a pre-heated hot oven, 200°C (400°F), until puffed, golden, firm and dry on the surface, or deep-fry in hot oil until cooked through. Set aside, keeping warm.

Very finely chop or mince (grind) the pork and sauté in 2-3 tablespoons of the oil until lightly coloured. Add the soy sauce, salt and pepper, sugar and rice wine and continue to stir-fry until there is no liquid left in the bottom of the wok.

Serve the pork with the warm buns, adding chopped fresh coriander or finely diced pickled vegetables.

CRISP DOUGH COATED WITH SUGAR AND POWDERED CANDIED ROSE

Sichuan 四川

CRISP DOUGH COATED WITH SUGAR AND POWDERED CANDIED ROSE

3 eggs
¾ cup (90g/3oz) flour
3 tablespoons water
¾ cup (185g/6oz) sugar
cornflour (cornstarch)
oil for deep-frying
1 tablespoon finely chopped candied rose petals*

Beat the eggs in a mixing bowl and add the flour and water. Stir until the batter is smooth, then pour into a lightly greased, heated wok and cook gently, stirring continually, until the batter forms into a soft ball. Lift out and press out on an oiled plate to about 1.25 cm (½ in) thickness. Leave to cool.
※ Pour the sugar into a saucepan, add about 3 tablespoons cold water and set aside.
※ Cut the cooled batter into strips. Cover a plate thickly with cornflour and press the strips into this, coating them evenly with the cornflour.
※ Heat the oil in a wok to smoking point, then reduce the heat slightly. Deep-fry the strips, several at a time until puffed and golden, turning once. Lift out and drain well.
※ Bring the syrup to a slow boil and simmer for 2-3 minutes. When all of the wafers have been fried and well drained, dip them one by one into the syrup and pile on a serving plate. Sprinkle on the candied rose and serve at once.

If candied rose petals are unobtainable add 1 teaspoon of rose water essence to the sugar syrup.

Guangzhou 广州

STEAMED MILK BUNS

MAKES ABOUT 24

DOUGH STARTER

1 teaspoon dried yeast
3 tablespoons warm water
¾ cup (90g/3oz) flour

2 cups (250g/8oz) flour
½ cup (125mL/4floz) water
¾ cup (175mL/6floz) lukewarm milk
3 tablespoons sugar
2 tablespoons softened lard
pinch of bicarbonate of soda (baking soda)
2 cups (250g/8oz) flour
1½ cups (185g/6oz) wheat starch
1½ tablespoons baking powder

To make the dough starter, sprinkle the dried yeast into the warm water and stir until completely dissolved, then sift on the flour and work into a soft dough, kneading lightly. Set aside in a warm place for about 10 hours.
※ Mix the water with 2 cups (250g/8oz) flour, add the dough starter and work together to a soft dough, cover again and leave a further 8-10 hours until it has at least tripled its bulk.
※ Pour the milk into a bowl and add the sugar and softened lard. Mix the bicarbonate of soda with a little water and add to the above, then stir in the remaining flour, the wheat starch and baking powder and mix into the risen dough. Knead together until smooth and elastic.
※ Divide the mixture into about 24 balls and press a small piece of paper onto the back of each. Set in a bamboo steamer basket, cover and steam for about 10 minutes until firm textured, springy and well risen. Serve at once.
※ An assortment of fillings can be used inside steamed milk buns. Try barbecued pork lightly sauteed with spring onions and flavoured with oyster sauce, or sweetened lotus seed or red bean paste, or mashed dates.

Guangzhou 广州

FLAKY TARTS STUFFED WITH SHREDDED COCONUT

MAKES 24

PASTRY A

2½ cups (315g/10oz) flour
½-⅔ cup (125-150mL/4-5floz) water
90g (3oz) lard, melted

PASTRY B

1½ cups (185g/6oz) flour
125g (4oz) lard, melted

FILLING

¾ cup (185g/6oz) sugar
½ cup (125mL/4floz) water
1½ tablespoons butter
1½ cups (140g/4½oz) desiccated coconut
2 eggs, beaten
1 tablespoon lukewarm milk
½ teaspoon baking powder
½ teaspoon vanilla

Sift the flour for pastry A into a mixing bowl and make a well in the centre. Add the water and melted lard and work into a soft dough, then transfer to a board and knead until smooth and pliable.
※ Sift the flour for pastry B onto a board, make a well in the centre and work in the lard with your fingertips until the dough is smooth, adding just a few teaspoons of water to make the mixture hold together.
※ Cover the pastries and set aside.
※ Heat the sugar and water together in a saucepan for about 4 minutes, then add the butter and pour into a mixing bowl. Add the coconut, mix well and leave to cool. Add the remaining ingredients, working in well.
※ Roll out the two lots of pastry and cut with a fluted circular cutter into 24 rounds each. With practice they can be rolled out and cut together.
※ Place one round of pastry in the bottom of a patty pan and top with the other, pressing them lightly together. Place a portion of the filling in the centre of each.
※ Bake in a pre-heated hot oven, 200°C (400°F), for about 20 minutes until the filling is puffed and golden and feels dry to the touch, and the pastry is crisp and dry. Serve with tea.

Shanghai 上海

STEAMED SMALL MEAT BUNS

These tasty little meat buns are the speciality of Nan Xiang, a suburb of Shanghai. Their special feature is their perfectly symmetrical shape, resembling a water chestnut, or sometimes a pagoda.

When crab is in season it may be used as the stuffing instead of the pork and cabbage described in the following recipe. The crab buns are shaped so that the opening at the top is in the shape of a crucian carp's mouth, and after steaming the orange-coloured crab oil can be seen through the opening.

Although this type of savoury snack is very popular, it is rarely made at home.

WRAPPERS

2 cups (250 g/8 oz) flour
1 egg, beaten
3/4 cup (175 mL/6 fl oz) water
1 teaspoon baking powder
3/4 teaspoon salt

FILLING

185 g (6 oz) lean pork
2-3 fresh cabbage leaves
1 1/2 tablespoons peanut oil
1 spring onion (shallot/scallion), finely chopped
1 clove garlic, finely chopped
1 slice fresh (root) ginger, finely chopped

SEASONING

1 tablespoon light soy sauce
2 teaspoons rice wine or dry sherry
2 teaspoons sugar
pinch of white pepper
1/2 teaspoon sesame oil
2 tablespoons chicken stock (broth)
2 teaspoons cornflour (cornstarch)

Make the wrappers first by sifting in the flour into a mixing bowl and dropping the egg into the centre. Mix in lightly, then add the water, baking powder and salt and mix together thoroughly. Knead until smooth, then set aside and cover with a damp cloth for 5-6 minutes to activate the baking powder which will cause the dumpling wrappers to swell and become soft when steamed.

🌸 Finely mince (grind) the pork and finely chop the cabbage leaves. Heat the peanut oil in a wok and sauté the pork, cabbage leaves, spring onion, garlic and ginger until the pork turns white, then add the pre-mixed seasoning ingredients and stir-fry together until there is no liquid in the bottom of the wok.

🌸 Roll the dough out into a long sausage shape and cut into about 24 pieces. Roll out each piece into a thin round shape and place a spoonful of the filling in the centre of each.

🌸 Gather up the edges, pleating them together, then bring to a point, pinch together and twist to give the right shape. Flatten the bases so that they will stand upright, then stand in a lightly oiled steaming basket or on a rack in a wok, cover and steam for about 14 minutes over high heat until done. The dumplings can be placed on cabbage leaves in the steamer to give them extra flavour and prevent them from sinking through the slats in the steaming basket.

🌸 Serve with the traditional dips of shredded young ginger and brown rice vinegar.

BEAN FLOUR CAKES OR DONKEY ROLLING CAKES

Beijing 北京

BEAN FLOUR CAKES OR DONKEY ROLLING CAKES

Bean flour cakes make a delicious snack or dessert. In Beijing they used to be sold by hawkers, pushing their carts along the road and loudly announcing their products. The elderly people of Beijing remember these cakes as Donkey Rolling Cakes, because the hawkers often sprinkled a layer of dry bean flour over the cakes before giving them to the customers – reminding them of a donkey rolling on the sand and raising a cloud of dust.

1/2 cup (125 g/4 oz) sugar
1 cup (315 g/10 oz) red bean paste
3 cups (375 g/12 oz) glutinous rice flour
1 cup (250 mL/8 fl oz) boiling water
1/2 cup (60 g/2 oz) white sesame seeds
1 cup (185 g/6 oz) yellow lentils

Mix the sugar and red bean paste together in a saucepan or wok, stirring over gentle heat until dissolved, then remove and leave to cool completely.

🌸 Sift the glutinous rice flour into a mixing bowl, make a well in the centre and pour in the water. Work the mixture into a smooth dough, adding a little extra water if needed, then cover and leave for a few minutes until the flour softens.

🌸 Dry-fry the sesame seeds until golden and beginning to pop, then remove and grind to a powder. Dry-fry the lentils until golden brown and very crisp. Grind to a fine powder and mix with the sesame seed powder.

🌸 Spread the dough over a work top in a large rectangular shape, about 1 cm (1/3 in) thick. Cover with the bean paste, leaving a border at the top. Roll up from the bottom to form a thick roll, then place on a rack in a wok or in a steamer, cover and steam for about 8 minutes, until cooked through.

🌸 Roll in the sesame and lentil powder, coating thickly, then cut into thick slices and serve.

STEAMED PRAWNS WITH STUFFING

Guangzhou 广州

STEAMED PRAWNS WITH STUFFING

In Guangdong snacks the colour, flavour, aroma and shape are important elements. Colour is particularly highly regarded. There is a saying that "the colour is encountered before the flavour is sampled". In some snacks, artificial colouring is used to achieve the desired effect, but more often this is done by the use and blending of coloured ingredients.

6 large river prawns (freshwater shrimps)
125 g (4 oz) chicken breast
1 thin slice Yunnan or Virginia or other well-salted ham
6 small sprigs fresh coriander
½ recipe wheat starch wrappers (*see page 209*), using plain wheat flour
light soy sauce or vinegar

SEASONING

1 teaspoon rice wine or dry sherry
½ teaspoon sugar
pinch each of salt and white pepper

Peel the prawns, leaving the last section and the tail intact. Cut the chicken into six strips, about the size of the peeled parts of the prawns, or mince (grind) finely. Place the chicken in a dish and add the seasoning ingredients. Cut the ham into six strips.
❀ Cut the prawns along the underside without cutting through them completely. Remove the intestinal vein, and flatten each prawn out. Place a chicken strip or a portion of minced (ground) chicken, a ham strip and a coriander sprig on each prawn and fold up.
❀ Make the wrappers and roll out 6 large enough to enclose the filled prawns. Wrap up each prawn, leaving the tails exposed. Pinch the wrappers together underneath. Arrange on a lightly oiled heatproof plate and place on a rack in a wok, or in a steamer, over simmering water. Cover tightly and steam for about 12 minutes until the prawns are bright pink, the chicken meat white and the wrappers transparent.
❀ Serve with soy sauce, or a vinegar dip.

Sichuan 四川

GLUTINOUS RICE DUMPLINGS

The pyramid-shaped delicacies described in this recipe have a long history. They were originally made as an offering to the spirit of the great Chinese poet-statesman Qu Yuan who died in the third century BC. Although a loyal patriot, he was dismissed from the emperor's service because he complained about the corruption in the imperial court. Disappointed about his failure to save the country, he later committed suicide by jumping into the Mi Luo River in Hunan Province.

To commemorate his death and appease his spirit, every year on the fifth day of the fifth month, when the "Duan Wu" festival is celebrated, the locals fill sections of hollow bamboo with rice and throw them into the river.

Legend has it that the rice was originally thrown by people who went out in a boat to search for his body. They hoped the rice would lure the fish away and prevent them from devouring the body.

In later years bamboo leaves, reeds or rushes were used to wrap the glutinous rice into dumplings, and fillings of sweetened red bean paste, mashed dates or savoury meat were added. These specialities are now eaten during the "Duan Wu" festival.

DUMPLINGS

1 cup (125 g/4 oz) glutinous rice flour
3 tablespoons boiling water
2-3 tablespoons cold water
12 dried bamboo leaves, soaked to soften
oil for brushing leaves

SWEET FILLINGS

6 tablespoons canned sweetened red bean paste
or
6 tablespoons sweetened date paste*

SAVOURY FILLING

125 g (4 oz) minced (ground) lean pork
2 cloves garlic, crushed
2 tablespoons lard
2 tablespoons light soy sauce
½ teaspoon pepper
1 teaspoon sugar
pinch of salt

Place the rice flour in a mixing bowl and make a well in the centre. Add the boiling water and 2 tablespoons of the cold water and mix quickly into a pliable dough, adding the remaining cold water if needed. Knead until smooth, then roll out into a sausage shape and cut into 12 pieces.
❀ Drain the bamboo leaves, dry thoroughly and brush with the oil.
❀ To cook the savoury filling, stir-fry the pork and garlic in the lard until white, then add the remaining ingredients and continue frying until the liquid has been absorbed. Cool before using.
❀ Flatten the dough pieces and place half a tablespoon of the chosen filling in the centre. Pull the dough up around the filling, pinching the edges together to seal it smoothly.
❀ Place near the lower end of the bamboo leaf and wrap the leaf around it, so that it makes a pyramid shape. Set the dumplings on a rack in a wok or in a steamer, cover and steam over high heat for about 15 minutes, or until cooked through. Serve hot or cold. They can be dipped into sugar before eating.

*Dates simmered in water until tender, then sweetened with sugar, softened with a little lard and simmered further until all of the liquid has evaporated leaving a thick paste.

Guangzhou 广州

STEAMED SHAO MAI TOPPED WITH CRAB ROE

The steamed shao mai or dumpling of Guangdong is an adaptation of the northern xiao long shao mai. In Beijing there is a well-known shao mai shop, the Dou Yi Chu which opened for business over 200 years ago during the reign of Emperor Qian Long. It is said that when returning to the capital from a journey, the Emperor passed a small restaurant without a signboard. He entered, ordered the xiao long shao mai and found it unusually delicious. Full of praise, he named the shop the Dou Yi Chu, and through this royal patronage both the shop and the snack of shao mai became nationally famous.

185 g (6 oz) fatty pork
125 g (4 oz) fresh prawn (shrimp) meat
3 dried black mushrooms, soaked for 25 minutes
24 wonton wrappers*
2-3 tablespoons fresh crab roe or tiny carrot cubes
  or green peas
chilli sauce
hot mustard
light soy sauce

SEASONING

1 egg white
2 teaspoons Shuang Huang or other light soy sauce
1/3 teaspoon sesame oil
1/2 teaspoon salt
1 teaspoon sugar
pinch of white pepper
2 teaspoons cornflour (cornstarch)

Finely chop the pork, prawn meat and drained mushrooms and mix with the seasoning ingredients.

Use a circular cutter to cut wonton wrappers into circles of about 7 cm (3 in) diameter. To fill, place a single wrapper over the thumb and curled forefinger of the left hand and press a spoonful of filling onto the wrapper, forcing the dumpling between thumb and finger into the cupped hand. Squeeze gently, then tap on the work surface to flatten the bottom. The finished dumpling should be cup-shaped and filled right up to the edge of the pastry, the top left open to expose the filling. Place a few grains of crab roe on top of each dumpling.

Set in a lightly greased steamer, cover and steam over simmering water for about 12 minutes until cooked through. Serve with chilli sauce, hot mustard and soy sauce.

Available commercially, fresh or frozen.

Guangzhou 广州

SISTER ER'S DUMPLINGS

FILLING

125 g (4 oz) lean pork
75 g (2½ oz) fresh prawn (shrimp) meat
3 dried black mushrooms, soaked for 25 minutes
1 fresh or canned winter bamboo shoot, weighing approx
    75 g (2½ oz)
24 fresh coriander leaves or pieces of spring onion
    (shallot/scallion) tops
oil for frying

SEASONING

2 teaspoons superior or other light soy sauce
1 teaspoon rice wine or dry sherry
½ teaspoon sesame oil
½ teaspoon salt
¾ teaspoon sugar
pinch of white pepper

WHEAT STARCH WRAPPERS

1 cup (125 g/4 oz) wheat starch (gluten-free wheat flour)*
2 teaspoons cornflour (cornstarch)
½-⅔ cup (125-150 mL/4-5 fl oz) boiling water
½ teaspoon softened lard

Prepare the filling first and leave to cool while the wrappers are being made. Very finely dice the pork, prawn meat, drained mushrooms and bamboo shoot. In about 1 tablespoon of oil, stir-fry the pork until it whitens. Add the remaining ingredients, except the coriander, and stir-fry for 30-40 seconds. Add the seasoning ingredients and stir-fry a further 30-40 seconds. Transfer to a dish to cool.

※ Pour the flour into a mixing bowl, add the cornflour and make a well in the centre. Add the water, and, using the handle of a wooden spoon, very quickly work the hot liquid into the flour. When all is incorporated, cover with a cloth and leave for 5-6 minutes for the flour to soften. Rub the lard into the dough, kneading lightly for 1-2 minutes.

※ If wheat starch has been used the wrappers can be prepared in the traditional way. Roll the dough into a long sausage shape and cut into 24 pieces. Keep it covered while rolling each piece. Place a piece on a clean board, and use a blunt-bladed cleaver (these are especially made for the purpose) to spread the dough into a circle about 9 cm (3½ in) diameter. Turn over and place a spoonful of filling in the centre, top with a single coriander leaf, fold in half and pinch the edges together. Keep the board and the cleaver very lightly greased with lard.

※ Plain flour dough can simply be rolled into very thin circles with a rolling pin.

※ Place the dumplings side by side in a lightly greased steamer, cover and steam over briskly boiling water for about 15 minutes until the wrappers are clear.

※ Serve with soy sauce.

If wheat starch is unobtainable, plain (all-purpose) white flour can be used, although the dumplings will be less transparent and the wrappers slightly more chewy.

STEAMED SHAO MAI TOPPED WITH CRAB ROE

SISTER ER'S DUMPLINGS

THIN PASTRY DIM SUM STUFFED WITH FRESH PRAWNS – HAW GOW

Guangzhou 广州

THIN PASTRY DIM SUM STUFFED WITH FRESH PRAWNS – HAW GOW

The story behind this dish concerns the Empress Dowager Cixi who been created in a small teahouse in the Wu Chu village of Guangzhou city. Wu Chu used to be a scenic trading centre and the teahouse owner would often buy his prawns from the fishing boats of the area. But his original dumpling had a thick skin, and subsequent chefs replaced the original rice flour with wheat starch to produce the thin-skinned perfect snack known as Haw Gow.

1 recipe wheat starch wrappers (see Sister Er's Dumplings)
155 g (5 oz) fresh prawn (shrimp) meat
45 g (1½ oz) pork fat
45 g (1½ oz) bamboo shoots, cooked or canned
1 spring onion (shallot/scallion), white part only
hot mustard
light soy sauce

SEASONING

¼ teaspoon sesame oil
¾ teaspoon salt
½ teaspoon sugar
1 teaspoon cornflour (cornstarch)

Coarsely chop the prawn meat and finely chop the pork fat, bamboo shoots and spring onion. Mix with the seasoning ingredients, using your fingers to make it into a smooth and slightly sticky mass. Set aside while the wrappers are prepared.

※ As each wrapper is done, turn it over and place a spoonful of the filling in the centre. Fold the wrapper in half to enclose the filling and pinch the edges together firmly, at the same time pleating the edge of the dumplings so the smooth fold becomes the wider, curved side of the crescent shape (see photograph above).

※ Arrange on a lightly oiled rack in a wok or in a steamer, cover and steam over simmering water for about 7 minutes until the dumplings are as clear as crystal with the prawns showing pink inside.

※ Serve with hot mustard and soy sauce.

STEAMED RICE WRAPPED IN LOTUS LEAVES

Guangzhou 广州

STEAMED RICE WRAPPED IN LOTUS LEAVES

"Ten miles around Ban Tang are many lotus ponds/Sisters are busy picking lotus/They do not pick lotus flowers but only pick the leaves/Rice in lotus leaves is more fragrant than the flowers."

This is one of the songs from the Zhu Zi Ci collection composed during the final years of the Qing Dynasty (1644-1911 AD). Today, steamed rice wrapped in lotus leaves remains a popular dish.

6 dried lotus or 18 bamboo leaves
2 cups (315 g/10 oz) raw, long-grain white rice
125 g (4 oz) fresh prawn (shrimp) meat
125 g (4 oz) Chinese barbecued pork
90 g (3 oz) roast duck meat
125 g (4 oz) lean pork
4 dried black mushrooms, soaked for 25 minutes
2 eggs
2 tablespoons lard

SEASONING

1 tablespoon oyster sauce
1 tablespoon light soy sauce
2 teaspoons rice wine or dry sherry
½ teaspoon sesame oil
1½ teaspoons salt
1 teaspoon sugar
¼ teaspoon white pepper

Soak the lotus leaves to soften them, and drain well. Partially cook the rice until it is tender but still slightly chewy, drain and set aside.

※ Dice finely the prawn meat, barbecued pork, duck, pork and drained mushrooms. Beat the eggs lightly in a small dish.

※ Heat the wok, add the lard and heat to smoking point, then pour in the eggs. Cook quickly, stirring until set, then lift out with a slotted spoon and set aside. Add the diced ingredients and stir-fry for 2-3 minutes, add the seasoning ingredients and mix well. Stir this into the rice.

※ Place one-sixth of the rice mixture on the underside of each lotus leaf and fold into a square package to completely enclose the filling. Arrange the parcels side by side on a rack in a wok or in a steamer, cover and steam over simmering water for about 20 minutes. Use scissors to cut a cross in the top of each parcel to expose the contents before serving. The fragrance of the lotus leaf will thoroughly penetrate the rice, giving it a unique and tantalising taste.

Guangzhou 广州

RADISH PUDDING

Radish pudding is a traditional Guangdong snack, and is made in most households in early winter, when radishes appear in the markets. It is always enjoyed during the Chinese New Year celebrations.

250 g (8 oz) rice flour
875 g (1¾ lb) giant white radish (Japanese daikon or
   icicle radish)
1½ tablespoons sugar
½ teaspoon white pepper
2 Chinese sausages, steamed for 5 minutes
3-4 dried black mushrooms, soaked for 25 minutes
3 tablespoons dried shrimps, soaked for 25 minutes
1 slice Yunnan or other well-salted ham
3 spring onions (shallots/scallions)
2 tablespoons chopped fresh coriander
2 tablespoons lard
light soy sauce

Place the rice flour in a large mixing bowl and add enough cold water to make the flour evenly damp. Grate the radish and add to the rice flour paste with the sugar and pepper.

Finely dice the remaining ingredients, except the coriander and lard. Stir-fry in hot lard for 2-3 minutes, then add to the radish paste with the coriander. Mix well.

Line a deep 25 cm (10 in) square or round cake tin with a piece of greaseproof paper. Thickly grease the paper and the sides of the tin with lard. Pour in the radish mixture and smooth the top. Place on a rack in a large covered wok, or in a steamer, cover and steam for about 1½ hours, until the pudding feels firm on top and a chopstick inserted into the centre comes out clean.

Invert the pudding onto a plate, but do not remove the tin until almost cool. Cut into slices and then into large squares when cold.

Cook on a hot griddle plate with a very little oil or lard until slightly crisp and golden on the surface. Serve with soy sauce.

RADISH PUDDING

SWEET AND SOUR FISH WITH NOODLES

Beijing 北京

SWEET AND SOUR FISH WITH NOODLES

The story behind this dish concerns the Empress Dowager Cixi who was fleeing from a foreign aggressor and took refuge in Xian. On her return to Beijing, she passed through the Kai Feng Fu, one of China's ancient capitals in Henan Province.

Realising that the Empress was fond of sweet and sour dishes, a local cook prepared sweet and sour fish with noodles for her. The Empress thought the dish delicious, it became popular and was handed down through the generations.

1 x 625 g (1¼ lb) fresh carp or other meaty white fish
1 cup (125 g/4 oz) cornflour (cornstarch)
oil for deep-frying

SWEET AND SOUR SAUCE

2 tablespoons vegetable oil
½ cup (125 g/4 oz) sugar
½ cup (125 mL/4 fl oz) brown vinegar
1 tablespoon dark soy sauce
3 tablespoons superior or other light soy sauce
¾ cup (175 mL/6 fl oz) chicken stock (broth)
4 cloves garlic, chopped
1-2 pickled or fresh red chillies, chopped
1 spring onion (shallot/scallion), finely chopped
2½ teaspoons cornflour (cornstarch)

NOODLES*

2 small eggs
2 tablespoons cold water
3 cups (375 g/12 oz) flour

To make the noodles, break the eggs into a large bowl and beat well. Add the water and one-quarter of the flour and beat this mixture until very smooth.

🍜 Gradually work in the remaining flour, kneading it with your hands, then turn out onto a lightly floured surface and continue to knead until the dough feels elastic and is very smooth. Cover with a damp cloth and leave for 20 minutes.

🍜 Roll out as thinly as possible, then roll the sheet up into a cylinder and cut into very narrow strips. Toss in flour, then set aside.

🍜 Scale, clean and fillet the fish. Cut each fillet in half lengthways to give four long strips. Mix the cornflour with cold water to make a thick batter and coat the fish.

🍜 Heat the oil in a wok to smoking point, then reduce the heat slightly. Deep-fry the fish, two pieces at a time, until cooked through and lightly browned on the surface. Lift out and keep warm on a serving plate.

🍜 Reheat the oil to smoking point, reduce the heat and deep-fry the noodles in several batches until crisp and golden. Lift out and arrange on another serving dish.

🍜 In another wok heat the oil for the sauce and add the sugar. Cook until it turns to caramel, then add the remaining pre-mixed sauce ingredients, boiling until the sauce thickens and turns clear. Pour over the fish and serve.

*2-3 cakes of pre-prepared egg noodles can be used in place of these home-made noodles. They should be softened in water first, then drained well and allowed to partially dry before deep-frying.

Beijing 北京

RICE WITH PINEAPPLE AND ASSORTED FRUIT

2 cups (375 g/12 oz) raw, short-grain white rice
3 rings fresh pineapple
½ apple
1 Chinese pear or firm, unripe pear
2 tablespoons raisins
2 tablespoons chopped, candied melon
2 tablespoons chopped walnuts
2 tablespoons chopped glacé cherries
2 tablespoons lard
3 tablespoons sugar

Cook the rice with 3 cups (750 mL/24 fl oz) of cold water over very gentle heat until the rice is tender and the liquid completely absorbed.

🍚 Cut the pineapple into small fan shapes, peel, core and dice the apple and pear.

🍚 Heat a wok and add the lard, stir-fry the rice until each grain is coated with the fat. Add the nuts and fruit except the pineapple and continue to stir-fry for another minute. Sprinkle with sugar and stir-fry a further 2 minutes until the ingredients are tender and well mixed.

🍚 Arrange the pineapple around the edge of a serving plate and pile the rice in the centre.

RICE WITH PINEAPPLE AND ASSORTED FRUIT

Guangzhou 广州

GOLDEN RICE
WITH PIGEON EGGS

In China there are many ways to cook rice dishes, but this one is unique, and was originally known as Palace Golden Rice. In feudal China, Imperial chefs continually had to create new dishes to satisfy demanding empresses. One chef, Fang Shi, was said to have had the ability to turn things into gold, and as this recipe demonstrates, in the hands of a capable chef, plain white rice can, in fact, be transformed into "gold fragments".

4 cups (500 g/16 oz) freshly cooked white rice (about
   1½ cups [250 g/8 oz] raw rice)
3 cloves garlic
90 g (3 oz) prawn (shrimp) meat
2 chicken livers
5 medium-sized chicken eggs
½ cup (125 mL/4 fl oz) vegetable oil
6 pigeon or quail eggs
1 teaspoon sesame oil
6 stalks choy sum, or other Chinese green vegetable

SEASONING
2 tablespoons superior or other light soy sauce
1 teaspoon salt
1 teaspoon sugar
⅓ teaspoon white pepper

Spread the cooked rice on a tray to cool. Very finely chop the garlic, then dice the prawn meat and chicken livers. Beat the chicken eggs lightly in a small bowl, adding 1 tablespoon of water and a pinch of salt.

❋ Heat half the vegetable oil in a wok and stir-fry the garlic for 30 seconds. Add the prawns and chicken livers and stir-fry until they change colour and are beginning to firm up. Add the rice and stir-fry until the rice has warmed through. Add the seasoning ingredients and mix in well. Pour in the beaten eggs and continue to stir-fry over low heat until the eggs have mixed well with the rice. The eggs should still be quite moist and only half cooked.

❋ Pile onto a heatproof plate and shape into a flat mound. Make six small depressions in the top and break a pigeon egg into each.

❋ Heat the remaining vegetable oil in the wok and add the sesame oil. Put in the choy sum and stir-fry briefly, then add ½ cup (125 mL/4 fl oz) water, cover and cook until the vegetables are almost tender.

❋ Arrange around the rice dish, place the whole dish in a steamer, or on a rack in a wok, and steam over simmering water until the pigeon eggs are just cooked.

云南
Yunnan

云南

Yunnan

BELOW THE CLOUDS

POSSIBLY the most beautiful corner in all China is the southwest. It is also possibly the least known, a great pity because Yunnan and neighbouring Guizhou and western Guangxi are among the most fascinating as well as the most scenic areas in the land. The ravines are steep, the mountains covered in jungle, the rivers rush in fast turbulence towards the Gulf of Tonkin and the mighty Mekong slashes through Yunnan. Southeast Asia lies over the next hill; Yunnan borders Burma, Laos and Vietnam, and culinary ties are close.

A rich racial stew makes up the people of the three southwesterly provinces; minorities are probably a majority in Yunnan itself where dozens of different peoples inhabit the valleys. Some of them are tiny remnants of once-mighty tribes; peoples like the Achang, who now count themselves as only twenty thousand; the fifty-eight thousand Bulong and their cousins, the four thousand remaining Dulong; ten thousand Jinuo people and twenty-three thousand Nu. But there are also sizeable communities like the Bai (over a million); the Hani and the Yao (one million each) and hundreds of thousands of Tibetans. A million Miao live in Guizhou. Thais, too, who stayed behind when their forefathers left to form Thailand, remain in the hills. Five million Yi and fourteen million Zhuang are scattered through all three provinces. Every one of these races has its own culture and cuisine. All are mixed in with what is generally considered to be Chinese cooking to give a gastronomic treat that can be found nowhere else.

Yunnan means Below the Clouds, and the name signifies the remoteness of the land. The clouds referred to are those that eternally shroud the mountains that fringe Sichuan. In the past nobody knew what lay on the far side of the forbidding mountains that marked the limits of Chinese civilisation, so they just referred to it as "Below the Clouds". This lack of knowledge bred legends and myths of a fabulous land, a kind of Chinese El Dorado. Although the Yuan Dynasty deposed the

CROSSING THE RICE PADDIES

LEO MEIER

(previous page)

AUTUMNAL FIELDS IN NORTHERN YUNNAN

GREGORY HEISLER

217

A BAI GRANDMOTHER IN HER KITCHEN   GREGORY HEISLER

WATER BUFFALOES, ESSENTIAL TO TRADITIONAL FARMING LIFE   GREGORY HEISLER

Thai kings of Yunnan in the thirteenth century, the province still lay outside the pale of knowledge, wracked by ceaseless Muslim uprisings which were put down by successive dynasties with a bloodthirstiness outstanding even for the Manchus. Then in the early years of the twentieth century the great mineral wealth of Yunnan was discovered and the myth of an El Dorado in the misty hills turned out to be true.

The many races of the southwest provinces have borrowed freely from each others' kitchens. The culinary result is a splendid smorgasbord from hill tribes and hunters, farmers and fishermen, and the sophisticated gastronomy of Nanning, the capital of Guangxi and a city which can boast of a long and unique cuisine of its own. Kunming, Yunnan's capital, claims China's most perfect climate and is known as the city of perpetual spring. Its restaurants also have a well-deserved reputation for exotic dishes which carry the tangy flavour of Vietnamese herbs, steamed carp and perch from the cool waters of the high-country lakes, and noodles served with green peppers. The red peppers of Sichuan make guest appearances in many Yunnan dishes and one of the gifts of the Kunming kitchen is steamed chicken in a Yunnan pot which is the Chinese version of a French pot-au-feu.

Into the regional cooking pot go many influences. The various minorities who make up the colourful anthropological map of the southwest make their contribution. The largest recognised minority in China is the Zhuang who live in their own sprawling autonomous region occupying half of southern Guangxi Province. A happy, amiable people, the Zhuang have developed a rich and nutritious diet based on the abundance of the fertile southern coast and mountains. One specialty that features in their feasts is a giant pyramid-shaped dumpling stuffed with rice and ground pork. These dumplings are said to be the biggest in China and cook for many hours in sealed pottery jars over the embers of a slow fire.

PUPILS AT THE LI JIANG NATIONAL SCHOOL, YUNNAN PROVINCE

GREGORY HEISLER

China also has minorities within minorities, adding further colourful confusion to its gastronomic map. During the Yuan Dynasty (1206-1368 AD), the Mongols determined to bring the entire country under their central rule. The best way to do so was to establish colonies in the outer reaches of the empire. This they did, but as in later years their empire in China shrivelled the outposts were abandoned, leaving racial enclaves like the one on the shores of Lake Lugu, which lies like a spectacular pearl in the highlands on the Yunnan-Sichuan border. There today, Mosuo minority people still proudly claim Mongol origin and on feast days celebrate with dishes like stewed lamb. The descendants of the Mongols in Yunnan – Muslim colonists transplanted to take Yuan rule to the area – are the only sizeable group in south China who today appreciate lamb.

Other ingredients and ideas come from the bordering lands. Indian culture, including Buddhism, seeped into China through Yunnan and has left an underlying influence, and the Han Chinese have brought with them their own many cuisines. The results are a many-splendoured table. One dinner can include tribal, Islamic, Vietnamese, Sichuan and other dishes.

The cooking of Guizhou likewise reflects trends from neighbouring provinces – the red pepper of Hunan is a notable feature. For generations Guizhou was the

YOUNG BUDDHIST ACOLYTES   LEONG KA TAI

EVERY FERTILE PIECE OF ARABLE LAND IS UTILISED

MARY ELLEN MARK

A VILLAGE NESTLES AMIDST CAREFULLY TENDED TERRACES   GREGORY HEISLER

A VILLAGE COOK

poor, backward relation of southern China. It was said there was not one piece of flat land in the entire province, an exaggerated claim unhappily based on fact. The rice grows vertically in Guizhou, it is said, and seeing the terraces that have been adzed with agony out of the steep hillsides, each as small as a garden and built with enormous labour, one is prepared to believe it. But the rivers are rich, the woods provide game and the province has a selection of mushrooms and fungi second to none.

For generations landlocked, poor Guizhou was also desperately short of salt. There was none to be mined as in other inland provinces, and most people were too poor to buy the salt imported from the distant ports of the South China Sea. Salt was a luxury, and when it could be afforded a block of salt took pride of place in the centre of the table. Family and important guests would gather, take a piece of meat or vegetable in their chopsticks and rub it over the salt before eating the morsel. The exotic taste of salt was a rare and valued treat. Other provinces may cook sweet and sour, but Guizhou is known for its unique contribution of salt and sour cooking. Such a recipe calls for a fish to be rubbed inside and out with salt, then to be stuffed with strongly salted pickle and fried. When it is served it comes with yet more salt and pepper. Guizhou diners of today are making up for the salt their forebears could not afford.

GREGORY HEISLER

THE RICH FIELDS AND DRAMATIC LANDSCAPE OF NORTHWESTERN YUNNAN

GREGORY HEISLER

蔬果
Vegetables
& Fruit

Vegetables & Fruit

蔬果

HARALD SUND

FRUIT AND VEGETABLE SELLERS AT SHIMIAN MARKET, SICHUAN PROVINCE

THE daily food of the Chinese is among the healthiest in the world, due mainly to the preponderance of vegetables. Although no longer the incredible luxury it once was, the rarity of meat for most of the population over many centuries has helped to make a tradition in which vegetables play a vital culinary role at the centre of the gastronomic stage.

In any city or hamlet, seasonal vegetables can be seen for sale in busy street markets. Like a culinary kaleidoscope ceaselessly in motion, the colours, variety and types of vegetables on sale change with the locality and the season as new crops are harvested and reach the marketplace. Foreigners will recognise many familiar vegetables on sale, because for thousands of years the Chinese farmer has enthusiastically adopted plants brought back by returning traders and adventurers, and chefs have just as keenly adapted these newcomers to existing recipes. Vegetables from every continent grow in China today, but so do many others which have seldom made the gastronomic trip abroad.

With the economic reorganisation of recent years under which China's eight hundred million peasants have been encouraged to grow and sell their own private crops after meeting state quotas, the range of vegetables on sale has notably increased. Nowhere is this more evident than in the verdant south where a warm subtropical climate helps the diligent market gardeners coax a fresh vegetable crop from their tiny plots every two months. It is a very different story in the north. Any autumn visitor to Beijing can see loads of Tianjin cabbages – the big, elongated vegetables known as Chinese cabbages – trucked into the city from the state farms of Hebei Province. The cabbage is stored in every home to eke out the chill winter months when fresh vegetables do not grow, and ones that are on sale are expensive imports to the capital from more temperate zones. The hardy cabbages keep for months in the cold winters, and although the outer layers may become yellowish and dry, the inside remains tender and juicy until spring returns. Along with turnips and a vast variety of pickles, the humble cabbage plays a vital role in the daily diet of millions of northern Chinese for six months of the year.

One of the gastronomic tragedies of China's culinary history is that so many of the delightful regional specialties are unknown elsewhere. The blue turnip of Tianjin, for example, is still unknown to most people outside Hebei and Shandong. Similarly, some of the crunchy and deliciously fresh winter-garden crops of the south never make it to the northern markets where they would bring joy to the monotony of Manchurian tables in the long winter months. With the exception of the wealthy and the privileged, people have always had to make do with what is produced close at hand. This is, however, slowly changing with improvements in transport.

The Chinese chef in every regional kitchen insists, wherever possible on the freshest vegetables, preferably straight from the garden, but if that is impossible certainly direct from the market. This fastidiousness can be seen in any Chinese market where buyers prod, poke and peer at the goods on display to ensure they have not passed their peak. Many newcomers to a Chinese table may think they are eating some exotic new plant when they are merely enjoying an unfamiliar part of an old favourite. The leaves of the pea plant, for example, are generally discarded in the West, but are a prized delight in Guangzhou. Another example is the spinach root, usually unknown in Europe, but as eagerly cooked and eaten in China as the green leaves. For the uninitiated, China has a vast, baffling array of vegetables. This is because over the centuries China has borrowed with willing enthusiasm from every continent to add to its own rich garden heritage, and a nation of gardeners lets no small corner of ground go to waste – gourds, squashes and melons grow on vines covering storehouses in the fields; the bamboos that line village lanes provide food as well as building materials; seaweed gives a free, mineral-rich crop, while inland the prized water chestnut and valuable lotus grow in ponds which are home for duck and carp alike.

Vegetables in the Chinese cuisine have played an important role for four major reasons: religion, poverty, health and farm economics. Those who follow Buddhist teachings choose to avoid eating meat (though not necessarily fish), and vegetable dishes have been raised to glorious heights to provide a vibrant, exciting meatless cuisine. On the other hand, millions of peasants have traditionally been unable to afford meat – famine, in-

vasion, immigration or political instability have often caused culinary chaos making meat and fish too expensive for any but the wealthy or privileged.

Even in the good times there have been many cooks in the kitchens of China who prefer the healthy vitality of vegetables. Ancient herbalists have long recognised (although not always aware of the scientific and dietary reasons) that vegetables play a vital part in maintaining good health, and insisted that a variety of fresh garden foods should be on the menu at every meal. The growth of China's huge population has put immense pressure on the patient, ancient agricultural practices, and simple economics has dictated the intensive farming practices in use today; one field of carefully tended vegetables can keep many more people alive than if the same area is used to graze a couple of sheep or a cow. Hence the absence of grazing stock in most parts of the country: plants are more efficient people-feeders than animals.

A STRIKING SELECTION OF CHINESE VEGETABLES

SHUFUNOTOMO

Guangzhou 广州

STUFFED WINTER MELON SOUP

This is a traditional banquet delicacy to serve during summer and autumn. The melon takes on a jade colour, appears crystal-like and is translucent, the ingredients within the melon being half visible.

1 kg (2 lb) rounded end of a winter melon*
1 chicken carcass
125 g (4 oz) fresh prawn (shrimp) meat
125 g (4 oz) boneless frog or chicken meat
125 g (4 oz) duck meat
125 g (4 oz) lean pork
125 g (4 oz) lean ham
125 g (4 oz) fresh or canned straw mushrooms
125 g (4 oz) angled luffa or stalks of broccoli
6 cups (1½ L/48 fl oz) superior stock (*see page 124*) or chicken stock (broth)

SEASONING

1 teaspoon sesame oil
2 teaspoons salt
⅓ teaspoon white pepper
1 teaspoon sugar

Thinly skin the end of the melon, then scoop out the seeds and fibrous centre. Place in a large pot with the chicken carcass inside and add boiling water to cover. Simmer gently for about 20 minutes. Discard the chicken bones and the water and set the melon aside.

✻ Cut the meat and vegetables into small dice. Place in a large casserole and add the seasoning ingredients. Carefully turn over the melon so that it covers the diced ingredients, forming a dome in the casserole. Pour the stock into the casserole, then set it on a rack in a wok or in a steamer, cover and simmer over gentle heat for about 1 hour until the diced ingredients and the melon are completely tender and full of flavour. Garnish the melon top with coriander leaves or designs cut from melon or cucumber skin. Skilled chefs often cut the design directly onto the melon before cooking.

Substitute a hollowed water melon shell and add chopped choko (chayote) as a vegetable.

Sichuan 四川

STUFFED PEA SPROUT SOUP

Pea sprouts, in actual fact, are not sprouts at all but the tender round leaves of the sweet pea plant. They are bright green and have a delicate taste. Served as a vegetable accompaniment, pea sprouts are simply stir-fried, but in this interesting and unusual recipe, small balls of finely minced chicken are pressed onto the pea leaves to make a delicious and subtly flavoured soup. Giving the impression of a bouquet of white flowers, this dish is a favourite at springtime banquets.

125 g (4 oz) chicken breasts
1 small egg white
2-3 teaspoons cornflour (cornstarch)
500 g (1 lb) pea leaves
5 cups (1¼ L/40 fl oz) clear chicken stock (broth)
1 tomato
salt

Very finely mince (grind) the chicken breasts with a cleaver or in a food processor. Add the lightly beaten egg white and the cornflour and mix to a paste.

✻ Rinse the pea leaves in cold water, sorting out any tough stems and discoloured leaves. Drain well and wipe the larger leaves with a cloth to dry. Press a small ball of the chicken paste onto as many leaves as possible.

✻ Bring the stock to the boil, then reduce the heat and put in the pea leaves. Simmer for about 5 minutes, until the vegetable is tender and the chicken white, then add salt to taste. Do not overcook, or the leaves will turn yellow and become bitter.

✻ Drop the tomato into a saucepan of boiling water, remove and peel, cut it into wedges, then trim away the pulp and seeds leaving petal shapes. Arrange these on the top of the soup and serve at once.

228

Guangzhou 广州

HAINAN COCONUT POTAGE

Coconut trees are abundant in tropical China, particularly on Hainan Island where this dish originated. There are many stories about coconuts; one concerns Emperor Cheng Di who, in about 20 BC, chose Zhao Feiyan as his Empress. Her sister wove a mat with coconut leaves and sent it to her as a present to congratulate her, wishing her to be a mother to many sons, just like the fruitful coconut tree.

2 coconuts
30 g (1 oz) fresh mushrooms
125 g (4 oz) chicken breast meat
60 g (2 oz) lean ham
coconut or peanut oil
½ cup (125 mL/4 fl oz) coconut cream
3 cups (750 mL/24 fl oz) water or chicken stock (broth)
¾ teaspoon salt
fresh coriander

Saw the tops off the coconuts and use the liquid as a refreshing drink.

※ Cut the mushrooms, chicken and ham into small dice. Sauté briefly in a wok with a little coconut or peanut oil and place in a saucepan with the coconut cream, water and salt. Bring to the boil and simmer for about 5 minutes, then divide the soup between the two coconut shells, place the tops of the shells in position and set on a rack in a wok or in a steamer. Cover and steam for about 30 minutes until the soup has thoroughly absorbed the flavour of the coconut.

※ Garnish with chopped coriander and serve.

HAINAN COCONUT POTAGE

THICK JADEITE SOUP

Beijing 北京

THICK JADEITE SOUP

There is a touching story behind the creation of this dish concerning a beautiful young girl who was about to be married to a handsome prince when their tribe was invaded by foreigners. Before he departed to lead his army into battle, the prince gave the girl a piece of jade as a token of his love.

The girl gazed at the piece of jade night and day, thinking of her prince and could not eat or sleep. Her worried mother made this nutritious soup in which the bright green of spinach contrasted with the white of the chicken to represent the piece of jade she so coveted. She ate, regained her health and married the triumphant prince.

SPINACH SOUP

250 g (8 oz) fresh spinach leaves, finely chopped
1 teaspoon rice wine or dry sherry
1 teaspoon sugar
1½ tablespoons lard or vegetable oil
1½ cups (375 mL/12 fl oz) chicken stock (broth)
1 tablespoon cornflour (cornstarch)

CHICKEN SOUP

280 g (9 oz) chicken breast meat
1 teaspoon rice wine or dry sherry
½ teaspoon sugar
¾ teaspoon salt
2 teaspoons ginger juice
3 egg whites
1½ cups (375 mL/12 fl oz) chicken stock (broth)
1 tablespoon cornflour (cornstarch)
1 tablespoon lard or vegetable oil
cherry tomatoes (garnish)

Stir-fry the spinach in a wok with rice wine, sugar and lard until softened, then add the stock and cover. Simmer gently for about 7 minutes until the spinach is tender. Mix the cornflour with a little cold water or stock, stir into the soup and simmer, stirring, until thickened.

※ To prepare the chicken soup, very finely mince (grind) the chicken meat and season with the rice wine, sugar, salt and ginger juice. Beat in the egg whites, stirring until the mixture is very thick and smooth. Add the chicken stock and cornflour and beat again thoroughly.

※ Heat the wok and add the lard. Pour in the chicken mixture and simmer, stirring, for about 6 minutes over moderate heat until the chicken has cooked through and is very white.

※ Pour the chicken soup into a deep serving dish, keeping it as much to one side of the dish as possible. Reheat the spinach soup and carefully pour into the other side of the dish, using a wide spatula to push the chicken soup to the side, so that the two colours are clearly separated. Garnish with cherry tomatoes and serve.

BRAISED BAMBOO SHOOTS

STIR-FRIED DICED CARROTS

slices, make a short slit along the centre of each slice and pull one end through the centre slit so that the slice of bamboo shoot forms a curl. Coat with cornflour and fry in hot oil until the coating is lightly coloured. Lift out and drain.

In another wok heat 1½ tablespoons oil and fry the ginger slices for 30 seconds, then discard. Add the bamboo shoots and pour in the seasoning/sauce ingredients. Simmer until the bamboo shoots are tender.

Shred the capsicum finely and add to the pan. Heat until softened, then sprinkle with the sesame oil and serve.

To prepare the clear stock, stir-fry a handful of beans sprouts in a wok, then add 2 cups (500mL/16 floz) of water and simmer briefly until reduced by half. Separate the vegetables from the resultant stock and use for other purposes.

Beijing 北京

STIR-FRIED DICED CARROTS

This side dish originated in the days of the Manchurian invasion. During the battle the soldiers had no time to cook, so they would just roast over an open fire whatever meat or vegetables they could find, then add some brown bean sauce to enhance the flavour. Even after the establishment of the Qing Dynasty (1644-1911 AD) this style of cooking remained popular, although the imperial chefs improved the flavour by stir-frying and these dishes became daily side dishes at the imperial court.

125 g (4 oz) lean pork
250 g (8 oz) fresh young carrots
1 tablespoon sesame oil
2 cubes dried beancurd, soaked for 10 minutes
1 tablespoon dried shrimps, soaked for 25 minutes
2 tablespoons lard
2 spring onions (shallots/scallions), chopped
2 slices fresh (root) ginger, chopped
1 tablespoon brown bean sauce
1 tablespoon light soy sauce
2 teaspoons rice wine or dry sherry
⅓ cup (75 mL/2½ floz) chicken stock (broth)
1 teaspoon cornflour (cornstarch)

Dice the pork and carrots and sauté the carrots in the sesame oil in a wok for about 2 minutes until they turn red, then set aside. Squeeze the water from the dried beancurd and cut into small dice. Drain the shrimp.

In a wok, stir-fry the pork in the lard over high heat until it turns white, then add the spring onions, ginger and brown bean sauce and stir-fry for another minute.

Add the carrots, beancurd and dried shrimps and continue to stir-fry until the carrot is tender. Add the soy sauce and rice wine and fry again briefly, then add the stock mixed with the cornflour and stir-fry together until the sauce thickens. Add about 1 teaspoon of the sesame oil, used to stir-fry the carrots, and serve at once.

Beijing 北京

FRIED WINTER BAMBOO SHOOTS

Winter bamboo shoots are the very young shoots of a particular type of hairy bamboo. They have a distinct flavour and are considered to be tastier than other winter vegetables. In this dish they are combined with crisply fried lobe-leaf seaweed.

500 g (1 lb) fresh or canned winter bamboo shoots
¾ teaspoon salt
2 tablespoons rice wine or dry sherry
30 g (1 oz) lobe-leaf seaweed (wakame)
oil for deep-frying

Peel the coarse outer leaves from the fresh bamboo shoots and cut off their tough bases. Cut each shoot lengthways into quarters, place in a dish and season with the salt and wine.

Soak the seaweed in warm water to soften, then drain well and cut out the hard spine and any tough ribs. Rinse again in cold water, cut into small pieces and drain.

Heat the wok and add about ½ cup (125 mL/4 floz) of oil. When very hot, stir-fry the bamboo shoots until the edges are crisp, then remove with a slotted spoon and set aside.

Add another cup (250 mL/8 floz) of oil and heat to smoking point. Deep-fry the seaweed until crisp and bright green. Do not overcook or it will turn brown and taste bitter. Remove from the oil, mix with the bamboo shoots and serve immediately.

FRIED WINTER BAMBOO SHOOTS

TWO KINDS OF MUSHROOMS WITH GREEN VEGETABLES

MUSHROOM AND PORK PATTIES

Shanghai 上海

TWO KINDS OF MUSHROOMS WITH GREEN VEGETABLES

2 hearts of young Chinese cabbage (bok choy)
peanut or vegetable oil
250 g (8 oz) fresh button mushrooms
12 dried black mushrooms, soaked for 25 minutes

SAUCE A

1 cup (250 mL/8 fl oz) liquid from the soaked dried mushrooms
1 tablespoon dark soy sauce
1 teaspoon sugar
1 teaspoon cornflour (cornstarch)

SAUCE B

½ cup (125 mL/4 fl oz) chicken stock (broth)
¼ teaspoon salt
½ teaspoon sugar
1 teaspoon cornflour (cornstarch)
1 tablespoon milk or cream
½ teaspoon sesame oil

Cut the vegetable hearts in halves lengthways, remove the ends of the stems and discard any wilting or loose leaves. Rinse well in cold water, then shake out as much water as possible.

Stir-fry the cabbage in a wok with 1 tablespoon of oil for 1 minute, add 3 tablespoons water, cover and braise until tender. Lift out, drain and keep warm.

Trim the fresh button mushrooms and rinse with cold water, then dry well. Drain the black mushrooms, squeeze the water out and cut off the stems.

Heat about 2 tablespoons of oil in a wok and stir-fry the black mushrooms for 1 minute. Mix the sauce A ingredients together and pour into the wok. Simmer for about 3 minutes until the liquid is well reduced and the mushrooms are tender. Spoon onto one end of an oval serving plate and arrange the green vegetables across the centre.

Rinse out the wok and heat 2 tablespoons of oil. Stir-fry the button mushrooms quickly, add the sauce B ingredients and simmer until softened. Check the seasoning, dish onto the other end of the serving plate and serve at once.

Beijing 北京

MUSHROOM AND PORK PATTIES

Black mushrooms are considered to be the queen of the mushrooms, not only because of their exceptional taste, but also because of their high nutritional and medicinal value. People who work with black mushrooms are said never to suffer from influenza because they are constantly inhaling the powder from the dried mushrooms.

24 medium-sized dried black mushrooms
185 g (6 oz) lean pork, preferably fillet/tenderloin
1 tablespoon cornflour (cornstarch)
1 cup (250 mL/8 fl oz) oil or lard for frying
3-4 slices canned, or fresh and cooked bamboo shoot

SEASONING

2 teaspoons ginger juice
½ teaspoon salt
1 egg white

SAUCE

¾ cup (175 mL/6 fl oz) reserved mushroom liquid or chicken stock (broth)
1 tablespoon rice wine or dry sherry
1 tablespoon light soy sauce
1½ teaspoons sugar
1-2 teaspoons oyster sauce
2½ teaspoons cornflour (cornstarch)

Place the mushrooms in a heatproof dish and cover with warm water, leave to soak for at least 25 minutes until soft, then place the dish on a rack in a wok or steamer, cover and steam for 10 minutes. Remove and drain well, then cut off the stems, squeeze the excess liquid from the caps and set aside.

Very finely mince (grind) the pork, add the seasoning ingredients and stir the mixture in one direction only until smooth. Dust the inside of the mushroom caps lightly with cornflour and fill with a portion of the pork paste, smoothing the tops with a wet spoon.

Heat the oil or lard in a wok and fry the mushrooms, filling downwards, for about 1½ minutes, then remove and drain well.

Pour off the oil, add the pre-mixed sauce ingredients except the cornflour to the wok and bring to the boil. Slide in the mushrooms and simmer for about 4 minutes, then transfer to a serving plate and garnish with the bamboo shoot slices.

Mix the cornflour with a little cold water and stir into the sauce. Stir over moderate heat until thickened, then pour over the mushroom patties and serve at once.

Guangzhou 广州

STUFFED MUSHROOMS

10 dried black mushrooms, soaked for 25 minutes
½ teaspoon salt
2 tablespoons cornflour (cornstarch)
185 g (6 oz) chicken breast meat
1 tablespoon chicken stock (broth) or water
1 teaspoon rice wine or dry sherry
1 egg white
1½ teaspoons lard
pinch each of salt and pepper
½ slice Yunnan or other well-salted ham
10 fresh rape or coriander leaves
1 tablespoon rendered chicken fat, melted (optional)

SAUCE

½ cup (125 mL/4 fl oz) chicken stock (broth)
1 teaspoon rice wine or dry sherry
1 teaspoon cornflour (cornstarch)
pinch each of salt and pepper

Drain and rinse the mushrooms in boiling water and add the salt. Drain again, then squeeze to remove excess liquid. Trim the stems close to the caps and dust inside each cap with cornflour.

Very finely mince (grind) the chicken meat using a cleaver or a food processor. Add the stock, egg white, lard, salt and pepper, and mix in one direction only until the filling is smooth and sticky. Use a wet spoon to mound it into the mushroom caps, smoothing the tops.

Lightly oil a wide, flat, heatproof plate and arrange the mushrooms on this with the filling on top. Chop the ham very finely, sprinkle a little over each mushroom and add a rape or coriander leaf.

Set the plate on a rack in a wok or in a steamer, cover and steam for about 15 minutes until the mushrooms are tender and the filling cooked through.

Mix the sauce ingredients together in another wok and simmer until thickened. Pour the sauce over the mushrooms and sprinkle with the chicken fat, if used, before serving.

STUFFED MUSHROOMS

SNOWFLAKE WALNUT PASTE

Beijing 北京

SNOWFLAKE WALNUT PASTE

Walnuts are good for the skin, hair (making it more black and shiny), lungs and kidneys, and are said to stimulate the appetite. This rich combination of ground walnuts and dried fruits makes a dessert suitable to serve after a banquet or important dinner.

4 slices white or wholemeal bread
90 g (3 oz) halved walnuts
1½ cups (375 mL/12 fl oz) clean vegetable oil
30 g (1 oz) raisins
30 g (1 oz) candied winter melon or mango,
    pawpaw/papaya or pineapple
45 g (1½ oz) pitted dates
30 g (1 oz) dried apricots
3 eggs
1½ tablespoons lard
3 tablespoons sugar
strips of dried fruit and peel

Remove the crusts from the bread, tear into pieces and soak in a dish with water until softened, then drain and squeeze out as much water as possible.

Drop the walnuts into a saucepan of boiling water, leave for 3 minutes, then drain and carefully peel off all the skin. This is time-consuming, but the skin must be removed or the dish will have a bitter aftertaste.

Heat the oil in a wok and fry the peeled walnuts for about 3 minutes over moderate heat until lightly coloured. Remove and drain well, then chop very finely and mix with the bread.

Finely chop the dried fruit and stir into the nut and bread mixture, adding the egg yolks.

Heat the wok, add the lard and gently fry the mixture over moderate to low heat for about 5 minutes, then add the sugar and continue cooking until it forms a glossy ball. Pile into an attractively shaped dish, press down firmly, then unmould onto a serving plate.

Beat the egg whites until stiff and pour into a lightly oiled, shallow heatproof dish. Decorate with strips of dried fruit and peel and place on a rack in a wok or in a steamer. Cover and steam for about 6 minutes until firmly set, then slide on top of the walnut paste and serve at once.

FRESH FRUITS IN WATERMELON

Shanghai 上海

FRESH FRUITS IN WATERMELON

Long ago, folk artists south of the Yangtze River developed the "watermelon lamp" by carving historical and legendary scenes into the skin of a watermelon, scooping out the flesh and placing a lighted candle inside the melon to illuminate the illustrations.

This carving art is used in modern cuisine and melons are decorated with traditional designs of flora and fauna and suitable calligraphy.

1 round watermelon, plus 1 watermelon end
2 kg (4 lb) diced fresh fruit, including orange and
    mandarine segments, pear, apple and pineapple
glacé or maraschino cherries

Wash the round melon and cut off the top to form a lid. Decorate the edge of the melon and lid with a scalloped or zig-zag design.

Scoop out the flesh, pick out the seeds and cut half of the flesh into cubes. Mix with the diced fresh fruit and glacé cherries and set aside.

Carve the desired design into the rind of the melon, then shape the extra watermelon end to use as a base.

Stand the base on a serving platter and position the carved melon shell on top. Fill with the prepared fruit. Place the lid in position and serve.

CANDIED APPLE

Beijing 北京

CANDIED APPLE

This northern-style dessert has become popular in Beijing restaurants around the world, and consists of slivers of apple coated with piping-hot sugar toffee. They are dipped into a dish of iced water before eating so that the outer coating of toffee is crisp, while the apple is tender and sweet inside.

3-4 ripe apples
½ cup (60 g/2 oz) flour
3 tablespoons cornflour (cornstarch)
1 egg white, lightly beaten
oil for deep-frying
1-2 teaspoons sesame oil
iced water

TOFFEE

2 tablespoons water
1 tablespoon lard
½ cup (125 g/4 oz) sugar

Peel and core the apples, then cut into wedges. Place the flour in a plastic bag, add the apple wedges, close the top and shake vigorously to coat the apple evenly with flour. Remove the apple and mix the remaining flour with the cornflour and egg white to make a thick batter, adding a little cold water as needed.

Heat the oil in a wok until almost smoking and add the sesame oil. Dip each piece of apple into the batter and deep-fry in several batches until golden, turning once or twice. Drain well.

Spread a little sesame oil over a serving plate and pour the iced water into a bowl.

Drain the wok and add the toffee ingredients. Cook over moderate heat without stirring until the sugar has turned a caramel colour, then quickly turn off the heat.

Dip each piece of apple into the toffee using wooden chopsticks, and place on the oiled plate. Serve immediately, dipping into the iced water before eating.

STUFFED PEARS

Sichuan 四川

STUFFED PEARS

The snow pear from Sichuan has a crisp firm texture, is very sweet and juicy, and is thought to be beneficial for the lungs and throat. The unique dish described in this recipe is often served as dessert at winter banquets.

8 snow pears or other ripe fresh pears
1 tablespoon glutinous rice
1 tablespoon pearl barley
8 lotus seeds, fresh, dried or canned
8 fox nuts
4 dates
16 glacé cherries
1½ tablespoons chopped candied melon or pineapple
½ cup (125 g/4 oz) crushed rock sugar

Peel and core the pears, and remove the stems. Rinse the rice, barley, lotus seeds and fox nuts, place in a heatproof dish on a rack in a wok or steamer, cover and steam until cooked.

❈ Wash the dates, stone and chop them with the glacé cherries and melon. Add to the cooked ingredients and stuff the filling into the prepared pears.

❈ Stand upright on a heatproof plate and steam for about 15 minutes, or until the pears are tender. Decorate each with a cherry.

❈ Melt the rock sugar in a wok, adding 1 tablespoon of water. Cook gently until golden, then pour over the pears and serve.

Sichuan 四川

LOQUAT JELLY

The serving of dried and fresh fruits at banquets goes back some two thousand years in China. We can find such terms as "Bian Shi" in ancient books. "Bian" indicates a kind of food basket made of split bamboo, which was used to hold fruit or dried meat at banquets and when offering sacrifices to gods or ancestors.

Although actual desserts made a late appearance in Chinese menus, many varieties of jellied fruit desserts became popular once the gelatinous seaweed extract agar agar became available. This recipe can be adapted for seasonal availability of fruits, loquats being a refreshing summer dessert.

24 fresh loquats
15 g (½ oz) agar agar strips or powder*
3 cups (750 mL/24 fl oz) cold water
½ cup (125 g/4 oz) sugar
glacé cherries

Skin the loquats and remove the seeds, then place one each in the bottom of 24 Chinese teacups or other small dishes.

❈ Place the agar agar in a wok or saucepan, add the water and slowly bring to the boil, stirring constantly. Simmer for 2-3 minutes, then add the sugar and stir slowly until dissolved and simmer for another 2-3 minutes.

❈ Strain through a fine mesh strainer over the loquats. Allow to cool, then chill in the refrigerator.

❈ Unmould the jellies onto a serving plate and decorate the dish with glacé cherries. Serve cold.

Strip agar agar may require more time to dissolve than powdered types. Jellies made with agar agar do not require refrigeration once they have set.

Glossary

ABALONE The king of the molluscs in Chinese cuisine. Canned or dried, it is widely available but, like most other ingredients in any Chinese recipe, the fresher the better.

AGAR AGAR Sheets of dried, pressed seaweed that feature in some Chinese and Manchurian dishes. It is used like gelatin, which can act as a substitute. Can be bought in sheets or powdered form.

BALSAM PEAR (CHINESE BITTER MELON) A small and wrinkled, cucumber-like vegetable with soft flesh and a central seed core. It adds a tart taste to stews and braised dishes, and is sold fresh or canned. Cucumber is a pleasant alternative.

BAMBOO SHOOTS These look like the horn of a small water buffalo. Different species vary in size, texture and taste. Originally, the shoot was used in northern and western cuisines but in recent years has also appeared on the Guangdong table. They can be bought in cans in Chinese stores. Celery hearts make a passable substitute.

BEANCURD The processed extract of the soy bean which comes in the form of jelly, custard, and dried, fried, hard or soft cakes of all shapes and sizes. Takes on the taste and aroma of whatever it is cooked with.

Beancurd sheets come in dry layers and are used to wrap other ingredients, usually for stews. When slowly cooked, the sheets dissolve and produce a rich broth of soy milk in which the vegetables and meat are cooked. Soak or dampen before use.

Preserved or *fermented beancurd* comes in tough-skinned squares in a pickle of chilli and brine. Known as Chinese cheese, the taste often seems offensive to Western palates, in the same way as dairy cheeses are often unpleasant in taste and odour to the Chinese.

BEAN PASTE There are many varieties made from different ingredients added to a basic fermented paste usually made from soy beans. Pastes can be found in cans and jars in every Chinese food shop. Even if the colourful labels are in Chinese only, the pictures give a good indication of what the contents will taste like.

Hot bean paste is served with every Sichuan and Hunan meal. It is made from the basic soy paste with hot red peppers crushed and fried in oil. Salty and palate-jarringly hot, it gives Sichuan food its distinctive taste.

Hot black bean paste is one of the most tasty of all the seasonings, and a marvellous accompaniment to crab. This fermented sauce comes in many brands and styles. All are delicious.

Sweet bean paste is a rich, salty, sweet sauce made from soy beans fermented with salt, sugar and seasonings. Used in marinades, as a seasoning and as a dip.

Yellow bean paste comes from the yellow soy bean and is very salty. Used sparingly it is delicious, but too much can kill rather than complement other tastes.

BEAN PASTE, SWEETENED RED This is a thick sweet mixture made from red beans. Used as a filling for cakes, dumplings and buns.

BEAN SAUCES *Brown bean sauce* is a more liquid version of the fermented bean paste, being quite salty in taste but mildly flavoured. *Hot bean sauce* is a mixture of fermented soy bean and chilli preserved in salt.

BEAN SPROUTS Available fresh or canned. The fresh ones will last at least a week in a sealed plastic bag or box, and are vastly superior to the canned variety.

To grow them at home, soak a handful of dried soy or mung beans. Put dampened cheese cloth in a colander, place the beans on top, put another layer of cloth over that and pour on a cup of warm water. Suspend the colander in a large saucepan and place in a warm cupboard. Give the beans another soaking through the cloth four times a day for five days, by which time you should have a nice crop of beans ready for the pot or wok.

BEAN THREAD NOODLES Made from the flour of the mung bean. The light, translucent threads are used to thicken stews and hotpots or as the base for a meal of vegetables.

BOK CHOY Choy means vegetables in Chinese and bok means white. The chef in the Chinese kitchen has an enormous range from which to choose. Generally, the generous southern gardens provide the widest selection of fresh greens and the further north one goes the narrower becomes the range. The Chinese "white cabbage" is a small, white-stemmed cabbage with deep-green leaves, a favourite of the Guangdong kitchen and a staple green accompaniment for many a meat or beancurd dish. There are hundreds of different varieties of cabbage, scores of assorted types of bok choy. Some cousins of this family are as small as 10 cm (4 in) long, others grow three times as large. It should be cooked as swiftly as possible, no more than two or three minutes, and served immediately to keep the succulent taste and goodness of the leaves.

CABBAGE Comes in a great variety from tiny delicate bok choy to the solid northern Tianjin cabbage. It is an essential and delicious part of many meals. Any cabbage can be used with magnificent effect in its place.

CAMPHOR Woodchips used to smoke poultry, particularly chicken for Jiangsu, Henan and Anhui dishes. Black tea leaves do the job equally well.

CASSIA A variety of cinnamon found in southern China.

CHICKEN FAT The rendered fat of a chicken, reduced during fast boiling in a double boiler. Used for stir-frying and to add flavour and shine to sauces and finished dishes. Duck fat is treated in the same way.

CHILLI OIL Used in spicy dishes, it is made by heating 1/2 cup (125 mL/4 fl oz) of good quality sesame or vegetable oil and adding 2½ tablespoons of chilli powder, flakes or, best of all, whole chillies. The oil is then allowed to cool and strained. It keeps indefinitely in a jar.

CHILLI PASTE Can be added to the food when cooking or placed in a side dish into which diners can dip their chopsticks to make their food as hot as they can take it.

CHOY SUM A sparsely leafed, green vegetable with small yellow flowerheads and a slightly bitter flavour.

CHRYSANTHEMUM The fresh petals of white chrysanthemum flowers are used as a garnish and for their delicate flavour in some dishes.

CLOUD EAR FUNGUS One of the countless varieties of dried fungi, this one is a tiny, crinkled, dry fungus which turns gelatinous in soups and stews. Another variety is called wood ear fungus. Soak to soften.

CORIANDER Also called Chinese parsley, it is much stronger than the Western variety, which can be used as a poor substitute. Coriander will grow like a weed in a windowbox or garden, and every serious amateur chef should have some growing.

FEN LIQUOR A strong spirit used mainly in marinades. Vodka, white rum or brandy can be used instead with little cost to taste.

FERMENTED BLACK BEANS Soft, dried, salted black beans used as a flavouring.

FERMENTED GLUTINOUS RICE JUICE The result of cooked glutinous rice being treated with brewer's yeast to produce a fermentation with a strong brewed flavour.

FISH SAUCE More familiar in the Vietnamese kitchen, but originally Chinese and still used in many country recipes. The pale brown, light sauce can be used to cook (sparingly) or as a condiment in which to dip vegetables.

FIVE-SPICE POWDER Made from cinnamon, brown Sichuan peppercorns, cloves, fennel and anise. Different chefs call for different proportions of the mixture and trial and error is the best way to find a suitable blend. It is available commercially.

FUNGI Countless varieties of dried fungi are available, including *cloud ear fungus* and *wood ear fungus*. Soak to soften.

GALANGAL The aromatic rootstock of certain plants of the ginger family.

GINGER One of the major ingredients in Chinese cuisine. Its taste is as pleasing as the appearance of the knobbly, gnarled root is ugly. With meat, fowl, fish and vegetable dishes, steamed, stir-fried or stewed, finely chopped ginger is an indispensable essential for almost every Chinese meal. It can be stored for weeks in a refrigerator, but use it fresh wherever possible. Make sure all skin is peeled off before use.

GINGER JUICE Made by squeezing slices of fresh (root) ginger in a garlic crusher.

GINGKO NUTS Small, oval nuts, sometimes called white nuts. Used mainly in vegetarian dishes, stuffings, soups, or as a garnish. Sold fresh, canned or dried, the bitter core must be removed before use.

GLUTINOUS RICE Available as long or short grain varieties, it has a cloudy, white appearance, unlike the usual pearly, white rice. When cooked it forms a sticky mass, and is often used in sweets and cakes.

GOLDEN NEEDLES The dried flower buds of the tiger lily. Used in simmered winter dishes and stir-fried to both give and take flavour from other ingredients. Usually knotted before being added to the dish.

HOISIN SAUCE Made from soy beans and chillies with sugar and salt added to give it a sweet but biting taste. A delicious partner for meat and poultry dishes.

LARD Rendered pork fat used for stir-frying and for sweets and pastry making.

LOQUATS Look like apricots but taste like peaches.

LOTUS The floating leaves of the lotus, immortalised in Chinese paintings, are only the most obvious part of the plant. The seeds, pale yellow when they are dried, are used for decorating desserts or for casual nibbling. The root looks like a string of plump, firm sausages, the sweet flesh inside something like a ripe cucumber. The delicacy can be braised, stir-fried or boiled and at festivals is sold as a candied sweet.

LOTUS SEED PASTE   Boiled and mashed with oil and sugar, a dry but rich paste.

LUFFA   A long, green gourd halfway between a skinny pumpkin and an okra. It can be distinguished in markets by the heavy ridges running along the skin. It is sometimes known as angled luffa because of the angles made by these ridges. The squash-like flesh, with little taste of its own, is usually stir-fried with other vegetables or meat.

LYCHEES   Justly famed as one of the best ways to finish a feast. The rough red skin peels off to reveal the ripe, plump, juicy pulp. Also available canned.

MAO TAI   A potent (some might say lethal) clear spirit with an overwhelming odour and a memorable after effect. Not for nothing is it known as White Lightning. Mao Tai is a common accompaniment for a Chinese banquet, along with wines of the Shaoxing sort and some of China's excellent beers. Newcomers to the table should beware of overindulgence in Mao Tai and similar spirits such as the equally fearsome Kaoliang.

MELONS   Come in all shapes and sizes, but the most commonly used are the globe-shaped, light green *winter melons*. The white, juicy flesh can be cut out and cooked as the main ingredient in the famed Winter Melon Soup, then served on the table in the original gourd which has been carved into a superb dining top decoration. Substitute hollowed water melon for the shell and chokos (chayotes) for the flesh.

MONOSODIUM GLUTAMATE (MSG)   You either swear by it or curse it. Many professional Chinese chefs call MSG "the master" because a handful of the composition allows them to serve just about anything and make it taste good. But in recent years there has been a wide backlash against the use of the substance and many people doubt its value from a culinary angle and fear its side effects from the point of view of health. Originally made from wheat gluten which had been dried and fermented, MSG has for decades been made chemically. Overuse of it causes various effects in diners such as headaches, hot flushes, dryness and tiredness. Many discriminating chefs and experienced cooks refuse to use MSG and in such culinary capitals as Hong Kong there is a move in a number of leading Chinese restaurants to ban its use. Some of these establishments proudly boast that they do not use MSG; the result is that they attract hordes of knowledgeable gourmets who want to savour real tastes instead of chemicals.

MUSHROOMS   These come in infinite varieties. Every province has its prize varieties, but *dried black mushrooms* are universal. They can be purchased in most Chinese food stores and must be soaked to soften before use. Any type of mushroom makes a palatable and acceptable alternative in home cooking, although European varieties have a foreign flavour. The most common Chinese types are the *button mushrooms, yellow straw mushrooms,* the *golden needle mushrooms,* the *black forest* and the large *umbrella mushrooms* of Hunan.

MUSTARD   The green leaves, which come in a number of versions, mostly dark green and sometimes pickled, are used in stir-fried dishes and some stews. The thick stem/root section needs to be shredded or diced before use.

NOODLES   Fat, thin, long, short, broad, slender – take your pick because they come in all shapes and sizes. They can be made of mung bean flour like the delicate, transparent vermicelli, from wheat flour or from rice. Home cooks in non-Asian countries can use Italian pastas in place of noodles in most Chinese recipes.

OIL FOR STIR-FRYING   Almost invariably vegetable oil. It can be flavoured with chilli (*see* chilli oil) or, more rarely, with onion, ginger or five spices.

ORANGE PEEL   Is used to add a dash of sweetness to spicy Hunan and Sichuan dishes. You can buy it dried or canned, or make your own.

OYSTER SAUCE   A delicious and classic accompaniment to swiftly stir-fried greens. The rich flavouring comes from steamed oysters judiciously blended with soy sauce and salt.

PEA LEAVES   The small, bright green leaves from the sweet pea plant. Young spinach will do instead.

PEPPER   The black and white varieties were introduced during the Tang Dynasty (618-907 AD), when pepper was called for in almost every dish at the tables of the wealthy.

PEPPER, SICHUAN   The brown peppercorn of western China – the flower pepper of Sichuan – is still favoured above the "barbarian" pepper, and the whole peppercorn is often cooked rather than being ground. It is in fact the seed of the prickly ash tree (*Xanthoxylum pipertum*). Also known as Fagara pepper, and sold under the Japanese name Sansho.

PEPPERCORN SALT   A mixture of ground Sichuan brown peppercorns and salt. Used as a seasoning and condiment.

PICKLES   Served at the start of a meal or to add a pungent, salty flavour to Chinese cooking, they differ depending on the region and the season. There are countless varieties of vegetables and solutions but among the most popular are cabbages, mustard greens and roots, radishes, turnips and cucumbers. Chillies are often added to the brine to give a spicy taste.

PLUM SAUCE   Tart and sweet at the same time, has a taste that seems heaven-made to go with roast goose or duck. It also contains apricots, chilli and vinegar, which explains the exciting reddish brown tone.

PORK FAT NET (CAUL LINING)   A large sheet of pork fat, used to wrap food to form rolls or to prevent dryness. It holds the food together while frying but eventually melts away unless coated with batter or flour, when it makes a crisp crust. Available from Chinese food stores.

PRAWN CRACKERS   Also called "krupuk", they are compressed slivers of prawn and flour paste. They expand into large translucent crisps when deep-fried.

PRAWNS (SHRIMPS)   The heads and tails are generally left on to add flavour and colour to the dish. To devein prawns, hold with the back curling upwards, push a toothpick into the centre back and gently hook out the dark vein. You can also cut along the back with a sharp knife and pull out the vein.

Cooked prawns are easily peeled by sliding the shell off. To peel uncooked prawns, cut the shell along the underside between the rows of legs and remove the whole shell.

PRESERVED VEGETABLES   Used to give a pungent, salty flavour to Chinese dishes. They are sold by weight in Chinese food stores, and are also known as spiced vegetables. Preserved mustard is the most common. Mustard greens are the leaves, and mustard root the stem or root, and must be shredded or diced before use.

QUAIL EGGS   Readily available hard-boiled in cans. Substitute very small chicken eggs.

RAPE   The plant of the Brassica group, the leaves of which are used in some Chinese cooking. *Rapeseed oil* has been used in China as a fine cooking oil for many centuries.

RED FERMENTED RICE (WINE LEES)   A mash of red rice and wine. Called for in some strong, regional recipes and virtually impossible to obtain in a non-Chinese society. Japanese miso paste can be used instead, but should first be diluted with water.

RICE WINE   Many varieties are available, but *Shaoxing rice wine* is possibly the most famous in China and essential to many Shanghai and Yangtze Valley recipes. Available in most Chinese food stores worldwide, any shopowner will be delighted to chat about the different wines he stocks. As a drink to accompany food, it should be served warm from a teapot-like container in small cups without handles. Dry sherry can be used as a substitute in cooking.

SCALLION OIL   Used to give extra flavour when stir-frying. It is made by frying roughly chopped spring onions (shallots/scallions) in oil until they are light-brown. Use 4 spring onions to 3 tablespoons of oil, and remove with a slotted spoon before using the oil. Peanut oil is preferred by Guangzhou cooks, although other vegetable oil is suitable.

SEA CUCUMBER (BÊCHE-DE-MER)   A delicacy among southern gourmets who prize its rubbery texture. Known also as sea bear (because of its resemblance to bear's paw) it is the basis of expensive specialty dishes in some of the world's top Chinese restaurants. Soak, remove stomach, then pre-cook for one to several hours, depending on cooking time of final dish.

SEAWEEDS   Mostly used in conjunction with other vegetables in soups. They must be soaked before use, preferably overnight, and should be rinsed thoroughly before and after soaking.

SESAME OIL   Comes from the crushed and roasted seeds of the sesame plant. This treatment gives the oil its rich, nutty taste. It is used mainly as an aromatic garnish, and occasionally for cooking.

SESAME PASTE (TAHINA)   A thick yellow paste made from ground sesame seeds. Peanut butter is a rather poor substitute for the aromatic, thick richness of sesame.

SHARKS' FINS   Can be bought from well-stocked Chinese stores, but they are extremely expensive and daunting to prepare.

SHRIMP PASTE   Is sold dried and should be cooked before being eaten. It has an unpleasant smell before being cooked but adds a distinctive flavour to certain dishes. Anchovy concentrate can be used instead if necessary.

SILVER SPROUTS   Mung bean sprouts with the roots and seed pods removed. They are silvery when cooked.

SOY SAUCE   Makes a Chinese meal. It is hard to imagine picking up your chopsticks without this familiar friend at your elbow. Salty, pungent and essential for cooking and as a garnish, it is absolutely indispensable for enjoyment of Chinese food. *Light soy sauce* is thinner and lighter in flavour than *black soy sauce* which is used mainly in stews. *Sweet soy sauce* is thick, black and sweet.

STAR ANISE   Comes from a shrub that is cousin to the magnolia. It gets its name from the star-like splay of its pod. Western anise, although not from the same botanical family, can be used as a substitute.

STOCKS   Vary from region to region, and are made by boiling meat, bones, poultry or vegetables in water for hours, skimming and filtering. Stock cubes are a poor substitute. Clear stock is made by simply frying a handful

of bean sprouts and then boiling them in 1 or 2 cups (250-500 mL/8-16 fl oz) of water.

VERMICELLI   Usually a transparent bean thread pasta made from mung bean flour; can also be made from rice flour. Sold dried, in bundles. Both types can be deep-fried, or used in soups and stews.

VINEGAR   Plays an important, often overlooked role in every regional kitchen. Each province prides itself on the quality and clarity of its vinegar. *Rice vinegar,* light and clear with a sharp taste, is the most common. Any good quality vinegar is an acceptable alternative.

Several other types of vinegar are used in Chinese cooking. Distilled from fermented rice, the range includes *red vinegar,* which is mildly flavoured and used in sauces and dips;

brown or *black vinegar,* stronger in taste and colour, and with a slight sweetness and fine aroma; *sweet black vinegar* is an especially sweetened dark rice vinegar used only occasionally.

WATER CHESTNUTS   Really the bulb of wild rushes. Very expensive and a lot of trouble to prepare, but now available in cans. The powdered flour called for in some exotic recipes is also available outside China.

WHITE RADISH   A popular cold starter, sliced thinly and eaten either raw with chilli or pickled. Its sharp taste turns sweet when cooked. Sweet white turnip can be substituted in cooked dishes.

YUNNAN HAM   Reputedly the finest in China. There is nothing quite the same, but you can substitute another well-salted ham.

WAGUO INN, NEAR SHIMIAN VILLAGE, SICHUAN PROVINCE

HARALD SUND

AUTHENTIC RECIPES FROM THE REGIONS OF THAILAND

THAILAND
THE BEAUTIFUL
COOKBOOK

ในน้ำมีปลา ในนามีข้าว
ไพร่ฟ้า หน้าใส

หลักศิลาจารึกของพ่อขุนรามคำแหงแห่งสุโขทัย ปีพุทธศักราช 1292

"In the water there are fish, in the fields there is rice ...
The faces of the people shine bright."

Stone inscription dated 1292, attributed to King Ramkhamhaeng the Great of Sukhothai

NORTHEAST BARBECUED CHICKEN (LEFT, RECIPE PAGE 376) AND CHARCOAL BEEF (RECIPE PAGE 386)

AUTHENTIC RECIPES FROM THE REGIONS OF THAILAND

THAILAND

THE BEAUTIFUL
COOKBOOK

RECIPES BY
PANURAT POLADITMONTRI
AND JUDY LEW

TEXT BY
WILLIAM WARREN

PHOTOGRAPHY BY
LUCA INVERNIZZI TETTONI
JOHN HAY

HarperCollinsPublishers

First published in USA 1992 by
Collins Publishers San Francisco.
Reprinted in 1992; 1995; 1998; 1999.

Conceived and produced by Weldon Owen Inc.
814 Montgomery Street, San Francisco, CA 94133, USA
Fax (415) 291 8841
A member of the Weldon International Group of Companies
Sydney • San Francisco • London

Chairman: Kevin Weldon
President: John Owen
General Manager: Stuart Laurence
Publisher: Wendely Harvey
Co-Editions Director: Derek Barton
Project Director: Dawn Low
Editor: Margaret Olds
Assistant Editor: Kate Etherington
Editorial Assistant: Tristan Phillips
Indexer: Susan Leipa – Comsearch Information Services
Picture Editor: Jenny Mills
Designer: John Bull – The Book Design Company
Production Director: Mick Bagnato
Maps: Stan Lamond – Lamond Art & Design
Illustrations: Yolande Bull
Food Stylist: Ann Creber
Food Photography: John Hay
Scenic Photography: Luca Invernizzi Tettoni
Associate Project Director, Thailand: Yvan Van Outrive
Project Coordinator, Thailand: Wongvipa Thephasdin
    Na Ayudhaya

Library of Congress
Cataloging-in-Publication Data

Poladitmontri, Panurat,
    Thailand the beautiful cookbook; authentic recipes
from the regions of Thailand/recipes by Panurat
Poladitmontri and Judy Lew; text by William Warren;
photography by Luca Invernizzi Tettoni, John Hay.
    p. cm.
    Includes index.
    ISBN 0-00-255029-6
    1. Cookery, Thai. 2. Thailand – Social life and customs.
    I. Lew, Judy. II. Warren, William, 1930- III. Title.
    TX724.5 T5P66 1992
641.59593–dc 20   91-33549

ISBN 0-06-757595-1 (pbk.)

Printed by Toppan in China

A Weldon Owen Production

ENDPAPERS: GRAND STAIRCASE MURAL, THE REGENT OF BANGKOK.
PAINTED BY PAIBOON SUWANNAKUDT TO COMMEMORATE THE
BICENTENNIAL OF BANGKOK AND THE ESTABLISHMENT OF THE
CURRENT CHAKRI DYNASTY
PHOTO: LUCA INVERNIZZI TETTONI/PHOTOBANK

PAGES 2-3: SINGHA, BURMESE STYLE LIONS, LOOK OUT OVER
THE MIST-FILLED MAE HONG SON VALLEY FROM WAT PHRA
THAT DOI KONG MU
PHOTO: LUCA INVERNIZZI TETTONI/PHOTOBANK

PAGES 6-7: RAKING UNHUSKED RICE IN THE FIELDS NEAR AYUTTHAYA
PHOTO: MICHAEL FREEMAN

PAGES 8-9: A FLOATING MARKET IN RATCHABURI PROVINCE, WHERE
VENDORS PADDLE THEIR FLAT-BOTTOMED BOATS ALONG THE CANALS
PHOTO: LUCA INVERNIZZI TETTONI/PHOTOBANK

MICHAEL FREEMAN

BARBECUED CHICKEN (RECIPE PAGE 382)

CONTENTS

MONKS IN A MONASTERY IN CHIANG MAI

INTRODUCTION

EXCEPT FOR TWO BRIEF INTERLUDES in the sixteenth and eighteenth centuries, when the Burmese occupied the capital and some other parts of the kingdom, Thailand has enjoyed more than seven hundred years of independence—a distinction that can be claimed by no other country in Southeast Asia—and that has had a powerful effect on its social and political development.

But this is not to say that the Thais have been untouched by outside influences. Indeed, another great distinction, perhaps an even more important one, lies in their remarkable capacity for selective adaptation, taking certain foreign aspects and altering them in ways that make them uniquely Thai. Like the cuisine of the country, with its subtle, sometimes surprising blend of hot, sweet, and sour flavors, Thai culture is an artful amalgam, its individual components often recognizable but its overall effect highly distinctive.

China, where the Thais are generally believed to have originated as a minority ethnic group, certainly provided significant ingredients. So did India, Java, and Cambodia, all of which exerted strong influences on pre-Thai cultures. Later Sri Lanka made contributions, especially to Buddhist art and architecture, and later still there were borrowings from various European countries. The influences may, in the opinion of some historians, go back much further, to the very dawn of history: excavations in northeastern Thailand during the 1960s found evidence of rice cultivation as long ago as 3500 B.C., a thousand years before either China or India.

The earliest Thai principalities were established in the far north, centered around such cities as Chiang Rai and Chiang Mai and forming a loose federation known as Lanna. True independence came in the mid-thirteenth century when two Thai chieftains in the north central region overthrew their Khmer overlords and established the kingdom of Sukhothai, a name that in its Sanskrit form means "Dawn of Happiness". To judge from the scanty records that survive, the appellation was appropriate; for Sukhothai at the height of its short-lived power was indeed a happy place, a mystic Thai version of Camelot, which still continues to exert a potent power over the national imagination.

It had wise paternalistic rulers, who were alert to the needs of their people and very different from the aloof god-kings of the Khmers. It was abundant; "in the water there is fish, in the fields there is rice" reads part of a famous inscription of 1292. Its power, for a time at least, was considerable; less by means of conflict than through strategic alliances it managed to forge a sphere of influence that covered nearly all of present-day Thailand. And it was extraordinarily creative; the Buddhist architecture and art of Sukhothai, all produced in a few centuries, were never to be equalled for originality and sheer beauty.

We know little about the food of Sukhothai, though one familiar present-day ingredient certainly not in use was the chili pepper, which reached Southeast Asia from its Central American homeland a few centuries later. On the other hand, there is no reason to think that the early Thai view differed much from that given by a contemporary writer: "Wherever we are and whatever we are doing, we like first and best to eat." Very likely, ordinary people sat down to the basic fare described by a French visitor to Ayutthaya, the next capital. "A Siamese," he wrote, "makes a very good meal with a pound of rice a day, which amounts to not more than a farthing; and with a little dry or salt fish, which costs no more … Their sauces are plain, a little water with some spices, garlic, or some sweet herb. They do very much esteem a liquid sauce, like mustard, which is only crayfish corrupted because they are ill-salted; they call it Kepi."

By contrast, it is interesting to note the Thai opinion of French cuisine at about the same time, as recorded by an envoy from Ayutthaya to the court of King Louis XIV in 1684. When he was given some wine at a reception in his honor, he noted that it "helps give taste to the food which would otherwise be insipid to our palates; here are few spices and much meat, and an attraction of quantity replaces piquant wholesomeness."

With the rise of Ayutthaya in the fourteenth century, perhaps the most cosmopolitan of all cities in the region, other ingredients were added to the Thai blend. At the peak of its power in the seventeenth century, Ayutthaya had a population of more than a million, among them Laotians, Cambodians, Chinese, Indians, Japanese, Persians, Dutch, Portuguese, English, and French, many of whom left some kind of lasting imprint. Thai sweets based on sugar and egg yolks, for instance, are nearly all derived from the Portuguese,

THAI CLASSICAL DANCE, OF INDIAN ORIGIN, HAS TWO
MAIN FORMS: KHON—MASKED DRAMA; AND LAKON—DRAMA

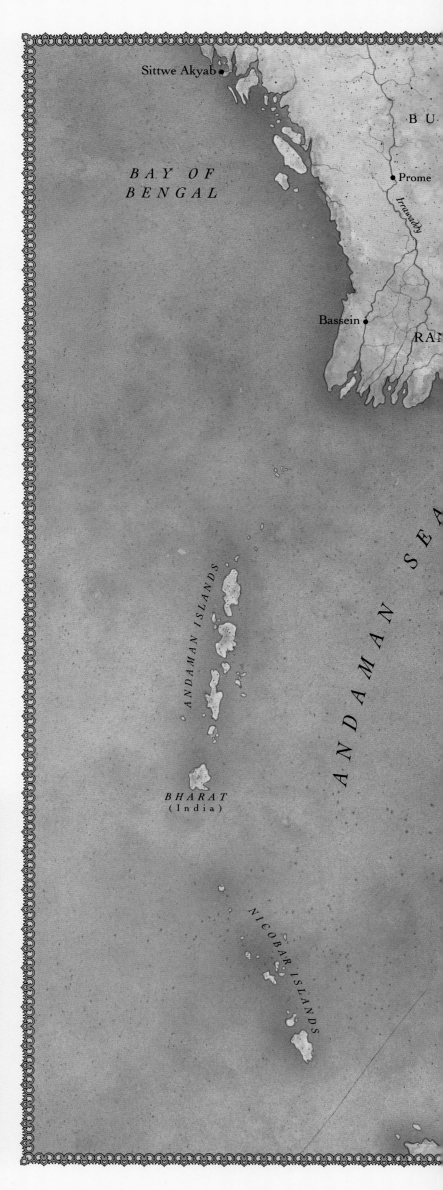

269

WAT RATBURANA AT AYUTTHAYA, ONCE THE CAPITAL OF SIAM.
THE CITY WAS DESTROYED BY BURMESE INVADERS IN 1767

UPCOUNTRY, RURAL PEOPLE LEAD A SIMPLE LIFE. HERE A MAN
CARRIES HIS WARES ON A POLE OVER HIS SHOULDER

and the Indians contributed a milder form of curry. The Portuguese were also probably responsible for introducing that now-essential ingredient, the chili pepper, shortly after they opened relations with Ayutthaya in 1511, and may have brought the tomato as well.

Surrounding Ayutthaya and stretching all the way to the gulf was the real source of Thailand's wealth: the vast, fertile Chao Phraya River valley, an ancient checkerboard of paddy fields, fruit orchards, and waterways, which not only fed most of the kingdom but also supplied most of its foreign exchange. This great resource remained after Ayutthaya was destroyed by the Burmese in 1767 and sustained subsequent capitals established further down the river, first at Thonburi and finally, in 1782, across the river on the site of a small trading port called Bangkok.

Visitors today, as in the past, often fail to perceive Thailand's cultural and geographical variety—confined as so many of them are to cities and resort areas, where Western

A JUNK ON PHANGNGA BAY. CHINESE STYLE
SAILING BOATS ARE NOW USED BY TOURISTS

and other influences (mainly Chinese) tend to predominate. The overwhelming majority of Thais, however, still live in rural areas, mostly in villages of between 100 and 150 households, and still abide by regional mores that are only superficially affected by modern changes.

Geographically the country is divided into four main regions. The North, sharing borders (and many cultural affinities) with Burma and Laos, has mountains and secret valleys that until fairly recent years were all but inaccessible. It experiences temperatures that drop sufficiently in the winter months to permit cultivation of temperate-zone fruits and vegetables. The Northeast is a rolling plateau stretching to the Mekong River which separates Thailand from Laos, and also, in its southern part, bordering on Cambodia. Once densely forested and fertile, it is now semi-arid, a condition that influences both the psychology and cuisine of its inhabitants. The Central Plains region, which includes the provinces along the eastern coast of the gulf, is one of the

271

world's greatest rice-growing areas and has been the scene of Thailand's most intense cultural and economic development. The South, a peninsula stretching like a long finger all the way down to Malaysia, is characterized by craggy limestone mountains, dense jungles, and a rich abundance of seafood from the waters off its two coastlines.

Equally varied are the approximately 56 million people who live in Thailand. In addition to the Thai majority the population includes numerous other ethnic groups—semi-nomadic hill tribes, Chinese, Vietnamese, Laotians, Malays, Cambodians, Indians and Burmese, to mention only some—nearly all of whom have been politically assimilated, yet who also display marked cultural differences.

Buddhism is the faith followed by most, reflected not only by the country's 27,000 temples, dazzling creations that manage to be at once fantastical and serene, but also, less visibly, by countless modes of instinctive behavior that range from a fatalistic acceptance of misfortune to a passion for social harmony. The domed Muslim mosque, however, is almost as common as the Buddhist monastery in the far south; astrologers and fortune tellers figure prominently in daily life; and every village and town has its shrines to the countless far more ancient spirits who bring rain, prosperity, fecundity, or even a winning ticket in the lottery.

As a country, as a culture, Thailand can be likened to one of its most popular traditional arts, that of fitting countless fragments of brightly colored glass or porcelain to form mosaics for the adornment of such celebrated structures as Bangkok's Wat Arun, the Temple of Dawn. From a distance the effect is that of a seamless pattern of sparkling jewel-like hues, shading imperceptibly into one another. Only on closer inspection do the individual parts of the design become clear; only then can the outsider begin to appreciate the ingenuity that has produced this remarkably complex creation.

JENNY MILLS

LONG-TAILED BOATS TAKE VISITORS TO THE ISLANDS OF THE ANDAMAN SEA IN THAILAND'S SOUTHWEST

THE COUNTRY SWARMS WITH BICYCLES AND MOTORBIKES. HERE NEIGHBORS STOP FOR A CHAT OUTSIDE CHIANG MAI

JOHN HAY

THE ROYAL PALACE AND THE TEMPLE OF THE EMERALD BUDDHA IN BANGKOK
LUCA INVERNIZZI TETTONI / PHOTOBANK

GIRLS AT A FESTIVAL TAKING TIME OUT FOR A BOWL OF VEGETABLES

EATING A THAI MEAL

"THE THAIS TAKE THEIR REPASTS seated on a mat or carpet," reported Bishop Jean-Baptiste Pallegoix, a missionary who lived in Bangkok during the early nineteenth century. "The dishes are great brazen vases with a cover, over which a red cloth is placed; the meat is cut into small pieces, and the rice is kept apart in a deep porringer on one side of the floor, while a great basin of water is on the other, having in it a drinking cup. The guests have neither knives or forks, but use a mother-of-pearl spoon to dip into the various dishes, of which having eaten a sufficiency, they drink pure water or tea. To help themselves one after another from the same plate, to drink one after another from the same cup, has nothing strange."

Though the Bishop clearly moved in lofty circles, in which accoutrements like brazen vases and mother-of-pearl spoons were taken for granted, certain features of

the Thai meal he describes will be familiar to any contemporary diner.

Almost always, eating Thai style will involve a number of people, usually a family group, for being forced to eat alone ranks high on the Thai scale of misfortunes.

A visit to a Thai house for dinner begins with the warm welcome that is the hallmark of Thai hospitality. The host will likely offer some refreshing cool water as a prelude to a session of light-hearted conversation—Thai people enjoy telling jokes and teasing each other so that talk, not food, may occupy much of the early part of the visit. But then comes the time to enjoy a meal together.

Dishes are usually comprised of bite-sized portions, and meal service typically includes only a fork and a spoon. In fact a century or so ago no cutlery (apart from serving utensils) was used at traditional meals. The rice, whether ordinary or glutinous, was pressed into small

274

balls with fingers and then dipped into the other dishes. European spoons and forks appeared during the nineteenth century, at first in royal circles and later taken up by the general population; the custom today is to actually eat with a dessert-sized spoon, using the fork mainly to move food around on the plate. A Chinese-style ceramic spoon is often provided if there is a soup, in which case each guest will have a small bowl as well as a plate. Knives are rarely used, since meats are already cut into bite-sized pieces, and chopsticks only when Chinese-type noodles are included.

Almost always there will be a variety of dishes, for it takes more than one or two preparations to achieve the blend of flavors Thais like. An ample supply of rice is always the centerpiece. Traditionally all of the dishes are served at the same time. The Thai cook strives for a balance of flavors, textures and colors.

Ideally, a Thai meal offers a combination of flavors: sweet, hot, sour, salty and bitter. Sometimes several of these are present in a single creation, subtly blending, while in other dishes one flavor predominates. Most often, in addition to the obligatory bowl of rice, there will be a soup of some kind, a curry, a steamed dish, a fried one, a salad, and one or more of the basic sauces, probably based on *nam prik* and/or *nam pla.*

There is generally enough food to accommodate any unexpected guests who may drop in. All the dishes are placed on the table at the same time and can be eaten in no particular order. Nor are there any rigid rules about what goes with what: diners are free to mix dishes according to individual taste. Diners at the table serve themselves only one or two mouthfuls of a dish at a time, allowing everyone

A TRADITIONAL KITCHEN IN NORTHERN THAILAND

to share the same dishes. Serving plates are replenished as they empty. Dessert for a formal meal often consists of several dishes—usually fruit of some kind as well as a solid and a liquid sweet. Water and tea are still the most common liquid accompaniments, though a bottle of Thai whisky is often present at festive gatherings, to be drunk with soda and fresh lime juice.

The preferences of individual cooks will dictate how strongly the various flavors are emphasized. When using these recipes Western cooks may wish to alter them so that the flavors are sweeter, less salty or less hot. In the event that some of the ingredients may not be available outside Thailand (such as specific noodles), alternative suggestions and explanations are provided for the cook's benefit.

OUTDOOR RESTAURANTS ARE POPULAR WITH THAIS
AND TOURISTS ALIKE

THE NORTH

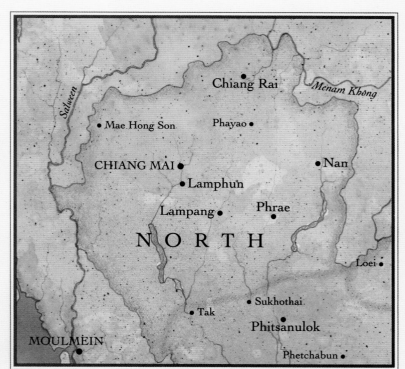

THE NORTH

L IKE OTHER PARTS OF MODERN THAILAND, the North is currently undergoing dramatic changes, most vividly apparent in the construction boom in once-quiet provincial capitals such as Chiang Mai and Chiang Rai and the network of new highways reaching far into the surrounding country-side. At the same time, however, the North retains a large measure of its traditional culture, in part because of geography but equally perhaps because of a long history that provides its people with a strong sense of their own identity. Even the most casual visitor immediately senses that there is some-thing "different" about the North—not just its weather, which is often much cooler than the rest of the country, but also its crafts, architecture, food, language, and everyday social behavior.

Bordered by Burma and Laos, the North is a rugged mountainous region rising to 8,451 feet (2,576 meters) at its highest point on the summit of Doi Inthanon and watered by a number of rivers including the Ping, the Wang, the Yom, the Nan, and the mighty Mekong. Once it was thickly forested with hardwood trees, particularly teak, and timber was a major source of wealth for Thai princes and, later, European companies which were granted concessions; but indiscriminate logging, together with an increasing demand for more arable land, has resulted in the destruction of much of the old-growth forest, though some tracts are preserved in national parks and serious efforts at reafforestation are being undertaken by the government.

CELEBRATING THAI NEW YEAR, SONGKRAN

PREVIOUS PAGES: LIMESTONE OUTCROPPINGS ON THE WAY FROM PHAYAO TO CHIANG RAI
LUCA INVERNIZZI TETTONI / PHOTOBANK

JOHN HAY

A RICE PLANTER WEARS A BROAD-BRIMMED HAT
FOR PROTECTION FROM THE SUN

PLANTING RICE SEEDLINGS IN CHIANG RAI PROVINCE

LUCA INVERNIZZI TETTONI / PHOTOBANK

It is a region of precipitous slopes, accessible only by good-weather trails, and verdant valleys where hamlets and rice fields are clustered along rivers and streams, of Buddhist temples flashing in the sunlight, and thick mists that roll suddenly down from the hills, obscuring everything. Nearly a thousand species of orchids are native to the North, festooning trees in the dry summer months with a spectrum of colors ranging from bright gold to rare blue. There are elephants, too, no longer roaming wild or being used for transport as in the not-so-distant past but still playing a vital role in what remains of the timber industry; a Young Elephant Training Center in Lampang province has a five-year course to teach student pachyderms such skills as dragging, carrying, pushing and stacking huge logs. In a few less-populated areas, especially near the Burmese border, there are still secret fields of pink opium poppies, tended by people in bizarre costumes that might have been taken from a medieval illustration.

Historically the culture of northern Thailand goes back to the seventh century when the Mons, an ethnic group who had already established important city-states in the Central Plains region, founded a kingdom called Haripunchai in the valley of the Ping River. Located on the site of the present-day town of Lamphun, this was an important religious center whose artistic influence continued long after its power waned. The Thais began arriving later—exactly when is a matter of scholarly dispute—and became predominant in the

CHIANG MAI AT DUSK. THE CITY STILL RETAINS
PARTS OF THE OLD WALLS AND MOATS

mid-thirteenth century, when one of them, King Mengrai, embarked on an ambitious campaign to unite the whole of the northern region under his rule.

Beginning in his home principality on the bank of the Mekong River, King Mengrai moved southward, founding first Chiang Rai as his capital in 1262 and then Chiang Mai in 1297. According to northern chronicles he was killed by a bolt of lightning in 1317, having ruled for more than fifty years and having established a kingdom that would control the region for the next two centuries.

Chiang Mai was the heart of Lanna, as the kingdom was known, and during its golden age around the middle of the fifteenth century it was celebrated for its Buddhist scholarship, its splendid temples, and the skills of its superb artisans. The famous Emerald Buddha, a small green jadeite image now enshrined at Wat Phra Keo in Bangkok, is believed to be of Lanna origin, probably produced by a Chiang Mai sculptor. Even today Chiang Mai has an exceptionally large number of monasteries—more than a hundred scattered through the metropolitan area—and it is also still the principal source of Thailand's best handicrafts.

Despite its cultural achievements, the Lanna kingdom was often at war, sometimes with another rising Thai state of Ayutthaya to the south, but more often with neighboring Burma. Beginning in 1558 the North entered two centuries of domination by the Burmese who, while they never actually occupied the region in the military sense, neverthe-

less appointed local chiefs to carry out their orders and exerted a strong cultural influence which is reflected today in northern art and food. In 1774 King Kawila of Lampang, a city not far from Chiang Mai, managed to regain Lanna independence, but only for a short time; he soon pledged his allegiance to King Rama I, founder of Bangkok, and technically at least the North became a part of the Thai kingdom.

Administrative control, however, remained weak during most of the nineteenth century and to some degree well into the twentieth. This was mainly because of the difficulty of getting from Bangkok to Chiang Mai, which lay on the other side of a formidable mountain chain that effectively sealed off the North from the Central Plains region. During the rainy season the journey took fifty-five days by river, buffalo cart, and elephant back, and even in the dry months it required thirty-five days of hard travel.

Among the few outsiders willing to undergo such discomforts were a small group of American Protestant missionaries, who established the first schools and hospitals while also managing to convert more locals to Christianity than anywhere else in Thailand. Another early visitor, in 1883, was a Danish traveler named Carl Bock, who referred to Chiang Mai as "the most powerful of all the Lao states" and found that real power remained in the hands of local princes, descendants of the ancient Lanna royalty. Bock paid a visit to the daily Chiang Mai market, where "as in the island of Bali, the women do all the selling. They all sit on the ground, with a basket on each side of them, sometimes with the contents emptied out and spread on a couple of plantain-leaves. The principal articles offered for sale are provisions, fruits and vegetables; tobacco, betel-nuts, and lime; fish, dried salted, and stewed, but always more or less stinking; buffalo-meat, and pieces of buffalo-hide, also eaten and considered good; ... mushrooms, of which the Laotians are very fond; wax and cotton; earthenware pots, jars and jugs, so brittle they almost break at a touch; and always a good stock of flowers that would be the envy of a Parisian."

Later during his stay Carl Bock was invited to dinner with the highest ranking "Chow", or prince. He was surprised to find that the meal included potatoes, "which had been introduced along with other vegetables into this country by the American missionaries, and which the Chow ate with great relish, helping himself to them sans ceremonie, in the good old-fashioned peasant style, and blowing his fingers to keep them cool".

Not until the northern railway line reached Chiang Mai in 1921—a major feat of engineering by any standard—did central Thais begin to come north in any appreciable numbers, and it was not until 1928 that the people of the North gained their first glimpse of their ruler, when King Rama VII came on a royal visit, riding through the city on a splendidly caparisoned elephant.

This long period of isolation explains many of the characteristics that so impress visitors to the North today, for it meant that its people were relatively unexposed to the changes going on elsewhere in the country, and their own customs and traditions remained strong for much longer.

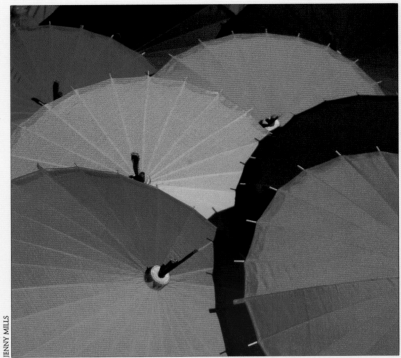

BRIGHTLY PAINTED PAPER UMBRELLAS ARE MADE BY LOCALS ON THE OUTSKIRTS OF CHIANG MAI

Language and manners are two notable examples. Northern Thai even today differs from that spoken in the Central Plains region (about as much as Spanish does from Portuguese), and as used in daily life it contains a greater number of polite expressions and sounds much more soothing to the ear. Northern Thais themselves are renowned for their gentle ways and hospitality to strangers; an old custom of the region, still widely practiced, is the placing of an earthenware jar of cool water outside houses so any thirsty passerby can refresh himself. Observe, too, the smiles that still flash so readily even in busy cities, the friendliness of vendors in marketplaces, the willingness to assist in countless small ways. On the rare occasion when impolite behavior is encountered, the offender will almost always turn out to be an outsider, and when northerners have to go to Bangkok for one reason or another they are usually shocked by its brash impersonal ways. The people of Chiang Mai in particular have a tendency to look down disapprovingly on the bumptious residents of the far younger capital, often protesting loudly (sometimes successfully) when the latter attempt to intrude with their money-making innovations.

All Thais attach great importance to the pursuit of *sanuk*—a term usually translated as "fun", though in fact covering a far wider range of pleasures—but northerners seem to go much further and with more exuberance than almost anybody else. Loi Krathong, for instance, the loveliest of traditional Thai festivals, when little lighted boats are set adrift in rivers and canals to pay homage to the water spirits, is in other regions merely a one-night affair in November—*sanuk*, to be sure, but not a major interruption to daily life. In Chiang Mai, three full days are devoted to the festivities and almost the entire city participates in some way, along with thousands of visitors who book hotel rooms months in advance. Similarly, both the Western and the old Thai New Year's celebrations are major events in the North, with shows, gala parades, and contests to select a beauty queen. Some occasions are purely local and give the impression of having been organized mainly to provide a pleasant break in routine: the Chiang Mai Flower Festival, for instance, when blossom-bedecked floats stop city traffic; or the Lamphun

TAPAE ROAD IS THE BUSIEST STREET IN CHIANG MAI, NORTHERN THAILAND'S CULTURAL AND COMMERCIAL CENTER

MONKS SWEEPING THE COURTYARD AT WAT PHRA DOI KHONG MU IN MAE HONG SON

JENNY MILLS

A GROUP OF YOUNG GIRLS IN EMBROIDERED COSTUMES
AT ONE OF THE MANY REGIONAL FESTIVALS

EATING A KHANTOKE DINNER, THE TRADITIONAL NORTHERN
MEAL. SOMETIMES A RED LACQUERWARE TABLE IS USED

JENNY MILLS

Garlic Festival, where the climax comes with the choice of *Nang Kratiem*, or "Miss Garlic", and her crowning with a garland of pungent bulbs.

Even religious observances there have an added zest. About a third of Thailand's 27,000 Buddhist temples are in the North, and at the end of the rainy season it is hard to go anywhere in the region without coming across one or more *thot kathin*, merit-making ceremonies when groups of people present new robes and other necessities to monks, usually in out-of-the-way monasteries. Solemn as they are essentially, these too are nevertheless still opportunities for *sanuk* in the form of music, dancing, and convivial meals prepared by outstanding local cooks.

Like nearly all traditional Thai houses, those of the North are elevated from the ground on stout pillars, offering protection from floods and wild animals as well as a working area below, but they differ from the airy Central Plains style in a number of significant respects. The prefabricated walls slant outward rather than inward, the windows are smaller, and the overall effect is that of a sturdier structure built for life in a cooler climate. The roof-peaks, especially of houses in the Chiang Mai area, are often adorned with a graceful V-shaped decoration which is unique to the region and may once have had magical significance. Temples are often different, too, with their lavish woodcarvings and frequent use of Burmese ornamental techniques.

Northern cuisine also remains quite distinctive. Instead of the soft, boiled rice of the Central Plains region, northerners

A HILLTRIBE VILLAGE ON DOI MAE SALONG, THE NORTHERNMOST
POINT OF THAILAND, AT THE BORDER WITH BURMA

A YOUNG MONK PLAYS WITH A ROOSTER DURING
A QUIET MOMENT AT A CHIANG MAI TEMPLE

prefer a steamed glutinous variety and traditionally eat it with the fingers, kneading small handfuls into balls with which to scoop up more liquid dishes. (As well as the white variety of glutinous rice there is also one with black grains, which has a nutty flavor reminiscent of American wild rice, but Thais usually eat this sweetened as a dessert.)

Coconut milk, which is widely used as an ingredient in much of central and southern Thai cooking, plays an insignificant role in the North, where the curries tend to be clear rather than thickened.

The fondness for *khao neow*, or "steamed sticky rice", reflects the influence of neighboring Laos, as do the northern versions of *nam prik*, that basic sauce that accompanies every Thai meal, which range from a relatively mild minced pork and tomato mixture (*nam prik ong*) to a fiery *nam prik tadaeng* composed mainly of dried red chilies. Burmese influence is evident as well, particularly in such popular dishes as *gaeng hang lay*, a pork curry that employs ginger, tamarind and turmeric for its distinctive flavor, and *khao soi*, a curry broth with egg noodles and chicken, pork or beef, topped with shallots, pickled vegetables and slices of lime. One of the favorite regional specialties is *naem*, a spicy pork sausage eaten in a wide variety of ways and probably the delicacy northerners miss most when they move away. While some are highly seasoned, the curries and salads (*yams*) of the North are generally milder than those of central and northeastern Thailand, although chili-hot sauces are always available for those who want a stronger flavor.

JENNY MILLS

285

JENNY MILLS

THE NAGA IS THE MYTHICAL KING OF SERPENTS. THESE TWO
CARVED NAGAS ARE ON A CHIANG MAI TEMPLE BALUSTRADE

Other northern foods are perhaps best appreciated by true connoisseurs: crisply fried cicadas, for example, or cow's placenta (a much-prized treat in Phayao province), or a version of *laab* consisting of minced raw buffalo meat, pulverized rice, chilies, mint and a dash of buffalo bile to provide the bitter flavor common to many traditional dishes of the region. Popular, too, is the giant waterbeetle called *maengda*, which when pounded in a mortar adds an aromatic flavor to certain dishes; the beetles are also eaten fried or, when out of season, pickled. Some of the tribal people who live in the mountains are quite partial to dog meat and raise a black chow-like variety in order to have a guaranteed supply on hand for feast days.

The traditional form of meal in the North, especially when guests are being entertained, is the *khantoke* dinner—*khan*, meaning "bowl", and *toke* a low round table made of woven bamboo, or, in a fancier version, red lacquerware. Diners sit on the floor around the table and help themselves to assorted dishes placed on it, in no particular order. Glutinous rice is always provided, and nowadays ordinary rice as well, along with one or two curries, a minced-meat dish, a salad, raw and pickled vegetables, fried pork rind, and a variety of sauces and condiments. Dessert will generally be fruit—most memorably, if it is in season, the succulent lychee-like longan, harvested from the trees that grow in almost every compound. Longan, known in Thai as *lamyai*, is sent all over the country during August and September and also exported by air to fanciers in Singapore and Hong Kong.

In central Thailand, particularly in Bangkok, one significant result of increased relations with the West during the nineteenth century was a rapid decline of local handicrafts. Wealthy families who had once maintained their own personal groups of artisans—weavers and woodcarvers, goldsmiths and jewelers—turned to the European goods that began flooding the markets, prompted partly by a desire for novelty and partly by the fact that their rulers were urging Westernization as proof that Thailand was a "civilized" country and thus not ripe for colonization.

Few of these innovations reached the remote North, where artisans continued to produce their ancient crafts and to hand down their skills through the generations. There were the silversmiths who hammered out the thin, exquisitely decorated bowls used in so many regional rituals; the woodcarvers who produced the elaborate panels, sometimes inlaid with pieces of colored glass, that adorned every temple; the lacquerware makers who wove delicate objects of bamboo and then patiently applied coat after coat of thin resin to achieve the desired thickness; the weavers who used primitive looms to create shimmering lengths of brocaded silk, often in patterns so intricate that months were required to complete a single piece. Moreover, there were specialists in pottery and fine rice paper, jewelry and hand-painted umbrellas, embroidery and bronze-casting.

All these have survived to the present day, often in the same villages that produced them a century ago. Chiang Mai's famous Night Bazaar offers a wide selection of northern crafts, which has made it one of the region's leading tourist attractions, and there are numerous "factories"—often nothing more than a few simple sheds—in which the various processes can be observed. Such skills are playing a significant role in the modern regional economy, as evidenced by a visit to the subdistrict of Hang Dong, just outside Chiang Mai, where hundreds of artisans are busily turning out furniture and woodcarvings for wholesale exporters with clients throughout the world.

Among the most exotic sights of the far North are the tribal people who live in the hills. There are seven principal tribes—Karen, Hmong (Meo), Akha, Lahu, Lawa, Lisu, and Yao—and their numbers have been variously estimated at somewhere between 250,000 and 500,000. Arriving at a precise figure would be all but impossible, however, for by nature most of the groups are nomadic and move more or less freely across national borders. Each has its own distinctive culture, differing not only in language and racial origin, but also, most vividly, in their costumes. Yao women, for instance, are noted for their skill at embroidery and wear elaborately decorated loose trousers, huge indigo turbans, and a bright pink boa-like puff around the neck. Those of the Lisu tribe favor bold red and turquoise dresses and, during festivals, spectacular silver jewelry that covers them almost like a suit of armor, while the Hmong are gifted at producing subtly patterned batik cloth and display their wealth by wearing masses of silver ornaments.

In previous times the members of these tribes rarely descended to towns from their lofty homes, and only a few intrepid missionaries bothered to learn much about their lifestyles. Today they are far more visible, partly because of a growing demand for their distinctive crafts but more because their presence has given rise to a number of problems, both social and ecological.

ELEPHANTS ARE NO LONGER USED AS PACK ANIMALS, BUT
IN THE HILLS THEY ARE STILL SOMETIMES USED TO HAUL LOGS

The traditional tribal cash crop—indeed, for many, the only means of earning any money at all—was opium poppy, refined in secret factories by middlemen and smuggled out as heroin to dealers of the West. Equally harmful in terms of Thailand's future was their slash-and-burn method of clearing forests for the poppy fields, working the thin soil until it was exhausted and then moving on to a new location, leaving behind a trail of wasted, eroded slopes.

It was Thailand's King Bhumibol Adulyadej who first called attention to these destructive practices in the late 1960s. Traveling extensively by helicopter, jeep, and foot through the region from his palace atop Doi Suthep overlooking Chiang Mai, the King visited numerous tribal sites and eventually established a pioneering Royal Project to bring them better social welfare and introduce alternative crops to replace the poppy. As a result, although opium continues to be grown in Burma and Laos (and to transit illegally through Thailand), Thai production has fallen from a high of about 250 tons (250 tonnes) a year during the 1970s to only about 15–30 tons (15–30 tonnes). More and more hill tribes have now settled in permanent villages with schools and adequate medical services, and they earn a better living through the cultivation of coffee, strawberries, peaches, and such temperate-zone vegetables as asparagus, kidney beans, and lettuce. Thanks to processing facilities and improved transportation, these are now adding to the variety of Bangkok markets as well as being exported as fresh and canned products and so earning money for the country.

In addition the hill tribes have been assisted by Queen Sirikit, who popularized their crafts by using them prominently in her own fashions and also opened training centers for artisans through her SUPPORT Foundation.

Tourism is now the major source of income in the North, with Chiang Mai as the focal point. Whereas three decades ago there were only one or two proper hotels in the city, now there are dozens, along with an even greater number of condominiums and housing projects catering to people from Bangkok who want a place for holidays during the cool winter months. The impact is also being felt much further afield: in the once-mysterious "Golden Triangle", where warlords battled for control of the opium traffic and where resorts with views of three national borders are now rising; and in the scenic valley of Mae Hong Sorn, formerly known as "the Siberia of Thailand" because it was regarded as a suitably remote place to exile erring officials, although now it is only a short plane trip from Chiang Mai. Trekkers with backpacks are exploring the slopes of Doi Inthanon, and tour groups are thrilling to the novelty of a two-hour elephant ride in the jungle.

For all its recent development, however, the North is still probably Thailand's most distinctive region, with a culture that has so far proved remarkably resistant to change. Its "differences", which derive in part from Burmese and Lao influences, are undoubtedly its most valuable asset, making it a place where Thais as well as foreign visitors go in search of traditional customs that have been diluted elsewhere.

SOUPS AND APPETIZERS

PREPARING SNACKS AT A BUSY MARKET

LUCA INVERNIZZI TETTONI / PHOTOBANK

SOUPS AND APPETIZERS

THE THAIS "snack" all through the day and into the night and so in the city and village markets streetside vendors offer a multitude of good things to eat. Some dishes are small, others, like the popular noodle dishes, are more substantial and can even make a meal in themselves: all can be regarded as snacks to eat separately or as appetizers forming the first part of a meal. Appetizers, snacks, hors d'oeuvres—however you treat them, they are delicious.

Stir-fried Thai noodles *(pad thai)* are often served as an appetizer in Thai restaurants. This is a colorful dish of fried rice noodles and shrimp accompanied by fresh vegetables like crispy bean sprouts and banana blossoms.

Another appetizer which will tantalize the palate is fish cakes *(taud man pla)*, which are especially good when served with refreshing cucumber salad *(tam taeng)*.

Satay, yet another popular appetizer, consists of curry-marinated chicken or beef strips charcoal-broiled on skewers. They are usually served with a peanut dipping sauce *(nam jim satay)* although other sauces can be served.

The huge variety of appetizers means that, whatever dishes are served later in the meal, a complementary appetizer can be served first, to ready the diner for the taste sensations to follow. Unlike Western-style cuisine, soup is not served as an appetizer in a Thai meal.

While a soup dish is included in a full Thai meal to provide liquid refreshment throughout the meal, soup is

LUCA INVERNIZZI TETTONI / PHOTOBANK

PREVIOUS PAGES: SPICY MIXED VEGETABLE SOUP (TOP, RECIPE PAGE 292), CHICKEN COCONUT SOUP (BOTTOM, RECIPE PAGE 292) AND RICE SOUP WITH SHRIMP (RIGHT, RECIPE PAGE 293)

290

A WOMAN SELLING HATS ON A KLONG TAKES A FEW MOMENTS OFF TO ENJOY A BOWL OF SOUP

AN EAGER CUSTOMER MAKING A SELECTION FROM A
TEMPTING ARRAY OF DISHES AT A MARKET STALL

also used as a snack or a meal on its own. Rice soup is a favorite light nourishment at both the beginning and end of the day. Rice soup with pork *(khao tom moo)* and glass noodle soup *(gaeng jued woon sen)* are popular for breakfast. These and other light soups like Thai wonton soup *(geow nam moo)* are also used as snacks or as a light luncheon dish. Thai wonton soup contains wontons cooked in a thin salty stock, with bok choy and bean sprouts spiced up with green onions, cilantro and fried garlic.

Other soups served at lunchtime are more substantial. Red Sea noodles *(yen ta fo)*, for example, is a striking noodle soup. A mouthful initially resonates with a salty and sour tone, punctuated by a slight note of sweetness. *Yen ta fo* contains pork, fish cakes, squid and fried wontons and is garnished with fried garlic.

A soup dish is also an essential part of a full Thai meal. Diners refresh their palates with small sips in-between the flavors of the various other dishes. A full Thai meal is an ensemble of distinctive flavors: the citrus freshness of lemon grass, mint and kaffir lime leaf; the aromatic freshness imparted by spices such as cardamon, star anise, turmeric and cinnamon; the pungency of garlic, ginger, cilantro and basil; and the fierce bite of chilies and pepper.

Soups play an important role in this symphony of flavors. Hot and sour shrimp soup *(tom yam goong)*, for example, gives a taste that is sour, savory and hot. This

TRAYS OF BITE-SIZED SAVORY APPETIZERS FOR SALE
ON A ROADSIDE CART IN BANGKOK

refreshing and tart soup includes lemon grass and fresh lime juice. Tamarind flavor soup *(gaeng som pla chon)* is an orange-colored fish soup containing swamp cabbage. The color derives from dried chili peppers and the subtle sourness comes from tamarind juice. Another popular soup, chicken coconut soup *(tom kha gai)* bathes tender pieces of chicken in the silky creaminess of coconut milk. The "kha" in the name refers to galangal, a root which resembles ginger in appearance but its inimitable flavor contains a mint-like jolt.

291

FRIED EGG SOUP

Bangkok and the Central Plains

GAENG JUED KAI

แกงจืดไข่

Fried Egg Soup

Easy to prepare, this mild-flavored soup is a good accompaniment for any meal.

¼ cup (2 fl oz/60 ml) oil
4 garlic cloves (*kratiem*), chopped
½ cup chopped onions
6 eggs, beaten
6 cups (1½ qt/1.5 l) water
8 oz (250 g) pork, thinly sliced in 2-in (5-cm) lengths
⅓ cup (3 fl oz/90 ml) fish sauce (*nam pla*)
1 cup sliced cabbage
2 green onions/scallions/spring onions, cut into 1-in (2.5-cm) slices
¼ teaspoon white pepper

▩ Heat a small skillet and add half the oil. Fry the garlic until golden brown. Set aside the garlic, then fry the onion.
▩ In another small skillet, add the rest of the oil and fry the beaten eggs until golden brown, about 2 minutes on each side. Remove carefully, keeping in one piece, and set aside. When cool, cut into 1-in x 2-in (2.5-cm x 5-cm) strips.
▩ In a large saucepan, heat the water to boiling and add the pork. Reheat to boiling and when the pork is cooked add the egg strips, onion and the remaining ingredients. Remove to a serving bowl and top with the fried garlic before serving.

SERVES 4

Bangkok and the Central Plains

TOM KHA GAI

ต้มข่าไก่

Chicken Coconut Soup

A rich, aromatic dinner soup, which is enjoyed throughout the meal. Whenever possible, fresh kaffir lime leaves should be used, and their flavor and aroma is increased when they are torn instead of cut with a knife. Young galangal (kha orn) is pale yellow, with firm unwrinkled pink shoots. Fresh young ginger can be substituted if necessary, but the flavor will not be quite the same.

2 cups (16 fl oz/500 ml) coconut milk
6 thin slices young galangal (*kha orn*)
2 stalks lemon grass/citronella (*ta-krai*), lower ⅓ portion only, cut into 1-in (2.5-cm) lengths and crushed
5 fresh kaffir lime leaves (*bai ma-grood*), torn in half
8 oz (250 g) boned chicken breast, sliced
5 tablespoons (2½ fl oz/75 ml) fish sauce (*nam pla*)
2 tablespoons sugar
½ cup (4 fl oz/125 ml) lime juice
1 teaspoon black chili paste (*nam prik pow*) (see page 493)
¼ cup cilantro/coriander leaves (*bai pak chee*), torn
5 green Thai chili peppers (*prik khee noo*), crushed

▩ Combine half the coconut milk with the galangal, lemon grass and lime leaves in a large saucepan and heat to boiling. Add the chicken, fish sauce and sugar.
▩ Simmer for about 4 minutes, or until the chicken is cooked. Add the remaining coconut milk to the saucepan and heat just to boiling.
▩ Place the lime juice and chili paste in a serving bowl then pour the soup into the serving bowl.
▩ Garnish with the torn cilantro leaves and crushed chili peppers, and serve.

SERVES 4 *Photograph pages 288–289*

Bangkok and the Central Plains

GAENG LIANG

แกงเลียง

Spicy Mixed Vegetable Soup

A traditional soup, which in some variations is extremely hot and spicy. This version, however, is quite mild.

½ cup fresh shrimp/prawn meat, chopped
½ cup dried shrimp/prawns, chopped
8 shallots, chopped
2 tablespoons shrimp paste (*gapi*)
1 teaspoon white pepper
⅓ cup (3 fl oz/90 ml) fish sauce (*nam pla*)
4 cups (1 qt/1 l) water
½ cup chopped spinach, in 3-in (7.5-cm) lengths
½ firm fresh yellow gourd, cut into ½-in (1-cm) wedges
¼ cup bush basil leaves (*bai manglak*)

▩ Place the fresh and dried shrimp, shallots, shrimp paste and pepper in a mortar. Pound with a pestle until smooth. A blender can also be used.
▩ Place the fish sauce and water in a large saucepan, heat to boiling and add the blended mixture and the other ingredients. Stir thoroughly, bring to the boil and cook for 3 minutes. Remove to a soup tureen and serve.

SERVES 4 *Photograph pages 288–289*

DRIED FISH BELLY SOUP, GARNISHED WITH DRIED PUFFY PORKSKIN

Bangkok and the Central Plains

KHAO TOM GOONG

ข้าวต้มกุ้ง

Rice Soup with Shrimp

Rice soups are easy to prepare. Cooked rice is usually used, although uncooked rice will produce the same result, only over longer time. The use of different types of shellfish or fish can provide endless variations of this flavorful dish.

2 cups (16 fl oz/500 ml) water
2 stalks celery, chopped
¼ teaspoon white pepper
1 tablespoon Maggi seasoning
8 oz (250 g) shrimp/prawns, shelled, deveined
  and butterflied
1 cup steamed jasmine rice (*khao suay*) (see page 350)
2 tablespoons fish sauce (*nam pla*)
2 tablespoons oil
1 teaspoon thinly sliced garlic cloves (*kratiem*)
cilantro/coriander leaves (*bai pak chee*), for garnish

▓ Heat the water to boiling in a large saucepan and add the chopped celery, white pepper and Maggi seasoning.
▓ Add the shrimp, rice and fish sauce.
▓ Heat to boiling and cook for 3 minutes, or until shrimp are cooked.
▓ Heat the oil in a small skillet and sauté the garlic until golden brown.
▓ Serve the soup with the fried garlic sprinkled over it and garnished with cilantro leaves.

SERVES 4   *Photograph pages 288–289*

Bangkok and the Central Plains

KAPAW PLA

กระเพาะปลา

Dried Fish Belly Soup

If fish belly is difficult to find you can substitute with dried puffy porkskin instead.

4 cups (1qt/1 l) water
1 whole chicken breast, about 1 lb (500 g)
8 oz (250 g) dried fish belly/fish maw, soaked in hot
  water until soft
⅓ cup (3 fl oz/90 ml) light soy sauce
1 tablespoon sweet soy sauce
½ cup bamboo shoot strips (see glossary)
¼ teaspoon white pepper
4 small hard-cooked/hard-boiled eggs, shelled and sliced
¼ cup cilantro/coriander leaves (*bai pak chee*), minced

▓ Heat the water to boiling in a large saucepan and simmer the chicken breast for about 10–15 minutes or until done. Reserve the chicken stock.
▓ Place the cooked chicken breast in cold water to·cool. Remove the meat from the bone and discard the skin. Shred the meat and set aside.
▓ Drain the dried fish belly, squeeze out any excess water and cut into 1-in (2.5-cm) pieces.
▓ Heat the chicken stock to boiling, add the dried fish belly and all the remaining ingredients except the eggs and the cilantro. Stir in the shredded chicken and cook until hot. Pour into a serving bowl and garnish with egg slices and cilantro.

SERVES 4

CRISPY FISH SPICY SOUP

Bangkok and the Central Plains

Tom Yam Pla Grob

ต้มยำปลากรอบ

Crispy Fish Spicy Soup

In earlier times catfish were brought in from Cambodia. Today the grilled crispy fish are sold in markets throughout Thailand.

3 cups (24 fl oz/750 ml) water
8 oz (250 g) grilled crispy fish (see glossary)
4 thin slices galangal *(kha)*
4 shallots
4 dried jalapeño peppers *(prik chee fa haeng)*
2 garlic cloves *(kratiem)*
2 stalks lemon grass/citronella *(ta-krai)*, halved
⅓ cup (3 fl oz/90 ml) fish sauce *(nam pla)*
½ cup (4 fl oz/125 ml) tamarind juice *(ma-kaam piag)*
   (see glossary)

▨ Heat the water to boiling in a large saucepan. Meanwhile, break the fish into 2-in (5-cm) pieces.
▨ Place the galangal, shallots, peppers, garlic and lemon grass on top of a charcoal grill and broil/grill until they are slightly burned. Allow to cool then crush using a mortar and pestle.
▨ Add with the fish and all the other ingredients to the boiling water and simmer for 20 minutes.

SERVES 4

Bangkok and the Central Plains

Gaeng Jued Pakkaad Dong

แกงจืดผักกาดดอง

Chinese Mustard Pickle Soup

Sips of soup between other dishes cleanse the palate for the interplay of flavors that is so much a part of a Thai meal. This one is a very refreshing soup. Chinese mustard pickles are available from Asian food stores.

1 tablespoon oil
4 garlic cloves *(kratiem)*, minced
4 cups (1 qt/1 l) water
1 lb (500 g) pork ribs, cut into 2-in (5-cm) pieces
1 lb (500 g) Chinese mustard pickle, cut into 2-in
   (5-cm) pieces
¼ cup (2 fl oz/60 ml) fish sauce *(nam pla)*
¼ teaspoon white pepper

▨ Heat a small skillet and add the oil. Stir-fry the garlic until golden brown. Reserve the garlic.
▨ Heat the water to boiling and add the pork ribs. Cover and simmer for 15 minutes.
▨ Mix in the Chinese mustard pickle pieces, the fish sauce and the pepper, stirring until warmed through.
▨ Remove to a serving bowl and top with the fried garlic.

SERVES 4

CHINESE MUSTARD PICKLE SOUP (BOTTOM) AND
THAI WONTON SOUP (TOP, RECIPE PAGE 296)

Bangkok and the Central Plains

GEOW NAM MOO

เกี๊ยวน้ำหมู

Thai Wonton Soup

Wonton soup is a delicious light meal. Both the wonton fillings and the soup vegetables can be varied according to personal preference.

2 tablespoons oil
2 tablespoons chopped garlic cloves *(kratiem)*

FILLING FOR WONTONS

8 oz (250 g) ground/minced pork
1 teaspoon chopped garlic cloves *(kratiem)*
¼ teaspoon white pepper
1 teaspoon Maggi seasoning
2 tablespoons fish sauce *(nam pla)*

8 oz (250 g) wonton wrappers
6 cups (1½ qt/1.5 l) water
1 lb (500 g) pork or chicken bones
3 tablespoons fish sauce *(nam pla)*
1 teaspoon salt
8 oz (250 g) bok choy, cut into 1-in (2.5-cm)
   lengths, diagonally
8 oz (250 g) bean sprouts
2 green onions/scallions/spring onions, cut into 1-in
   (2.5-cm) lengths
¼ cup chopped cilantro/coriander leaves *(bai pak chee)*

▨ Heat the oil in a small skillet and fry the garlic until golden brown. Set aside.
▨ Combine the filling ingredients. Fill each wonton wrapper with 1 heaped teaspoon of filling then fold it in half, sealing the edges with water. To complete the wonton, form some pleats by pinching the edge above the meat filling.
▨ Heat the water to boiling in a large saucepan and simmer the pork bones for 5 minutes. Discard the bones, reserving the stock.
▨ Heat another large pot of water to boiling. Add the wontons and cook for 30 seconds, then remove them with a strainer and add directly to the stock from the bones. Add the fish sauce and salt.
▨ Add the bok choy and reheat the soup to boiling.
▨ To serve, put a small bed of bean sprouts in a soup tureen. Spoon in the wonton soup and garnish with green onions and cilantro. Sprinkle with the fried garlic.

SERVES 4   *Photograph page 295*

Bangkok and the Central Plains

POH TAEK

โป๊ะแตก

Seafood Combination Soup

Vary this dish by adding or substituting other seafoods and adapting the number of chili peppers to taste. Its lovely aroma comes from the galangal and kaffir lime leaves.

2 ½ cups (20 fl oz/625 ml) water
2 stalks lemon grass/citronella *(ta-krai)*, cut into 1-in
   (2.5-cm) slices
6 thin slices galangal *(kha)*
6 kaffir lime leaves *(bai ma-grood)*, torn in half

TAMARIND FLAVOR SOUP (LEFT) AND
SEAFOOD COMBINATION SOUP (RIGHT)

3–4 green Thai chili peppers *(prik khee noo)*
2 green jalapeño peppers *(prik chee fa)*
4 oz (250 g) white fish fillets, cut into ½-in x 2-in (1-cm x
   5-cm) pieces
4 oz (250 g) squid, cleaned, scored and sliced
4 oz (250 g) large shrimp/prawns, with shells
4 oz (250 g) small crabs (2 small crabs), cleaned and cut in
   half with top shell removed
4 oz (250 g) mussels
4 oz (250 g) clams
3 oyster mushrooms, sliced
¼ cup (2 fl oz/60 ml) fish sauce *(nam pla)*
¼ cup (2 fl oz/60 ml) lime juice

▨ In a large saucepan heat the water, lemon grass, galangal, lime leaves and peppers to boiling.
▨ Add the prepared fish fillets, squid, shrimp, crabs, mussels, clams and mushrooms and boil for 30 seconds. Reduce the temperature and add the fish sauce and lime juice and stir carefully.
▨ Remove to an attractive serving bowl.

SERVES 4

GAENG SOM PLA CHON

แกงส้มปลาช่อน

Tamarind Flavor Soup

Gaeng som pla chon *is orange in color, with a sour and sweet taste given by the tamarind used in the recipe. This should be served with fried* sun-dried fish (pla kem taud)*, on page 374, and steamed jasmine rice* (khao suay)*, on page 350.*

1½ lb (750 g) whole snapper
4 cups (1 qt/1 l) water
4 garlic cloves (kratiem)
8 shallots
6 large dried red jalapeño peppers (prik chee fa haeng)
1 teaspoon shrimp paste (gapi)
1 teaspoon salt
¼ cup (2 fl oz/60 ml) fish sauce (nam pla)

2 tablespoons sugar
⅓ cup (3 fl oz/90 ml) tamarind juice (ma-kaam piag) (see glossary)
8 oz (250 g) swamp cabbage or spinach, cut in 1-in (2.5-cm) lengths

▨ Clean the snapper and discard the head of the fish. Cut the fish in half and cut 4 steaks from the top half.
▨ Heat the water to boiling in a large pot and cook the tail half of the fish for about 5 minutes. Remove the fish, keeping aside the stock. Take the flesh off the fish and discard the other parts.
▨ Combine the flesh from the fish with the garlic, shallots, peppers, shrimp paste and salt in a processor and blend well.
▨ Heat the fish stock to boiling and add the fish steaks and the blended ingredients along with the fish sauce, sugar and tamarind juice. Cook at a slow boil until the fish steaks are done. When the fish steaks are cooked, add the swamp cabbage and cook until just done (about 15 seconds).
▨ Serve in individual bowls.

SERVES 4

RICE SOUP WITH PORK (LEFT) AND GLASS NOODLE SOUP (RIGHT)

Bangkok and the Central Plains
GAENG JUED WOON SEN

แกงจืดวุ้นเส้น

Glass Noodle Soup

The glass, or cellophane, noodles become translucent when cooked, giving this soup a most attractive appearance.

MARINADE

1 tablespoon fish sauce (*nam pla*)
1 tablespoon Maggi seasoning
2 garlic cloves (*kratiem*), minced
¼ teaspoon white pepper
1 teaspoon cornstarch/cornflour

8 oz (250 g) ground/minced pork
1 tablespoon oil
2 garlic cloves (*kratiem*), minced
4 cups (1 qt/1 l) water
2 oz (60 g) dried cellophane noodles (*woon sen*), soaked in
　　warm water until soft
¼ cup (2 fl oz/60 ml) fish sauce (*nam pla*)
1 cup sliced cabbage
2 green onions/scallions/spring onions, cut into 1-in
　　(2.5-cm) pieces
¼ cup minced cilantro/coriander leaves (*bai pak chee*)
¼ teaspoon white pepper

▨ Mix together the ingredients for the marinade, then combine with the pork. Form the mixture into 1-in (2.5-cm) diameter meatballs, and set aside.
▨ Heat the oil in a small skillet and fry the garlic until light golden brown. Remove, drain, and set aside.
▨ Heat the water to boiling in a large saucepan, add the meatballs and reheat to boiling. Continue to cook until the meatballs rise to the surface. Add all the remaining ingredients except the fried garlic and heat to boiling. Carefully pour into a soup tureen and scatter the fried garlic on top.

SERVES 4

Bangkok and the Central Plains
KHAO TOM MOO

ข้าวต้มหมู

Rice Soup with Pork

A rice soup such as this one is usually the most substantial part of a Thai breakfast.

2 cups (16 fl oz/500 ml) water
1 tablespoon Maggi seasoning
¼ teaspoon white pepper
½ teaspoon galangal powder (*kha pon*)
2 stalks celery, chopped
8 oz (250 g) ground/minced pork
1 cup steamed jasmine rice (*khao suay*) (see page 350)
2 tablespoons fish sauce (*nam pla*)
2 tablespoons oil
1 teaspoon sliced garlic (*kratiem*)
cilantro/coriander leaves (*bai pak chee*), for garnish

▨ Heat the water to boiling in a large pot and add the Maggi seasoning, white pepper, galangal powder and chopped celery.
▨ Add the pork, rice and fish sauce. Stir thoroughly so that the ground pork is broken up, then heat to boiling and simmer until the pork is cooked.
▨ Heat the oil in a small skillet and fry the garlic on medium-high heat until golden brown.
▨ Carefully pour the rice soup into a serving bowl. Sprinkle the fried garlic slices over the top of the soup, and garnish with the cilantro leaves.

SERVES 4

Bangkok and the Central Plains
KHAO TOM PLA GAPONG

ข้าวต้มปลากะพง

Rice Soup with Red Snapper

This is a good dish for a light luncheon or snack, providing energy without being too heavy.

3 tablespoons oil
6 garlic cloves (*kratiem*), chopped
4 cups (1 qt/1 l) water
½ teaspoon powdered galangal (*kha pon*)
1 lb (500 g) red snapper or other firm-fleshed fish fillets,
　　cut in 1-in (2.5 cm) slices
2 cups cooked rice
1 cup chopped celery
½ teaspoon white pepper
⅓ cup (3 fl oz/90 ml) fish sauce (*nam pla*)
¼ cup chopped green onions/scallions/spring onions
¼ cup chopped cilantro/coriander leaves (*bai pak chee*)

▨ Heat a small saucepan and add the oil and garlic. Stir-fry the garlic until golden brown, remove the pan from the heat and set aside.
▨ Add the water to a large saucepan and heat to boiling. Add the remaining ingredients except the green onions and cilantro and heat to boiling. Simmer until the fish is cooked.
▨ Pour carefully into a serving bowl and garnish with the fried garlic and oil spread on the surface. Sprinkle with the green onions and cilantro.

SERVES 4

RICE SOUP WITH RED SNAPPER (LEFT)
AND HOT AND SOUR SHRIMP SOUP (RIGHT)

Bangkok and the Central Plains

Tom Yam Goong

ต้มยำกุ้ง

Hot and Sour Shrimp Soup

A subtle blend of hot and sour with citrus overtones, tom yam goong
*is the most famous of all Thai soups. Each region has its own particular
variation of the recipe.*

8 oz (250 g) shrimp/prawns, shelled and deveined, with
  shells reserved
3 cups (24 fl oz/750 ml) water
2 garlic cloves (*kratiem*), minced
5 kaffir lime leaves (*bai ma-grood*)
3 thin slices fresh or dried galangal (*kha*)
¼ cup (2 fl oz/60 ml) fish sauce (*nam pla*)

2 stalks lemon grass/citronella (*ta-krai*), lower ⅓ portion only,
  cut into 1-in (2.5-cm) lengths
2 shallots, sliced
½ cup sliced straw mushrooms
5 green Thai chili peppers (*prik khee noo*), optional
¼ cup (2 fl oz/60 ml) lime juice
1 teaspoon black chili paste (*nam prik pow*) (see page 493)
1 tablespoon chopped cilantro/coriander leaves (*bai pak chee*)

▓ Rinse the prawn shells and place them in a large pot with the
water. Heat to boiling, strain the broth and discard the shells.
▓ Add the garlic, lime leaves, galangal, fish sauce, lemon grass
and shallots to the stock, then the mushrooms and chili peppers, if using. Cook gently for 2 minutes.
▓ Add the shrimp to the soup, and reheat to boiling. When
the shrimp are cooked, place the lime juice and black chili
paste in a serving bowl. Pour the soup into the bowl, stir,
garnish with the cilantro leaves, and serve.

SERVES 4

SHRIMP PASTE FRIED RICE (LEFT) AND CRISPY OMELETS (RIGHT)

Bangkok and the Central Plains

KANOM BUENG YUAN

ขนมเบื้องญวน

Crispy Omelets

Originally from Vietnam, the Thai version of this recipe varies according to the availability of ingredients for the filling.

FILLING FOR OMELETS

2 tablespoons oil
8 garlic cloves *(kratiem)*, chopped
1 lb (500 g) shredded coconut meat
1 lb (500 g) shelled shrimp/prawns
½ cup chopped salted dried turnip
½ cup (4 oz/125 g) ground roasted peanuts
½ cup chopped fried tofu (see glossary)
½ teaspoon white pepper
¼ cup cilantro/coriander leaves *(bai pak chee)*
1 cup bean sprouts

CRISPY OMELET BATTER

1½ cups (6 oz/185 g) rice flour
½ teaspoon baking soda/bicarbonate of soda

1½ cups (12 fl oz/375 ml) coconut milk
2 eggs
½ cup (4 fl oz/125 ml) water
1 teaspoon turmeric
¼ teaspoon salt
¼ cup (2 fl oz/60 ml) oil

▦ Heat a large skillet and add the oil, garlic, coconut meat, and shrimp and cook until the shrimp are almost done. Add all the remaining filling ingredients except the bean sprouts and continue to cook for 3 more minutes. When the filling is cooked, stir in the bean sprouts and remove from the heat. Set filling aside.

▦ Mix the omelet batter by combining all the ingredients and gently beating until smooth.

▦ Heat a 10-in (25-cm) skillet on medium-high heat and add just enough oil to coat the skillet, pouring out any excess.

▦ Pour in enough of the batter to coat the surface of the skillet, reducing the temperature if necessary. When the omelet is cooked remove it from the pan. Repeat until all the batter is used—makes 6–8 omelets.

▦ When all the omelets are cooked, divide the filling between them. Arrange it on one half of each omelet so that the rest of the omelet can be folded over to cover the filling.

▦ Carefully remove the omelets to a serving plate and serve with northeast cucumber salad *(tam taeng)*, on page 428.

SERVES 6–8

Bangkok and the Central Plains

KHAO CLOOK GAPI

ข้าวคลุกกะปิ

Shrimp Paste Fried Rice

The salty shrimp paste which gives this fried rice its unique flavor is an essential ingredient in many Thai recipes.

½ cup (2 fl oz/60 ml) oil
½ cup (1 oz/30 g) dried shrimp/prawns
2 eggs, beaten
4 shallots, sliced
4 garlic cloves (*kratiem*), thinly sliced
½ cup shredded green mango
4 wedges lime
2 tablespoons oil
4 cups cooked rice
2 tablespoons shrimp paste (*gapi*)
3 tablespoons fish sauce (*nam pla*)

※ Heat the oil to 375°F (190°C). Fry the shrimp for 30 seconds then remove and set aside.

※ Pour out most of the oil, leaving 1 tablespoon. Pour the eggs into the pan and cook without stirring on medium heat. Carefully remove in one piece and set aside. Roll the egg sheet into a cylinder and slice thinly.

※ Arrange the fried shrimp on the side of a serving plate and pile the egg strips on another section of the plate. Arrange the shallots, garlic, mango and lime wedges attractively on the same plate.

※ Heat a large skillet, add the oil and then the rice, shrimp paste and fish sauce. Stir-fry until all the ingredients are well combined and heated through. Remove to a serving platter and serve with the condiment plate.

SERVES 4

Bangkok and the Central Plains

KHAO GRIAB PAAK MAW

ข้าวเกรียบปากหม้อ

Folded Rice Skin Dumplings

A very common and popular dish offered at the street markets of Bangkok and in the surrounding villages, this is a perfect snack for any time of day.

FILLING

1 tablespoon oil
8 oz (250 g) ground/minced pork
½ cup (4 oz/125 g) ground roasted peanuts
4 garlic cloves (*kratiem*), minced
¼ cup chopped cilantro/coriander leaves (*bai pak chee*)
½ teaspoon white pepper
3 tablespoons fish sauce (*nam pla*)
2 tablespoons sugar

6 garlic cloves (*kratiem*), chopped
¼ cup (2 fl oz/60 ml) oil
24 Thai rice papers
½ cup coriander/cilantro leaves (*bai pak chee*)

※ Heat a medium skillet and add the oil, then add the rest of the filling ingredients. Cook on medium-high heat until the pork is cooked and the liquid is all reduced and clinging to the other ingredients. Set aside.

※ Using a small skillet, fry the garlic cloves in the ¼ cup of oil until golden, then discard the garlic, reserving the garlic oil.

※ Prepare a steaming pot using a large pot of boiling water 2–3 in (5–7.5 cm) deep. Cover the top of the pot with a piece of wet muslin cloth and tie around the rim with string to keep the surface taut. Cut a 2-in (5-cm) opening near the edge to release the steam.

※ Moisten each sheet of rice paper with water and cut to size, making circles 5 in (12.5 cm) in diameter, and then place on the muslin surface to heat for 1–2 minutes. Remove and place on a plate. Repeat, stacking with a layer of wax/greaseproof paper between each one.

※ When the rice skins are ready, spoon on 1 teaspoon of the filling on each. Use a small paddle or the handle of a spoon to fold the rice skin in half to cover the filling. Overlap the sides and crimp around the edges softly to give it shape. As each dumpling is made, remove it to a plate and brush with the garlic oil to keep it from sticking to the others.

※ To serve, wrap each dumpling in a small piece of lettuce and eat with cilantro on the side.

SERVES 4

CRISPY NOODLES (TOP, RECIPE PAGE 302) AND
FOLDED RICE SKIN DUMPLINGS (BOTTOM)

301

Bangkok and the Central Plains

Mee Grob

หมี่กรอบ

Crispy Noodles

Originally a village favorite, this dish then became popular in the cities.

4 cups (1 qt/1 l) oil
6 oz (200 g) rice vermicelli *(sen mee)*

SAUCE

½ cup (4 fl oz/125 ml) vinegar
½ cup (4 oz/125 g) sugar
1 teaspoon salt
1 teaspoon tomato paste
3 tablespoons garlic pickle *(kratiem dong)* (see page 497)

GARNISH

2 eggs, beaten (optional)
¼ cup chopped green onions/scallions/spring onions
¼ cup chopped red bell pepper/capsicum
⅛ cup 1-in (2.5-cm) lengths chopped chives
4 oz (125 g) fried tofu, cut into small pieces (see glossary)
1 tablespoon chopped cilantro/coriander leaves *(bai pak chee)*

In a deep-fryer or wok, heat the oil to 375°F (190°C) and fry the rice vermicelli until puffed. Remove and set aside.

Combine the sauce ingredients in a large skillet and cook for 4 minutes over medium heat, until of syrupy consistency.

If desired, fry the beaten eggs in a small pan. When cooked remove carefully and slice into thin strips. Set aside.

Add the noodles to the pan and mix quickly with the sauce so that they are evenly coated. Place on a serving dish and sprinkle with the garnish. Serve immediately.

SERVES 4 *Photograph page 301*

Bangkok and the Central Plains

Po Pia Sod

ปอเปี๊ยะสด

Fresh Spring Rolls

These rolls are not fried and so are ideal for the health-conscious.

12 spring roll wrappers
12 leaves green leaf lettuce/Chinese lettuce
3 Chinese sausages, cut into ½-in (1-cm) cubes
1 cup fried tofu (see glossary)
1 cucumber, peeled, cut into ½-in (1-cm) strips
2 cups bean sprouts, blanched
2 cups spinach, blanched
½ cup (4 fl oz/125 ml) peanut sauce *(nam jim satay)* (see page 490)

Steam the spring roll wrappers. Place one wrapper on a flat surface, then place a 6-in (15-cm) square piece of lettuce leaf on the lower portion of the wrapper. Arrange a twelfth of each of the Chinese sausage, tofu, cucumber, bean sprouts and spinach on top of the lettuce leaf.

Roll the bottom of the wrapper up, bring the sides in and continue to roll all the way up. Repeat for the rest of the wrappers.

Slice the rolls and serve with the peanut sauce.

SERVES 4

FRESH SPRING ROLLS (LEFT) AND SPRING ROLLS (RIGHT, RECIPE PAGE 304)

Bangkok and the Central Plains

PO PIA TAUD

ปอเปี๊ยะทอด

Spring Rolls

These spring rolls are a perfect appetizer for any meal and they are also a favorite when entertaining.

2 tablespoons oil
1 teaspoon minced garlic (*kratiem*)
8 oz (250 g) ground/minced pork
2 cups grated carrots
2 cups chopped celery
¼ cup (2 fl oz/60 ml) fish sauce (*nam pla*)
1 tablespoon Maggi seasoning
2 tablespoons sugar
⅛ teaspoon white pepper
1 cup bean sprouts
20 spring roll wrappers
2 egg yolks, beaten
3 cups (24 fl oz/750 ml) oil, for deep-frying

⁂ Heat a large skillet and add the oil, garlic and pork. Sauté until the pork is cooked.
⁂ Add the carrots, celery, sauces, sugar and pepper. Cook for 1 minute on high heat to reduce the sauce. Drain whatever liquid is left from the pan.
⁂ Allow the filling to cool, then add the bean sprouts to the filling.
⁂ Place a wrapper as a diamond with a corner towards you. Place 2 tablespoons of the filling in the lower portion of the wrapper. Fold the corner up, rolling once. Bring the sides in and brush the upper portion of the wrapper with egg yolk.
⁂ Roll the wrapper up, sealing the entire spring roll. Fill and roll up the rest of the wrappers in the same way.
⁂ Heat the oil to 350°F (180°C) and deep-fry the spring rolls in batches until golden brown all over, turning as needed.
⁂ Serve with a sweet and sour sauce or other dip of your choice.

SERVES 4   *Photograph page 303*

COCONUT NOODLES

⁂ Heat a large skillet and add the oil and tomatoes; cook on medium-high heat for 5 minutes and add the noodles. Cook until the noodles are soft, then set aside in a large serving dish.
⁂ Combine the remaining ingredients, except the chives, in a large skillet and cook on medium-high heat for 5 minutes. Garnish with the chives and pour the mixture over the noodles.

SERVES 8

Bangkok and the Central Plains

MEE GA-THI

หมี่กะทิ

Coconut Noodles

Vendors with carts sell these noodles around Bangkok. People can buy a little to eat as a snack or buy more for a complete meal.

1 lb (500 g) rice vermicelli (*sen mee*)
2 tablespoons oil
1 cup (8 oz/250 g) wedged tomatoes
1 lb (500 g) shrimps/prawns, shelled and deveined
½ lb (250 g) pork, cut in 1-in (2.5-cm) slices
3 cups (24 fl oz/750 ml) coconut milk
¼ cup (2 fl oz/60 ml) yellow bean sauce (*tao jeow*)
5 shallots, sliced
½ cup tofu, cut in 1-in (2.5-cm) cubes
2 tablespoons fish sauce (*nam pla*)
½ cup (4 oz/125 g) sugar
1 lb (500 g) bean sprouts
½ cup 1-in (2.5-cm) lengths chopped chives

⁂ Soak the rice vermicelli for 30 minutes in water to cover, then drain and set aside.

Bangkok and the Central Plains

PAD THAI

ผัดไทย

Stir-Fried Thai Noodles

One of Thailand's best known noodle dishes. It is eaten as a light meal at any time of the day or night, and is especially popular at the night markets throughout the country.

8 oz (250 g) rice noodles (*sen lek*)
3 tablespoons oil
3 garlic cloves (*kratiem*), minced
¼ cup dried shrimp/prawns
¼ cup (2 fl oz/60 ml) fish sauce (*nam pla*)
¼ cup (2 oz/60 g) sugar
2 tablespoons tamarind juice (*ma-kaam piag*) (see glossary)
1 tablespoon paprika
½ cup fried tofu (see glossary)
2 tablespoons dried unsalted turnip, cut into small pieces
1 egg, beaten
¼ cup 1-in (2.5-cm) lengths chopped chives
¼ cup (2 oz/60 g) ground roasted peanuts
1 cup bean sprouts

STIR-FRIED THAI NOODLES

GARNISH

½ cup bean sprouts
½ cup chopped chives
¼ small banana blossom, cut into strips
½ lime, cut into wedges

▨ Soak the rice noodles in cold water for 30 minutes, or until soft. Drain, and set aside.

▨ Heat a large skillet until hot, then add the oil. Add the garlic and dried shrimp, and stir-fry. Add the noodles and stir-fry until translucent. It may be necessary to reduce the heat if the mixture is cooking too quickly and the noodles stick.

▨ Add the fish sauce, sugar, tamarind juice and paprika. Stir-fry the mixture until thoroughly combined. Stir in the tofu, turnip and egg.

▨ Turn the heat to high and cook until the egg sets, stirring gently. Thoroughly combine the mixture, and continue cooking over medium-high heat for about 2 minutes until most of the liquid is reduced.

▨ Mix in the chives, peanuts and bean sprouts. Place on a serving dish, arrange the bean sprouts, chives, banana blossom and lime attractively and serve.

SERVES 4

305

COCONUT RICE

The North

KHAO SOI

ข้าวซอย

Chiang Mai Noodles

These fine egg noodles, which also come in a flat form, are a favorite fresh noodle dish from Lam Poon Lam Pang to Chiang Mai. They can be eaten as part of a luncheon or just as a light snack.

2 tablespoons oil
3 garlic cloves (*kratiem*), crushed
3 shallots, chopped
4 cups (1 qt/1 l) coconut milk
2 tablespoons curry powder
1 tablespoon red curry paste (*nam prik gaeng ped*)
  (see page 488)
8 oz (250 g) beef, cut into 1-in (2.5-cm) cubes
½ cup (4 fl oz/125 ml) fish sauce (*nam pla*)
¼ cup (2 oz/60 g) sugar
½ teaspoon turmeric
1 tablespoon lime juice
3 cups (24 fl oz/750 ml) water
6 oz (185 g) fresh thin egg noodles (*ba mee*)
1 green onion/scallion/spring onion, chopped
1 tablespoon chopped cilantro/coriander leaves (*bai pak chee*)

GARNISH

2 shallots, sliced
½ lime, cut into wedges
¼ cup sliced Chinese mustard pickles

▨ Heat a large saucepan and add the oil. When the oil is hot, stir-fry the garlic and shallots for 30 seconds. Add the coconut milk, curry powder, red curry paste and then the beef. Heat to boiling, reduce to medium heat and simmer for approximately 30 minutes.

▨ Add the fish sauce, sugar, turmeric and lime juice. Stir to combine all the ingredients and bring to a slow boil. Continue to cook for 10 minutes.
▨ In a medium saucepan, heat the water to boiling. Stir in the fresh noodles and cook for 1 minute in rapidly boiling water. Drain the noodles and place in a serving bowl.
▨ Pour the curry mixture over the noodles and top with the green onion and the cilantro. Serve with the garnish ingredients arranged on the side.

SERVES 4

Bangkok and the Central Plains

KHAO MAN

ข้าวมัน

Coconut Rice

When this dish is served it is usually accompanied by papaya salad (som tam Esan) on page 424, with dried shrimp served on the side. A lunch dish only, this is an example of palace style dining.

4 cups jasmine rice
1 cup (8 fl oz/250 ml) water
3 cups (24 fl oz/750 ml) coconut milk
1 teaspoon salt
2 tablespoons sugar

▨ Rinse the rice in running water until the water stays clear. Place the water, coconut milk, salt and sugar in a large saucepan.
▨ Add the rice and heat to boiling on high heat, stirring to prevent the rice from sticking to the bottom of the pan.
▨ Cover and simmer until the rice is tender and cooked through.

SERVES 4

CHIANG MAI NOODLES

Bangkok and the Central Plains

GUAY TEOW RAAD NAA

ก๋วยเตี๋ยวราดหน้า

Wide Noodles with Cream Sauce

This recipe produces a dish similar to Western fettucine dishes. The stir-fry method is easy, while other meat and vegetable combinations can be used to take advantage of regional abundances.

MARINADE

1 tablespoon cornstarch/cornflour
1 egg
2 teaspoons Oriental sesame oil
½ teaspoon white pepper
1 tablespoon Maggi seasoning

8 oz (250 g) pork loin, thinly sliced
8 oz (250 g) wide rice noodles (*sen yai*) or other noodles
¼ cup (2 fl oz/60 ml) oil
2 tablespoons sweet soy sauce
1 tablespoon crushed garlic (*kratiem*)
1 cup (8 fl oz/250 ml) water
3 tablespoons fish sauce (*nam pla*)
2 tablespoons sugar
2 tablespoons cornstarch/cornflour, mixed in a little water
1 cup broccoli flowerets
½ cup sliced carrots
¼ cup sliced red bell pepper/capsicum
½ cup sugar peas/snow peas
¼ cup straw mushrooms
1 green onion/scallion/spring onion, cut in 1-in (2.5-cm) pieces

▨ Mix together the marinade ingredients and pour over the pork slices, turning to make sure all surfaces are coated. Marinate pork for 10 minutes.
▨ Soak the noodles in warm water until soft—about 10 minutes—then drain.
▨ Heat a large skillet, add half the oil and stir-fry the noodles with the sweet soy sauce. Stir continually as these noodles are apt to stick. When thoroughly mixed, remove and set aside.
▨ Heat a large saucepan, add the rest of the oil, garlic, water, fish sauce and sugar. Add the pork and heat the mixture to boiling. Add enough cornstarch mixture to form a medium-thick sauce.
▨ Add all the remaining ingredients and reheat the mixture to boiling, cooking for 3 more minutes. Pour the mixture over the noodles and serve.

SERVES 4

Bangkok and the Central Plains

GUAY TEOW NUEA

ก๋วยเตี๋ยวเนื้อ

Noodles with Meatballs

A hearty noodle dish, this can also be served as a complete meal. Either use the instructions for meatballs contained in the recipe for glass noodle soup (gaeng jued woon sen) *on page 298 or purchase the meatballs from an Asian grocery store.*

3 tablespoons oil
6 garlic cloves (*kratiem*), minced
1 lb (500 g) wheat noodles
1 lb (500 g) bean sprouts, blanched
1 cup chopped celery, blanched

SAUCE

6 cups (1½ qt/1.5 l) water
1 lb (500 g) meatballs
8 oz (250 g) beef, cut into ⅛-in (3-mm) thick slices
8 garlic cloves (*kratiem*), minced
½ cup chopped cilantro/coriander roots (*raak pak chee*) and leaves (*bai pak chee*)
½ teaspoon white peppercorns
6 clusters of star anise (about 8 pods per cluster)

6 whole cardamon
2 sticks cinnamon
1 teaspoon salt
2 tablespoons Maggi seasoning
¼ cup (2 fl oz/60 ml) light soy sauce
2 tablespoons sweet soy sauce
3 oz (90 g) palm sugar (*nam taan peep*)

▨ Heat the oil in a small skillet and fry the garlic until golden brown. Remove contents from pan and set aside.

▨ Cook the noodles in boiling water and drain, then place into a serving bowl and top with the bean sprouts and celery.
▨ Heat the water to boiling and add the meatballs and beef. Secure the raw garlic, coriander, peppercorns, anise, cardamon and cinnamon in a piece of muslin and place in the same pot. Simmer for 20 minutes then remove the seasonings.
▨ Stir in the remaining ingredients, and pour the mixture over the noodles. Sprinkle the fried garlic over the top before serving.

SERVES 6–8

NOODLES WITH MEATBALLS (LEFT), WIDE NOODLES WITH CREAM SAUCE (RIGHT)

RED SEA NOODLES

Bangkok and the Central Plains

YEN TA FO

เย็นตาโฟ

Red Sea Noodles

A favorite dish for lunch served by many restaurants and street vendors, this is a flavorful noodle dish which could also be used to make a complete and healthy meal for four. This is a good way to use up leftover wontons, fish balls and fish cakes, but they can also be purchased ready-made at Asian food stores.

8 wontons
1 cup (8 fl oz/250 ml) oil, for deep-frying
4 garlic cloves (*kratiem*), minced

SOUP

6 cups water
8 oz (250 g) pork loin, in one piece
1 teaspoon salt
8 oz (250 g) fish balls
4 oz (125 g) cleaned sliced squid
4 oz (125 g) sliced fish cakes

1 lb (500 g) wheat noodles
1 lb (500 g) swamp cabbage or spinach, cut into 4-in (10-cm) lengths and blanched
½ cup (4 fl oz/125 ml) fish sauce (*nam pla*)
½ cup (4 fl oz/125 ml) chili in vinegar (*prik dong*) (see page 241)
½ cup (4 oz/125 g) sugar
1 cup (8 fl oz/250 ml) ketchup/tomato sauce
2 cups fried pork skin/pork rind (*kaep moo*) (see page 326)

▓ Deep-fry the wontons in the oil at 350°F (180°C) for 2 minutes or until golden brown. Set aside.

▓ Pour 2 tablespoons of the oil into a small skillet and fry the garlic until golden brown. Remove the garlic and set it aside.
▓ Heat the water to boiling and cook the pork for 15 minutes or until done. Remove the pork and slice into thin pieces. Set aside, reserving the stock.
▓ Add the salt, fish balls, squid and fish cakes to the stock. Heat to boiling.
▓ While the pork is cooking, heat another large pot of water to boiling to cook the noodles. Boil the noodles just until tender, remove and divide between eight individual bowls. Add the cabbage to the individual bowls, dividing into eight equal servings.
▓ Place in each bowl 1 tablespoon each of the fish sauce, vinegar and sugar and 2 tablespoons ketchup. Stir to combine, adding an eighth of the soup and sliced pork. Top each bowl with a fried wonton and some fried pork skin. Serve immediately with the fried garlic sprinkled on top.

SERVES 8

Bangkok and the Central Plains

KANOM JEEN NAM PRIK

ขนมจีนน้ำพริก

Noodles in Sweet Curry Sauce

Celebrations, whether religious or personal, are an important part of Thai life. This is a dish served at celebrations like weddings or house-warmings.

1 cup (8 oz/250 g) dried mung beans, soaked in water to cover overnight
6 cups (1½ qt/1.5 l) water
1 lb (500 g) dried thin wheat noodles or fresh noodles
1 cup shrimp/prawn meat
4 cups (1 qt/1 l) coconut milk
¼ cup (2 fl oz/60 ml) red curry paste (*nam prik gaeng ped*) (see page 488)
½ cup (4 fl oz/125 ml) fish sauce (*nam pla*)
¼ cup (2 oz/60 g) sugar
¼ cup (2 fl oz/60 ml) lime juice
2 kaffir limes (*ma-grood*), cut into halves
½ cup chopped green onions/scallions/spring onions, in 1-in (2.5-cm) pieces
½ cup sliced garlic (*kratiem*), fried in oil until golden brown
1 cup chopped blanched swamp cabbage or spinach
¼ banana blossom, sliced thinly lengthwise
¼ cup dried Thai chili peppers (*prik khee noo haeng*), fried in oil until golden brown

▓ Drain the mung beans and steam in a steamer for 15 minutes or until soft. Remove and set aside.
▓ Heat the water to boiling and boil the noodles until soft, then drain and rinse in cold water. Lift a small amount of noodles up and twist them into a bundle. Repeat until all the noodles are in bundles and set aside on a large plate.
▓ Using a mortar and pestle, grind the steamed mung beans and shrimp meat together to form a smooth paste.
▓ Heat a large saucepan and add the coconut milk, red curry paste, fish sauce, sugar and shrimp and bean mixture and heat to boiling. Add the lime juice and limes and reheat to boiling.
▓ Toss in the green onions and half of the fried garlic.
▓ Arrange the swamp cabbage, banana blossom, chilies and the rest of the fried garlic over the bundles of noodles.
▓ Pour the curry sauce, including the limes, over the noodles and serve.

SERVES 4

NOODLES IN SWEET CURRY SAUCE (TOP) AND
STIR-FRIED WIDE NOODLES (BOTTOM, RECIPE PAGE 312)

311

Bangkok and the Central Plains

GUAY TEOW PAD SE-IEW

ก๋วยเตี๋ยวผัดซีอิ๊ว

Stir-Fried Wide Noodles

A popular luncheon dish in Bangkok, this is a drier, though equally delicious, version of the cream sauce style.

MARINADE

1 garlic clove (*kratiem*), minced
1 egg, beaten
1 tablespoon cornstarch/cornflour
1 tablespoon wine
1 tablespoon fish sauce (*nam pla*)
1 tablespoon oyster sauce
1 tablespoon sugar
1 teaspoon Oriental sesame oil
½ teaspoon white pepper

8 oz (250 g) beef, thinly sliced
8 oz (250 g) fresh rice noodles (*sen yai*), ½ in (1 cm) wide
2 tablespoons oil
1 tablespoon fish sauce (*nam pla*)
1 tablespoon sugar
1 tablespoon oyster sauce
1 tablespoon sweet soy sauce
1 cup broccoli flowerets
⅛ cup sliced carrot

Mix together all the ingredients for the marinade, then combine with the beef. Marinate the beef for 10 minutes.
Cook the noodles until tender in a large pot of boiling water.
Heat a large skillet and add the oil. Stir-fry the beef until done.
Add the noodles and all remaining ingredients. Continue to cook until liquid is reduced slightly and all ingredients are hot.

SERVES 4 *Photograph page 311*

Bangkok and the Central Plains

POO JAA

ปูจ๋า

Crab in Shell

A dish elegant enough for any party, showcasing the rich crab meat.

2 large whole crab shells, cleaned and cut in halves,
    or 4 small crab shells, cleaned
1 lb (500 g) crab meat
1 lb (500 g) ground/minced pork
6 garlic cloves (*kratiem*), minced
½ teaspoon white pepper
3 tablespoons Maggi seasoning
2 tablespoons fish sauce (*nam pla*)
6 eggs, beaten
4 cups (1 qt/1 l) oil, for deep-frying

Dry the cleaned crab shells. Combine all the remaining ingredients except the eggs and oil.
Stuff the filling mixture into the crab shell and place in a steamer. Steam for 20 minutes or until the filling is cooked. Remove the crab shells from the steamer.
Heat the oil in a wok or deep skillet to 350°F (180°C). Dip each crab shell into the beaten egg and then deep-fry until golden brown.

SERVES 4

CRAB IN SHELL (TOP) AND BROILED MUSSELS WITH CHILI SAUCE (BOTTOM, RECIPE PAGE 314)

The South

Hoi Ma-Laeng Poo Pow

หอยแมลงภู่เผา

Broiled Mussels with Chili Sauce

Broiling over charcoal is a common method of cooking seafood. Because the cooking method is very simple it is the sauce that makes each dish unique.

2 lb (1 kg) mussels

DIPPING SAUCE

6 garlic cloves (*kratiem*), finely minced
8 green Thai chili peppers (*prik khee noo*), finely chopped
⅓ cup (3 fl oz/90 ml) fish sauce (*nam pla*)
½ cup (4 fl oz/125 ml) lime juice
3 tablespoons sugar
2 tablespoons chopped cilantro/coriander root
  (*raak pak chee*)
2 tablespoons chopped mint
2 tablespoons thinly sliced green onion/scallion/spring
  onion

▦ Clean the mussels well by scrubbing the shells and removing the beards. Broil/grill the mussels over charcoal until they open. Then turn each one over to broil the other side until the mussel is heated through.
▦ Combine all the dipping sauce ingredients.
▦ Each mussel is removed from its shell and dipped into the sauce before eating.
▦ Serve hot.

SERVES 4   *Photograph pages 312–313*

SHRIMP CAKES (TOP) AND SUN-DRIED SHRIMP (BOTTOM)

The South

Goong Haeng Yam

กุ้งแห้งยำ

Sun-Dried Shrimp

These sun-dried shrimp act as a very good substitute for meat when a lighter dish is desired. Frequently they are served with a rice soup or just as a light meal with rice.

8 oz (250 g) dried shrimp
4 shallots, sliced
2 garlic cloves (*kratiem*), sliced
1 tablespoon sliced green Thai chili pepper (*prik khee noo*)
3 tablespoons fish sauce (*nam pla*)
¼ cup (2 fl oz/60 ml) lime juice
1 tablespoon sugar

▦ Soak the dried shrimp in water for 10 minutes, then drain.
▦ Combine the shrimp with the remaining ingredients and toss. Transfer to a serving plate.

SERVES 4

Bangkok and the Central Plains

Taud Man Goong

ทอดมันกุ้ง

Shrimp Cakes

This is a dish not usually sold by the Bangkok street vendors—more often it is served in restaurants or in private homes.

1 lb (500 g) shrimp/prawns, shelled, deveined and cleaned
3 tablespoons red curry paste (*nam prik gaeng ped*)
  (see page 488)
2 eggs, beaten
3 tablespoons fish sauce (*nam pla*)
¼ cup (1 oz/30 g) cornstarch/cornflour
4 cups (1 qt/1 l) oil, for deep-frying

▦ Place the shrimp in a food processor with all the other ingredients, except the oil, and blend into a smooth paste.
▦ Heat the oil to 375°F (190°C). Form the paste into about 24 patties, each 2 in (5 cm) in diameter and ½ in (1 cm) thick. Drop the patties into the hot oil and deep-fry until they are golden brown and puffed.
▦ Serve with cucumber salad (*tam taeng*), on page 428.

SERVES 4

Bangkok and the Central Plains

Pla Dook Foo Nam Prik Ma-Muang

ปลาดุกฟูน้ำพริกมะม่วง

Puffy Catfish with Mango Sauce

A favorite deep-fried fish dish which is usually served as a first course. The mango sauce is a perfect accompaniment to the crispy flesh.

1 catfish, about 1½ lb (750 g), cleaned, retaining the head
1 egg, beaten
¼ cup (1 oz/30 g) cornstarch/cornflour
3 cups (24 fl oz/750 ml) oil, for deep-frying

MANGO SAUCE

½ cup shredded green mango
¼ cup sliced shallots
2 tablespoons chopped green Thai chili peppers
 (*prik khee noo*)
3 tablespoons fish sauce (*nam pla*)
2 tablespoons lime juice
2 tablespoons palm sugar (*nam taan peep*)

green leaf lettuce/Chinese lettuce

❋ Cook the catfish by steaming or broiling/grilling.
❋ Shred the meat along either side of the backbone with a fork so that the surface is rough, then brush the fish with the beaten egg and roll it in the cornflour.
❋ Heat the oil in a deep skillet to 350°F (180°C). Deep-fry the fish until it is golden and puffy. Remove and set aside.
❋ Thoroughly combine all the ingredients for the mango sauce in a bowl.
❋ Line a serving plate with the green leaf lettuce. Place the puffy fish on top of the lettuce and serve the mango sauce on the side.

SERVES 4

PUFFY CATFISH WITH MANGO SAUCE

The South

PLA MUK YANG

ปลาหมึกย่าง

Charcoaled Squid

The aroma of charcoal broiling squid to perfection attracts customers to the street stalls of many of the cities and small towns in this region. The flavor would be enhanced by any number of dipping sauces.

1 whole squid, about 1 lb (500 g)
2 tablespoons fish sauce *(nam pla)*
1 tablespoon soy sauce

SAUCE

6 garlic cloves *(kratiem)*, minced
1 tablespoon chopped cilantro/coriander leaves *(bai pak chee)*
1 tablespoon chopped onion
3 tablespoons fish sauce *(nam pla)*
3 tablespoons lime juice
1 tablespoon palm sugar *(nam taan peep)*

Cut open the squid and remove the entrails, leaving the tentacles intact. Remove the skin carefully.

Place on a rack and charcoal-broil for 2 minutes on each side. Brush with the combined fish sauce and soy sauce during broiling to add color and more flavor.

Mix together the sauce ingredients and pour into a bowl.

Cut open the squid and remove the entrails, leaving the tentacles intact. Remove the skin carefully.

SERVES 4

Bangkok and the Central Plains

KANOM PANG NAA GOONG

ขนมปังหน้ากุ้ง

Shrimp Toast

Wonderful as an appetizer with your favorite sauce or dip, this recipe is also a delicious snack.

TOPPING

8 oz (250 g) minced shrimp/prawn meat
8 oz (250 g) ground/minced pork
4 egg yolks
1 tablespoon cornstarch/cornflour
4 garlic cloves *(kratiem)*, minced
¼ teaspoon white pepper
1 tablespoon minced cilantro/coriander leaves *(bai pak chee)*

8 slices white bread, crust removed, and sliced in
  half diagonally
4 cups (1 qt/1 l) oil, for deep-frying

Mix together all the topping ingredients. Spread one-eighth of the topping on each bread piece in an even layer.

Heat the oil to 350°F (180°C) and deep-fry the bread until the topping is cooked and the bread is light golden brown, turning as required.

SERVES 4

NOODLES IN FISH CURRY SAUCE (LEFT, RECIPE PAGE 318),
SHRIMP TOAST (TOP) AND CHARCOALED SQUID (RIGHT)

PAN-STEAMED MUSSELS

Bangkok and the Central Plains

HOI MA-LAENG POO OB

หอยแมลงภู่อบ

Pan-Steamed Mussels

Mussels are a favorite shellfish of Thai cuisine. In this dish the flavor of lemon grass adds a fresh tang to the mussels.

4 lb (2 kg) mussels, cleaned and debearded
3 stalks lemon grass/citronella (*ta-krai*), chopped
5 shallots, chopped
1 cup sweet basil leaves (*bai horapa*)
4 green jalapeño peppers (*prik chee fa*), sliced
2 tablespoons fish sauce (*nam pla*)
2 tablespoons lime juice

Place all the ingredients in a large skillet and stir thoroughly. Then cover and steam for 5 minutes or until the mussels open and are hot. Remove to a serving plate and serve.

SERVES 4

Bangkok and the Central Plains

KANOM JEEN NAM YAA

ขนมจีนน้ำยา

Noodles in Fish Curry Sauce

Nam yaa is a medicinal soup using herbs such as lemon grass, lesser ginger, galangal and garlic. This recipe uses all of these ingredients and is considered a very healthy dish.

1 lb (500 g) thin wheat noodles

FISH CURRY SAUCE

2 lb (1 kg) fish or 1 lb (500 g) canned tuna
6 cups (1½ qt/1.5 l) water
6 tablespoons lesser ginger (*krachai*), chopped
8 garlic cloves (*kratiem*), chopped
2 tablespoons shrimp paste (*gapi*)
8 shallots, chopped
6 thin slices galangal (*kha*), chopped
3 tablespoons chopped lemon grass/citronella (*ta-krai*)

8 dried jalapeño peppers (*prik chee fa haeng*), soaked in water until soft
4 cups (1 qt/1 l) coconut milk
½ cup (4 fl oz/125 ml) fish sauce (*nam pla*)

VEGETABLES

string beans
basil stems, with leaves (*bai horapa*)
bean sprouts
swamp cabbage or spinach
Chinese mustard pickles

🔣 Heat a large pot of water to boiling and cook the noodles until just soft. Rinse and drain the noodles and arrange in eight small bundles on a large plate.

🔣 If using fresh fish cut it into 2-in (5-cm) chunks. Heat the water to boiling and cook the fish for 10 minutes. Remove the fish and debone, retaining the shredded meat.

🔣 Place the lesser ginger, garlic, shrimp paste, shallots, galangal, lemon grass and peppers in a mortar and blend with the pestle until smoothly mashed.

🔣 In a large saucepan, heat the coconut milk, fish sauce and blended ingredients to boiling. Add the fish meat, boil again and cook for 5 minutes. Pour the entire mixture over the noodle bundles and arrange the raw vegetables and pickles around the plate.

SERVES 8   *Photograph pages 316–317*

Bangkok and the Central Plains

TAUD MAN PLA

ทอดมันปลา

Fish Cakes

Taud man pla are eaten in many areas of Thailand, made with whatever fish is available. On the streets of Bangkok there are stands where these fish cakes are freshly made and cooked while you wait.

8 oz (250 g) white fish fillets, minced
3 tablespoons red curry paste (*nam prik gaeng ped*) (see page 488)
2 tablespoons fish sauce (*nam pla*)
2 eggs, beaten
3 tablespoons cornstarch/cornflour
¼ teaspoon baking soda/bicarbonate of soda
6 kaffir lime leaves (*bai ma-grood*) or sweet basil leaves (*bai horapa*), very thinly sliced
3 cups (24 fl oz/750 ml) oil, for deep-frying

🔣 Combine the fish with the next five ingredients in a food processor or mix thoroughly by hand. After the mixture is combined, continue to blend, adding the lime leaves. If using your hands, keep wetting them as you mix.

🔣 Shape the mixture into 1-in (2.5-cm) thick patties about 2 in (5 cm) in diameter. Set aside on a tray until ready to fry.

🔣 Heat the oil to 325°F (160°C) and deep-fry the fish cakes until light golden brown.

🔣 Serve with cucumber salad *(tam taeng),* on page 428.

SERVES 4

STEAMED BLOODY CLAMS WITH DIPPING SAUCE (LEFT, RECIPE PAGE 320) AND FISH CAKES (RIGHT)

Bangkok and the Central Plains

HOI KRAENG LUAK

หอยแครงลวก

Steamed Bloody Clams with Dipping Sauce

The flavor of the clams is balanced by the sweet and sour taste of the tamarind dip.

SAUCE

½ cup (4 fl oz/125 ml) tamarind juice (*ma-kaam piag*)
  (see glossary)
⅓ cup (3 fl oz/90 ml) fish sauce (*nam pla*)
¼ cup (2 oz/60 g) sugar
½ cup (4 oz/125 g) ground roasted peanuts
¼ cup minced green Thai chili peppers (*prik khee noo*)
½ cup cilantro/coriander leaves (*bai pak chee*), chopped

2 lb (1 kg) bloody clams in the shell (see glossary)
2 cups (16 fl oz/500 ml) water

▨ Place all the sauce ingredients in a small saucepan. Heat to boiling then simmer until the sauce is reduced by a quarter and is thick.
▨ Place the clams in a large pot with the water and heat to boiling. Continue to cook until the clams open. Remove to a serving platter, and serve with the dip in a bowl alongside.

SERVES 4   *Photograph page 319*

Bangkok and the Central Plains

KHAO MAN GAI

ข้าวมันไก่

Chicken Rice

Rice dishes like this are very popular as "lunch box" meals in Thailand. Although usually served as part of a complete meal, this is an ideal dish to be served for luncheon or a quick meal.

6 cups (1½ qt/1.5 l) water
1 chicken, about 3 lb (1.5 kg)
1 teaspoon salt
3 cups (1 lb 6 oz/700 g) jasmine rice
8 garlic cloves (*kratiem*), minced
½ teaspoon white pepper
¼ cup slivered ginger
1 teaspoon salt

SAUCE

¼ cup (2 fl oz/60 ml) yellow bean sauce (*tao jeow*)
¼ cup (2 fl oz/60 ml) lime juice
¼ cup minced garlic (*kratiem*)
¼ cup minced ginger
5 green Thai chili peppers (*prik khee noo*), chopped
¼ cup (2 fl oz/60 ml) light soy sauce
¼ cup (2 oz/60 g) sugar

1 cup cucumber slices
1 cup cilantro/coriander leaves (*bai pak chee*)

▨ Heat the water to boiling in a large steamer. Rub the chicken with salt and steam the chicken for about 45 minutes or until done. Reserving the liquid, remove the chicken and slice the meat. Set aside.

▨ Rinse the rice and drain. Measure 4 cups (1 qt/1 l) of the chicken stock and add to the rice in a medium saucepan. Heat the rice to boiling on high heat and boil for 2 minutes. Add the garlic, pepper, ginger and salt and stir into the rice. Cover and simmer for 10 minutes. More chicken stock may be added as needed if all the liquid is absorbed before the rice is cooked. Stir the rice after it is cooked.
▨ Thoroughly combine all the sauce ingredients. Arrange the slices of chicken with the rice on the side, garnished with the cucumber slices and cilantro leaves. Serve the sauce as a dip in a separate dish.

SERVES 6–8   *Photograph page 322*

The South

GAENG LUENG

แกงเหลือง

Light Yellow Curry

In the South, in the coastal regions, a great many fish dishes are served. Mackerel is found in quite a few of these recipes.

1 mackerel, or a number of smaller fish, about 1 lb (500 g), cleaned and sliced into 1-in (2.5-cm) steaks
6 cups (1½ qt/1.5 l) water
5 shallots
3 garlic cloves (*kratiem*)
1 teaspoon turmeric
1 tablespoon shrimp paste (*gapi*)
1 teaspoon salt
25 green Thai chili peppers (*prik khee noo*)
5 tablespoons (2½ fl oz/75 ml) fish sauce (*nam pla*)
2 tablespoons coconut sugar
⅓ cup (3 fl oz/90 ml) tamarind juice (*ma-kaam piag*)
  (see glossary) or lime juice
½ cup chopped string beans, in 1-in (2.5-cm) pieces
½ cup sliced bamboo shoots (see glossary), 1 in x 1 in x ⅛ in
  (2.5 cm x 2.5 cm x 0.3 cm) thick

▨ Dry the mackerel steaks with paper towels and set aside.
▨ In a blender place 1 cup (8 fl oz/250 ml) of the water, the shallots, garlic, turmeric, shrimp paste, salt and chilies. Blend until smooth.
▨ Pour this mixture into a large saucepan and add the remaining water. Heat to boiling and add the mackerel steaks, fish sauce, sugar, tamarind juice and the vegetables. Heat to boiling and reduce to medium heat. Continue cooking for 5 minutes, or until fish is cooked through. Serve hot with steamed jasmine rice (*khao suay*), on page 350.

SERVES 4

The South

PHLA HOI

พล่าหอย

Clam Salad

A popular appetizer with the people of the South, this recipe is served in many restaurants in the major cities of Thailand.

2 lb (1 kg) clams or mussels
¼ cup sliced lemon grass/citronella (*ta-krai*)
6 tablespoons sliced shallots

CLAM SALAD (TOP) AND LIGHT YELLOW CURRY (RIGHT)

1 tablespoon sliced kaffir lime leaves (*bai ma-grood*)
½ cup mint leaves
2 tablespoons chopped cilantro/coriander leaves (*bai pak chee*)
¼ cup chopped green onions/scallions/spring onions
5 green jalapeño peppers (*prik chee fa*), chopped
3 tablespoons fish sauce (*nam pla*)
3 tablespoons lime juice
1 bunch green leaf lettuce/Chinese lettuce

Heat a large pot of water to boiling. Add the clams and cook for 2 minutes. Rinse them in cold water and remove the shells. Discard the shells.

Place the clams in a bowl and add all the remaining ingredients except the green leaf lettuce. Toss to combine all ingredients.

Serve on a platter lined with green leaf lettuce.

SERVES 4

321

The North

PEAK GAI YANG

ปีกไก่ย่าง

Barbecued Chicken Wings

This is a favorite barbecue recipe. The enticing aroma of the sizzling meat on the grill makes it very popular with the street vendors' clientele.

MARINADE

1 teaspoon salt
¼ cup chopped lemon grass/citronella *(ta-krai)*
8 garlic cloves *(kratiem)*, chopped
½ teaspoon white pepper
¼ cup minced cilantro/coriander root *(raak pak chee)*
1 teaspoon turmeric

1½ lb (750 g) chicken wings

▨ Combine all the marinade ingredients and marinate the chicken wings overnight. Barbecue the wings over medium coals for 5–7 minutes on each side until they are cooked through and golden brown.
▨ Serve with steamed sticky rice *(khao neow)*, on page 350.

SERVES 4

The North

NUEA SAWAN

เนื้อสวรรค์

Heavenly Beef

In this recipe the beef is first sautéed to dry it out and then deep-fried to give a crispy effect. The flavor is delicious.

MARINADE

3 tablespoons fish sauce *(nam pla)*
1 tablespoon soy sauce
1 teaspoon cilantro/coriander powder *(pak chee pon)*
 (see glossary)
3 tablespoons sugar

1 lb (500 g) sirloin or tenderloin/fillet beef, thinly sliced
2 cups (16 fl oz/500 ml) oil, for deep-frying

▨ Mix together the marinade ingredients and marinate the beef for about 10 minutes.
▨ Heat a skillet and cover with a thin coating of oil. Pan-fry the meat and marinade until the marinade is reduced.
▨ Heat the rest of the oil in another pan and deep-fry the beef on medium heat in small batches until the pieces float to the top. Serve with steamed sticky rice *(khao neow)*, on page 350.

SERVES 4

The North

KHAO NEOW NUEA

ข้าวเหนียวเนื้อ

Sticky Rice with Beef

The beef is sun-dried and then deep-fried. It is especially tasty served with the sticky rice of the North.

STICKY RICE WITH BEEF (TOP) AND HEAVENLY BEEF (BOTTOM)

½ cup (4 fl oz/125 ml) fish sauce *(nam pla)*
3 tablespoons sugar
2 tablespoons cilantro/coriander powder *(pak chee pon)*
 (see glossary)
2 lb (1 kg) tender beef, sliced into thin 4-in x 4-in
 (10-cm x 10-cm) squares
3 cups (24 fl oz/750 ml) oil, for deep-frying
4 cups steamed sticky rice *(khao neow)* (see page 350)

▨ Mix together the fish sauce, sugar and cilantro powder, and add the beef. Marinate for 20 minutes. Arrange the pieces of beef on a rack and allow to dry in the hot sun for half a day. Turn the pieces over and sun-dry for another half a day. Alternatively, bake the beef strips at 325°F (165°C) for 25 minutes.
▨ Heat the oil to 350°F (180°C). Deep-fry the beef for 2–3 minutes. Serve with the sticky rice.

SERVES 6–8

Bangkok and the Central Plains

NUEA SATAY

เนื้อสะเต๊ะ

Satay Beef

Satays are one of Thailand's most popular appetizers.

MARINADE

⅓ cup (3 fl oz/90 ml) coconut milk
2 tablespoons fresh cilantro/coriander leaves (*bai pak chee*)
3 tablespoons sugar
1 tablespoon yellow curry powder
⅓ cup (3 fl oz/90 ml) fish sauce (*nam pla*)
1 tablespoon oil

8 oz (250 g) sirloin or flank steak, cut in long narrow
   strips 1 in (2.5 cm) wide and 3 in (7.5 cm) long

In a large bowl mix together all the ingredients for the marinade. Dip each piece of meat in the sauce and set aside. Cover and leave in refrigerator for 15 minutes.

Weave each strip of meat onto an 8-in (20-cm) skewer lengthwise.

Broil/grill for 5 minutes on each side or pan-fry. To pan-fry, brush a large non-stick pan with coconut milk or leftover marinade and pan-fry meat for 2–3 minutes on each side. Brush the meat with the sauce as it is turned.

Serve with peanut sauce (*nam jim satay*), on page 490.

SERVES 4

Bangkok and the Central Plains

GUAY TEOW NUEA SAB

ก๋วยเตี๋ยวเนื้อสับ

Noodles with Ground Beef

This easy and delicious appetizer can also be served as a light meal.

1 lb (500 g) wide rice noodles (*sen yai*), cooked
2 tablespoons sweet soy sauce
3 tablespoons oil
1 lb (500 g) ground/minced beef
8 garlic cloves (*kratiem*), minced
¼ cup minced cilantro/coriander leaves (*bai pak chee*)
½ teaspoon white pepper
1 tomato, cut into wedges
½ cup sliced onions
¼ cup (2 fl oz/60 ml) fish sauce (*nam pla*)
2 tablespoons oyster sauce
1 tablespoon Maggi seasoning
3 tablespoons sugar
2 tablespoons cornstarch/cornflour, dissolved in ¼ cup
   (2 fl oz/60 ml) water
1 bunch green leaf lettuce/Chinese lettuce

Rub the noodles with the sweet soy sauce. Heat a large skillet with 2 tablespoons of the oil and stir the noodles continually until they are hot. Set the noodles aside.

Heat the rest of the oil in the same skillet and stir-fry the beef with the garlic until the beef is cooked. Add the next eight ingredients and heat to boiling.

Stir constantly, adding the cornstarch mixture to thicken.

Cover the base of a serving platter with green leaf lettuce. Arrange the noodles on top and pour the beef mixture over the noodles and serve.

SERVES 6–8

NOODLES WITH GROUND BEEF (TOP) AND SATAY BEEF (BOTTOM)

FRESH SAUSAGE (TOP) AND TAPIOCA PORK (BOTTOM)

The North

NAEM SOD

แหนมสด

Fresh Sausage

This sausage mixture is not served in a casing in the traditional manner. The ground mixture can be served with a side salad of fresh vegetables or with green lettuce leaves to use as wrappers.

4 cups (1qt/1 l) water
8 oz (250 g) pork skin/pork rind
8 oz (250 g) ground/minced pork
4 garlic cloves (*kratiem*), sliced
¼ cup slivered ginger
½ cup (2½ oz/75 g) whole roasted peanuts
¼ cup fried dried Thai chili peppers
 (*prik khee noo haeng*)
¼ cup (2 fl oz/60 ml) fish sauce (*nam pla*)
¼ cup (2 fl oz/60 ml) lime juice
¼ cup chopped green onions/scallions/spring onions
¼ cup chopped cilantro/coriander leaves (*bai pak chee*)

▓ Heat the water to boiling in a medium saucepan and add the pork skin. Reheat to boiling then simmer for about 40 minutes or until the pork skin is tender.

▓ Remove the pork skin from the water, allow to cool, then slice into very thin 2-in x ¼-in (5-cm x 6-mm) strips.

▓ In a medium skillet on medium-high heat, cook the ground pork for about 4 minutes or until it is done, stirring to break up the meat.

▓ Combine the pork skin strips, ground pork and remaining ingredients except the green onion and cilantro. Place the mixture on a serving dish and sprinkle the green onion and cilantro on top.

▓ Serve with lettuce leaves and garnish if desired.

SERVES 4–6

Bangkok and the Central Plains

SA-KOO SAI MOO

สาคูไส้หมู

Tapioca Pork

Enjoy this as a snack or as a first course for four to six people.

2 tablespoons oil
½ cup garlic cloves (*kratiem*), minced
1 lb (500 g) ground/minced pork
3 tablespoons fish sauce (*nam pla*)
¼ cup (2 oz/60 g) sugar
¼ cup chopped salted turnip
1 cup (8 oz/250 g) ground roasted peanuts
8 oz (250 g) small pearl tapioca
½ cup (2 oz/60g) cornstarch/cornflour

ACCOMPANIMENTS

green leaf lettuce/Chinese lettuce
chopped green Thai chili peppers (*prik khee noo*)
cilantro/coriander leaves (*bai pak chee*)

▓ Heat the oil in a medium skillet, then add the garlic. Fry for 30 seconds, then remove half the garlic and reserve.

▓ Add the pork to the remaining garlic and oil and stir-fry until cooked. Add the fish sauce, sugar, turnip and peanuts. Mix well to combine, then reduce heat and stir until the sauce is absorbed. Remove from heat and allow to cool.

▓ Cover the tapioca pearls with warm water and soak for about 30 minutes, or until swollen. Drain. Add the cornstarch and mix with hands to form a soft dough.

▓ With wet hands pinch off about 1 tablespoonful of dough and shape into a 2-in (5-cm) diameter circle. Center 1 teaspoonful of the pork mixture on the circle then seal by wrapping the dough around the filling. Continue until all the dough is used.

▓ Heat some water to boiling in a large pot, then add the tapioca balls. Cook for 3–4 minutes, or until the dough is translucent, on high heat. Drain.

▓ Serve the tapioca balls on the lettuce, with the chilies, cilantro and reserved cooked garlic. The diners sprinkle these on each tapioca ball, which is wrapped inside a lettuce leaf.

MAKES 24 BALLS

The North

KAEP MOO

แคบหมู

Fried Pork Skin

Beautifully crisp pork skin's flavor is enhanced by a tasty dip.

4 cups (1 qt/1 l) water
1 lb (500 g) pork skin/pork rind, cut in 2-in x 2-in
 (5-cm x 5-cm) squares
1 teaspoon salt
4 cups (1 qt/1 l) oil, for deep-frying

▓ Heat the water to boiling in a large saucepan. Add the pork skin and return to the boil. Reduce heat and simmer for 40 minutes or until the pork skin is soft and tender. Drain. Rub with the salt.

▓ Place the cooked pork skin on a rack in a 350°F (180°C) oven and bake for 30 minutes or until it is dry.

▓ Heat the oil to 375°F (190°C) and deep-fry the pork skin until crisp. Serve with your favorite dipping sauce.

SERVES 4

FRIED PORK SKIN (LEFT), CHARCOAL-BROILED
PORK NECK (TOP, RECIPE PAGE 328) AND FRIED
NORTHEAST SAUSAGE (BOTTOM, RECIPE PAGE 328)

The Northeast

SAI GROG TAUD

ไส้กรอกทอด

Fried Northeast Sausage

This northeastern sausage specialty is most often fried to bring out the flavor of the meat, retaining the juices within the casing. It is often served with vegetables, which perfectly complement the spiciness of the sausage.

1 cup (8 fl oz/250 ml) oil
1 lb (500 g) northeast sausages *(sai grog Esan)* (see page 392)

ACCOMPANIMENTS

⅓ cup (2 oz/60 g) roasted peanuts
¼ cup sliced ginger
¼ cup sliced shallots
¼ cup sliced lemon grass/citronella *(ta-krai)*
¼ cup sliced green Thai chili peppers *(prik khee noo)*

▨ Heat a large skillet and add the oil. Use medium-high heat to bring the oil to approximately 350°F (180°C).
▨ Place half the sausages in the skillet and slowly fry for 6 minutes, turning the sausages to cook evenly. Remove and set aside. Cook the other sausages in the same manner.
▨ Slice the sausages and place on a serving plate. Combine the accompaniments and arrange beside the sausages.

SERVES 6 *Photograph page 327*

The Northeast

KAW MOO YANG

คอหมูย่าง

Charcoal-Broiled Pork Neck

In the Northeast not much food is wasted and every part of an animal is used. This is an easy recipe, with a dip that enhances the flavor of the broiled meat.

1 pork neck, 1 lb (500 g)

MARINADE

6 garlic cloves *(kratiem)*, minced
3 tablespoons minced cilantro/coriander root *(raak pak chee)*
1 teaspoon white pepper
2 tablespoons sugar
2 tablespoons soy sauce
2 tablespoons fish sauce *(nam pla)*

DIPPING SAUCE

2 tablespoons fish sauce *(nam pla)*
1 tablespoon sliced green Thai chili pepper *(prik khee noo)*
1 tablespoon sliced garlic *(kratiem)*
2 tablespoons lime juice
1 tablespoon sliced shallot
1 tablespoon chopped cilantro/coriander leaves *(bai pak chee)*
1 tablespoon chopped green onion/scallion/spring onion

▨ Place the pork neck in a dish with the combined marinade ingredients. Let stand for 15 minutes.
▨ Charcoal-broil for 10 minutes on each side or bake at 350°F (180°C) for 30 minutes. While this is cooking combine the dipping sauce ingredients.
▨ Slice the meat and place on a platter; serve with the dipping sauce.

SERVES 4 *Photograph page 327*

Bangkok and the Central Plains

KHAO MOO DAENG

ข้าวหมูแดง

Barbecued Pork with Rice

A delicious accompaniment to any noodle dish as well as being an appetizer, this recipe is easy to prepare.

2 lb (1 kg) pork, cut into 2-in x 6-in (5-cm x 15-cm) strips

MARINADE

6 garlic cloves *(kratiem)*, minced
½ teaspoon white pepper
1 cup (8 fl oz/ 250 ml) soy sauce
½ cup (3 oz/90 g) brown sugar
1 teaspoon red food coloring

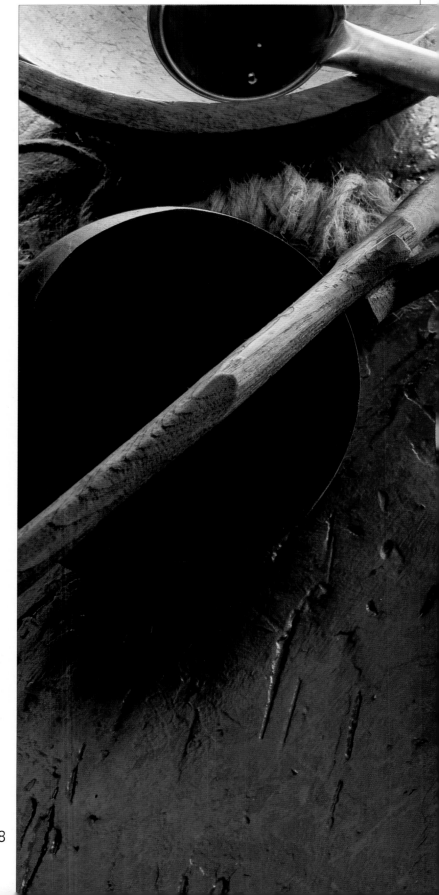

GRAVY

2 tablespoons oil
¼ cup minced garlic cloves *(kratiem)*
½ teaspoon salt
½ cup (4 oz/125 g) ground roasted peanuts
½–1 cup (4–8 oz/125–250 ml) pan juices from pork
2 tablespoons cornstarch/cornflour dissolved in
   3 tablespoons water

4 cups steamed jasmine rice *(khao suay)* (see page 350)
1 cup cucumber slices
6–8 green onions/scallions/spring onions
½ cup cilantro-coriander leaves *(bai pak chee)*
½ cup (4 fl oz/125 ml) chili in vinegar *(prik dong)*
   (see page 493)

✥ Combine the pork strips with the combined marinade ingredients and marinate for 30 minutes. Place the strips on a rack in a baking pan and bake at 350°F (180°C) for 45 minutes. Reserve

all the pan juices for making the gravy, but skim off some of the fat. If the pan juices from the pork are too diluted reduce the sauce to achieve a greater concentration of flavor.

✥ To prepare the gravy, heat a small skillet and add the oil. Fry the garlic until golden brown. Add the remaining ingredients, stirring in the cornstarch and water mixture. Heat to boiling. Set aside.

✥ Slice the pork. Place a portion of cooked rice on each plate. Arrange slices of pork around the rice and pour some gravy over the pork. Garnish with cucumber slices, green onion and cilantro leaves. Serve with the chili in vinegar. If the pork and gravy are served on a platter with the garnish the rice must be served separately.

SERVES 6–8

BARBECUED PORK WITH RICE

CHIANG MAI SAUSAGE (LEFT) AND EGG NOODLES
WITH BARBECUED PORK (RIGHT)

The North

KANOM JEEN NAM NGEOW

ขนมจีนน้ำเงี้ยว

Noodle Rib Curry

Noodles are second only to rice as a favorite staple and the great variety of noodles provides many taste delights. Curry noodles make a very satisfying meal.

3 tablespoons oil
8 garlic cloves *(kratiem)*, chopped
¼ cup (2 fl oz/60 ml) red curry paste *(nam prik gaeng ped)*
  (see page 488)
2 lb (1 kg) pork ribs, cut into 1-in x 1-in
  (2.5-cm x 2.5-cm) pieces
2 tablespoons yellow bean sauce *(tao jeow)*
1 cup diced tomatoes
¼ teaspoon turmeric
⅓ cup (3 fl oz/90 ml) fish sauce *(nam pla)*
4 cups (1 qt/1 l) water
8 oz (250 g) egg noodles *(ba mee)*, cooked
1 green onion/scallion/spring onion, chopped
¼ cup cilantro/coriander leaves *(bai pak chee)*

CONDIMENTS

1 cup bean sprouts
1 cup string beans, cut in 2-in (5-cm) pieces
½ cup chopped vegetable pickles

▨ Heat a small skillet, add 2 tablespoons of the oil and brown the garlic, then remove and set aside.
▨ Heat a large saucepan, add the rest of the oil and fry the curry paste for 3 minutes on medium heat. Add the pork ribs and bean sauce and continue to brown for 3 more minutes.
▨ Add the tomatoes, turmeric, fish sauce and water. Continue to cook for 15 minutes on medium-high heat.
▨ Separate the noodles into individual bowls, and spoon some of the soup mixture over them. Top with the green onion, cilantro leaves and all the condiments and carefully pour more soup on top before serving.
▨ Serve the browned garlic separately, to be added as desired for extra flavor.

SERVES 4–6

Bangkok and the Central Plains

KHAO PAD MOO BAI GA-PROW

ข้าวผัดหมูใบกะเพรา

Pork Fried Rice with Basil Leaf

Fried rice is a favorite food of Thailand. This version has a delicate aroma imparted by the flavor of the basil leaf.

3 tablespoons oil
4 oz (125 g) pork loin, thinly sliced
3 garlic cloves *(kratiem)*, minced
½ cup sliced green jalapeño peppers *(prik chee fa)*
¼ cup sliced onions
4 cups cooked rice
⅓ cup (3 fl oz/90 ml) fish sauce *(nam pla)*
2 tablespoons sugar

1 tablespoon sweet soy sauce
¼ teaspoon white pepper
1 cup hot basil leaves *(bai ga-prow)*
1 small tomato, cut into wedges
½ cup sliced cucumber
4 green onions/scallions/spring onions, cut in 4-in
  (20-cm) lengths
1 carrot, thinly sliced

NOODLE RIB CURRY (LEFT) AND PORK
FRIED RICE WITH BASIL LEAF (RIGHT)

Heat a large skillet until hot and add the oil. Add the pork, garlic, peppers and onions and cook for 30 seconds. Add the rice, fish sauce, sugar, soy sauce and pepper and continue to cook until the rice is hot.

Toss in the basil leaves and stir to combine. Remove to a serving plate and garnish with tomato, cucumber, carrot and green onions.

SERVES 4

THE NORTHEAST

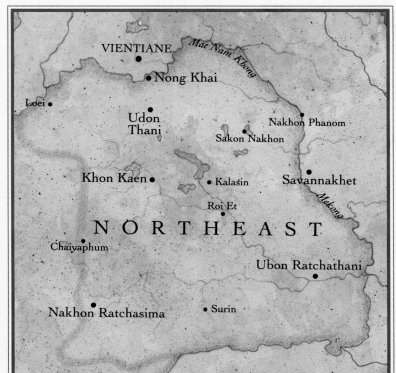

THE NORTHEAST

I N THE SUMMER of 1966 a young American student, the son of a former U.S. ambassador, happened to pass through an obscure hamlet called Ban Chiang in the northeastern province of Udon Thani. A road was being constructed in the area, and among the debris piled up along it the student noticed a large number of unusual pottery shards: buff-colored and adorned with bold, swirling red designs. He collected a few and brought them back to an art-collecting Thai princess with whom he was staying in Bangkok; she in turn showed them to a representative of an American museum, who thought they should be sent to the United States for precise dating.

Thus, quite accidentally, began one of the most exciting chapters in contemporary archeology. Later excavations by the Thai Fine Arts Department and the University of Pennsylvania revealed that an extraordinary prehistoric culture had flourished on Thailand's northeastern plateau, going back to nearly 4000 B.C. and numbering among its achievements the use of sophisticated bronze metallurgy as well as rice cultivation, fine pottery, and possibly even textiles. Indeed, some archeologists who worked on the site have become convinced that the so-called Ban Chiang culture ranks among humankind's first "cradles of civiliz-ation", thus challenging the traditional assumption of a gradual spread from the Middle East to Asia.

The findings are still incomplete, and many tantalizing mysteries remain about the people of Ban Chiang: where

ELEPHANTS AT THE ANNUAL SURIN ROUND-UP

PREVIOUS PAGES: PRASAT MUANG THAM, IN BURIRAM PROVINCE, BUILT BY THE KHMERS ONE THOUSAND YEARS AGO

JOHN HAY

THE FRIENDLY SMILE OF A FARMER BUSY AT WORK IN THE FIELDS

they came from, where they went, and why, with all their accomplishments, they never apparently developed an urban society. Enough is known, however, to dispel the old theory that Southeast Asia was a "cultural backwater", as a French historian once described it, and also to add a much-needed flavor of romance to the region the Thais call Esan.

For most of the present century, Esan, or the Northeast, has been known as Thailand's chronic problem region, in spite of the fact that it is almost a third of the country's total area and includes seven of the most populous provinces plus the second-largest Thai city, Khon Kaen. In many parts the soil is poor and yields only a subsistence livelihood for those who work it. Prolonged droughts are frequent; and when rain does come it often results in disastrous floods, especially along the Mekong River which serves as a border with Laos. Temperatures can also be extreme, ranging from some of the coldest in Thailand in provinces such as Loei, where it can drop to almost freezing, to some of the hottest, at more than 110 degrees Fahrenheit (over 43 degrees Celsius) recorded at Udon Thani. Despite considerable progress in recent years, real hardship is still more prevalent in the Northeast than in most other parts of Thailand, and many of its people are still forced to seek temporary employment in Bangkok, where they form the great majority of low-income construction laborers, taxi drivers, and domestic servants.

This was not always true. At the time of the Ban Chiang culture and probably for some time afterward, the Northeast was thickly forested and rich in animal life. In historical ·times, between the ninth and fourteenth centuries, it was an important center of Khmer culture, the remains of which constitute one of its principal tourist attractions today. The

great temple of Phimai, for instance, not far from the provincial capital of Nakhon Ratchasima, was linked by a direct road to Angkor and is artistically regarded as one of the finest examples of classical Khmer architecture. The recently restored Prasat Phanom Rung, near the Dongrek Mountains along the frontier of Cambodia, is another imposing ruin which has splendid stone figures and friezes; one of these, stolen in the 1960s, was retrieved from an American museum after a much-publicized protest a few years ago. Altogether there are more than thirty such sites scattered around the Northeast, and until Cambodia itself becomes accessible again they offer the best opportunity to view Khmer artistry outside a museum.

Following the decline of Khmer power in the fourteenth century, Thai kingdoms rose, ruling first from Sukhothai and then, for much longer, from Ayutthaya. Though the Northeast was theoretically under the control of both, and though armies sometimes marched through it to do battle in Laos and Cambodia, the region was actually as isolated as the far North and remained so even after Bangkok became the capital, its forests gradually diminishing and the life of its people growing steadily harder.

Immigrants filtered across the borders from both Laos and Cambodia, bringing various elements of those cultures; indeed, until recent years at least, ethnic Lao comprised the major part of the population in several large northeastern provinces, and there has long been an active trade across the Mekong River. Later Vietnamese refugees came in a series of waves, as well as hill tribes and other minority groups fleeing the turmoil in Indochina. Like elsewhere in Thailand, sizeable numbers of Chinese settled in the cities, where they opened businesses, became middlemen for the region's farmers, and added their own flavor to the ethnic mixture.

Though a railway line was built to link Bangkok with Nakhon Ratchasima in 1900 and extended eastwards to Ubon Ratchathani in 1926, and though an airmail service was started in the region in 1922—the first airmail service in all of Southeast Asia—travel in most of the Northeast remained difficult until relatively recent years. There were almost no paved roads as late as the early 1960s, only rutted tracks that became impassable during the rainy season, and few people from the capital ever went to the more distant

GLASS BRACELETS AND BEAD NECKLACES FROM THE BAN CHIANG PRE-HISTORIC CULTURE, SHOWN AT THE SUAN PAKAAD PALACE MUSEUM

LUCA INVERNIZZI TETTONI/PHOTOBANK

THE TEMPLE OF PRASAT HIN PHIMAI, NEAR KORAT, BUILT BY THE KHMERS IN THE LATE ELEVENTH AND EARLY TWELFTH CENTURIES

AN OPEN-AIR DUCK FARM, WHERE POULTRY IS RAISED
FOR MEAT RATHER THAN EGGS

provinces. When King Bhumibol Adulyadej and Queen Sirikit made a three-week tour of the northeastern provinces in the mid-1950s, it was the first time a ruling monarch had ever been seen by most residents. It also marked the beginning of the determined efforts to improve rural life that have characterized King Bhumibol's long rule.

At least one reason for the previous lack of development was a perceptible prejudice against northeasterners, especially on the part of Bangkok people. Many of their popular foods, too, were regarded as "strange" by sophisticated city dwellers, and in Bangkok northeastern restaurants tended to be very modest establishments tucked away on obscure side-streets, patronized mainly by immigrants from the region. When William Klausner, an American anthropologist, announced in 1955 that he was going to do ethnographic research in a northeastern village, he was strongly advised against it by several government officials who warned that "the area was remote, the food unpalatable, the women not very attractive". And the most telling criticism: "It wouldn't be sanuk", meaning it wouldn't be fun.

All these factors have powerfully influenced northeastern life and culture as it exists today. Having usually worked on their own land, however infertile it might be, typically northeasterners have a strong sense of independence which they are willing to assert; it is no accident that many of Thailand's most outspoken writers and politicians in modern times have come from Esan backgrounds. They are also resourceful, able to derive a livelihood (and also a distinctive cuisine) from meager resources. Not surprisingly, they have a fatalistic bent that helps them accept the natural disasters that

so often afflict them, but they are by no means gloomy or brooding. Like Thais everywhere, they have devised numerous local forms of amusement, from building huge rockets to fire in a ceremony believed to bring rain, to staging impromptu battles between two of the giant horned beetles native to the region. Despite the recent growth of several large northeastern cities, they are more than likely to live in a small village and to leave it only when forced by dire economic need; even after years of driving a Bangkok taxi or loading ships at the capital's port, northeasterners still think of the village as the home to be returned to one day.

Many northeasterners from the provinces along the Mekong River speak Lao as fluently as they do Thai, and those in the southern part speak Khmer. Northeastern food reflects the influence of both cultures as well, particularly the former, just as it reflects a past when staples were often unavailable. "Esan people eat anything," Bangkok residents often remark, and so it may seem to a finicky outsider invited for a meal in one of the more distant hamlets, for this is a region where little is wasted, however unusual. Fried grub worms or grasshoppers are likely to be offered as a snack, or perhaps grilled lizard, ant eggs, snail curry, or a dried semi-decayed fish of exceptional pungency (and also, to its many admirers, of exceptional flavor).

William Klausner, contrary to official warnings, managed to settle down quite happily in the northeastern village of his choice and ultimately to marry one of the local girls. He did, however, have certain problems with food at first. "I developed my own cooked variations of such staples as ... raw fermented fish and the cold salad of unripe papaya, raw fermented fish, peppers, tomatoes, and onions. I soon became accustomed to glutinous rice but remained wary of cooked silkworms, frogs, crickets and red ants. It is often said that the way to a villager's heart is through speaking the village dialect and eating such favorite village staples as uncooked fermented fish. After sampling the latter, I decided to stress my linguistic ability," he wrote.

But such exotica is actually the exception rather than the rule, especially in larger communities where better supplies are available. Indeed, more and more frequently, one hears connoisseurs of Thai cuisine proclaiming that northeastern fare is the best in all the country. Typical Esan dishes can now be found on the menus of the smartest Thai restaurants in Bangkok, and many of those humble side-street food shops are crowded with well-dressed diners as well as taxi drivers. As in Laos (and also in northern Thailand) glutinous rice is the staple, eaten either as a base for other dishes or as a sweet when steamed in a hollow piece of bamboo with coconut milk and black beans. Typical Laotian herbs such as dill (called *pak chee Lao*, or Lao cilantro or coriander, by Thais) also often turn up as seasonings. Another popular dish of Lao origin is *khanom buang*, a thin crispy crepe stuffed with dried shrimp, bean sprouts, and other assorted ingredients, which requires considerable skill to prepare properly and is thus usually served only on special occasions.

Laab, spicy minced meat or chicken, is a specialty of the region—the methods of preparation varying from province to province—along with *som tam* (green papaya salad), barbecued chicken, *hor mok* (fish with curry paste and steamed in

BRIGHTLY COLORED UMBRELLAS SHADE MELONS FROM
THE SUN ON A ROADSIDE STALL

banana leaf), catfish curry, and entrails cooked in numerous ways. Since meat is often scarce in villages, freshwater fish and shrimps are the principal sources of protein, either in the fermented form that William Klausner found difficult to appreciate or cooked with herbs and spices. One of the great regional delicacies for those who live along the Mekong is a giant catfish called *pla buk*, which can reach 10 feet (3 meters) in length and weigh more than 550 pounds (250 kilograms). Perhaps in a sort of culinary reaction to their difficult lives, or perhaps merely because some of the traditional ingredients

A BOY FROM THE NORTHEAST TENDING HIS FAMILY'S BUFFALOES
AT THE END OF THE DAY

JOHN HAY

A COLLECTION OF FRESHLY MADE SAUSAGES LOOPED
OVER A POLE FOR DISPLAY AT THE MARKET

needed strong seasoning to make them more palatable, northeasterners like their food not just spicy but very hot, and chili peppers are used with a greater abandon than almost anywhere else.

Certain foods are reserved for festivals and ceremonial days, among them a noodle dish called *khaw pun* made from non-glutinous rice flour. The noodles take a long time to prepare, and the long thin strands are said to resemble the sacred thread used in Brahmanical blessing ceremonies, giving them a special symbolic quality not regarded as proper for ordinary meals.

Cut off from the outside world, northeastern villagers in the past made most of the items needed in their daily life, from cooking pots and rice baskets to fish traps and textiles. Silk is probably the most noted regional handicraft, especially a subtly colored traditional form of tie-and-dye ikat known as *mudmee* which has been popularized in recent years by Queen Sirikit. (Pierre Balmain, who often designed for the Queen, once did an entire fashion collection based on *mudmee*.) Weaving and sericulture continued to be important home industries in this region long after they had declined in areas more exposed to Western culture, and to a large extent northeastern skills were responsible for the great Thai silk revival that took place shortly after the Second World War. One especially active weaving center was in a village called Pakthongchai just outside Nakhon Ratchasima, and it was here that Jim Thompson, the American who led the revival, supervised most of the dazzling silks produced for the original Broadway production of *The King and I*, a break-through exposure that brought international fame to the fabric. At that time, in the late 1940s, it took Thompson an exhausting eleven hours to reach his weavers by train and local bus from Bangkok; today it takes less than two hours. The company that Thompson founded maintains the largest hand-weaving silk facility in the world at Pakthongchai.

A number of factors were responsible for finally opening the Northeast to the outside world. One of the most important of these was a military and political leader named Field Marshal Sarit Thanarat, who came from the region himself—like many northeasterners, he also had close relatives across the border in Laos—and was determined to bring development to it when he came to power toward the end of the 1950s. Among his achievements was the construction of the Friendship Highway, a joint Thai-American undertaking that linked Saraburi, just north of Bangkok, with Nakhon Ratchasima and thereby made travel to the Korat Plateau by car relatively easy for the first time. Sarit also launched many other projects to raise the standard of living in the Northeast, including rural electrification, much-needed reservoirs and expanded irrigation.

The Indochina War accelerated the building of more all-weather roads to move military equipment to sensitive areas along the Cambodian and Laotian borders. Several large American military bases were built during the conflict, pumping money into the region and virtually overnight turning once-sleepy provincial capitals like Ubon Ratchathani and Udon Thani into boomtowns. Though the Americans (and much of the money) disappeared in due course once the war had ended, some of the innovations they brought profoundly altered local ways of life.

Communist insurgents, too, played a role in awakening Bangkok authorities to northeastern needs. Esan's poverty made it a natural target for those trying to destabilize the government and for a time in the mid-1970s the area probably contained more openly discontented people than any other in the country. This problem was met by a number of enlightened military commanders—among them the future Prime Minister, General Prem Tinsulanonda—who recognized that greater prosperity was the key to winning the support of the people and who launched a massive campaign of development that continues today.

King Bhumibol Adulyadej, as already mentioned, became aware of northeastern problems early in his reign, and hundreds of royally initiated projects have resulted throughout the region. The royal family now maintains a residence at Sakon Nakhon which is used as a base when overseeing regional activities and when making regular visits to remote hamlets. Another, newer palace is located in mountainous Phetchabun at the western extremity of the Northeast, once a notorious center for insurgents but now a peaceful scenic area of farms and fruit orchards being promoted by local travel writers as "the Switzerland of Thailand".

Among the other signs of a renewed sense of purpose in the Northeast was the opening of a university in Khon Kaen, the first to be established outside the capital. Modern highways now connect every major provincial town, and there is regular air service within the region as well. An extensive reafforestation program, known as "Green Esan", is underway, and farmers are beginning to learn that while rice may have been the traditional crop of their forefathers, it is not necessarily the right one for a region where the rains often fail. Other crops may be better suited to local conditions—soya beans, vegetables, and fruit, for example—and may also bring a better income. Many of Thailand's avocados, a relatively recent introduction to local markets, are being grown on the Korat Plateau.

Tourism still ranks low on the list of income-earners, but an increasing number of outsiders are discovering that their preconception of the Northeast as a barren wasteland devoid of cultural or scenic interest is untrue. Though much of the region's original forest cover has been destroyed, some tracts still remain, particularly in a number of splendid national forests in the more mountainous areas. The best known, thanks to its easy accessibility to Bangkok, is Khao Yai, which covers more than 770 square miles (2,000 square

LUCA INVERNIZZI TETTONI/PHOTOBANK

SILK WEAVING IS A HOME INDUSTRY IN THE NORTHEAST, THE BEST
KNOWN BEING THE TIE-AND-DYE IKAT KNOWN AS MUDMEE

kilometers) in four provinces and accounts for about a tenth of Thailand's total area of national parks and game preserves. Khao Yai offers usually cool fresh air, impressive scenery with evergreen tropical trees, native orchids, and waterfalls, and a chance to glimpse nearly all of the two hundred species of protected wildlife in Thailand, including elephants, tigers, deer, and a wide assortment of birds. In 1987 a herd of more than fifty wild elephants was spotted in the park, delighting conservationists who had doubted that such large numbers of the species still existed in Thailand.

Another extensive park is Phu Kadung in Loei province, centered on a mountain topped by a plateau of 23 square miles (60 square kilometers) of exceptional natural beauty. Though there is no road to the plateau and the ascent involves a strenuous four-hour climb, it is becoming a popular holiday destination for nature-loving (and athletic) student groups from Bangkok and elsewhere.

Others are coming to see the archeological sites, not only the great Khmer ruins mentioned previously but newer discoveries such as Ban Chiang, which now has an excellent museum displaying relics which were found in the excavations. A famous mountaintop Khmer temple called Khao Phra Vihar was awarded to Cambodia in a controversial decision by the World Court during the 1950s and remains inaccessible from the Thai side; if the political situation improves and visitors are once more allowed, this will undoubtedly be another major attraction.

The Tourism Authority of Thailand, which is actively promoting the Northeast, has helped to publicize a number of traditional festivals in the region. One is the Elephant Roundup, held every November in Surin province, when nearly two hundred of the huge animals take part in a four-

hour show enjoyed by thousands of spectators. Surin people have long been noted for their skill at training elephants, which in former days they captured in the forests of Cambodia; that source, obviously, is no longer available, but Surin elephants and their enterprising mahouts appear in many parts of the country, including the streets of Bangkok, to earn a little money from performances.

Boon Bang Fais, or rocket festivals, are held in several northeastern provinces, though the most famous is undoubtedly the one in Yasothon province in May, just before rice is planted. Enormous rockets almost 30 feet (9 meters) long are fired at the peak of the lively celebrations, the purpose being to ensure a plentiful supply of rain as well as to provide an opportunity for villagers to enjoy themselves.

A more solemn occasion is *Khao Phansa* in July, marking the start of the three-month Buddhist Lent, or "Rains Retreat", when the monks are supposed to remain in their temples. This is of course observed throughout Thailand, but Ubon Ratchathani, in the heart of the Northeast, has become especially renowned for the huge imaginative candles carved by local people and paraded proudly through the streets in a two-day festival.

No longer isolated, no longer ignored by authorities in the capital, the Northeast is now a center of purposeful activity—"the region of the future", as one government official recently described it in a discussion of the role it will play when peace and economic stability return to the countries that share its borders. Already, in the space of just a few decades, its distinctive customs and cuisine are better known and more appreciated than ever before, and the time when "Esan" was a term heavily weighted with pejorative connotations may finally be drawing to an end.

CURRIES AND MAIN COURSES

SORTING CHILIES AT A MARKET IN BANGKOK

Curries and Main Courses

A TEEMING, NOISY SEA OF DUCKS AT ONE OF THE
FARMS THAT SUPPLY BANGKOK'S NUMEROUS MARKETS

THERE IS A SAYING that there are two seasons in Thailand: hot and hotter. What better way to thrive in the tropical warmth of this country than with a cuisine whose spicy heat helps to cool down the body.

The intensity of many curries owes itself to Thai chili peppers (*prik khee noo*).

Prik khee noo are found in Thailand's famous green curry (*gaeng keow wan gai*), whose cool, lime green color deceives the unwary diner tasting this most incendiary of Thai curries. Take a bite of green curry, and it bites back. But it can become habit-forming, and make you want to return for more. The green color comes from the fresh green jalapeño peppers and the smaller *prik khee noo*.

The perfect complement to the searing assault of chilies is rice, which is usually served at every meal. Thai jasmine rice, a long-grained rice, is the best choice of rice, possessing a faint fragrance like jasmine.

For those who favor milder curries, the choices are many. Red curry uses long red chili peppers and lemon grass, with an array of other spices and herbs. Equally flavorful, but less fiery, are some curries from central Thailand like Panaeng curry (*panaeng nuea*) and Massaman curry (*massaman nuea*).

All curry-making begins with the curry paste. In days past, when the lifestyle was more relaxed, time allowed the making of curry paste by each household from the freshest ingredients available, using a stone mortar and

PREVIOUS PAGES: BARBECUED CHICKEN (RIGHT, RECIPE PAGE 376), GREEN CURRY WITH CHICKEN AND THAI EGGPLANT (TOP LEFT, RECIPE PAGE 376) AND RED CURRY CHICKEN (LEFT, RECIPE PAGE 376)

pestle. Because each family devised its own recipe for the paste, the balance of ingredients was based upon personal taste, giving rise to subtle differences in the recipes, even though curries employ a common ingredient, chili peppers. Homemade curry paste is always the best because all the ingredients are fresh. But for those living in cities with their unrelenting schedules, prepared curry paste can be purchased at most markets.

In the making of fresh, traditional Thai curry paste, one first pounds the dried spices such as cumin and peppercorns in a mortar with a pestle. A visitor to a Thai village can hear the rhythmic pounding that accompanies this most time-consuming step in the curry-making process. The other ingredients, such as fresh or dried chilies, lemon grass, garlic and shallots, are incorporated to yield a smooth paste.

Most Thai curries, unlike Indian curries, are very easy to make because the cooking stage only requires a short time. Massaman curry (*massaman nuea*) is one of the few exceptions to this rule. Indian curries are usually simmered for many hours.

Curries, like other main courses, draw upon a rich variety of seafood, vegetables and meats.

Thailand's coastal regions yield an abundance of fresh fish, crab, shrimp, clams and mussels. The harvest from the land is similarly bountiful. In rural areas, villagers in long, narrow boats glide along shallow canals, selling a variety of produce at the floating marketplace. It is also a time to share the latest news of the day and is an important part of the people's social life.

For seafood and meat dishes, barbecuing is one of the most preferred cooking styles. Simple dips or sauces can be served on the side. Other cooking methods include frying and steaming. Seafood is also sun-dried: a visitor to a dried-fish stall can find anything from squid to prawns, all neatly laid out on platters.

The liquid essence of Thai cuisine is fish sauce (*nam pla*), made by fermenting fish with salt. *Nam pla* is found in many Thai recipes, heightening the flavor of any meat, seafood or vegetable dish. Another key flavoring is shrimp paste (*gapi*).

In a typical Thai dinner, at least four or five different dishes are served together, each having equal importance in the enjoyment of the meal. A nicely balanced meal would include a soup, a curry, a vegetable or salad dish, a seafood dish, perhaps a meat dish, and, of course, rice.

ROADSIDE FOOD STALLS IN BANGKOK OFFER THE PASSERBY
A SELECTION OF DELICIOUS CURRIES TO SAMPLE

JENNY MILLS

349

STEAMED JASMINE RICE

Bangkok and the Central Plains

KHAO SUAY

ข้าวสวย

Steamed Jasmine Rice

The wonderful aroma and subtle flavor of jasmine rice complement every dish perfectly. Thais cook rice almost instinctively—it is their staple food.

3 cups (1 lb/500 g) jasmine rice
3 cups (24 fl oz/750 ml) water

▨ Place the rice in a large saucepan. Rinse twice to clean the rice, draining thoroughly. Add the water to the rice.
▨ Cover the saucepan and heat to boiling. Allow to boil on high heat for 1 minute. Turn the temperature to low and steam for 10 minutes. Reduce the heat to the lowest setting and allow to steam for 10 minutes more.

SERVES 4

The North

KHAO NEOW

ข้าวเหนียว

Steamed Sticky Rice

Sticky rice is a glutinous rice eaten by the people of the North and Northeast. The rice is sometimes referred to as sweet rice because it has a sweet flavor. It is often used to make rice wine and vinegar.

4 cups (2 lb/1 kg) sticky rice

▨ Place the rice in a saucepan or bowl and add enough water to cover. Rub the rice between your hands several times and drain off the milky water. Add clean water and repeat the process until the water runs clear.
▨ Soak the rice overnight in enough water to cover or, to save time, the rice can be soaked in hot water for 3 hours before steaming, rather than overnight.
▨ Drain the rice and place in a cloth-lined steamer or in a steaming basket. Place the basket over a pot of boiling water, making sure that the basket does not touch the water. Cover the steamer and steam for approximately 30 minutes.

SERVES 4

Bangkok and the Central Plains

KAI LOOK-KUEY

ไข่ลูกเขย

Eggs with Tamarind Sauce

Whether just fried, used as toppings, or as an essential component of many desserts, eggs are a favorite food in Thailand. In this dish, deep-frying boiled eggs gives them a different texture while their flavor is enhanced by the accompanying sauce.

STEAMED STICKY RICE (TOP)
AND EGGS WITH TAMARIND SAUCE (BOTTOM)

4 cups (1 qt/1 l) water
6 eggs
2 cups (16 fl oz/500 ml) oil, for deep-frying
½ cup chopped shallots

TAMARIND SAUCE

½ cup (4 fl oz/125 ml) tamarind juice (*ma-kaam piag*)
  (see glossary)
½ cup (4 fl oz/125 ml) fish sauce (*nam pla*)
¼ cup (2 oz/60 g) sugar

❀ Pour the water into a large pot and boil the eggs for 5 minutes.

❀ Remove from the heat and plunge the eggs into cold water. Peel the eggs and set aside.

❀ In a large saucepan heat the oil to 325°F (165°C). Dry the eggs and deep-fry them until they are golden brown. Remove and set aside. With the same oil, deep-fry the shallots until golden brown. Drain and set aside.

❀ Combine all the ingredients for the sauce. Heat to boiling and simmer for 5 minutes.

❀ To serve, cut the eggs in half, lengthwise. Pour the sauce over the eggs and sprinkle with the fried shallots.

SERVES 4

351

Bangkok and the Central Plains

GAENG KUA SAPPAROD

แกงคั่วสับปะรด

Pineapple Curry

The delicate sweet and sour flavor of this curry sauce comes from the pineapple. It is also delicious with mussels or smoked salmon instead of shrimp.

2 cups (16 fl oz/500 ml) coconut milk
1 cup crushed fresh pineapple
2 tablespoons red curry paste *(nam prik gaeng ped)* (see page 488)
¼ cup (2 fl oz/60 ml) fish sauce *(nam pla)*
1½ tablespoons sugar
8 oz (250 g) shrimp/prawns, shelled and deveined

▦ Combine all the ingredients except the shrimp in a large saucepan and heat to boiling.
▦ Add the shrimp, reheat to boiling and cook for about 3 minutes or until done.
▦ Serve with steamed jasmine rice *(khao suay)*, on page 350.

SERVES 4

The South

POO NEUNG

ปูนึ่ง

Steamed Crab with Hot Sauce

As soon as the fishing boats return to harbor in the South the locals want to taste the sweetness of the fresh crabs. Simple cooking methods allow the natural taste of these crabs to be enjoyed.

1 crab, about 2 lb (1 kg), cleaned

HOT SAUCE

8 garlic cloves *(kratiem)*, minced
10 green Thai chili peppers *(prik khee noo)*, minced
2 tablespoons finely chopped cilantro/coriander root *(raak pak chee)* and leaves *(bai pak chee)*
¼ cup (2 fl oz/60 ml) fish sauce *(nam pla)*
¼ cup (2 fl oz/60 ml) lime juice
2 tablespoons sugar

▦ Leaving the shell intact, place the crab in a large steamer and steam for 10 minutes on high heat. After the crab is cooked, remove and set aside.
▦ Prepare the hot sauce by combining all the ingredients in a small bowl. Use as a dipping sauce. Crack the crab and dip into the sauce before eating.

SERVES 4

STEAMED CRAB WITH HOT SAUCE (LEFT),
PINEAPPLE CURRY (TOP RIGHT) AND CLAMS WITH
CHILI SAUCE (BOTTOM RIGHT, RECIPE PAGE 354

Bangkok and the Central Plains

HOI PAD NAM PRIK POW

หอยผัดน้ำพริกเผา

Clams with Chili Sauce

An easy cooking method gives delicious results. Mussels or other shellfish can be used as an alternative to clams or as an added extra.

2 tablespoons oil
1 teaspoon red curry paste (*nam prik gaeng ped*) (see page 488)
2 lb (1 kg) clams in their shells
2 tablespoons fish sauce (*nam pla*)
2 teaspoons sugar
¼ cup sliced green bell pepper/capsicum
¼ cup sliced red bell pepper/capsicum
1 tablespoon slivered fresh ginger
¼ cup sweet basil leaves (*bai horapa*)

Heat a large skillet, add the oil and the curry paste and sauté the clams for 1 minute.

Add the fish sauce, sugar, peppers, ginger and basil, stir thoroughly then cover the pan and cook for 6 minutes on medium heat.

SERVES 4   *Photograph pages 352–353*

Bangkok and the Central Plains

HAW MOK

ห่อหมก

Steamed Fish in Banana Leaf

While these folded packets are a delight to serve in small numbers, for a larger group the leaves can be folded into a large boat shape and the mixture steamed in larger portions with an extended cooking time.

1 lb (500 g) white fish fillets, cut into chunks

SAUCE

½ cup (4 fl oz/125 ml) red curry paste (*nam prik gaeng ped*)
   (see page 488)
2 cups (16 fl oz/500 ml) coconut milk
4 egg yolks (reserve whites for topping)
2 tablespoons fish sauce (*nam pla*)
2 tablespoons cornstarch/cornflour

TOPPING

1 cup (8 fl oz/250 ml) coconut cream
4 egg whites

1 large banana leaf, cut into 4 pieces, each 8 in x 8 in
   (20 cm x 20 cm)
1 cup shredded lettuce, blanched
1 cup sliced zucchini/courgette, blanched
1 cup sweet basil leaves (*bai horapa*)
2 green jalapeño peppers (*prik chee fa*), sliced
¼ cup cilantro/coriander leaves (*bai pak chee*)

Marinate the fish chunks with the combined sauce ingredients and place in the refrigerator to chill for about 15 minutes.

Beat the topping ingredients together with a fork.

Wipe each piece of banana leaf with a damp cloth before use. Place a quarter of each of the blanched vegetables and of the fish in the center of each piece of banana leaf. Spoon on a quarter of the topping. Top with a scattering of basil leaves, pepper slices and cilantro leaves.

Bring the sides of each square together and fold in the ends. Secure with a small piece of wood or a toothpick.

Arrange the packets in a steamer and steam for 15 minutes or until done. Alternatively, the packets can be baked in the oven at 350°F (180°C) for 20 minutes.

SERVES 4

Bangkok and the Central Plains

PLA NEUNG KIAMBOUY

ปลานึ่งเกี้ยมบ๊วย

Steamed Whole Fish with Plum Pickles

Different methods of preparation are used to give variety to the abundance of fresh fish in Thailand. This recipe uses the popular method of steaming, and the saltiness of the plum pickles adds a unique flavor.

1 rock cod or other white-fleshed fish, about 1–1½ lb
   (500–750 g)
½ teaspoon salt
½ teaspoon ground white pepper
1 tablespoon fish sauce (*nam pla*)
1 tablespoon white wine
3 whole pickled plums, cut into small pieces
2 tablespoons slivered fresh ginger
2 green jalapeño peppers (*prik chee fa*), sliced
2 tablespoons lime juice

Clean the fish, retaining the head, and make three slashes to the backbone on each side of the fish.

Rub the fish with the salt and pepper and place on a steaming plate. Add all the other ingredients. Place in the steamer, cover, and steam for 30 minutes until the fish is cooked.

SERVES 4

The Northeast

GAENG NAW MAI

แกงหน่อไม้

Bamboo Shoot Curry

A delicious curry supplemented with fresh fish and enhanced with the flavor of pickled fish. More sauce can be added for a wetter curry.

CURRY PASTE

6 garlic cloves (*kratiem*), chopped
8 shallots, sliced
½ cup sliced green jalapeño peppers (*prik chee fa*)
1 stalk lemon grass/citronella (*ta-krai*), chopped
1 tablespoon chopped galangal (*kha*)

1 lb (500 g) pickled fish
2 cups (16 fl oz/500 ml) water
1 lb (500 g) freshwater fish fillets, cut into 2-in (5-cm) slices
1 cup sliced tender bamboo shoots (see glossary)
2 tablespoons fish sauce (*nam pla*)
3 tablespoons tamarind juice (*ma-kaam piag*) (see glossary)

Prepare the curry paste by mashing the ingredients in a mortar with a pestle, or by combining in a blender, until a paste is formed. Set aside.

Boil the pickled fish in the water for 10 minutes and strain to retain the juice. Discard the pickled fish. Add the curry paste to the fish stock and heat to boiling. Add all the other ingredients and reheat to boiling. Remove to a serving bowl.

SERVES 4

BAMBOO SHOOT CURRY (LEFT), STEAMED WHOLE FISH WITH PLUM PICKLES (FRONT) AND STEAMED FISH IN BANANA LEAF (TOP RIGHT)

Bangkok and the Central Plains

PLA KAPONG KEEMOW

ปลากะพงขี้เมา

Whole Fish with Garlic Sauce

Cooking a fish whole ensures that the flesh remains juicy, and the skin is crisp. The blending of the garlic with the flavors of the peppers provides a dish worthy for any celebration.

1 whole fish, about 1 lb (500 g), cleaned, head retained
½ cup (2 oz/60 g) all-purpose/plain flour
4 cups (1 qt/1 l) oil, for deep-frying

SAUCE

8 garlic cloves *(kratiem)*
¼ cup chopped green jalapeño pepper *(prik chee fa)*
¼ cup chopped red jalapeño pepper *(prik chee fa daeng)*
¼ cup chopped green onions/scallions/spring onions
¼ cup chopped cilantro/coriander root *(raak pak chee)*

3 tablespoons oil
⅓ cup (3 fl oz/90 ml) fish sauce *(nam pla)*
3 tablespoons sugar
3 tablespoons lime juice
¼ teaspoon white pepper
6 kaffir lime leaves *(bai ma-grood)*, torn in half
¼ cup sweet basil leaves *(bai horapa)*

Cut three slashes to the bone on both sides of the fish, then coat with flour on both sides. This will prevent it from sticking to the skillet and will also make the skin crisp.

Heat the oil in a wok or large skillet to 350°F (180°C). Carefully lay the fish in the oil and deep-fry for approximately 5 minutes. Turn the fish with the aid of a large spatula and deep-fry the other side for 5 minutes. Remove from the oil and set on a large plate.

Heat a medium skillet on medium-high heat, then add the oil and the blended sauce ingredients. Stir and cook for 3 minutes.

Add the fish sauce, sugar, lime juice and pepper and cook for a further 2 minutes. Stir in the lime leaves and the basil.

Pour the sauce over the fish and serve.

SERVES 4

WHOLE FISH WITH GARLIC SAUCE

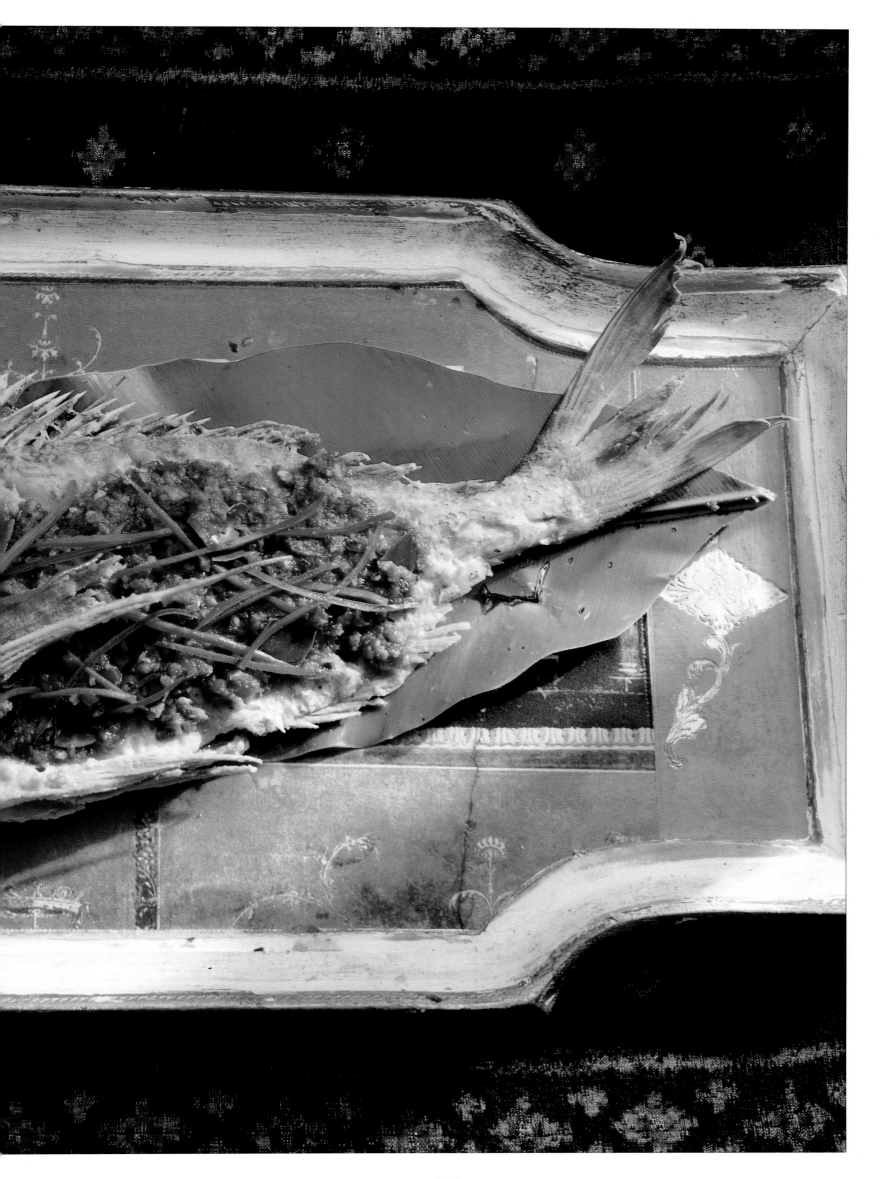

CRAB WITH LEEKS

Bangkok and the Central Plains

POO PAD TON KRATIEM

ปูผัดต้นกระเทียม

Crab with Leeks

This simple cooking method nevertheless results in a delicious dish, in which the richness of crab is lightened by the fresh flavor of leeks.

1 crab, about 2 lb (1 kg)
3 tablespoons Oriental sesame oil
4 garlic cloves (*kratiem*), minced
1 cup sliced leeks
2 tablespoons fish sauce (*nam pla*)
2 tablespoons sugar
½ cup sliced onions
1 egg

▨ Remove the crab's body shell, discard the internal gills and clean the cavity. Cut the crab in half. Separate the legs and claws and crack gently, and remove tips from legs. Rinse all the pieces.
▨ Heat a large skillet and add the sesame oil and garlic. Add the crab and stir-fry for 30 seconds to blend the flavors.
▨ Add all the remaining ingredients except the egg and stir-fry for 30 seconds, then cover the skillet and allow to steam for 3 minutes.
▨ Remove the lid, crack in the egg and stir until the egg is blended and cooked. Remove to a serving platter.

SERVES 4

Bangkok and the Central Plains

PAE-SA BANRAI

แป๊ะซะบ้านไร่

Steamed Fish Country Style

Steaming seafood makes sure that the moistness of the flesh is retained, and that the flavor of herbs and spices permeates through.

1 red fin, snapper or rock cod, about 1½ lb (750 g)
2 tablespoons rice wine
½ teaspoon salt
½ teaspoon white pepper
3 tablespoons fish sauce (*nam pla*)
¼ cup (2 fl oz/60 ml) lime juice
2 stalks lemon grass/citronella (*ta-krai*), crushed and cut into large pieces
¼ cup sliced onions
2 garlic cloves (*kratiem*), crushed
2 green onions/scallions/spring onions, sliced in halves and crushed
4 fresh or dried green Thai chili peppers (*prik khee noo*), crushed
¼ cup sweet basil leaves (*bai horapa*)
¼ cup slivered galangal (*kha*)

▨ Slash the fish on both sides.
▨ Place the fish on a steaming plate. Spread the remaining ingredients evenly over it.
▨ Steam for 25 minutes. Serve with your favorite dipping sauce.

SERVES 4

BROILED RED SNAPPER (TOP, RECIPE PAGE 360)
AND STEAMED FISH COUNTRY STYLE (BOTTOM)

The South

PLA KAPONG POW

ปลากะพงเผา

Broiled Red Snapper

Fish cooked in this way is particularly flavorful, with the marinade enhancing the delicate taste of fresh fish. Fish fillets can be substituted for the whole fish.

1 whole red snapper, about 1 lb (500 g)

MARINADE

2 tablespoons red curry paste (*nam prik gaeng ped*) (see page 488)
1¾ cups (14 fl oz/440 ml) coconut milk
3 tablespoons fish sauce (*nam pla*)
2 tablespoons sugar
5 kaffir lime leaves (*bai ma-grood*)

banana leaf or foil for wrapping fish
green and red bell pepper/capsicum slices, for garnish
kaffir lime leaves (*bai ma-grood*), for garnish

▨ Clean the fish and cut three slashes to the bone on both sides.
▨ Combine the marinade ingredients in a large bowl. Marinate the fish for 20 minutes.
▨ Wrap the fish in a banana leaf or in foil. Broil/grill or bake at 350°F (180°C) for 15 minutes per side or until done. Place on a serving dish and add the garnish.

SERVES 4   *Photograph page 359*

Bangkok and the Central Plains

GAAM POO OB WOON SEN

ก้ามปูอบวุ้นเส้น

Baked Crab Claws

A classic dish distinguished by the flavor of crab claws, which is usually served in the casserole it is cooked in.

3 tablespoons oil
2 lb (1 kg) crab claws, cracked
6 garlic cloves (*kratiem*), minced
1 teaspoon ground black peppercorns
2 tablespoons Maggi seasoning
3 tablespoons fish sauce (*nam pla*)
2 tablespoons sugar
2 oz (60 g) cellophane noodles (*woon sen*), soaked for 10 minutes
   in warm water.
2 stems cilantro/coriander (*pak chee*) including roots, chopped
2 green onions/scallions/spring onions, cut into 1-in
   (2.5-cm) pieces
cilantro/coriander leaves (*bai pak chee*), for garnish

▨ Heat a large skillet, add the oil, crab claws, garlic and black pepper. Add the sauces, sugar and cellophane noodles. Stir to combine the flavors and cook for 1 minute.
▨ Place the crab pieces in a metal or clay casserole dish then add the rest of the mixture.
▨ Scatter the cilantro and green onions on top, cover the casserole and bake at 350°F (180°C) for 10–15 minutes, taking care not to let the liquid dry out.
▨ Garnish with the cilantro leaves before serving.

SERVES 4

361

BAKED CRAB CLAWS (LEFT) AND CURRIED SHRIMP
(RIGHT, RECIPE PAGE 362)

The South

GOONG PAD PONG GAREE

กุ้งผัดผงกะหรี่

Curried Shrimp

The subtle flavor of the curry complements the fresh flavor of the shrimp very well in this quick and easy recipe.

2 tablespoons oil
3 garlic cloves (*kratiem*), minced
8 oz (250 g) shrimp/prawns, shelled and deveined
1 teaspoon curry powder
2 tablespoons fish sauce (*nam pla*)
1 tablespoon oyster sauce
1½ tablespoons sugar
¼ cup slivered green bell pepper/capsicum
¼ cup slivered red bell pepper/capsicum
¼ cup sweet basil leaves (*bai horapa*)
¼ cup sliced onions

▨ Heat a large skillet and add the oil, garlic and shrimp. Sauté for 1 minute. Add all the other ingredients and cook for 2 minutes.
▨ Serve with steamed jasmine rice (*khao suay*), on page 350.

SERVES 4   *Photograph pages 360–361*

Bangkok and the Central Plains

PLA RAD PRIK

ปลาราดพริก

Whole Crispy Fish with Chili Sauce

The presentation of a whole fish is always the highlight of a meal. The crispy outside surface contrasts with the juiciness of the flesh, the whole perfectly balanced with the sauce.

1 whole fish, 1 lb (500 g), cleaned
1 tablespoon white rice wine
½ cup (2 oz/60 g) all-purpose/plain flour
4 cups (1 qt/1 l) oil, for deep-frying

SAUCE

3 tablespoons oil
6 garlic cloves (*kratiem*), crushed
¼ cup sliced green bell pepper/capsicum
¼ cup sliced red bell pepper/capsicum
¼ cup sliced onions
⅛ cup cilantro/coriander leaves (*bai pak chee*)
¼ cup (2 fl oz/60 ml) fish sauce (*nam pla*)
2 tablespoons sugar
¼ cup sweet basil leaves (*bai horapa*)

▨ Cut three slashes to the bone on each side of the fish, then sprinkle it with rice wine. Flour the fish on all sides.
▨ Heat the oil to 350°F (180°C) and carefully immerse the fish in the hot oil.
▨ Deep-fry the fish until done (about 6 minutes on each side).
▨ While the fish is cooking, heat a medium skillet, add the oil and then all the sauce ingredients except the basil. Cook the mixture for 5 minutes on medium-high heat. Add the basil and mix.
▨ Place the fish on a serving dish and pour the sauce over the fish.
▨ Serve with fish sauce with chili (*nam pla prik*), on page 494.

SERVES 4

Bangkok and the Central Plains

PLA MUK PAD PED

ปลาหมึกผัดเผ็ด

Spicy Calamari

Squid is marinated in wine and fish sauce to both tenderize it and add flavor, and is then decorated with carved cucumber, carrot and tomato.

1 lb (500g) cleaned squid

MARINADE

5 garlic cloves (*kratiem*), minced
2 tablespoons white wine
⅛ teaspoon white pepper
1 tablespoon cornstarch/cornflour
2 tablespoons fish sauce (*nam pla*)
1 tablespoon soy sauce
1 tablespoon sugar

2 tablespoons oil

GARNISH

green leaf lettuce/Chinese lettuce
cucumber slices
tomato slices
carrot slices
cilantro/coriander leaves (*bai pak chee*)

▨ Slash the mantle/hood of the squid diagonally, then cut diagonal slashes in the opposite direction. Slice into 2-in (5-cm) pieces.
▨ Mix together all the marinade ingredients, then add the squid and marinate for 10 minutes.
▨ Heat a large skillet, add the oil and sauté the squid on medium-high heat until all the squid curls.
▨ Garnish with the ingredients listed above, or with any decoratively carved vegetables, and serve.

SERVES 2   *Photograph page 364*

Bangkok and the Central Plains

PAD PLA KAPONG KUNCHAI

ผัดปลากระพงขึ้นฉ่าย

Stir-Fried Snapper with Celery

Celery's pleasing taste gives extra flavor to this popular dish.

3 tablespoons oil
1 lb (500 g) snapper fillets, sliced into 2-in (5-cm) pieces
1 cup sliced celery
4 garlic cloves (*kratiem*), minced
½ teaspoon white pepper
½ cup chopped green onions/scallions/spring onions, in 1-in (2.5-cm) pieces
3 tablespoons fish sauce (*nam pla*)
1 tablespoon Maggi seasoning
mint leaves for garnish

▨ Heat a large saucepan, add the oil, then all the other ingredients except the mint.
▨ Stir-fry to mix then cover the saucepan and cook for 3 minutes.
▨ Serve with sprigs of mint leaves.

SERVES 4

WHOLE CRISPY FISH WITH CHILI SAUCE (TOP)
AND STIR-FRIED SNAPPER WITH CELERY (BOTTOM)

SPICY CALAMARI (LEFT, RECIPE PAGE 362) AND
BROILED LOBSTER WITH SWEET SAUCE (RIGHT)

Bangkok and the Central Plains

GOONG POW NAM PLA WAN

กุ้งเผา น้ำปลาหวาน

Broiled Lobster with Sweet Sauce

One of the best methods of cooking lobster is simply to broil it until just cooked. The tamarind sauce provides added flavor.

1 lobster, about 2 lb (1 kg), cleaned and left whole
2 tablespoons oil
6 shallots, sliced

SAUCE

½ cup (4 fl oz/125 ml) fish sauce (*nam pla*)
½ cup (4 fl oz/125 ml) tamarind juice (*ma-kaam piag*)
   (see glossary)
¼ cup (2 oz/60 g) sugar

▩ Broil/grill the lobster over charcoal for 5 minutes on each side or until done. After broiling cut the lobster in half lengthwise. Meanwhile heat a small skillet and add the oil. Stir-fry the shallots until golden brown; remove from the oil.
▩ Heat another small skillet and combine the fish sauce, tamarind juice and sugar. Cook the sauce for 3 minutes on high heat to reduce some of the liquid. Pour the sauce into a serving bowl and top with shallots. Use as a dip for the lobster.
▩ If desired crack the claws and legs and remove the meat from the body.

SERVES 4

Bangkok and the Central Plains

GOONG KRATIEM PRIK THAI

กุ้งกระเทียมพริกไทย

Garlic Shrimp

The garnish of tomato and cucumber slices adds freshness to this rich spicy dish, which should be served with plenty of fresh vegetables.

MARINADE

8 garlic cloves (*kratiem*), crushed
2 tablespoons minced cilantro/coriander root (*raak pak chee*)
1 teaspoon white pepper
½ teaspoon salt
2 tablespoons fish sauce (*nam pla*)
1½ tablespoons sugar

1 lb (500 g) shrimp/prawns, shelled, deveined and cleaned
3 tablespoons oil
1 tomato, cut into wedges
1 cucumber, sliced

▩ Thoroughly mix together all the marinade ingredients. Combine the shrimp with the marinade and set aside to marinate for 10 minutes.
▩ Heat a medium skillet, add the oil and sauté the marinated shrimp for 4 minutes.
▩ Remove to a serving plate and garnish with the tomato and cucumber.

SERVES 4

CRAB FRIED RICE (TOP LEFT, RECIPE PAGE 366), GARLIC
SHRIMP (TOP RIGHT) AND STIR-FRIED LOBSTER WITH
GINGER SAUCE (BOTTOM, RECIPE PAGE 366)

The South

PAD GOONG MANG-GORN

ผัดกุ้งมังกร

Stir-Fried Lobster with Ginger Sauce

The lobster in the southern part of Thailand is considered a large shrimp and is therefore called goong mang-gom—dragon shrimp.

1 cooked lobster, about 1½ lb (750 g)
2 tablespoons oil
4 garlic cloves (*kratiem*), minced
6 slices (about 2 tablespoons) fresh ginger
¼ cup sliced green jalapeño peppers (*prik chee fa*)
½ cup green onions/scallions/spring onions, chopped
1 egg, beaten
1 teaspoon freshly ground peppercorns
2 tablespoons oyster sauce
1 tablespoon fish sauce (*nam pla*)
1 tablespoon sugar

▓ Scrub the lobster clean and separate into large 2-in (5-cm) pieces. Cut the tail into individual sections.
▓ Heat a large skillet on high and add the oil. Add all the remaining ingredients except the lobster and stir-fry for 30 seconds. Add the lobster pieces to the skillet, cover, and steam on medium-high heat for 2 more minutes. Remove to a platter and serve.

SERVES 4   *Photograph page 365*

Bangkok and the Central Plains

KHAO PAD POO

ข้าวผัดปู

Crab Fried Rice

A delicious accompaniment for any dish. Vary the number of chili peppers in the sauce according to personal taste.

2 tablespoons oil
1 garlic clove (*kratiem*), chopped
1 cup crab meat, cooked
2 eggs, beaten
3 cups cooked rice
2 tablespoons Maggi seasoning
2 tablespoons fish sauce (*nam pla*)
2 tablespoons sugar
1 green onion/scallion/spring onion, chopped

SAUCE

¼ cup (2 fl oz/60 ml) fish sauce (*nam pla*)
5 green Thai chili peppers (*prik khee noo*), finely chopped

GARNISH

1 tomato, sliced
½ cup sliced cucumber
cilantro/coriander leaves (*bai pak chee*)
4 lemons, cut in wedges

▓ Heat a large skillet and add the oil. Stir-fry the garlic, crab and eggs together until the egg is cooked.
▓ Add the rice, Maggi seasoning, fish sauce and sugar. Continue to stir-fry until the mixture is hot. Add the green onion.
▓ Mix together the sauce ingredients. Remove the rice to a serving dish, decorate with the garnish, and serve with the sauce on the side.

SERVES 4   *Photograph page 365*

Bangkok and the Central Plains

PAD PED PLA LAI

ผัดเผ็ดปลาไหล

Eel Curry

Fresh eel cooked in this style is firm and juicy. Any seafood or firm-fleshed fish can be substituted.

3 tablespoons corn oil
1 eel, about 1 lb (500 g), skinned, cleaned, and cut into ½-in (1-cm) sections
2 tablespoons red curry paste (*nam prik gaeng ped*) (see page 488)
3 tablespoons fish sauce (*nam pla*)
½ cup sweet basil leaves (*bai horapa*)
¼ cup thinly sliced lesser ginger (*krachai*)
5 kaffir lime leaves (*bai ma-grood*), thinly sliced

▓ Heat a large saucepan, add the oil, eel slices and curry paste and stir-fry for 30 seconds. Add the remaining ingredients and continue cooking for 5 minutes more.

SERVES 4

EEL CURRY

Bangkok and the Central Plains

GAENG SOM PAE-SA

แกงส้มแป๊ะซะ

Crispy Fish with Tamarind Sauce

With the crispy outer surface of the fish contrasting with its firm moist flesh, and the sourness of the tamarind sauce balancing the garlic and onion, this dish offers a variety of flavors and textures.

TAMARIND SAUCE

5 large dried jalapeño peppers *(prik chee fa haeng)*
1 cup (8 fl oz/250 ml) warm water
4 garlic cloves *(kratiem)*
1 cup sliced onions
1 teaspoon shrimp paste *(gapi)*
½ cup (4 fl oz/125 ml) tamarind juice *(ma-kaam piag)*
  (see glossary)
¼ cup (2 fl oz/60 ml) fish sauce *(nam pla)*
2 tablespoons sugar

1 whole fish, about 1–1½ lb (500–750 g), with head removed if
  preferred
1 teaspoon salt
4 cups (1 qt/1 l) oil, for deep-frying
5 sprigs of swamp cabbage or young spinach leaves,
  for garnish
green jalapeño peppers *(prik chee fa)*, for garnish

▓ Soak the dried peppers in the warm water for 10 minutes to soften.

▓ Combine the soaked peppers with the water and all the remaining sauce ingredients in a blender. Process until the peppers, garlic and onions are coarsely chopped. Pour into a saucepan and heat to boiling. Cook for 1 minute.

▓ Cut three slashes on each side of the fish and rub with salt. Heat the oil to 350°F (180°C) in a large skillet and deep-fry the fish for 10–15 minutes.

▓ Remove the fish when it is fried to a golden brown and cooked through. Place on a serving dish, then pour the cooked sauce over the fish and garnish with the sprigs of swamp cabbage and green jalapeño peppers.

SERVES 4

Bangkok and the Central Plains

TOM SOM PLA TOO

ต้มส้มปลาทู

Mackerel in Tamarind Sauce·

Tamarind juice is used to add richness to this sauce, which beautifully complements the sweet flesh of the mackerel. This combination of flavors is a feature of Thai seafood cookery.

1 mackerel, about 2 lb (1 kg) or 2 lb (1 kg) smaller mackerel
3 cups (24 fl oz/750 ml) water
6 shallots, minced
¼ cup minced cilantro/coriander root (raak pak chee)
1 teaspoon white pepper
½ teaspoon salt
⅓ cup (3 fl oz/90 ml) fish sauce (nam pla)
⅓ cup (3 fl oz/90 ml) tamarind juice (ma-kaam piag)
   (see glossary)
3 tablespoons sugar
¼ cup sliced ginger
6 green onions/scallions/spring onions

Clean the mackerel and remove the backbone. Cut into four serving pieces.

Heat the water to boiling in a large saucepan and add the fish and all the other ingredients except the ginger and green onions. Simmer for 10 minutes, then add the ginger and four of the green onions, cut into 1-in (2.5-cm) pieces.

Remove from the heat and allow to rest for 2 minutes. Place the fish pieces on a serving plate and drizzle with some of the sauce. Garnish with the extra green onions.

SERVES 4

Bangkok and the Central Plains

PLA CHON PAE-SA

ปลาช่อนแป๊ะซะ

Steamed Whole Fish

Although rock cod is a freshwater fish, snapper or sole can be substituted. In fact this is delicious with any saltwater fish.

1 rock cod, about 1–1½ lb (500–750 g)
1 teaspoon salt
½ teaspoon white pepper
2 garlic cloves (kratiem), minced
1 cup chopped celery
2 tablespoons white wine
1 tablespoon fish sauce (nam pla)
2 green jalapeño peppers (prik chee fa), sliced
1 cup chopped green onions/scallions/spring onions

Clean the fish and slash to the bone three times on each side. Rub with salt and pepper. Place on a steaming plate and top with the remaining ingredients.

Place in a steamer, cover and steam for 15 minutes on high heat. Remove and serve.

SERVES 4

STEAMED WHOLE FISH (FRONT) AND MACKEREL
IN TAMARIND SAUCE (TOP)

The South

GOONG NEUNG KRATIEM

กุ้งนึ่งกระเทียม

Steamed Garlic Shrimp

Steaming the shrimp with the shells intact keeps them very moist and juicy. With the addition of garlic and cilantro this is a favorite Thai style of cooking seafood.

1 lb (500 g) shrimp/prawns, with shells
2 tablespoons oil
1/2 teaspoon salt
1/2 teaspoon white pepper
1 tablespoon Maggi seasoning
8 garlic cloves (*kratiem*), minced
3 tablespoons chopped cilantro/coriander leaves (*bai pak chee*)

▨ Rinse the shrimp and drain thoroughly. Place on a plate that will fit in a steamer. Combine the remaining ingredients with the shrimp.
▨ Place the entire plate of shrimp with the sauce in a steamer. Heat the steamer to boiling then reduce the temperature to medium-high. Continue steaming for 10 minutes. Serve hot.

SERVES 4

The South

POO PAD PONG GAREE

ปูผัดผงกะหรี่

Stir-Fried Crab Curry

Cooking fresh crab in its shell retains the sweetness of the meat. Eating crab cooked in this manner is an informal affair, allowing enjoyment of the company and much conversation between friends.

1 whole crab, about 1 1/2 lb (750 g)
3 tablespoons oil
4 garlic cloves (*kratiem*), minced
1 small onion, sliced
1/4 cup (2 fl oz/60 ml) fish sauce (*nam pla*)
2 tablespoons sugar
2 tablespoons curry powder
1 tablespoon Oriental sesame oil
1/4 teaspoon white pepper
1 egg, beaten
1 tablespoon chopped cilantro/coriander leaves (*bai pak chee*)
2 green onions/shallots/spring onions, cut into 1-in (2.5-cm) lengths

▨ Clean the crab by removing the shell from the body only. Disjoint the legs and crack the shell of the legs with a mallet. Rinse to remove small pieces of shell, drain and set aside.
▨ Heat a wok or large skillet on medium-high heat. Add the oil, garlic and onion. Stir-fry for 30 seconds. Add the cracked crab pieces and stir-fry for 2 minutes.
▨ Add all remaining ingredients except the egg, cilantro and green onions. Cover the skillet and continue cooking on medium-high heat for another 3 minutes, or until the crab is cooked.
▨ Add the egg and stir to combine thoroughly.
▨ Remove to a serving dish and garnish with the cilantro and green onions.

SERVES 4

STIR-FRIED CRAB CURRY (FRONT) AND STEAMED GARLIC SHRIMP (TOP)

SPICY CATFISH (BOTTOM) AND JUNGLE CURRY WITH CATFISH (TOP, RECIPE PAGE 372)

Bangkok and the Central Plains

PAD PED PLA DOOK

ผัดเผ็ดปลาดุก

Spicy Catfish

The abundance of freshwater fish in Thailand has led to the development of many ways in which to cook them. This recipe is a favorite and catfish is a popular choice although other types of freshwater fish can also be used. Both whole fish and fillets are suitable.

2 tablespoons oil
1 lb (500 g) catfish, cleaned and cut into 1/2-in (1-cm) wide sections
1/2 cup Thai eggplant (*ma-khue puang*), cut into wedges
6 garlic cloves (*kratiem*), minced
2 stalks lemon grass/citronella (*ta-krai*), cut into 1-in (2.5-cm) pieces
1/4 cup thinly sliced lesser ginger (*krachai*)
1/2 cup sweet basil leaves (*bai horapa*)
1/4 cup (2 fl oz/60 ml) fish sauce (*nam pla*)
1 tablespoon sugar

▨ Heat a large skillet and add the oil. Wait for 1 minute for the oil to heat then add all the ingredients. Stir thoroughly then cover and cook for 3 minutes on high heat. Remove to a serving dish.

SERVES 4

Bangkok and the Central Plains

GAENG PAA PLA DOOK

แกงป่าปลาดุก

Jungle Curry with Catfish

In the days when travel through various parts of Thailand required journeying through areas of jungle, the people had to make do with what was available there. This recipe is so named because the ingredients and cooking method made it a suitable dish for the jungle. Best eaten in the presence of monkeys, tigers and snakes to keep it more authentic!

CURRY PASTE

2 tablespoons chopped lemon grass/citronella (*ta-krai*)
8 shallots
6 garlic cloves (*kratiem*)
¼ cup chopped lesser ginger (*krachai*)
8 dried jalapeño peppers (*prik chee fa haeng*)
1 teaspoon canned peppercorns
1 teaspoon shrimp paste (*gapi*)
½ teaspoon salt

2 tablespoons oil
1 whole catfish, 1½ lb (750 g), cut into 1-in (2.5-cm) slices
¼ cup (2 fl oz/60 ml) fish sauce (*nam pla*)
3 cups (24 fl oz/750 ml) water
½ cup Thai eggplant (*ma-khue puang*)
¼ cup sliced green jalapeño pepper (*prik chee fa*)
½ cup sweet basil leaves (*bai horapa*)
10 whole kaffir lime leaves (*bai ma-grood*)

▧ Combine all the ingredients for the curry paste, using a mortar and pestle or a blender.
▧ Heat a large saucepan and add the oil and curry paste. Stir-fry for 1 minute on medium-high heat.
▧ Add the fish, fish sauce, water and eggplant and heat to boiling. Cook, stirring, for 3 minutes. Add the remaining ingredients and remove from the heat. Serve.

SERVES 4 *Photograph page 371*

The South

PLA KEM

ปลาเค็ม

Sun-Dried Salty Fish

One day of bright hot sunlight is an essential part of this recipe. This method of food preservation is particularly suitable for fish of all types, although mackerel is a favorite.

1 mackerel, 2 lb (1 kg) or 2 lb (1 kg) smaller mackerel
3 tablespoons salt
½ cup (4 fl oz/125 ml) water

▧ Remove only the entrails and rinse the fish until clean. Dissolve the salt in the water and soak the fish overnight in the salt solution. The next day, hang the fish in bright sunlight and allow it to dry for at least one whole day. Alternatively, bake the fish at 325° F (165°C) for 45 minutes.
▧ Seafood dried by this method keeps indefinitely, and can be used in other recipes, such as fried sun-dried fish (*pla kem taud*), on page 374.

SERVES 4

The South

PAD PO TAEK

ผัดโป๊ะแตก

Lemon Grass Seafood Combination

The flavor of fresh lemon grass balances the flavor of the seafood, serving the same purpose as the fresh lemon wedges served with seafood in other cuisines.

SUN-DRIED SALTY FISH (LEFT) AND LEMON
GRASS SEAFOOD COMBINATION (RIGHT)

2 tablespoons oil
4 oz (125 g) shrimp/prawns, shelled and deveined
4 oz (125 g) scallops
4 oz (125 g) fish fillets, sliced ½ in (1 cm) thick
4 oz (125 g) mussels, cleaned
¼ cup green curry paste (*nam prik gaeng keow wan*) (see page 488)
¼ cup (2 fl oz/60 ml) coconut milk
¼ cup (2 fl oz/60 ml) fish sauce (*nam pla*)
1 tablespoon sugar
⅛ cup slivered bamboo shoots

1 stalk lemon grass/citronella (*ta-krai*), in 1-in (2.5-cm) lengths
¼ cup sliced green bell pepper/capsicum
⅓ cup sweet basil leaves (*bai horapa*)

▨ Heat a large skillet and add the oil. Add all the seafood and sauté for 2 minutes on high heat.
▨ Add the remaining ingredients and gently combine. Cover the pan and continue cooking for about 3 minutes.
▨ Remove to a serving plate.

SERVES 4

FRIED SUN-DRIED FISH (BOTTOM) AND STEAMED FISH (TOP)

The Northeast

PLA NEUNG

ปลานึ่ง

Steamed Fish

Northeastern Thailand has many recipes for freshwater fish and one of the most popular cooking methods is steaming, which retains the flavor and moistness of the fish.

1 whole fish, about 1–1½ lb (500–750 g)
5 shallots, sliced
4 garlic cloves (*kratiem*), minced
4 green jalapeño peppers (*prik chee fa*)
½ teaspoon salt
¼ teaspoon white pepper
3 tablespoons fish sauce (*nam pla*)
3 tablespoons tamarind juice (*ma-kaam piag*) (see glossary)
2 tablespoons lime juice
4 thin slices galangal (*kha*)
2 kaffir lime leaves (*bai ma-grood*), thinly sliced
1 tablespoon oil

❊ Clean the fish and then make three slashes on each side with a sharp knife.
❊ Place on a steaming plate. Sprinkle the remaining ingredients over the fish.
❊ Place in a steamer and steam on high heat for 20 minutes. Present on a serving dish or a banana leaf.

SERVES 4

Bangkok and the Central Plains

NAM PRIK PLA TOO

น้ำพริกปลาทู

Fried Mackerel with Shrimp Paste Sauce

Although mackerel is traditionally used, other favorite fish may be substituted. The sauce will still give the dish the authentic flavor.

4 small mackerel, 1–1½ lb (500–750 g) altogether
1 teaspoon salt
4 cups (1 qt/1 l) oil, for deep-frying

SHRIMP PASTE SAUCE

½ cup dried shrimp paste
6 garlic cloves (*kratiem*)
6 green Thai chili peppers (*prik khee noo*)
3 tablespoons shrimp paste (*gapi*)
¼ cup (2 fl oz/60 ml) fish sauce (*nam pla*)
⅓ cup (3 fl oz/90 g) lime juice
2 tablespoons palm sugar (*nam taan peep*)

2 Thai eggplants (*ma-khue puang*), thinly sliced
4 Thai eggplants, cut into 1-in (2.5-cm) slices
4 snake beans, cut into 4-in (10-cm) lengths
4 red and yellow jalapeño peppers (*prik chee fa daeng*)

❊ Clean the mackerel and rub them with the salt. Steam for 20 minutes then heat the oil to 375°F (190°C) and deep-fry the mackerel until golden brown. Remove and set aside.
❊ Place the dried shrimp paste, garlic, chilies and shrimp paste in a mortar and, with the pestle, press for 30 seconds. Then add the remaining ingredients for the shrimp paste sauce and mix together. Remove to a serving bowl and place the thinly sliced eggplant on top of the sauce.
❊ Serve the fish with the dip and the assorted raw vegetables.

SERVES 4

The South

PLA KEM TAUD

ปลาเค็มทอด

Fried Sun-Dried Fish

The South is known for its abundance of seafood and supplies much of the seafood of Thailand. This is one of the many easy but delicious recipes for simply prepared fish. Sun-dried mackerel is available already prepared, but its flavor may be too strong for Western palates. Other fish may be substituted if desired.

4 steaks, 2 in (5 cm) thick, cut from sun-dried mackerel (*pla kem*) (see page 372)
3 tablespoons oil
2 shallots, thinly sliced
1 tablespoon chopped green Thai chili peppers (*prik khee noo*)
2 tablespoons fresh lime juice

❊ Rinse the mackerel steaks and dry them thoroughly with paper towels, removing as much moisture as possible.
❊ Heat the oil in a large skillet on medium-high heat. Carefully lay the mackerel steaks onto the oil and fry for 5 minutes on each side, or until the outside of the fish is golden brown and the inside is hot.
❊ Remove the steaks to a serving dish and scatter the shallots and chili peppers on top. Drizzle with lime juice and serve immediately.

SERVES 4

Bangkok and the Central Plains

CHOO CHEE PLA

ฉู่ฉี่ปลา

Whole Fish with Curry Sauce

Steaming is one of the best methods of cooking fish. This fish is steamed in the pan with a curry sauce, offering simplicity with flavor.

1 whole snapper, about 1½ lb (750 g), or 2 smaller fish
2 tablespoons oil
2 tablespoons red curry paste (*nam prik gaeng ped*) (see page 488)

2 cups (16 fl oz/500 ml) coconut milk
¼ cup (2 fl oz/60 ml) fish sauce (*nam pla*)
3 tablespoons sugar
5 kaffir lime leaves (*bai ma-grood*), thinly sliced

▓ Clean the fish, retaining the head and tail. Make three slashes on each side of the fish.
▓ Heat a large skillet and add the oil and curry paste. Stir-fry for 1 minute and add the coconut milk, fish sauce, sugar and the whole fish.
▓ Cover and cook for 20 minutes, carefully turning the fish once.
▓ Remove to a serving dish and sprinkle with the lime leaves before serving.

SERVES 4

FRIED MACKEREL WITH SHRIMP PASTE SAUCE (TOP)
AND WHOLE FISH WITH CURRY SAUCE (BOTTOM)

GREEN CURRY WITH CHICKEN AND THAI EGGPLANT
(TOP) AND RED CURRY CHICKEN (BOTTOM)

The Northeast

GAI YANG ESAN

ไก่ย่างอีสาน

Northeast Barbecued Chicken

Barbecuing is a premier method of cooking marinated meats. Served with sticky jasmine rice, a staple of the northeastern part of Thailand, gai yang Esan makes for a very memorable meal. The aroma and the golden brown color entice both the palate and the eye.

1 chicken, about 2 lb (1 kg)
1 teaspoon salt
8 garlic cloves (*kratiem*), minced
1 teaspoon white pepper
¼ cup chopped cilantro/coriander leaves (*bai pak chee*)
¼ cup chopped lemon grass/citronella (*ta-krai*)

▓ Clean the chicken and split it in half lengthwise. Marinate the chicken in the remaining ingredients overnight.
▓ Prepare charcoal 30 minutes in advance, so that the coals reach a stage of low heat. Barbecue the chicken over coals for 20 minutes on each side or until the chicken is golden brown and cooked through.
▓ Serve this dish with spicy anchovy dip (*nam prik jaew*), on page 495, and sticky rice (*khao neow*), on page 350.

SERVES 4   *Photograph pages 346–347*

Bangkok and the Central Plains

GAENG PED GAI

แกงเผ็ดไก่

Red Curry Chicken

This curry is best eaten as soon as it is made and served with steamed jasmine rice (khao suay), on page 350. The coconut flavor is enhanced by adding half the coconut milk towards the end of the cooking process.

2 cups (16 fl oz/500 ml) coconut milk
2 tablespoons red curry paste (*nam prik gaeng ped*) (see page 488)
1 lb (500 g) chicken breast, cut into 1-in (2.5-cm) pieces
¼ cup (2 fl oz/60 ml) fish sauce (*nam pla*)
3 tablespoons sugar
½ cup canned bamboo shoots, in strips
¼ cup Thai eggplant (*ma-khue puang*), cut into wedges
5 to 8 kaffir lime leaves (*bai ma-grood*)
¼ cup sweet basil leaves (*bai horapa*)

▓ Heat half the coconut milk in a large saucepan and add the red curry paste. Heat to boiling and cook for 2 minutes.
▓ Add the chicken and boil for 2 minutes. Add the fish sauce, sugar, canned bamboo shoot strips and eggplant, and reheat to boiling.
▓ Add the remaining coconut milk, lime leaves and basil leaves and heat just to boiling. Remove from heat and serve.

SERVES 4

Bangkok and the Central Plains

GAENG KEOW WAN GAI

แกงเขียวหวานไก่

Green Curry with Chicken and Thai Eggplant

This curry is always hot, the heat being determined by the amount of green chilies that are used. To make the dish more flavorful, 1 / 2 cup of fresh green peppercorns can also be added to the curry mixture.

GREEN CURRY PASTE

2 stalks lemon grass/citronella (*ta-krai*), cut into ½-in (1-cm) pieces
1 tablespoon sliced galangal (*kha*)
1 teaspoon cumin
½ cup chopped fresh cilantro/coriander root (*raak pak chee*)
8 garlic cloves (*kratiem*)
10 green Thai chili peppers (*prik khee noo*)
10 green jalapeño peppers (*prik chee fa*)
1 teaspoon shrimp paste (*gapi*)
1 tablespoon chopped shallot
¼ teaspoon minced kaffir lime skin (*piew ma-grood*)

2 cups (16 fl oz/500 ml) coconut milk
1 lb (500 g) boned chicken breast, sliced in 1/2-in x 2-in (1-cm x 2.5-cm) pieces
¼ cup (2 fl oz/60 ml) fish sauce (*nam pla*)
3 tablespoons sugar
1 cup Thai eggplant (*ma-khue puang*) or 1 cup canned bamboo shoots
½ cup (4 fl oz/125 ml) coconut cream
6 fresh kaffir lime leaves (*bai ma-grood*)
¼ cup sweet basil leaves (*bai horapa*)
red jalapeño pepper (*prik chee fa daeng*), for garnish

▓ Place all the green curry paste ingredients in an electric blender and process until the mixture is smooth, or pound in a pestle and mortar.
▓ Pour the coconut milk and the green curry paste into a large saucepan. Heat to boiling and add the chicken, fish sauce and sugar. Cook for 5 minutes at a slow boil. Add the eggplant and reheat to boiling, simmering for 2 minutes. Add the coconut cream and stir to combine. Add the kaffir lime leaves and basil leaves. Remove the contents to a serving bowl, garnish with the red pepper and serve.

SERVES 4

Bangkok and the Central Plains

GAI PAD BAI GA-PROW

ไก่ผัดใบกะเพรา

Spicy Chicken with Basil

This is a quick and easy dish which is a favorite of the people of downtown Bangkok. Sometimes it is served over rice with a fried egg.

6 garlic cloves (*kratiem*), minced
4 shallots, minced
12 mixed green and red jalapeño peppers (*prik chee fa* and *prik chee fa daeng*), sliced
1 teaspoon canned green peppercorns
1 tablespoon oil
1 lb (500 g) ground/minced chicken
¼ cup (2 fl oz/60 ml) fish sauce (*nam pla*)
2 tablespoons sugar
1 cup hot basil leaves (*bai ga-prow*)

▓ Place the garlic, shallots, peppers and peppercorns in a mortar and mash with a pestle until a paste is formed.
▓ Heat a large sauté pan to medium-high heat and add the oil. Add the garlic paste and stir for 1 minute, then add the ground chicken, fish sauce and sugar. Continue to cook until the sauce is reduced. Toss in the basil leaves.
▓ As a luncheon dish, serve over rice with a fried egg.
▓ As a dinner dish, serve separately with rice and with an accompaniment such as hot and sour shrimp soup (*tom yam goong*), on page 299.

SERVES 4

Bangkok and the Central Plains

GAI PAD MED MA-MUANG HIMAPAN

ไก่ผัดเม็ดมะม่วงหิมพานต์

Cashew Chicken

Vegetables can be added while the chicken is cooking, if desired.

¼ cup (2 fl oz/60 ml) oil
4 garlic cloves (*kratiem*), minced
1 lb (500 g) boned chicken, thinly sliced

SAUCE

2 tablespoons fish sauce (*nam pla*)
2 tablespoons oyster sauce
2 tablespoons sugar
⅛ teaspoon white pepper
1 teaspoon cornstarch/cornflour dissolved in a little water, optional

½ cup (70 g/2½ oz) roasted cashew nuts
1 green onion/scallion/spring onion, chopped
¼ cup sliced red bell pepper/capsicum

▓ Heat a large skillet then add the oil, garlic, chicken, the sauces, sugar and pepper.
▓ Turn the heat to high and reduce the sauce until a glaze forms. If the sauce is not reduced and is thin, add enough of the cornstarch mixture to produce a thick sauce. Add the cornstarch and water mixture only if you prefer a richer looking sauce.
▓ Mix in the roasted cashews and then turn the mixture onto a serving dish. Garnish with the green onion and bell pepper.

SERVES 4

CASHEW CHICKEN (LEFT) AND SPICY CHICKEN WITH BASIL (RIGHT)

STEAMED DUCK

Bangkok and the Central Plains
PET PALO

เป็ดพะโล้

Steamed Duck

The flavors in this dish reflect the influence of Chinese cuisine on that of Thailand.

1 whole duck, 4 lb (2 kg)

SAUCE

6 cups (1½ qt/1.5 l) water
8 garlic cloves (*kratiem*)
¼ cup minced cilantro/coriander root (*raak pak chee*)
1 teaspoon white pepper
1 teaspoon salt
½ cup (4 fl oz/125 ml) Maggi seasoning
1 cup (8 fl oz/250 ml) mushroom soy sauce
1 cup (8 fl oz/250 ml) sweet soy sauce
½ cup (4 oz/125 g) sugar

▦ Clean the duck and rinse it inside and out. Set aside.
▦ Pour the water into a steamer large enough to enclose the duck. Add the remaining ingredients to the water in the steamer and place the duck in the steamer.
▦ Cover and heat to boiling. Turn the heat to medium-high and steam for 45 minutes.
▦ Allow the duck to cool then fillet out the meat from the bones, reserving the legs and wings. Arrange the meat, legs and wings on a large platter. Skim the fat from the sauce from the steamer and pour some of the sauce over the duck before serving.

SERVES 4

The North
GAI TAUD

ไก่ทอด

Chiang Mai Fried Chicken

Chicken cooked in this way makes a good picnic dish, as it can be eaten hot or cold.

1 chicken, about 3 lb (1.5 kg), cut into 12 pieces

MARINADE

1 tablespoon fish sauce (*nam pla*)
1 teaspoon salt
6 garlic cloves (*kratiem*), finely minced
1 teaspoon white pepper

3–4 cups (24–32 fl oz/750–1000 ml) oil, for deep-frying

▦ Rinse the chicken and pat dry with paper towels. Mix the marinade ingredients together and then rub the mixture evenly over the pieces of chicken to coat them.
▦ Allow to marinate for 30 minutes.
▦ Heat the oil in a wok or deep-fryer to 350°F (180°C). Deep-fry the chicken for approximately 10 minutes until golden brown, turning the pieces often so as to achieve an even color.
▦ Serve with hot or cold young tamarind paste (*nam prik makaam*), on page 496.

SERVES 4

The North
GAENG GAI BAMA

แกงไก่พม่า

Burmese Chicken Curry

This recipe, with its rich tastes, shows a definite Burmese influence.

4 tablespoons (2 oz/60 g) butter
8 shallots, thinly sliced
2 tablespoons red curry paste (*nam prik gaeng ped*) (see page 488)
2 tablespoons yellow curry powder
1 chicken, about 3 lb (1.5 kg), cut into 12 pieces
6 cups (1½ qt/1.5 l) water
⅓ cup (3 fl oz/90 ml) fish sauce (*nam pla*)
3 tablespoons sugar
1 cup (8 fl oz/250 ml) milk
1 cup tomato wedges

▦ Heat a large pan and add three-quarters of the butter and the shallot slices. Stir and cook until the shallots are golden brown. Remove the shallots and set aside.
▦ Heat the same pan and add the rest of the butter. Add the curry paste and curry powder, stir, and cook for 2 minutes. Add the chicken and continue to cook on high heat for 5 more minutes. Add the water and all the remaining ingredients except the fried shallots and reheat to boiling. Cook for 30 minutes.
▦ Remove to a serving bowl and sprinkle with the fried shallots.

SERVES 4

CHIANG MAI FRIED CHICKEN (TOP LEFT) AND
BURMESE CHICKEN CURRY (RIGHT)

The North

GAENG HOH

แกงโฮะ

Mixed Curry

This dish is a rich blend of many flavors and textures.

2 tablespoons oil
2 garlic cloves (*kratiem*), minced
4 oz (125 g) pork, cut into 1-in (2.5-cm) cubes
4 oz (125 g) chicken, cut into ½-in x 2-in (1-cm x 5-cm) slices
2 tablespoons red curry paste (*nam prik gaeng ped*) (see page 488)
1 tablespoon yellow bean sauce (*tao jeow*)
1 oz (30 g) cellophane noodles (*woon sen*), soaked in warm
    water for 15 minutes, until soft, then drained and set aside
½ teaspoon turmeric
1 teaspoon curry powder
¼ cup (2 fl oz/60 ml) fish sauce (*nam pla*)
3 tablespoons coconut sugar or brown sugar
½ cup Thai eggplant (*ma-khue puang*)
½ cup slivered bamboo shoots
½ cup chopped string beans, in 1-in (2.5-cm) pieces
½ cup straw mushrooms
½ cup sliced Chinese mustard pickles
1 tomato, cut into ¼-in (6-mm) dice

Heat a large saucepan then add the oil, garlic, pork and chicken. Stir-fry for 4 minutes to cook the meat. Add the curry paste and yellow bean sauce and stir to combine.

Mix in the drained noodles, turmeric, curry powder, fish sauce and sugar. Stir-fry for 4 minutes.

Add the remaining vegetables and continue cooking for a further 2 minutes or serve the vegetables separately.

SERVES 4

Bangkok and the Central Plains

GAENG GAREE GAI

แกงกะหรี่ไก่

Yellow Curry Chicken

Thai curries are usually quickly and easily prepared. This one is especially popular with families with busy lifestyles.

2 tablespoons oil
¼ cup onion, chopped
¼ cup garlic (*kratiem*), chopped
3 cups (24 fl oz/750 ml) coconut milk
1 lb (500 g) boned chicken, sliced
3 tablespoons yellow curry powder
¼ cup (2 fl oz/60 ml) fish sauce (*nam pla*)
2 tablespoons sugar

Heat a large saucepan then add the oil, onion and garlic. Stir-fry the onion and garlic until almost golden brown, then remove and set aside.

Pour the coconut milk into the pan, heat to boiling and add the chicken. Reheat to boiling and cook for 3 minutes.

Add the remaining ingredients, including the fried onion and garlic, and simmer for 1 minute. Place the mixture in a serving bowl and serve with steamed rice.

SERVES 4

YELLOW CURRY CHICKEN (LEFT) AND MIXED CURRY (TOP AND RIGHT)

BAKED RICE WITH PINEAPPLE

Bangkok and the Central Plains

Khao Ob Sapparod

ข้าวอบสับปะรด

Baked Rice with Pineapple

The pineapple in this recipe serves dual purposes: first to enhance the flavor, and second to provide an attractive presentation.

1 pineapple
3 tablespoons oil
8 oz (250 g) boned chicken, diced

SEASONINGS

¼ cup (2 fl oz/60 ml) fish sauce (*nam pla*)
1 tablespoon Maggi seasoning
¼ cup (2 oz/60 g) sugar
2 cups coconut milk
¼ teaspoon white pepper
¼ cup cilantro/coriander leaves (*bai pak chee*), chopped

½ cup toasted cashew nuts
½ cup (3 oz/90 g) raisins
1 tablespoon chopped cilantro/coriander leaves (*bai pak chee*)
4 cups steamed jasmine rice (*khao suay*) (see page 350)

❀ Cut the pineapple in half lengthwise and remove the fruit so both pineapple shells can be used as containers. Place ½ cup of the fruit in a blender and process until finely chopped. Set aside. The rest of the fruit is not needed for this dish.

❀ Heat a large skillet and add the oil. Sauté the chicken until done. Add all the seasonings and allow the mixture to cook until it foams.

❀ Add the cashews, pineapple, raisins, cilantro and rice. Remove from the heat and mix thoroughly.

❀ Stuff the rice mixture into pineapple halves and bake in a 350°F (180°C) oven until hot, about 15 minutes, or microwave for 5 minutes. Cover the pineapple leaves with foil before baking so that they are not burned.

❀ If fresh pineapple is unavailable, the rice mixture could also be wrapped in banana leaves and baked at 350°F (180°C) for 15 minutes or until hot.

SERVES 4

381

SURAT BAKED CHICKEN (TOP LEFT) AND STIR-FRIED CHICKEN
WITH BASIL AND GREEN CURRY (BOTTOM)

Bangkok and the Central Plains

PAD BAI GA-PROW
KEOW WAN GAI

ผัดใบกะเพราเขียวหวานไก่

Stir-Fried Chicken with Basil
and Green Curry

The strong flavors in this dish make it a good partner for steamed rice.

3 tablespoons oil
3 tablespoons green curry paste (*nam prik gaeng keow wan*)
  (see page 488)
1 lb (500 g) boned chicken, sliced
½ cup bamboo shoots (see glossary)
½ cup sliced green and red jalapeño peppers (*prik chee fa* and *prik
  chee fa daeng*)
¼ cup (2 fl oz/60 ml) coconut milk
3 tablespoons fish sauce (*nam pla*)
3 tablespoons sugar
1 cup hot basil leaves (*bai ga-prow*)
3 tablespoons coconut cream

▨ Heat a large skillet and add the oil and green curry paste.
Add the chicken and stir-fry for 3 minutes, then add all but
the last two ingredients. Cook on high heat for 4 minutes.
▨ Toss in the basil leaves and pour the coconut cream on top.
Remove to a serving plate.

SERVES 4

The South

GAI OB SURAT

ไก่อบสุราษฎร์

Surat Baked Chicken

*Southern Thailand style baked chicken is usually served in large portions
and is a very good single main course.*

MARINADE

3 garlic cloves (*kratiem*), minced
⅛ teaspoon white pepper
¼ cup (2 fl oz/60 ml) fish sauce (*nam pla*)
2 tablespoons cognac or whiskey or wine
2 tablespoons chopped lemon grass/citronella (*ta-krai*)
3 tablespoons coconut milk
1 tablespoon red curry paste (*nam prik gaeng ped*) (see page 488)
1 teaspoon salt

1 whole chicken, 3 lb (1.5 kg)

▨ Mix together the ingredients for the marinade. Thoroughly
coat the chicken with the marinade and set aside for 15 minutes.
▨ Bake the chicken for 1 hour, or until done, at 325°F (165°C).
▨ Present the chicken whole, or carve into portions of legs,
thighs, breast, and serve with a dipping sauce.

SERVES 4

Bangkok and the Central Plains

GAI YANG

ไก่ย่าง

Barbecued Chicken

*Barbecued meats are sold by street vendors and restaurants throughout
Thailand. This is a popular recipe for chicken, which is a favorite meat.
A good picnic recipe.*

1 whole chicken, about 3 lb (1.5 kg), cut in half

MARINADE

1 teaspoon salt
4 garlic cloves (*kratiem*), chopped
1 teaspoon white pepper
1 tablespoon minced cilantro/coriander leaves (*bai pak chee*) and
  root (*raak pak chee*)
2 tablespoons cognac or whiskey or rice wine
2 tablespoons coconut milk
1 tablespoon fish sauce (*nam pla*)
1 teaspoon chopped fresh ginger
2 tablespoons soy sauce

sliced raw vegetables for garnish

▨ Rub the entire chicken with the combined marinade ingredi-
ents. Allow to marinate for 15 minutes.
▨ Bake at 350°F (180°C) for 45 minutes and then broil/grill
for 10 minutes or until done.
▨ Cut into serving-sized pieces and garnish before serving.
Serve with any chili sauce dip.

SERVES 4

BARBECUED CHICKEN

Bangkok and the Central Plains

PAD TAP GAI

ผัดตับไก่

Chicken Liver with Onion

Liver is a good source of iron and is quite a popular meat. This recipe uses one of the most common methods of cooking liver, although broiling and barbecuing are also used.

3 tablespoons oil
1 small onion, sliced
6 garlic cloves (*kratiem*), minced
1 lb (500 g) chicken livers, thinly sliced
2 tablespoons Maggi seasoning
2 tablespoons fish sauce (*nam pla*)
2 tablespoons sugar
2 tablespoons red wine or whiskey
2 green onions/scallions/spring onions, cut into 1-in (2.5-cm) pieces

▨ Heat a large skillet, add the oil, onion and garlic and stir for 30 seconds. Add the chicken livers and turn the heat to high.
▨ Add the remaining ingredients and cook for 3 more minutes or until the livers are just cooked through. Remove to a serving dish.

SERVES 4

Bangkok and the Central Plains

NUEA PAD KANAA

เนื้อผัดคะน้า

Beef with Chinese Broccoli

This combination of fresh broccoli and meat is delicious. However, this recipe is very easy to vary with different fresh vegetables in season.

MARINADE

4 garlic cloves (*kratiem*), minced
1 egg
2 tablespoons sugar
¼ teaspoon white pepper
1 teaspoon Oriental sesame oil
2 tablespoons rice wine
1 tablespoon cornstarch/cornflour
2 tablespoons fish sauce (*nam pla*)

8 oz (250 g) tender beef, thinly sliced
1 lb (500 g) Chinese broccoli or broccoli
2 tablespoons oil
¼ cup straw mushrooms
3 tablespoons oyster sauce

▨ Combine the marinade ingredients, then add the beef pieces and marinate for 5 minutes.
▨ Wash the broccoli and cut it into 3-in (7.5-cm) pieces and set aside.
▨ Heat a large skillet and add the oil. Sauté the beef until almost cooked.
▨ Add the broccoli and the other ingredients and continue to cook for another 3 minutes.

SERVES 4

GINGER CHICKEN (BOTTOM) AND CHICKEN LIVER WITH ONION (TOP)

Bangkok and the Central Plains

GAI PAD KHING

ไก่ผัดขิง

Ginger Chicken

A quick and easy recipe for a healthy meal, this is one of the most popular dishes in Thai restaurants. However, it is equally suitable for home kitchen preparation.

2 tablespoons oil
8 oz (250 g) boned chicken breast, thinly sliced
2 garlic cloves (*kratiem*), minced
2 tablespoons fish sauce (*nam pla*)
1 tablespoon oyster sauce
1 tablespoon sugar
pinch white pepper
⅛ cup slivered ginger
⅛ cup sliced green bell pepper/capsicum
⅛ cup sliced red bell pepper/capsicum
⅛ cup sliced mushrooms
⅛ cup sliced onion
cilantro/coriander leaves (*bai pak chee*), for garnish (optional)

▨ Heat a large skillet, add the oil, chicken and garlic. Cook for 2 minutes.
▨ Add the remaining ingredients and stir-fry for another 3 minutes. Transfer to an attractive serving dish and garnish with cilantro if desired.

SERVES 1–2

PEPPER STEAK (TOP LEFT, RECIPE PAGE 386) AND
BEEF WITH CHINESE BROCCOLI (BOTTOM RIGHT)

CHARCOAL BEEF

Bangkok and the Central Plains

NUEA PAD PRIK

เนื้อผัดพริก

Pepper Steak

A delicious dish usually served over steamed jasmine rice (khao suay), on page 350, with a garnish of fried egg as a variation.

MARINADE

1 teaspoon fish sauce (*nam pla*)
1 tablespoon cornstarch/cornflour
¼ teaspoon white pepper

1 lb (500 g) tender beef, sliced
2 tablespoons oil
4 garlic cloves (*kratiem*), minced
¼ cup sliced onion
¼ cup sliced green bell pepper/capsicum
¼ cup sliced red bell pepper/capsicum
3 tablespoons fish sauce (*nam pla*)
1 tablespoon Maggi seasoning
2 tablespoons sugar
1 tablespoon Oriental sesame oil

☒ Mix the marinade ingredients together, then combine with the beef and set aside for 10 minutes.
☒ Heat a large skillet, add the oil and sauté the beef with the garlic, onion and bell peppers for 3 minutes. Add the remaining ingredients and continue cooking for 2 minutes.

SERVES 4   *Photograph page 384*

The Northeast

NUEA YANG

เนื้อย่าง

Charcoal Beef

This recipe is served with a side dish of fresh local vegetables as well as its fiery dipping sauce.

1 lb (500 g) beef sirloin, cut into 1-in x 1-in x 6-in (2.5-cm x 2.5-cm x 15-cm) strips
3 tablespoons fish sauce (*nam pla*)

DIPPING SAUCE

¼ cup (2 fl oz/60 ml) fish sauce (*nam pla*)
5 tablespoons (2½ fl oz/75 ml) lime juice
1 teaspoon ground chili pepper (*prik khee noo pon*)
1 tablespoon chopped green onion/scallion/spring onion
1 teaspoon chopped cilantro/coriander leaves (*bai pak chee*)

VEGETABLES

cucumber slices
swamp cabbage or spinach
sweet basil stems with leaves (*bai horapa*)
mint stems with leaves
green onions/scallions/spring onions

☒ Place the beef strips in a bowl and rub the fish sauce into the meat. Allow to marinate for 5 minutes. Then charcoal-broil/grill the strips for approximately 3 minutes on each side. Remove.
☒ Combine all the dipping sauce ingredients in a small bowl and serve with the beef slices and a selection of the raw vegetables for dipping.

SERVES 4

Bangkok and the Central Plains

PAD PED NUEA

ผัดเผ็ดเนื้อ

Stir-Fried Curry Beef with Long Beans

Other meats can be substituted for the ground beef to vary the flavor of this quick and easy recipe. The addition of hot peppers will give a spicier taste if that is preferred.

2 tablespoons oil
1 garlic clove (*kratiem*), minced
8 oz (250 g) lean ground/minced beef
2 cups chopped snake beans or string beans, in 1-in (2.5-cm) pieces
3 tablespoons fish sauce (*nam pla*)
1 teaspoon red curry paste (*nam prik gaeng ped*) (see page 488)
1 tablespoon sugar
¼ cup sliced green bell pepper/capsicum
¼ cup sliced red bell pepper/capsicum
¼ teaspoon white pepper
5–8 green Thai chili peppers (*prik khee noo*), sliced (optional)

☒ Heat a large skillet and add the oil and garlic. Add the ground beef and sauté on medium-high heat until done.
☒ Add the beans and all the other ingredients, including the chilies if desired, and continue to cook for about 30 seconds or until the beans are tender.

SERVES 4

STIR-FRIED CURRY BEEF WITH LONG BEANS (TOP LEFT)
AND CHIANG MAI CURRY (TOP RIGHT)

The North

Gaeng Hang Lay

แกงฮังเล

Chiang Mai Curry

Because the meat is simmered in coconut milk to tenderize it, less expensive cuts can be used. A popular variation involves the substitution of side pork/pork flap for the beef.

1 lb (500 g) beef, cut into ½-in (1-cm) slices
2 cups (16 fl oz/500 ml) coconut milk
¼ cup chopped lemon grass/citronella *(ta-krai)*
1 teaspoon shrimp paste *(gapi)*

5 dried green jalapeño peppers *(prik chee fa haeng)*
2 tablespoons yellow bean sauce *(tao jeow)*
6 garlic cloves *(kratiem)*, chopped
1 tablespoon chopped ginger
3 tablespoons palm sugar *(nam taan peep)*
2 shallots
¼ cup (2 fl oz/60 ml) tamarind juice *(ma-kaam piag)* (see glossary)
2 tablespoons curry powder

Simmer the beef slices in the coconut milk for 30 minutes in a large covered saucepan.

Blend together the remaining ingredients to make a paste, add to the beef and continue to simmer, covered, for another 10 minutes.

SERVES 4

WATERFALL BEEF (LEFT) AND MASSAMAN STEAK (RIGHT)

The Northeast

NUEA YANG NAM TOK

เนื้อย่างน้ำตก

Waterfall Beef

The rhythmic sound of the dripping juices from the steak as it cooks over a charcoal grill gives this dish its poetic name.

1 lb (500 g) beef sirloin steak
⅓ cup (3 fl oz/90 ml) fish sauce (*nam pla*)
¼ cup (2 fl oz/60 ml) lime juice
2 tablespoons chopped green onion/scallion/spring onion
2 tablespoons chopped cilantro/coriander leaves (*bai pak chee*)
¼ cup mint leaves
1½ tablespoons ground roasted sticky rice (see glossary)
1 tablespoon toasted sesame seeds
½ teaspoon ground chili pepper (*prik khee noo pon*)

▧ Place the steak in a dish and rub both sides with 1 tablespoon of the fish sauce and marinate for 5 minutes. Charcoal-broil/grill the steak for 3 minutes on each side, or until the steak is medium rare. Remove the steak from the broiler and slice into ⅛-in (3-mm) thin pieces which are about 1 in x 2 in (2.5 cm x 5 cm).
▧ Place the strips in a medium saucepan and add the remaining fish sauce and the lime juice. Stir on medium-high heat for 1 minute. Remove from heat, and add the green onion, cilantro, mint, ground roasted rice, sesame seeds and chili pepper. Combine the entire mixture thoroughly.
▧ Place the beef on a serving plate with a selection of raw or blanched vegetables.

SERVES 4

Bangkok and the Central Plains

MASSAMAN NUEA

มัสมั่นเนื้อ

Massaman Steak

This popular recipe, like many from Bangkok, shows a Muslim influence.

1 lb (500 g) round steak, cut into 1-in (2.5-cm) cubes
3 ½ cups (28 fl oz/880 ml) coconut milk
2 tablespoons oil
⅓ cup (2 oz/60 g) peeled peanuts
¼ cup sliced onion
¼ cup minced garlic (*kratiem*)
6 large dried red jalapeño peppers (*prik chee fa daeng haeng*)
3 tablespoons massaman curry paste (*nam prik gaeng massaman*)
 (see page 493)
¼ cup (2 fl oz/60 ml) fish sauce (*nam pla*)
3 tablespoons sugar

▧ Combine the beef with half the coconut milk in a medium saucepan and simmer for 45 minutes to tenderize the meat.
▧ Heat a skillet, add the oil and fry the peanuts until golden brown. Remove the peanuts and set aside.
▧ Using the same oil, fry the onion, garlic and peppers.
▧ Place the fried onion, garlic and chili peppers in a blender and process until a smooth paste forms.
▧ Combine in a large saucepan the remaining coconut milk, massaman curry paste, fish sauce and sugar. Add the beef mixture, blended mixture and fried peanuts. Heat to boiling and cook for 5 minutes.

SERVES 4

The Northeast

TAP WAAN

ตับหวาน

Sweet Liver

Make sure the liver is not overcooked, so that the flavorful sauce ingredients can be better absorbed.

1 lb (500 g) beef liver, thinly sliced
¼ cup (2 fl oz/60 ml) fish sauce (*nam pla*)
¼ cup (2 fl oz/60 ml) lime juice
½ teaspoon ground chili pepper (*prik khee noo pon*)
1 tablespoon ground roasted sticky rice (see glossary)
4 shallots, thinly sliced
¼ cup lemon grass/citronella (*ta-krai*), thinly sliced
¼ cup mint leaves
selection of raw vegetables

▨ Heat a large saucepan of water to boiling. Blanch the liver slices in the boiling water for 30 seconds or until they are almost cooked. Drain and set aside.

▨ Place the liver slices in a large skillet, add the fish sauce and lime juice and cook on medium-high heat for 1 minute. Remove from heat and add the chili, rice, shallots and lemon grass. Stir to combine. Sprinkle with the mint leaves and remove the contents of skillet to a serving plate.

▨ Arrange the vegetables around the liver slices.

SERVES 4

Bangkok and the Central Plains

PANAENG NUEA

พะแนงเนื้อ

Stir-Fried Beef Curry

Its rich thick sauce helps to make this a very popular dish. Try replacing the beef with chicken for an interesting variation.

SAUCE

3 fl oz (90 ml) coconut milk
2 tablespoons fish sauce (*nam pla*)
2 tablespoons sugar
6 kaffir lime leaves (*bai ma-grood*)

1 tablespoon oil
2 tablespoons Panaeng curry paste (*nam prik panaeng*)
 (see page 493)
8 oz (250 g) tender beef, sliced
⅛ cup sliced green bell pepper/capsicum
⅛ cup sliced red bell pepper/capsicum
¼ cup sliced onions
2 tablespoons ground roasted peanuts
1 tablespoon coconut cream
1 kaffir lime leaf (*bai ma-grood*), very thinly sliced

▨ Mix together the ingredients for the sauce and set aside.

▨ Heat a large skillet and add the oil and curry paste. Cook for 1 minute on low heat. Return the temperature to high and sauté the beef, adding the sauce. Cook until the sauce is thick.

▨ Add the sliced peppers, onions and ground peanuts. Cook for 2 minutes, then pour the mixture into a serving bowl. Top with the coconut cream and lime leaf strips.

SERVES 4

STIR-FRIED BEEF CURRY (BOTTOM) AND SWEET LIVER (TOP RIGHT)

The Northeast

SAI GROG ESAN

ไส้กรอกอีสาน

Northeast Sausage

This is a specialty of the Northeast and is always made with cooked sticky jasmine rice. The rice gives the sausage a firm yet delicate texture.

FILLING

1 lb (500 g) ground/minced pork
¼ cup chopped garlic cloves (*kratiem*)
½ cup steamed sticky rice (*khao neow*) (see page 350)
1 teaspoon white pepper
1 teaspoon salt
¼ cup (2 fl oz/60 ml) lime juice
2 tablespoons fish sauce (*nam pla*)

1 sausage casing for 1 lb (500 g) of ground/minced pork,
    2 ft (60 cm) long

▧ Combine all the filling ingredients thoroughly. Fill the sausage casing. Allow the flavors to combine overnight.
▧ On the next day the sausage can be steamed for 30 minutes or hung outside to be dried in the sun.
▧ Fry the sausage or broil/grill before using in other recipes, such as fried northeast sausage (*sai grog taud*), on page 328.

MAKES 12 SAUSAGES

The South

KUA HAENG MOO PAA

คั่วแห้งหมูป่า

Wild Pig Curry (Dry Style)

This recipe was designed to use the meat from wild pigs but it tastes just as good with pork from domestic sources.

3 tablespoons oil
1 lb (500 g) side pork/pork flap with skin, cut in ½-in
    (1-cm) cubes
2 tablespoons red curry paste (*nam prik gaeng ped*) (see page 488)
3 tablespoons fish sauce (*nam pla*)
2 tablespoons sugar

▧ Heat a large skillet and add the oil and the other ingredients.
▧ Cook on medium-high heat until the sauce is reduced and the pork is cooked, about 10 minutes.
▧ Serve with light yellow curry (*gaeng lueng*), on page 320.

SERVES 4

Bangkok and the Central Plains

MOO PAD WOON SEN

หมูผัดวุ้นเส้น

Stir-Fried Glass Noodles with Pork

These noodles become clear when soaked and so have been given the name cellophane or glass noodles. They are frequently used in soups and stir-fried dishes.

PORK CURRY

2 oz (60 g) cellophane noodles (*woon sen*)
2 tablespoons oil
8 oz (250 g) ground/minced pork
2 eggs
4 garlic cloves (*kratiem*), minced
½ cup sliced cabbage
½ cup chopped green onions/scallions/spring onions, in 1-in
    (2.5-cm) pieces
3 tablespoons fish sauce (*nam pla*)
1 tablespoon Maggi seasoning
2 tablespoons sugar

▧ Soak the noodles in warm water for 10 minutes.
▧ Heat a large skillet and add the oil, pork, eggs and garlic. Stir-fry for 2 minutes, then add the remaining ingredients, and continue to cook (on lower heat if necessary) until the noodles are tender and the sauce has reduced. Remove to a serving platter.

SERVES 4

Bangkok and the Central Plains

GAENG MOO TAY PO

แกงหมูเทโพ

Pork Curry

Most of the curries in Thailand are made with chicken, beef or seafood. When pork curry is made, this is always used as a base.

3 cups (24 fl oz/750 ml) coconut milk
3 tablespoons red curry paste (*nam prik gaeng ped*) (see page 488)
1 lb (500 g) pork, cut into ½-in (1-cm) cubes
¼ cup (2 fl oz/60 ml) fish sauce (*nam pla*)
2 tablespoons sugar
¼ cup (2 fl oz/60 ml) tamarind juice (*ma-kaam piag*)
    (see glossary)
8 whole kaffir lime leaves (*bai ma-grood*)
4 cups swamp cabbage or spinach, cut into 1-in
    (2.5-cm) sections

▧ Combine one-third of the coconut milk with the curry paste in a large saucepan and cook for 1 minute.
▧ Add the pork and continue to cook until tender. Add all the remaining ingredients and bring to a slow boil. Remove from heat and serve.

SERVES 4

NORTHEAST SAUSAGE (TOP LEFT), STIR-FRIED GLASS NOODLES
WITH PORK (BOTTOM) AND WILD PIG CURRY (DRY STYLE) (RIGHT)

Bangkok and the Central Plains

PAD PRIK KHING MOO

ผัดพริกขิงหมู

Stir-Fried Crispy Pork with Swamp Cabbage

In olden times, side pork was used to render fat to be used for cooking. The resulting crispy pork was then used in other recipes.

3 tablespoons oil
1 lb (500 g) side pork/pork flap, thinly sliced
2 tablespoons oil
3 tablespoons curry paste
¼ cup (2 fl oz/60 ml) fish sauce (*nam pla*)
2 tablespoons sugar
1 cup chopped swamp cabbage or spinach, in 2-in (5-cm) sections
5 kaffir lime leaves (*bai ma-grood*), sliced very thinly

Heat a large skillet and add 1 tablespoon of the oil and the pork. Stir-fry for 7 minutes or until the pork is crispy, then remove from the pan and set aside.

Pour out the excess fat and add the rest of the oil. Add the curry paste and cook for a few seconds. Add all the other ingredients except the kaffir lime leaves, heat to boiling, then stir in the crispy pork.

Remove to a serving bowl and garnish with the kaffir lime leaves.

SERVES 2–4

Bangkok and the Central Plains

KHAO PAD MOO

ข้าวผัดหมู

Pork Fried Rice

With the addition of more meat or vegetables on the side, this easy dish is a complete meal in itself.

2 tablespoons oil
2 garlic cloves (*kratiem*), minced
8 oz (250 g) sliced pork
2 eggs, beaten
4 cups cooked white rice
¼ cup (2 fl oz/60 ml) fish sauce (*nam pla*)
1 tablespoon sweet soy sauce
2 tablespoons sugar
¼ teaspoon white pepper
½ cup sliced onion
½ cup tomato chunks
1 green onion/scallion/spring onion, chopped
⅛ cup cilantro/coriander leaves (*bai pak chee*)
¼ cup cucumber slices

Heat a large skillet and add the oil. Stir-fry the garlic and pork until cooked.

Add the eggs and scramble until cooked. Add the rice, sauces, sugar and white pepper. Continue cooking until the rice is hot, reducing the temperature if necessary. Add the onion, tomato chunks and green onion. Garnish with the cilantro and cucumber slices. Serve with fish sauce with chili (*nam pla prik*), on page 494.

SERVES 4

PORK FRIED RICE (LEFT), STIR-FRIED CRISPY PORK WITH
SWAMP CABBAGE (FRONT) AND FIVE SPICE PORK SPARE RIBS
(TOP RIGHT, RECIPE PAGE 396)

Bangkok and the Central Plains

SEE-KRONG MOO OB

ซี่โครงหมูอบ

Five Spice Pork Spare Ribs

Baking the ribs in the oven is the modern-day approach to this recipe—barbecuing over charcoal is the traditional method. Here the best of both worlds is used, with flavor added by a spell on the barbecue while the oven gives the convenience of controlled heat for the rest of the cooking time.

MARINADE

½ cup (4 fl oz/125 ml) soy sauce
¼ cup (2 fl oz/60 ml) fish sauce (*nam pla*)
1 teaspoon five spice powder
1 tablespoon Oriental sesame oil
½ cup (4 oz/125 g) sugar
6 garlic cloves (*kratiem*), minced
¼ cup coriander/cilantro leaves (*bai pak chee*), minced
2 tablespoons rice wine or cognac

4 lbs (2 kg) pork spare ribs, cut into 1-in (2.5-cm) pieces
1 tablespoon oil

▨ Mix together the marinade ingredients, then rub the mixture into the ribs thoroughly and marinate for about 10 minutes.
▨ Brush barbecue grill with the oil. Place the ribs on the grill and barbecue for 10 minutes. Remove from the barbecue and bake at 350°F (180°C) for 30 minutes.
▨ Serve with fresh cucumber slices and whole green onions/scallions/spring onions.

SERVES 4   *Photograph pages 394–395*

Bangkok and the Central Plains

PAD KREUNG NAI MOO

ผัดเครื่องในหมู

Stir-Fried Pork Stomach with Liver

Many organ meats are cooked in this way, giving them a texture which is a favorite among Thai people.

8 oz (250 g) pork stomach
8 oz (250 g) pork liver
4 black mushrooms/Chinese mushrooms
4 cups (1 qt/1 l) water
3 tablespoons oil
4 garlic cloves (*kratiem*), minced
2 tablespoons light soy sauce
1 tablespoon fish sauce (*nam pla*)
1 tablespoon cornstarch/cornflour, dissolved in
    2 tablespoons water
2 green onions/scallions/spring onions, cut into 1-in
    (2.5-cm) pieces

▨ Scrub the pork stomach well and remove any fat attached to it. Rinse the liver. Slice the stomach and liver into ½-in (1-cm) wide slices.
▨ Soak the black mushrooms in very hot water for about 10 minutes or until soft. Drain carefully, then slice into ½-in (1-cm) thick slices.
▨ Heat the water to boiling in a large pot. Put the stomach in the water and cook for 10 minutes on high heat. Add the liver and cook for 1 minute. Remove from water, drain and set aside.

STIR-FRIED PORK STOMACH WITH LIVER

▨ Heat a large skillet then add the oil, garlic, liver, stomach, black mushrooms, light soy sauce and fish sauce. Continue to cook for 2 minutes. Add the prepared cornstarch mixture to the skillet. Cook for 2 minutes then add the green onions. Remove and serve.

SERVES 4

Bangkok and the Central Plains

MOO YANG TA-KRAI

หมูย่างตะไคร้

Lemon Grass Pork Chops

Broiling over charcoal is a common Thai cooking method which gives meat a distinctive flavor. Boneless pieces of pork threaded onto skewers can be substituted for the chops in a delicious variation of this recipe.

MARINADE

2 garlic cloves (*kratiem*), minced
½ teaspoon white pepper
2 tablespoons sugar
2 tablespoons fish sauce (*nam pla*)
2 tablespoons soy sauce
1 tablespoon Oriental sesame oil
1 tablespoon cognac or whiskey or wine
2 tablespoons chopped lemon grass/citronella (*ta-krai*)
1 tablespoon finely chopped green onion/scallion/spring onion
2 tablespoons coconut milk

4 pork chops, about 1 lb (500 g) altogether

▨ Mix together the marinade ingredients then thoroughly combine with the pork chops. Allow to sit for 10 minutes.
▨ Broil/grill the meat over charcoal for about 8 minutes on each side, or until done.
▨ Serve with sweet and sour sauce or other dip of your choice.

SERVES 4

Bangkok and the Central Plains

Moo Tom Kem Palo

หมูต้มเค็มพะโล้

Steamed Five Spice Pork

This dish can be prepared a day in advance and left to marinate, giving a richer flavor to the pork.

1 tablespoon oil
4 garlic cloves (*kratiem*), minced
1 lb (500 g) side pork/pork flap, cut in 1-in (2.5-cm) cubes
8 oz (250 g) fried tofu (see glossary)
1 teaspoon five spice powder
¼ cup coriander root (*raak pak chee*), minced
½ teaspoon white pepper
¼ cup (2 fl oz/60 ml) sweet soy sauce
2 tablespoons light soy sauce
¼ cup (2 fl oz/60 ml) fish sauce (*nam pla*)
3 tablespoons sugar or brown sugar
2 cups (16 fl oz/500 ml) water
6 hard-cooked (hard-boiled) eggs

Heat a large saucepan and add the oil and garlic. Add the pork and stir, then add all the remaining ingredients, leaving the eggs whole.

Cover and simmer for 15 minutes until the pork is tender. Remove to a serving bowl and serve with rice.

SERVES 4

Bangkok and the Central Plains

Kai Jeow Moo Sab

ไข่เจียวหมูสับ

Thai Pork Omelet

Egg dishes are among the favorites on Thai menus. This one is delicious for lunch or as an accompaniment to a curry.

2 eggs
2 tablespoons fish sauce (*nam pla*)
1 teaspoon Maggi seasoning
¼ cup chopped green onions/scallions/spring onions
8 oz (250 g) ground/minced pork
½ cup (4 fl oz/125 ml) oil

Combine the eggs with the fish sauce, Maggi seasoning and green onions. Beat the mixture well and add the ground pork. Continue to stir until the ground pork is evenly dispersed.

Heat an 8-in (20-cm) skillet and add a quarter of the oil. Wait for the pan to get hot, then pour in a quarter of the egg mixture. Turn down the temperature to medium-high and fry the mixture for 2 minutes or until cooked.

Turn the omelet on to a plate and continue to cook the remaining mixture in the extra oil until all four omelets are cooked. Serve with a choice of dips.

MAKES 4 OMELETS

THAI PORK OMELET (TOP) AND STEAMED FIVE SPICE PORK (FRONT)

STIR-FRIED SQUASH

Bangkok and the Central Plains

PAD FAK THONG

ผัดฟักทอง

Stir-Fried Squash

This is one of the many ways of cooking winter squash. It is easy, and does not take as long as baking large pieces.

3 tablespoons oil
6 garlic cloves (*kratiem*), minced
8 oz (250 g) pork, sliced into ½-in x 2-in (1-cm x 2.5-cm)
   thick pieces
1 lb (500 g) winter squash/pumpkin, peeled and cut into
   ½-in x 2-in (1-cm x 2.5-cm) slices
¼ cup (2 oz/60 g) fish sauce (*nam pla*)
2 tablespoons sugar
3 eggs, beaten

▦ Heat a large skillet, add the oil, garlic and pork and stir-fry for 1 minute.
▦ Add the squash, fish sauce and sugar. Cover and cook on medium heat for 6 minutes or until the squash is tender and the sauce is reduced. Add the eggs and mix with the ingredients in the skillet. Continue to cook until the eggs are cooked. Remove to a serving bowl.

SERVES 4

Bangkok and the Central Plains

PAD TAP MOO

ผัดตับหมู

Sautéed Pork Liver

Liver, a good source of iron, is often paired with chives or onions. Sometimes it is included in noodle soups and other dishes.

4 cups (1 qt/1 l) water
1 lb (500 g) pork liver, thinly sliced
2 tablespoons oil
6 garlic cloves (*kratiem*), chopped
1 cup sliced onions
1 tablespoon canned peppercorns
¼ cup (2 fl oz/60 ml) fish sauce (*nam pla*)
2 tablespoons sugar
¼ cup julienned carrot strips, for garnish
¼ cup chopped chives, in 1-in (2.5-cm) sections, for garnish

▦ Heat the water to boiling in a large saucepan. Blanch the liver for 1 minute and drain.
▦ Heat a large skillet on medium-high heat, then add the oil, liver, garlic, onion, peppercorns, fish sauce and sugar.
▦ Cook for 3 minutes then remove to a serving dish and garnish with the carrot and chives.

SERVES 4

SAUTÉED PORK LIVER (TOP) AND SWEET PORK
(BOTTOM, RECIPE PAGE 402)

The South

Moo Wan

หมูหวาน

Sweet Pork

To achieve a glazed effect, reduce the sauce further.

1 lb (500 g) pork belly, cut into 1-in (2.5-cm) strips
¼ cup (2 fl oz/60 ml) cooking oil
2 tablespoons sweet soy sauce
⅓ cup (3 fl oz/90 ml) fish sauce (*nam pla*)
¼ cup (1¼ oz/40 g) brown sugar or coconut sugar

▦ Heat a medium skillet and add the oil. Add the pork and all the other ingredients. Heat to boiling, reduce heat and cover the skillet. Simmer for 15 minutes, until the pork is tender.

SERVES 4   *Photograph page 401*

Bangkok and the Central Plains

Kai Yad Sai

ไข่ยัดไส้

Square Thai Omelets

Usually a luncheon dish, these omelets can also be served for breakfast.

4 oz (125 g) pork
4 oz (125 g) shrimp/prawns, shelled and deveined
3 tablespoons oil
1 garlic clove (*kratiem*), minced
2 tablespoons fish sauce (*nam pla*)
1 tablespoon Maggi seasoning
2 tablespoons sugar
¼ teaspoon white pepper
1 small tomato, chopped
1 small onion, chopped
2 tablespoons chopped sugar peas/snow peas or green peas
⅛ cup chopped carrots
6 eggs, beaten
chopped cilantro/coriander leaves (*bai pak chee*), for garnish
green onions/scallions/spring onions, for garnish

▦ Mince the pork and shrimp together. Heat a 10-in (25-cm) skillet and add 1 tablespoon of the oil, with the garlic. Add the pork and shrimp mixture and stir-fry for about 2 minutes over medium-high heat or until cooked. Add the fish sauce, Maggi seasoning, sugar and pepper. Continue to cook for about 1 minute until the sauce is reduced. Add the vegetables and stir to combine. Remove the mixture from the skillet, drain off excess juice, and set aside.
▦ Warm a medium skillet over medium heat and coat with a thin layer of oil. Add a quarter of the beaten eggs and roll to coat the skillet surface evenly. Place a quarter of the filling mixture in the center of the egg surface and allow the omelet to cook over low heat until set.
▦ Fold the omelet Thai-style by bringing the lower portion of the cooked egg sheet up to cover the filling mixture. Bring in the sides to overlap each other and then fold down the top portion to cover the entire top of the omelet, so that it forms a square. Invert the omelet by placing a plate over the skillet and turning the skillet upside-down. Keep warm.
▦ Make three more omelets, move to a serving plate and garnish with the cilantro leaves and green onions.

SERVES 4

SPICY WILD PIG (TOP LEFT, RECIPE PAGE 404)
AND SQUARE THAI OMELETS (RIGHT)

Bangkok and the Central Plains

PAD PED MOO PAA

ผัดเผ็ดหมูป่า

Spicy Wild Pig

Originally prepared using the very lean meat of the wild pig, this dish tastes just as good with the pork available today.

3 tablespoons oil
1 tablespoon red curry paste (*nam prik gaeng ped*) (see page 488)
1 lb (500 g) pork, thinly sliced (¼ in x 2 in x 1 in)
   (6 mm x 5 cm x 2.5 cm)
¼ cup canned green peppercorns
5 green jalapeño peppers (*prik chee fa*), sliced
3 tablespoons fish sauce (*nam pla*)
2 tablespoons sugar
¼ cup (2 fl oz/60 ml) coconut cream

❊ Heat a large skillet then add the oil and red curry paste and cook for 1 minute.
❊ Add the slices of pork, peppercorns, peppers, fish sauce and sugar. Cook on medium-high heat for 3 minutes.
❊ Remove from pan to a serving plate and top with the coconut cream.

SERVES 4   *Photograph pages 402–403*

The North

MOO YANG

หมูย่าง

Chiang Mai Barbecued Pork

Sweet and juicy skewered pork combines well with steamed sticky rice, and the addition of a spicy chili sauce as a dip would further enhance this dish. It can also be served as a cold meat.

1 lb (500 g) pork loin, sliced into ½-in x 1-in (1-cm x 2.5-cm) thin strips

MARINADE

1 cup (8 fl oz/250 ml) coconut milk
¼ cup (2 fl oz/60 ml) fish sauce (*nam pla*)
6 garlic cloves (*kratiem*), finely minced
6 cilantro/coriander roots (*raak pak chee*), finely chopped
2 tablespoons soy sauce
3 tablespoons sugar
1 teaspoon white pepper
1 tablespoon ground cilantro/coriander seed (*pak chee pon*)

❊ Skewer each piece of pork onto a bamboo skewer, making sure that the meat is flat and skewered in the center. Mix the marinade ingredients together and marinate the pork skewers in the mixture for 15 minutes.
❊ Barbecue the pork skewers, or cook on a pre-heated broiler/griller, for 4 minutes on each side, or until the meat is cooked through.
❊ Serve with steamed sticky rice (*khao neow*), on page 350.

SERVES 4

The South

PAD SA-TAW

ผัดสะตอ

Beans with Shrimp Paste

Southern beans grow only in the South and have a slightly bitter taste, similar to that of raw peanuts. Ordinary green beans can be substituted for these beans, but the flavor will be different.

8 oz (250 g) southern beans (*sa-taw*) or snake beans
10 green Thai chili peppers (*prik khee noo*)
8 garlic cloves (*kratiem*), finely minced
1 tablespoon shrimp paste (*gapi*)
3 tablespoons fish sauce (*nam pla*)
3 tablespoons lime juice
2 tablespoons coconut sugar or brown sugar
3 tablespoons oil
8 oz (250 g) ground/minced pork
8 oz (250 g) shrimp/prawns, peeled and deveined

❊ Remove the southern beans from their pods. Set aside.
❊ Using a pestle and mortar, pound together the chili peppers, garlic and shrimp paste until the mixture is well mashed. Stir in the fish sauce, lime juice and sugar. Set aside.
❊ Heat a large skillet and add the oil. When the oil is hot, add the pork.
❊ Stir-fry for 2 minutes and then add the shrimp, beans and shrimp paste mixture. Continue cooking for approximately 3 minutes on medium-high heat, then serve.

SERVES 4

CHIANG MAI BARBECUED PORK (LEFT) AND
BEANS WITH SHRIMP PASTE (RIGHT)

404

Bangkok and the Central Plains

GAENG OM MARA

แกงอ่อมมะระ

Bitter Melon Curry

The bitter melon which gives this curry a bitter flavor is an acquired taste.
There is nothing else which has the same flavor.

2 tablespoons oil
2 tablespoons red curry paste *(nam prik gaeng ped)* (see page 488)

8 oz (250 g) pork, sliced
1 lb (500 g) bitter melon, cut into ½-in (1-cm) thick
  lengthwise slices
2 cups (16 fl oz/500 ml) coconut milk
¼ cup (2 fl oz/60 ml) fish sauce *(nam pla)*
2 tablespoons sugar

▓ Heat a large skillet and add the oil. Add the curry paste and pork and stir-fry for 1 minute. Then add the bitter melon slices.
▓ Stir-fry for 3 minutes and add the remaining ingredients. Heat to boiling and serve.

SERVES 4

BITTER MELON CURRY

BANGKOK AND THE CENTRAL PLAINS

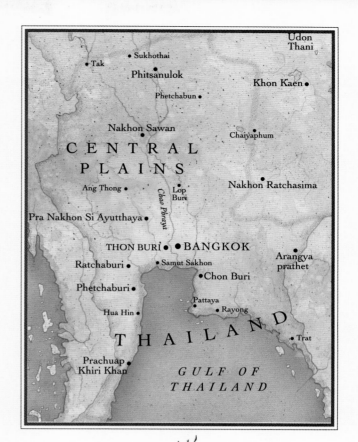

BANGKOK AND THE CENTRAL PLAINS

THE CENTRAL PLAINS region is a vast, flat, extremely fertile basin, regularly watered and enriched by the winding Chao Phraya River. It is the kingdom's geographical, cultural, and economic heart, the source of its agricultural strength and the stage where nearly all the major events in Thai history have been enacted.

On either side of the river, as far as the eye can see, extends a complex jigsaw puzzle of irrigation canals and rice fields, seas of acid green at the start of the rainy season, turning pale gold by harvest time. There are miles, too, of neat vegetable gardens, lush orchards of mangoes, durians, rambutans and citrus fruits, and canals and ponds that teem with a readily available supply of fish and shrimp. Not far from where the river empties into the gulf, rising out of the low-lying level earth like a sudden improbable dream, is the City—the only city, really—sprawling and splendid, chaotic and alluring. And then more fields, gardens, and orchards, wrapping around both sides of the sea.

The Thais were by no means the first to discover this wonderfully productive region, guarded by mountains on three sides, and to leave monuments scattered throughout it. There were the Mons, who established a distinctive Buddhist culture known as Dvaravati and built cities along the fringes of the Central Plains. There were the Khmers, who settled mostly in the Northeast

THE PLOUGHING CEREMONY IS HELD EVERY
APRIL AT SANAM LUANG IN BANGKOK

PREVIOUS PAGES: THE TEMPLE OF DAWN, WAT ARUN

THE DUSIT MAHAPRASAT, THE OLDEST BUILDING
IN THE ROYAL PALACE, HOUSES A THRONE THAT IS
STILL USED FOR STATE CEREMONIES

was destroyed by the Burmese in 1767 a new capital was built further downriver at Thonburi; in 1782 King Rama I, founder of the present Chakri dynasty, decided that the opposite bank offered better protection against future invasions and moved his palace to a small trading port known as Bangkok, literally "the village of the wild hog plum".

Although it appears on most foreign maps, Bangkok is not in fact the proper name of the Thai capital. When it was elevated to that high status a more imposing title was required, and King Rama I bestowed one so filled with honorifics that according to the Guinness Book of Records it ranks as the world's longest city name. The Thais shorten it to Krung Thep, "City of Angels", while outsiders have generally continued to use the older village appellation.

Whatever name is used, it would be difficult to overestimate the importance of the role played by the city in Thailand's modern development. King Rama I's aim—a highly ambitious one in view of the country's war-ravaged condition and the dearth of foreign trade at the time—was nothing less than a re-creation of magnificent Ayutthaya, then a moldering but still vividly remembered expanse of ruins. To this end he built a fortified city on an artificial island achieved by digging a canal at a point where the river curved. Its core was the Grand Palace, a dazzling collection of classic Thai structures covering nearly a square mile and containing, besides the royal residences and audience halls, a magnificent temple to house the sacred Emerald Buddha. Outside the walls but still adjacent to the river was a

STATUES OF KINNARI, A MYTHICAL BIRD-LIKE CREATURE,
STAND IN THE GRAND PALACE COMPOUND

but whose power extended over nearly all of the Chao Phraya basin during the eleventh and twelfth centuries. But it was the Thais who ultimately predominated and used the immense natural wealth of the Central Plains to create their own distinctive culture.

Their rise began at Sukhothai, near the ridge of the northern mountains and just above the point where three lesser rivers meet to form the Chao Phraya. Groups of Thais had been filtering down into the area for some time, drawn by a desire for better land and greater freedom, and by the early thirteenth century they probably outnumbered the Khmers who were theoretically in control. In 1238 two Thai chieftains combined forces and after overthrowing the local Khmer commander established an independent kingdom of their own.

Sukhothai's cultural and political achievements were considerable, exerting an influence still felt today in such key institutions as Buddhism and the monarchy. Its real power, however, lasted just a little more than a century before succumbing to another Thai state, Ayutthaya, which had risen on the Chao Phraya in the very heart of the river valley. Here over a period of four hundred years Thai culture was consolidated, absorbing a wide variety of outside influences that affected not only art and architecture but also cuisine and social life, yet maintaining a uniquely Thai identity.

The Chao Phraya remained the focal point of regional development, annually revitalizing the fields with deposits of silt from the northern highlands and serving as the gateway to contact with the outside world. When Ayutthaya

thriving community of Chinese merchants who had originally occupied the palace site and been relocated.

Ayutthaya had been known as the "Venice of the East" by European visitors, and Bangkok soon acquired the same sobriquet, for water also dominated its early life: the Chao Phraya served as the main highway, lined with double and sometimes triple rows of steep-roofed floating houses, while an intricate network of *klongs*, or canals, led off like streets into the countryside on either bank. Endless processions of huge hump-backed teak barges moved up and down the river loaded with rice and other produce from outlying provinces, and every household had a small dugout canoe for daily commuting. "Boats are the universal means of conveyance and communication," wrote Sir John Bowring in 1855. "Except about the palaces of the Kings, horses or carriages are rarely seen, and the sedan of the Chinese appears unknown in Siam."

But change was in the air even at the time of Bowring's visit to negotiate a historic treaty with King Rama IV. Almost from the beginning, as the threat of foreign invasion receded, Bangkok had prospered. Chinese junks sailed up the river in steadily increasing numbers, eager to buy high-quality Thai rice, which then, as now, was regarded as among the best in the world. They were soon joined by ships from more distant countries, and the Thai capital became a major Asian port of call. Immigrants came to seek their fortunes in the new capital, mainly Chinese but also Laotians, Indians, Cambodians, Malays, and *farangs*, or Westerners. Only a few years

A LACQUER PANEL FROM AYUTTHAYA, NOW IN THE SUAN PAKAAD PALACE IN BANGKOK, SHOWING WOMEN PREPARING NOODLES

LUCA INVERNIZZI TETTONI/PHOTOBANK

THE TRADITIONAL PROCESSION OF ROYAL BARGES NOW ONLY TAKES PLACE ON EXCEPTIONAL OCCASIONS, SUCH AS THE KING'S SIXTIETH BIRTHDAY

after Bowring's mission, the first proper road was constructed running parallel to the river for most of its length; according to some accounts, it was built as a result of European complaints to the king that their health was suffering for lack of a place to take an evening carriage ride. Bangkok's riverine character would remain intact for some time afterward—actually until the early years of the twentieth century—but its future as a Western-style city was already beginning to be clear.

Today, with an officially estimated population of about six million (though the true figure is probably closer to seven or eight million) and covering an area of some 2,311 square miles (5,986 square kilometers) on both sides of the Chao Phraya, Bangkok is sixty times the size of Khon Kaen, Thailand's second largest city. It dominates the country in more than just size, however. The king's permanent residence, all the government ministries, and most of the leading educational, medical, sporting, and cultural facilities are located in the capital, as well as the great majority of the biggest Thai and foreign business firms. It is the hub of air, rail, and bus transportation to all parts of the kingdom. Industry, until recent years at least, has been largely concentrated in the city or in nearby provinces, thus serving as a magnet for provincial Thais in search of work, and nearly all the country's exports and imports pass through its facilities. Its wealth is reflected not only in a relatively recent skyline of towering residential and office blocks, hotels, and shopping centers but also in notorious traffic jams arising from the fact that 90 percent of the motor vehicles in Thailand are registered there.

Bangkok's urban problems are manifest: squalid slums that house migrant workers, periodic floods caused partly by inadequate drainage and partly by indiscriminate pumping of underground water, alarming air pollution, traffic congestion that appears to defy solution. Yet in spite of these, it is vibrantly alive, a city of incredible diversity and serendipitous surprises, a city where one may be frustrated, perhaps bewildered, but never for an instant bored.

Nowhere is Bangkok's variety more apparent than in the culinary opportunities it offers. As an introduction, go to any of the city's great public markets and view the produce of the countryside piled in artful pyramids, spilling colorfully out of bamboo baskets, or arranged on trays in patterns like a display of rare jewels.

Spices are there in abundance, of course, essential for achieving the subtle gradations of flavor that characterize all Thai cooking. Some will be familiar to a visitor from the West: chili peppers both fresh and dried, in dozens of different varieties and sizes, from large and relatively mild to the deceptively tiny *prik khee noo* which is the hottest of all; cilantro (coriander), the fresh leaf sprinkled on almost everything and the root and seed used to flavor many meat dishes; basil of several kinds; black and white peppercorns; garlic; mint; dill; ginger root; and cardamon. Others may seem more exotic: sword-shaped pandanus leaves, which impart a delicate fragrance to anything cooked in them; lemon grass, a basic for several of the best known soups and salads; bumpy-skinned kaffir limes and their leaves; cinnamon-colored tamarind pods, from which a sharp-tasting liquid is extracted for many

THE LAYOUT OF THE ANCIENT THAI CITY OF SUKHOTHAI REFLECTS THE COSMOLOGICAL AND URBAN CONCEPTS OF THE EARLIER KHMER CIVILIZATION

THE TOWERING OFFICE BLOCKS OF BANGKOK

THE KLONGS AROUND BANGKOK ARE
CROWDED WITH SMALL CRAFT

JOHN HAY

dishes; tiny eggplants called *ma-khue puang*, with a distinctive bitter flavor; and galangal, a rhizome sometimes called Siamese ginger. In addition to such fresh or dried ingredients, there is also a wide selection of prepared seasonings found in every Thai kitchen, the most important of which are shrimp paste, fish sauce, and chili sauce in various degrees of potency.

Vegetables, which the Thais eat in large quantities, are imaginatively presented, too, and the choice is far more varied today than it was in the past: not only such traditional staples as cabbages, mushrooms, morning glory, bitter gourds, bamboo shoots, cucumber, celery, and tomatoes, but also newer ones such as asparagus, broccoli, lettuce, and tender baby corn. Elsewhere in the market there are displays of fresh beef and pork, chicken and duck, small game birds and, above all, fish, the main source of protein in the Thai diet, which is offered fresh, dried, and salted, and appears in some form at all meals.

Fresh fruits constitute one of Thailand's greatest treats. Thanks to improved methods of growing, many are now available throughout the year: oranges, limes, and huge succulent pomeloes which look like grapefruits but have a very different taste; some of the sweetest pineapples in the world, mostly grown along the western coast of the gulf; crispy cool guavas; mangosteens, the ruby-red shells encasing juicy white pearls; hairy rambutans; some twenty-eight different kinds of banana, from large to finger-sized; nutty-tasting sapodillas; papayas, or pawpaws, eaten both green and ripe; young coconuts with tender meat; custard apples, watermelons, cantaloupes, honeydews, and sweet grapes in varieties especially hybridized for tropical cultivation.

A number are seasonal, eagerly sought during the few months when the best specimens appear on the market. Perhaps the most controversial, at least among foreigners, is the celebrated durian: the size of a football, covered with lethal-looking spines, and, in the view of one early European traveler, smelling "like exceedingly defective sanitation". Thais, like many other Asians, think differently and would agree with the famous naturalist Alfred Russel Wallace, who was introduced to durian on the island of Borneo and later wrote, "The more you eat of it the less you feel inclined to stop." To them the durian is nothing less than the king of fruits, a treat well worth the high prices commanded by prized hybrids bearing such names as "Golden Pillow", "Long Stem", and "Gibbon". Each kind of durian has a special name, some of them useful to buyers. "Deception", for instance, is so-called because from the outside it looks as if it contains a large quantity of golden flesh but doesn't. "Transvestite", on the other hand, is quite meaty but the seeds won't germinate.

Another favorite is the mango, which in Thailand is a very different fruit from the large red or orange-fleshed varieties familiar to most Westerners. Here it is smaller and pale yellow, sweet but tempered with a slight hint of tartness, an altogether more subtle and delicate flavor. Thais eat mangoes fresh, often accompanied by sweetened glutinous rice, but the fruit is equally popular green, when it is used in salads or as a snack with sugar and salt.

As suggested by the abundance of its markets, eating is a major pastime in Bangkok and a highly visible one, too, since almost every street contains at least one sidewalk restaurant—usually several of them—along with countless itinerant vendors offering everything from tasty grilled baby squid and noodle soup to chunks of chilled fruit and brightly colored sweets. Until quite recently the most authentic Thai cooking was to be found principally in private homes, especially those of the wealthier class, where there were adequate servants and family members to take care of all the requisite chopping, mincing, and grinding; when they went out, city Thais preferred to eat Chinese food which even then was plentifully available, or occasionally at a Western restaurant. New lifestyles have changed that: today there are numerous elegantly decorated places specializing in properly prepared Thai dishes from all the country's regions as well as one style often described as "Royal" or "Palace" cooking, with a more refined taste and exquisite presentation, unique to the capital.

Ayutthaya was noted for its cosmopolitan atmosphere, and in this regard King Rama I's aspirations were amply fulfilled; for Bangkok, too, is a cultural melting pot composed of many flavors. Among the foreign influences, the most pervasive is Chinese, though thanks to long and successful assimilation it may now be more accurate to use the term Sino-Thai. Indians have established a prominent economic presence, especially in the past decade or so, and there are significant communities of Japanese, Malays, Laotians, and Burmese. The diversity of Westerners living in the capital is reflected in the fact that diners with a taste for *farang* food have a choice of French, British, German, Italian, Swiss, Spanish, Greek, and Mexican restaurants, not to mention American fast-food outlets and at least one place offering Louisiana Cajun cuisine.

But Bangkok, despite its power and glamor, is only one aspect of life in the Central Plains region. Beyond the urban sprawl lie the endless rice fields, and there, in villages consisting of a few dozen simple wooden houses and a local *wat*, or Buddhist temple, other Thais follow patterns and precepts that have remained remarkably unchanged and reveal the country's true culture far more accurately than those of the worldly city.

Village society is at once democratic—the head, or *phu-yai-ban*, is popularly elected—and highly organized, reflecting the Thai belief that social harmony is more important than individual freedom. Buddhist concepts, symbolized by the *wat* which serves as a social center for most community activities, are instilled in children almost from birth, and are prevalent at every level. William Klausner was writing of a northeastern village in the 1950s but his comments on ideal behavior apply equally to those in the Central Plains region today: "Being gentle is a highly valued character trait. One often hears the compliment 'he acts in a gentle way' as well as the criticism 'he did not speak or act in a gentle manner.' Gentle behavior flows from a 'cool heart' with avoidance of expressions of anger, hatred, and annoyance. Harmonious personal relationships must be preserved."

Families tend to be large, including not only parents and children but also grandparents and perhaps a few other relatives, all living under the same roof or in the same compound, a communal lifestyle that naturally

TRADITIONAL HOUSES ON STILTS ARE STILL A COMMON SIGHT ON THE CANALS AROUND AYUTTHAYA AND SINGHBURI

BUNCHES OF ROSES, THEIR BUDS STILL TIGHTLY CLOSED, AT BANGKOK'S WHOLESALE MARKET AT PAKLONG TALAT

414

calls for compromise and tact. Respect for elders is another important Thai value that begins in the family, extending from the youngest child up to the oldest grandparent and formulated through a complex system of words and gestures; this conditioning later determines behavior outside the immediate family, whether in village society or in the business and government offices of cosmopolitan life.

Life revolves around the seasonal cycles of planting and harvesting. Rice planting in the Central Plains usually begins in April or May, just before the arrival of the monsoon rains, and is a co-operative undertaking, with families joining to plough the fields, repair dikes, release water from nearby canals and irrigation ditches, and plant the young rice seedlings. Though many farmers now grow other crops—fruits, vegetables, or, especially in the eastern area, tapioca—rice remains the mainstay of Thai agriculture, with a significance that is not merely economic but almost mystical. *Kin khao* is the Thai expression for "to eat"; literally translated it means "to eat rice", reflecting the belief that any meal without the staple is incomplete. Central Thais prefer polished rice—the unhusked form is associated with poverty or with such unfortunate groups as prisoners and military conscripts—and usually steam it, though it is also fried in the Chinese manner or boiled for the traditional breakfast dish known as *khao tom*.

Phansa, the three-month Buddhist "Rains Retreat", commences after the rice plants are established. During this period monks are required to remain in their monasteries, meditating and studying the scriptures, and many young village men enter the monkhood for spiritual training. Such an experience is regarded as one of the essential steps in every male Thai's life, bringing merit to his family and also certifying his emergence as a mature adult. In many parts of the country a man who has not been ordained is called a *khon dip*, an "unripe person", and thus avoided by marriageable girls of the community.

By the end of the rains, usually in late November, Central Plains rice is ready for harvest, another co-operative effort that occupies most able-bodied villagers from early morning until late at night. Afterward, many farmers plant a second crop, sometimes more rice and sometimes vegetables, to supplement their incomes.

And so the cycle continues, as timeless as the great river that makes it possible: not an easy life (no farmer's is), though a far more profitable one in the fertile Central Plains region than elsewhere in the country. At the same time, the Thai penchant for *sanuk*, or pleasure, ensures that it is not a monotonous routine. Ordinations, marriages, auspicious birthdays, Buddhist holy days, all offer a welcome opportunity for villagers to get together and enjoy special foods, folk dancing, perhaps a demonstration of Thai-style boxing or a performance by an itinerant theater troupe, relaxing the natural conservatism that ordinarily prevails.

Widespread industrial development has come to the eastern part of the Central Plains region, thanks to offshore discoveries of oil and natural gas in the gulf; under the huge Eastern Seaboard Project, which will eventually extend into three provinces, gas separation plants and a petrochemical complex have already been

EVERY YOUNG THAI MAN HAS TO SPEND SOME TIME IN A MONASTERY. HERE A NOVICE IS BEING SHAVED BEFORE THE INITIATION CEREMONY

constructed and more facilities are scheduled over the coming decade. Tourism, too, has had an impact through such seaside resorts as Pattaya, once a quiet fishing community and now an internationally famous recreation center which stretches for miles along the coast.

Despite these changes, traditional village life continues in the area, though occupations may differ from those of the rice-oriented Chao Phraya valley. Both Chanthaburi and Rayong provinces, for example, are noted for their fruit orchards, producing some of the country's best pomeloes, rambutans, jackfruit, and durian. Rayong, not far from the bright lights of Pattaya, is also one of the best known sources of *nam pla*, the clear, amber-colored fish sauce that appears as a seasoning on every Thai dinner table, as well as of pungent shrimp paste. From countless ports on either side of the gulf, trawlers go out daily to bring back catches of seafood—the much-prized pomfret *(pla jaramet)*, snapper *(pla gapong)*, cotton fish *(pla samlii)*, grouper *(pla karang)*, squid, and an abundance of shellfish. A large number of residents have also taken up the profitable, relatively new career of raising large freshwater prawns, a delicacy popular locally and abroad.

Thailand's dynamic present is more apparent in the Central Plains region than in any other part of the country; at the same time, as the traditional heartland, its countryside probably offers some of the purest reflections of authentic Thai culture as it has gradually developed over the past seven centuries.

SALADS AND VEGETABLES

A FARMER CARRIES BUNCHES OF GREEN ONIONS, JUST PULLED FROM THE FIELDS

SALADS AND VEGETABLES

THAI FOODS ENTRANCE THE EYE as well as the palate—qualities well displayed in Thailand's appealing and appetizing variety of salads. These salads combine fresh raw vegetables with protein such as shrimp, squid or charcoal-broiled, thinly sliced beef. The paradigmatic salad resonates with three taste notes: a hint of sourness, followed by saltiness, then sweetness.

In preparing salads, one strives for a mix of colors to tantalize the diner, complementing the warm reds of peppers and tomatoes with the green of green onions. Salads are often presented on a bed of green leaf lettuce.

One of the most popular Thai salads is beef salad *(yam nuea)*. Beef strips are tossed with a dressing made of lime juice, minced Thai chili peppers, minced garlic and chopped green onions. The dish is embellished with a sprig of cilantro and slivers of green onions. So the salad not only tastes good but looks good too.

Another popular dish, papaya salad *(som tam Esan)*, originated in northeast Thailand. The salad is made from under-ripe, firm papaya that is peeled and shredded; raw, long string beans cut into 1-inch (2.5-centimeter) sections; and tomatoes. Seasonings include garlic, Thai

chili peppers, and lime juice or tamarind juice. Papaya salad can be assembled in a large mortar in which the vegetables and papaya are slightly crushed together, a technique that helps release the flavors and juices. The version cooked in the Bangkok style uses ground peanuts, fish sauce, palm sugar and, sometimes, fresh shrimp. In the Northeast style, anchovy sauce is used instead of fish sauce.

Regional variations in Thai cuisine echo the abundance or scarcity of certain ingredients. One finds that the cooking of the Bangkok area and the southern region of the country relies upon seafood to a larger extent than the cooking of the North and Northeast. The cuisine of these northern areas draws upon freshwater fish and freshwater shrimp.

Cooked vegetable dishes vary greatly. Some, like ten vegetable stew *(tom jabchai)*, are quite substantial, containing beef, pork, chicken, seafood or tofu as well as a variety of vegetables. Other dishes, like stir-fried Chinese broccoli with sun-dried fish *(pad kanaa pla kem)* and long string beans with egg *(pad tua fak yow kai)*, are quick, light and easy, using spicy sauces to complement the flavor of a particular vegetable.

PREVIOUS PAGES: SHRIMP SALAD NORTHEAST STYLE (LEFT, RECIPE PAGE 433), CRISPY FRIED EGG SALAD (BOTTOM, RECIPE PAGE 438) AND YOUNG CHILI SAUCE WITH VEGETABLES (RIGHT, RECIPE PAGE 433)

A PROFUSION OF CRISP, NEWLY PICKED VEGETABLES ON DISPLAY AT THE MARKETS IN PAK KLONG DALAT

The Northeast

SOOP NAW MAI

ซุปหน่อไม้

Bamboo Shoot Salad

There is an abundance of bamboo recipes in northeastern Thailand, and many are now also served elsewhere in the country. Bamboo shoot salad originated in the Northeast and is now popular in Bangkok.

2 cups (16 fl oz/500 ml) water
1 lb (500 g) young bamboo shoots (see glossary), shredded
6 bay leaves
¼ cup (2 oz/60 g) sticky rice
¼ cup (2 fl oz/60 ml) water
¼ cup (2 fl oz/60 ml) anchovy sauce
¼ cup (2 fl oz/60 ml) fish sauce (*nam pla*)
⅓ cup (3 fl oz/90 ml) lime juice
2 tablespoons toasted sesame seeds
1 teaspoon ground Thai chili pepper (*prik khee noo pon*)
¼ cup chopped green onions/scallions/spring onions
¼ cup mint leaves
¼ cup chopped cilantro/coriander leaves (*bai pak chee*)
1 bunch Chinese lettuce

Heat the water to boiling in a large saucepan. Add the shredded bamboo and bay leaves and cook for 10 minutes. Drain and set aside. Discard the bay leaves.

Heat a small skillet on medium-high heat and add the rice. Toast the rice, adding 1 tablespoon of water at a time to aid in the cooking. Continue to toast the rice in the dry pan until it is golden brown. Remove and grind in a mortar with a pestle.

Place the ground rice, drained bamboo, fish sauces, lime juice, toasted sesame seeds and ground chili pepper in a large saucepan. Heat to almost a boil. Add half of each of the green onions, the mint leaves and the cilantro leaves. Serve on a bed of Chinese lettuce and garnish with the remaining green onions, mint leaves and cilantro leaves. Serve cold.

SERVES 4

Bangkok and the Central Plains

MOO PAD TUA NGOK

หมูผัดถั่วงอก

Bean Sprout Pork

A favorite for a quick meal, this is an easy and simple recipe to make. Bean sprouts and green onions give it an attractive appearance.

3 tablespoons oil
4 garlic cloves (*kratiem*), minced
8 oz (250 g) ground/minced pork
¼ teaspoon white pepper
3 tablespoons fish sauce (*nam pla*)
1 lb (500 g) bean sprouts
1 teaspoon sugar
2 green onions/scallions/spring onions, cut into 1-in
  (2.5-cm) lengths

Heat a large skillet and add the oil, garlic and ground pork. When the pork is cooked, add the pepper and fish sauce and cook for 2 minutes to reduce the sauce. Add the bean sprouts, sugar and green onions and cook for 30 seconds on high.

Transfer to a serving dish and serve immediately.

SERVES 4

NORTHEAST SALAD WITH PORK SKIN (LEFT, RECIPE PAGE 423),
BEAN SPROUT PORK (TOP) AND BAMBOO SHOOT SALAD (RIGHT)

The Northeast

PHLA NANG MOO ESAN

พล่าหนังหมูอีสาน

Northeast Salad with Pork Skin

In the Northeast every part of the pig is put to good use, showing the Thais' creativity with recipes. This is an interesting and delicious recipe.

4 cups (1 qt/1 l) water
8 oz (250 g) pork skin/pork rind, cut into 2-in x ½-in (5-cm x 1-cm) strips
4 oz (125 g) ground/minced pork
¼ cup (2 fl oz/60 ml) fish sauce *(nam pla)*
¼ cup (2 fl oz/60 ml) lime juice
2 tablespoons ground roasted rice (see glossary)
4 stalks lemon grass/citronella *(ta-krai)*, thinly sliced
½ cup mint leaves
¼ cup chopped green onions/scallions/spring onions
¼ cup chopped cilantro/coriander leaves *(bai pak chee)*

▓ Heat the water to boiling and cook the pork skin for about 20 minutes or until tender. Drain and set aside.

▓ In a medium skillet, cook the ground pork on medium-high heat with the fish sauce, lime juice and pork skin. Add the roasted rice and toss with the remaining ingredients. Remove to a serving plate and serve with a few fresh vegetables of your own choice.

SERVES 4   *Photograph pages 420–421*

Bangkok and the Central Plains

TOM JABCHAI

ต้มจับฉ่าย

Ten Vegetable Stew

A very hearty dish, this can also be served as a complete meal.

1 tablespoon oil
6 garlic cloves *(kratiem)*, minced
1 lb (500 g) pork, cut into cubes
½ cup minced cilantro/coriander leaves *(bai pak chee)*
1 teaspoon salt
1 teaspoon white pepper
4 cups (1 qt/1 l) water
½ cup (4 fl oz/125 ml) light soy sauce
⅓ cup (3 oz/90 g) sugar

VEGETABLES

4 oz (125 g) bok choy
4 oz (125 g) cabbage
4 oz (125 g) Chinese broccoli
4 oz (125 g) napa cabbage
4 oz (125 g) celery
4 oz (125 g) green onions/scallions/spring onions
4 oz (125 g) sweet chard
4 oz (125 g) swamp cabbage
4 oz (125 g) carrots
4 oz (125 g) spinach

▓ Heat a large pot and add the oil and garlic. Add the pork and stir-fry for 3 minutes. Add all the ingredients except the vegetables. Heat to boiling, cover, and cook for 15 minutes.

▓ Slice all the vegetables, add them to the pot and cook for 10 minutes longer. Serve in a large soup tureen.

SERVES 4

TEN VEGETABLE STEW

The North

NAM PRIK ONG

น้ำพริกอ่อง

Vegetables with Chiang Mai Dipping Sauce

In the North most meats are barbecued and vegetables are served fresh on the side. This hearty sauce is a favorite among those used to add variety to the meals.

1 tablespoon oil
½ cup chopped garlic cloves *(kratiem)*
¼ cup chopped shallots
1 lb (500 g) diced red tomatoes
8 oz (250 g) ground/minced pork
⅓ cup (3 fl oz/90 ml) fish sauce *(nam pla)*
3 tablespoons sugar
2 tablespoons lime juice
1 cup cucumber slices
¼ cup cilantro/coriander leaves *(bai pak chee)*
4 green onions/scallions/spring onions

VEGETABLES

broccoli flowerets
carrots, sliced
cauliflower flowerets
shallots, cut into 2-in (5-cm) sections
sugar peas/snow peas

▩ Heat a large skillet and add the oil, garlic, shallots and tomatoes. Cook for 3 minutes and add the pork. Add the fish sauce, sugar and lime juice and cook for 4 minutes or until the pork is done.
▩ Remove to a serving dish with the cucumber, cilantro and green onions on the side. Serve with the vegetables for dipping.

SERVES 4

The Northeast

SOM TAM ESAN

ส้มตำอีสาน

Papaya Salad

This salad is delicious served with steamed sticky rice (khao neow), on page 350. The papaya must be dark green and firm.

1 medium dark green papaya/pawpaw
4 garlic cloves *(kratiem)*
6 green Thai chilies *(prik khee noo)*
2 tomatoes, cut into wedges
½ cup chopped green beans, in 1-in (2.5-cm) pieces
2 tablespoons anchovy sauce
½ teaspoon salt
¼ cup (2 fl oz/60 ml) lime juice or tamarind juice *(ma-kaam piag)* (see glossary)

▩ Peel the papaya and rinse with running water to remove the acid. Remove the seeds and shred the papaya with a grater. Set aside.
▩ Place the garlic cloves and the chilies in a mortar and mash with a pestle until crushed into chunks. Place the papaya and the remaining ingredients in the mortar and gently combine all ingredients by mixing with the pestle and a spoon. Serve cold.

SERVES 4

PAPAYA SALAD (LEFT) AND VEGETABLES WITH
CHIANG MAI DIPPING SAUCE (RIGHT)

RICE SALAD

The South

KHAO YAM

ข้าวยำ

Rice Salad

Like many salads from the South, khao yam *is a very light salad. Jasmine rice is used to complement the flavors of the many herbs, making this a very delicious light meal.*

SALAD

2 cups steamed jasmine rice (*khao suay*) (see page 350)
¼ cup thinly sliced ginger
½ cup ground dried shrimp/prawns
1 cup bean sprouts
1 cup chopped grapefruit flesh, in ½-in (1-cm) pieces
½ cup thinly sliced cucumber
2 stalks lemon grass/citronella (*ta-krai*), thinly sliced
6 fresh lime leaves, thinly sliced
6 shallots, thinly sliced

SAUCE

½ cup (4 fl oz/125 ml) fish sauce (*nam pla*)
2 tablespoons sugar
¼ cup (2 fl oz/60 ml) lime juice

🍲 Place all the salad ingredients in a large bowl. Thoroughly combine the ingredients for the sauce in a separate bowl. Pour the sauce over the salad and toss well just before serving.

SERVES 4

The North

PAK LUAK NAM PRIK

ผักลวกน้ำพริก

Vegetables with Dipping Sauce

While vegetables can be the highlight of any meal, dipping sauces make the vegetables more spicy and flavorful.

½ cup (1 oz/30 g) dried shrimp/prawns
1 lb (500 g) eggplant (long slender purple ones if available)
¼ cup (2 fl oz/60 ml) fish sauce (*nam pla*)
¼ cup (2 fl oz/60 ml) lime juice
2 tablespoons sugar

VEGETABLES

1 cup string beans, cut into 4-in (10-cm) lengths
4 oz (125 g) swamp cabbage
4 oz (125 g) spinach
1 cup sliced cucumber
4 baby eggplants

🍲 Soak the shrimp in warm water to cover for 10 minutes and drain.
🍲 Heat some water to boiling in a medium saucepan and cook the unpeeled eggplant until just soft and tender.
🍲 Drain, cool in cold water and peel the skin. Roughly dice the eggplant.
🍲 Put the eggplant, shrimp, fish sauce, lime juice and sugar in a mortar and gently mash with the pestle until all ingredients are combined and a coarse paste is formed. Spoon into an attractive serving bowl.
🍲 Arrange the raw or blanched vegetables on a platter and serve with the dip.

SERVES 4

Bangkok and the Central Plains

GAI PAD YOD KHAO POD

ไก่ผัดยอดข้าวโพด

Young Corn Chicken

A very easy recipe to prepare, this is especially delicious when served with hot steamed jasmine rice (khao suay), *on page 350.*

3 tablespoons oil
1 lb (500 g) boned chicken, thinly sliced
3 garlic cloves (*kratiem*), crushed
1 cup baby corn
½ cup halved straw mushrooms
2 tablespoons oyster sauce
2 tablespoons fish sauce (*nam pla*)
2 tablespoons sugar
½ teaspoon freshly ground peppercorns
2 green onions/scallions/spring onions, cut into 1-in (2.5-cm) pieces

🍲 Heat a medium skillet on high heat and add the oil, chicken and garlic. Stir-fry for 2 minutes and add all the remaining ingredients.
🍲 Continue to cook until the chicken is done and all ingredients are combined (about 2 minutes).
🍲 Remove to a serving plate and serve with steamed rice.

SERVES 4

YOUNG CORN CHICKEN (TOP) AND VEGETABLES
WITH DIPPING SAUCE (BOTTOM)

Bangkok and the Central Plains

YAM GOON CHIANG

ยำกุนเชียง

Chinese Sausage Salad

Offerings of plump, juicy and flavorful Chinese sausages can be found in many food markets in Bangkok. This salad is a favorite among them, although the vegetables can be varied.

DRESSING

2 tablespoons vinegar
1 tablespoon sugar
¼ teaspoon salt

2 cups (16 fl oz/500 ml) water
3–4 Chinese sausages
1 small onion, sliced
1 cup cucumber slices
½ cup cilantro/coriander leaves *(bai pak chee)*
3 tablespoons chopped green Thai chili peppers *(prik khee noo)*
green leaf lettuce/Chinese lettuce, for garnish
cilantro/coriander leaves *(bai pak chee)*, for garnish

▓ Mix together the dressing ingredients and set aside.
▓ Heat the water to boiling and cook the Chinese sausages, covered, for 3 minutes. Remove and slice in ¼-in (6-mm) thick slices.
▓ Arrange the sausages decoratively on a platter with the other ingredients, then trickle the dressing over.
▓ Garnish with the green leaf lettuce and cilantro leaves.

SERVES 4

The Northeast

TAM TAENG

ตำแตง

Northeast Cucumber Salad

Many of the broiled and barbecued meats of this region are complemented by this light salad.

1 lb (500 g) cucumbers
6 garlic cloves *(kratiem)*, minced
3 green Thai chili peppers *(prik khee noo)*, chopped
6 tablespoons tamarind juice *(ma-kaam piag)* (see glossary)
¼ cup (2 fl oz/60 ml) fish sauce *(nam pla)*
2 tablespoons sugar
6 cherry tomatoes, cut into quarters

▓ Peel the skin from the cucumbers, cut them in half lengthwise and remove the seeds. Cut into shreds the size of matchsticks.
▓ Mix together the remaining ingredients except the tomatoes, then mix with the cucumber shreds and tomatoes.

SERVES 4

NORTHEAST CUCUMBER SALAD (BOTTOM) AND
CHINESE SAUSAGE SALAD (TOP)

SHRIMP PASTE DIPPING SAUCE

The Northeast

SOOP NAW MAI PLA-RAA

ซุปหน่อไม้ใส่ปลาร้า

Bamboo Shoot Salad with Pickled Fish

The subtle flavor of bamboo shoots combines well with pickled anchovy. Served with its accompaniment of vegetables and with steamed sticky rice (khao neow), on page 350, this dish becomes a nutritious meal.

1 cup (8 fl oz/250 ml) water
1 lb (500 g) bamboo shoots (see glossary), shredded or in strips
5 bay leaves
4 oz/125 g pickled anchovy fish
¼ cup (2 fl oz/60 ml) fish sauce (nam pla)
¼ cup (2 fl oz/60 ml) lime juice
½ cup mint leaves
¼ cup chopped green onions/scallions/spring onions
1 teaspoon toasted sesame seeds
¼ teaspoon ground Thai chili pepper (prik khee noo pon)
1 tablespoon ground roasted sticky rice (see glossary)

ACCOMPANIMENT (OPTIONAL)

4 long string beans or snake beans, cut into 4-in (10-cm) lengths
8 leaves swamp cabbage or spinach
¼ head of cabbage, sliced into 1-in (2.5-cm) sections
4 stems of sweet basil leaves (bai horapa)

▦ Pour the water into a large saucepan. Add the bamboo shoots and bay leaves and heat to boiling. Cook for 1 minute. Drain the water and remove the bay leaves. Add the remaining ingredients to the bamboo shoots, mix well and reheat. Remove to a serving dish.
▦ If serving the accompaniment, mix the ingredients together and serve in a separate dish.

SERVES 4

The South

NAM PRIK GOONG SIAP

น้ำพริกกุ้งเสียบ

Shrimp Paste Dipping Sauce

Add your favorite vegetables to this recipe to make it even better.

8 green Thai chili peppers (prik khee noo)
6 garlic cloves (kratiem)
2 tablespoons shrimp paste (gapi)
¼ cup (2 fl oz/60 ml) fish sauce (nam pla)
⅓ cup (3 fl oz/90 ml) lime juice
3 tablespoons palm sugar (nam taan peep)
10 whole large dried shrimp/prawns, rinsed in warm water

VEGETABLES

snake beans or long string beans
green onions/scallions/spring onions
tomatoes
broccoli
sugar peas/snow peas

▦ Place the chilies, garlic and shrimp paste in a mortar and mash with a pestle until the garlic is crushed and combined with the other ingredients. Add the fish sauce, lime juice and sugar and gently mash together. Alternatively, use a blender.
▦ Add the whole dried shrimp and combine. Remove to a serving bowl and allow the shrimp to soak in the sauce for about 15 minutes.
▦ Serve as a dip for the raw or steamed vegetables.

SERVES 4

Bangkok and the Central Plains

YAM PLA SARDINE

ยำปลาซาร์ดีน

Sardine Salad

This combination of seafood and fresh vegetables is very popular.

8 oz (250 g) canned sardines
4–6 leaves green leaf lettuce/Chinese lettuce

TOPPING

8 shallots, sliced
2 stalks lemon grass/citronella (ta-krai), thinly sliced
4 garlic cloves (kratiem), sliced
¼ cup chopped green Thai chili peppers (prik khee noo)
¼ cup (2 fl oz/60 ml) fish sauce (nam pla)
¼ cup (2 fl oz/60 ml) lime juice

½ cup mint leaves
¼ cup cilantro/coriander leaves (bai pak chee)
2 green onions/scallions/spring onions, sliced in 1½-in (3.5-cm) pieces

▦ Split each sardine in half lengthwise. Remove the backbone.
▦ Cut the lettuce in 4-in (10-cm) sections and arrange on a plate. Place a sardine half on top of each piece of lettuce.
▦ Combine the topping ingredients and pour over the sardines. Garnish with the mint, cilantro and green onions.
▦ To eat, wrap each sardine in its piece of lettuce, including some of the topping and garnish ingredients.

SERVES 4

SARDINE SALAD (TOP) AND BAMBOO SHOOT SALAD
WITH PICKLED FISH (BOTTOM)

The North

NAM PRIK NOOM

น้ำพริกหนุ่ม

Young Chili Sauce with Vegetables

This dipping sauce is always included in the traditional Khantoke dinner of Chiang Mai.

15 green jalapeño peppers (*prik chee fa*)
10 garlic cloves (*kratiem*)
8 shallots
2 large tomatoes
1 oz (30 g) dried anchovies
2 tablespoons fish sauce (*nam pla*)
1 green onion/scallion/spring onion, chopped
2 tablespoons cilantro/coriander leaves (*bai pak chee*)

VEGETABLES

green beans, sliced
cabbage, chopped
cucumbers, sliced
baby eggplant, sliced

❊ Barbecue or broil/grill the peppers, garlic, shallots and tomatoes until they are slightly charred on the outside.
❊ Place the anchovies in a small pan with enough water to cover. Heat the water to boiling and cook the anchovies for 10 minutes at a slow boil, until the liquid is reduced to 2 tablespoons. Strain the juice and discard the anchovies.
❊ Combine the barbecued vegetables, the anchovy juice and the fish sauce in a blender and blend until the vegetables are coarsely chopped, or pound in a pestle and mortar.
❊ Pour the resulting dipping sauce into a serving dish and garnish with the chopped green onion and cilantro leaves. Serve with the vegetables.

SERVES 4

The Northeast

PHLA GOONG

พล่ากุ้ง

Shrimp Salad Northeast Style

The fresh, sweet, crisp taste of the shrimp will be lost if they are overcooked. The lemon grass and lime leaves add a delightful subtle flavor.

2 cups (16 fl oz/500 ml) water
1 lb (500 g) shrimp/prawns, shelled and deveined
2 stalks lemon grass/citronella (*ta-krai*), thinly sliced
4 kaffir lime leaves (*bai ma-grood*), thinly sliced
¼ cup mint leaves
2 tablespoons chopped green onion/scallion/spring onion
1 tablespoon chopped cilantro/coriander leaves (*bai pak chee*)
1 teaspoon ground Thai chili pepper (*prik khee noo pon*)
¼ cup (2 fl oz/60 ml) fish sauce (*nam pla*)
¼ cup (2 fl oz/60 ml) lime juice

❊ Heat the water to boiling in a large saucepan and add the shrimp. Blanch for 30 seconds and remove. Place in a bowl.
❊ Add the lemon grass, lime leaves, mint leaves, green onion and cilantro leaves, and mix. Sprinkle the ground chili pepper over the mixture, then pour in the fish sauce and lime juice.
❊ Gently toss to combine, then serve.

SERVES 4

SEAFOOD SALAD

The South

YAM PO TAEK

ยำโป๊ะแตก

Seafood Salad

The interesting combination of herbs and spices used in this dish creates an appetizing fresh taste. Alternative types of seafood can be used to give variation to this popular recipe.

1 cup (8 fl oz/250 ml) water
4 oz (125 g) shrimp/prawns, shelled and deveined
4 oz (125 g) white fish fillets, sliced
4 oz (125 g) clean squid, sliced into 2-in (5-cm) pieces
4 oz (125 g) clams or mussels

DRESSING

1 tablespoon black chili paste (*nam prik pow*) (see page 493)
¼ cup (2 fl oz/60 ml) fish sauce (*nam pla*)
¼ cup (2 fl oz/60 ml) lime juice
2 tablespoons sugar
6 garlic cloves (*kratiem*), sliced
1 teaspoon minced green Thai chili peppers (*prik khee noo*)
2 stalks lemon grass/citronella (*ta-krai*), thinly sliced
4 kaffir lime leaves (*bai ma-grood*), thinly sliced

green leaf lettuce/Chinese lettuce for garnish (optional)

❊ Heat the water to boiling in a large skillet and cook the seafood until done. Drain and set aside.
❊ Mix together the dressing ingredients and gently toss with the seafood just before serving. Serve on a large platter and garnish with green leaf lettuce if desired.

SERVES 4

VEGETARIAN DELIGHT

PAD KANAA PLA KEM

ผัดคะน้าปลาเค็ม

Stir-Fried Chinese Broccoli with Sun-Dried Fish

This delicious recipe is a quick and easy accompaniment for a rice soup, or it can be served with steamed jasmine rice (khao suay), *on page 350.*

3 tablespoons oil
4 oz (125 g) sun-dried fish, cut into 1-in (2.5-cm) pieces
6 garlic cloves (*kratiem*), crushed
1 tablespoon yellow bean sauce or black bean sauce
1 lb (500 g) Chinese broccoli, cut into 1-in (2.5-cm) pieces

Heat a large skillet and add the oil. Add the fish and stir-fry for 2 minutes on medium-high heat. Add the other ingredients and cook for 2 more minutes.

SERVES 4

YAM YAI

ยำใหญ่

Thai Chef Salad

Salads are among the favorite foods of the Thai people. This recipe allows for the creativity of each individual chef, because any vegetable or cooked meat can be added for a change of flavor.

DRESSING

2 tablespoons minced cilantro/coriander leaves (*bai pak chee*)
4 garlic cloves (*kratiem*), minced
3 tablespoons lime juice
1 tablespoon sugar

4–6 leaves green leaf lettuce/Chinese lettuce
4 hard-cooked/hard-boiled eggs, quartered
½ cup sliced white onion
1 tomato, cut into wedges
½ cup sliced cucumber
½ cup sliced red jalapeño pepper (*prik chee fa daeng*)
sprigs of cilantro/coriander (*pak chee*), for garnish
sprigs of mint, for garnish

Combine the ingredients for the dressing and set aside.
Arrange the green leaf lettuce attractively on a large platter with the eggs, onion, tomato, cucumber and pepper slices placed on top of the lettuce. Pour the dressing over and garnish with the sprigs of cilantro and mint.

SERVES 4

PAD PAK RUAM MIT

ผัดผักรวมมิตร

Vegetarian Delight

The variety of vegetables used in this dish gives it an attractive colorful appearance. It is very easy to prepare.

2 tablespoons oil
2 garlic cloves (*kratiem*), minced
¼ cup sliced onion
½ cup sliced carrots
1 cup sliced cabbage
1 cup broccoli flowerets
½ cup cauliflower flowerets
½ cup sliced red bell pepper/capsicum
¼ cup sugar peas/snow peas
¼ cup sliced mushrooms
¼ cup bean sprouts
1 tablespoon soy sauce
1 tablespoon sugar

Heat a large skillet and add the oil and garlic.
Add all the other ingredients. Stir-fry for 4 minutes, until the vegetables are crisp tender.
Serve with steamed jasmine rice (*khao suay*), on page 350.

SERVES 4

STIR-FRIED CHINESE BROCCOLI WITH SUN-DRIED FISH (LEFT)
AND THAI CHEF SALAD (RIGHT)

Bangkok and the Central Plains

PAD TUA FAK YOW KUB KAI

ผัดถั่วฝักยาวกับไข่

Long String Beans with Egg

This dish can be made very quickly and can be eaten before going to school or work. Serve it over rice.

3 tablespoons oil
8 oz (250 g) boned pork, sliced
1 lb (500 g) long string beans or snake beans, cut into 2½-in (6-cm) lengths
4 garlic cloves *(kratiem)*, minced
¼ cup (2 fl oz/60 ml) water
3 tablespoons fish sauce *(nam pla)*
1 tablespoon Maggi seasoning
2 tablespoons sugar
¼ teaspoon white pepper
2 eggs, beaten

Heat a large skillet and add the oil. When the oil is hot, add the pork, beans and garlic and stir-fry until the pork is done.

Add all the remaining ingredients except the eggs, then cover and cook for 2 minutes. Remove the lid, add the eggs, and stir until the eggs are cooked (about 1 minute).

SERVES 4

Bangkok and the Central Plains

KANAA NAMMAN HOI

คะน้าน้ำมันหอย

Chinese Broccoli with Oyster Sauce

Almost any fresh vegetable can be used in this recipe, which uses a simple cooking method and seasoning to provide a delicious dish.

2 tablespoons oil
4 garlic cloves *(kratiem)*, minced
1 lb (500 g) Chinese broccoli, cut into 1-in (2.5-cm) pieces
¼ cup (2 fl oz/60 ml) water
3 tablespoons oyster sauce
1 tablespoon fish sauce *(nam pla)*
3 green jalapeño peppers *(prik chee fa)*
1 tablespoon sugar

Heat a medium skillet on high heat then add the oil and garlic. Add the broccoli and the other ingredients. Stir-fry, cooking until the broccoli is crisp but tender. Remove to a serving dish.

SERVES 4

Bangkok and the Central Plains

PAD PAK TOW-HOO

ผัดผักเต้าหู้

Tofu with Vegetables

Tofu, which is extremely nutritious, tends to absorb the flavors of the various ingredients with which it is cooked.

3 tablespoons oil
3 garlic cloves *(kratiem)*, minced
¼ cup sliced onions
¼ cup bean sprouts
¼ cup sugar peas/snow peas
¼ cup sliced carrots
¼ cup sliced red bell pepper/capsicum
¾ cup cauliflower flowerets
¾ cup broccoli flowerets
¼ cup sliced mushrooms
2 cups fried tofu (see glossary)

CHINESE BROCCOLI WITH OYSTER SAUCE (TOP LEFT),
LONG STRING BEANS WITH EGG (BOTTOM LEFT)
AND TOFU WITH VEGETABLES (RIGHT)

2 tablespoons fish sauce *(nam pla)*
2 tablespoons oyster sauce
2 tablespoons sugar
¼ teaspoon white pepper

Heat a large skillet over high heat, then add the oil and garlic. Add all the vegetables and the fried tofu.

Add the fish sauce, oyster sauce, sugar and pepper and mix thoroughly. Reduce heat to medium and cook slowly for a further 2 minutes, until the vegetables are crisp but tender.

SERVES 4

GROUND BEEF SALAD

The Northeast

LAAB NUEA

ลาบเนื้อ

Ground Beef Salad

The blend of fresh herbs and lime juice makes this salad very refreshing. This laab recipe was taken to Bangkok by the people of the Northeast and is one of the favorite dishes of Thailand. Other meats such as chicken or pork can also be used.

1 lb (500 g) ground/minced beef
¼ cup (2 fl oz/60 ml) lime juice
2 tablespoons fish sauce (*nam pla*)
½ teaspoon galangal powder (*kha pon*)
6 shallots, thinly sliced
2 tablespoons chopped green onion/scallion/spring onion
2 tablespoons chopped cilantro/coriander leaves (*bai pak chee*)
2 tablespoons ground roasted sticky rice (see glossary)
1 teaspoon ground red Thai chili pepper (*prik khee noo pon*), optional
15 mint leaves

▧ Combine the ground beef with the lime juice, fish sauce, galangal powder and shallots.
▧ Heat a skillet and cook the ground beef mixture on medium-high heat for 5 minutes or until the beef is cooked.
▧ Remove the skillet from the heat and add the chopped green onion and cilantro and the ground roasted rice. Mix thoroughly so that everything is well combined.
▧ Remove to a serving plate, spoon the ground pepper on the side of the plate if desired, and garnish with the mint leaves.
▧ Serve with an accompaniment of raw vegetables, such as long string beans or snake beans, sliced cabbage, green leaf lettuce/Chinese lettuce, basil leaves and swamp cabbage or spinach.

SERVES 4

Bangkok and the Central Plains

YAM KAI DOW

ยำไข่ดาว

Crispy Fried Egg Salad

A delicious salad made from fried eggs, in which the eggs are fried until the whites of the eggs are golden brown and crispy. A very tasty way of cooking eggs.

SAUCE

8 garlic cloves (*kratiem*), minced
2 tablespoons chopped cilantro/coriander leaves (*bai pak chee*)
6 green Thai chili peppers (*prik khee noo*), minced
¼ cup (2 fl oz/60 ml) fish sauce (*nam pla*)
¼ cup (2 fl oz/60 ml) lime juice
2 tablespoons sugar

½ cup (4 fl oz/125 ml) oil
4 eggs
¼ cup sliced carrots
¼ cup sliced tomato
¼ cup sliced green bell pepper/capsicum
¼ cup sliced onion
¼ cup sliced red cabbage
6 leaves green leaf lettuce/Chinese lettuce, sliced

▧ Mix together all the ingredients for the sauce, and set aside.
▧ Heat the oil in a small skillet to 350°F (180°C). Fry the eggs individually until puffy and light golden brown. Remove and allow to cool. Then cut each fried egg into quarters.
▧ Arrange all the sliced vegetables on top of the sliced lettuce and top with the fried eggs.
▧ Serve the sauce on the side or toss it with the salad.

SERVES 4

Bangkok and the Central Plains

PAD PREW WAN MOO

ผัดเปรี้ยวหวานหมู

Sweet and Sour Pork

Unlike other styles of sweet and sour pork, the lean meat in this dish does not require coating and deep-frying. It is still delicious, but has fewer calories.

SAUCE

½ cup (4 fl oz/125 ml) vinegar
½ cup (4 oz/125 g) sugar
½ teaspoon salt
¼ cup (2 fl oz/60 ml) tomato paste

1 tablespoon oil
4 garlic cloves (*kratiem*), minced
8 oz (250 g) pork, cut into ¼-in x 2-in x 2-in
  (6-mm x 5-cm x 5-cm) pieces
½ cup tomato wedges
½ small onion, sliced
¼ cup chopped green jalapeño peppers (*prik chee fa*)
½ cup pineapple chunks
1 green onion/scallion/spring onion, cut into 1-in (2.5-cm) pieces
2 tablespoons cornstarch/cornflour, in 3 tablespoons water

▨ Mix the sauce ingredients in a small skillet and heat to boiling. Reduce to a simmer, cook for 3 minutes and set aside.
▨ Heat a large skillet and add the oil, garlic and pork. Cook for 30 seconds and add the sauce. Heat to boiling, add the remaining ingredients, except the green onion and the cornstarch mixture, and cook for 2 minutes, stirring intermittently.
▨ Add the green onion then stir in enough cornstarch mixture to thicken the sauce to a medium thickness.

SERVES 4

MUSTARD LEAF CHICKEN

Bangkok and the Central Plains

GAI PAD KIAMCHAI

ไก่ผัดเกี้ยมไฉ่

Mustard Leaf Chicken

The pickled mustard leaf is preserved in salt and should be rinsed before cooking. Its salty flavor is complemented by the chicken and the spiciness of the fresh ginger root.

3 tablespoons oil
4 garlic cloves (*kratiem*), minced
1 tablespoon slivered fresh ginger
8 oz (250 g) boned chicken, thinly sliced
1 cup mustard leaf pickle, cut into 1-in (2.5-cm) lengths
2 eggs, beaten
3 tablespoons fish sauce (*nam pla*)
2 tablespoons sugar

Heat a medium skillet and add the oil with the garlic and ginger. Add the chicken and stir-fry for 2 minutes. Add the mustard pickles and the eggs and stir to combine. Stir in the fish sauce and sugar and cook for 2 more minutes until the sauce thickens. Serve hot.

SERVES 4

Bangkok and the Central Plains

YAM NANG MOO

ยำหนังหมู

Pork Skin with Lemon Grass Salad

The skin of the pork in this salad has a unique texture resembling that of a translucent and elastic noodle. This is a popular salad in Bangkok.

4 cups (1 qt/1 l) water
1 lb (500 g) pork skin/pork rind
¼ cup (2 fl oz/60 ml) black chili paste (*nam prik pow*)
  (see page 493)
2 stalks lemon grass/citronella (*ta-krai*), thinly sliced
5 kaffir lime leaves (*bai ma-grood*), thinly sliced
1 cup mint leaves
½ cup (4 oz/125 g) ground roasted peanuts
2 tablespoons fish sauce (*nam pla*)
2 tablespoons lime juice
1 tablespoon sugar
green leaf lettuce/Chinese lettuce, for garnish
mint leaves, for garnish

Heat the water to boiling, add the pork skin and simmer for 30 minutes to soften and tenderize it. Drain the skin then slice into thin 2-in (5-cm) long strips. Set aside.

Mix the black chili paste with all the remaining ingredients except the lettuce and mint, and toss with the pork skin pieces. Garnish with the green leaf lettuce and mint before serving.

SERVES 4

PORK SKIN WITH LEMON GRASS SALAD (LEFT)
AND SWEET AND SOUR PORK (RIGHT)

BEEF SALAD

YAM NUEA

ยำเนื้อ

Beef Salad

In Bangkok, this recipe is one of the favorites in restaurants and home kitchens alike.

1 lb (500 g) tender beef steak

SALAD

¼ cup sliced onions
1 tomato, cut into wedges
¼ cup sliced cucumber
¼ cup thinly sliced red and green Thai chili peppers
    (*prik khee noo*)

SAUCE

¼ cup (2 fl oz/60 ml) fish sauce (*nam pla*)
¼ cup (2 fl oz/60 ml) lime juice
2 tablespoons minced garlic (*kratiem*)
2 tablespoons chopped cilantro/coriander leaves (*bai pak chee*)
¼ cup chopped green onions/scallions/spring onions, in 1-in
    (2.5-cm) pieces

⬛ Barbecue the beef over charcoal or broil/grill until medium to well done. Slice thinly and set aside.
⬛ Combine all the salad ingredients and add the sliced beef.
⬛ Make the sauce by mixing together all the ingredients, and toss with the salad just before serving.

SERVES 4

PAD PAK BOONG FI DAENG

ผัดผักบุ้งไฟแดง

Flamed Swamp Cabbage

This light dish tastes just as good with spinach, if swamp cabbage is not available.

2 tablespoons oil
1 lb (500 g) swamp cabbage or spinach, cut into 1-in
    (2.5-cm) pieces
6 garlic cloves (*kratiem*), minced
2 tablespoons black bean sauce
1 tablespoon fish sauce (*nam pla*)
1 teaspoon sugar
¼ cup sliced green jalapeño pepper (*prik chee fa*)

⬛ Heat a large skillet until very hot; add the oil and all the remaining ingredients. Quickly stir-fry for 30 seconds and serve.

SERVES 4

YAM PLA MUK

ยำปลาหมึก

Calamari Salad

Those who enjoy squid will want to eat this dish at every meal. Charcoal-broiling instead of sautéeing will provide added flavor.

8 oz (250 g) squid, thinly sliced (mantle/hood portion only)
1 teaspoon cornstarch/cornflour
1 teaspoon white wine
1 garlic clove (*kratiem*), minced
1 teaspoon grated fresh ginger
1 tablespoon oil

DRESSING

1 teaspoon red curry paste (*nam prik gaeng ped*) (see page 488)
1 teaspoon minced garlic (*kratiem*)
¼ cup (2 fl oz/60 ml) fresh lime juice
¼ cup (2 fl oz/60 ml) fish sauce (*nam pla*)
2 tablespoons sugar
1 tablespoon ground roasted sticky rice (see glossary)
¼ cup minced fresh cilantro/coriander leaves (*bai pak chee*)

2 cups shredded lettuce
¼ cup sliced red bell pepper/capsicum
¼ cup sliced green bell pepper/capsicum
¼ cup sliced mushrooms
¼ cup sliced sugar peas/snow peas
¼ cup sliced onions
⅛ cup mint leaves
¼ cup sliced lemon grass/citronella (*ta-krai*)
1 tomato, cut into wedges
¼ cup sliced cucumber

green onions/scallions/spring onions, sliced, for garnish
cilantro/coriander leaves (*bai pak chee*), for garnish
fresh ginger, grated, for garnish

⬛ Marinate the squid slices in the combined cornstarch and white wine, and garlic and ginger for about 10 minutes.
⬛ Heat a medium skillet and add the oil. Sauté the squid quickly and remove. Set aside.
⬛ Mix together the dressing ingredients.
⬛ Combine the squid with the vegetables and toss with the dressing just before serving. Garnish with the green onions, cilantro leaves and grated ginger.

SERVES 4

CALAMARI SALAD (TOP) AND FLAMED
SWAMP CABBAGE (BOTTOM)

THE SOUTH

LUCA INVERNIZZI TETTONI/PHOTOBANK

THE SOUTH

A LONG, SLENDER ARM reaching down to Malaysia, southern Thailand seems dramatically different from the country's other three regions, even to Thai travelers. It is much wetter, for one thing. Rain falls for some eight months of the year in brief but heavy showers or in sweeping monsoon storms, nurturing a luxuriant jungle that spills over the chain of rugged limestone mountains along the spine of the peninsula. Livelihoods differ, too. Rice fields, fruit orchards and vegetable gardens form their familiar patterns in the upper part, but more common as one proceeds farther south are long regimented rows of rubber trees and vast plantations of graceful coconut palms sloping down to the sea.

With two coastlines—1,165 miles (1,875 kilometers) long on the Gulf of Thailand, and 460 miles (740 kilometers) long on the Indian Ocean—the sea is an omnipresent part of life. Thousands of boats, comprising the world's eleventh-largest fishing fleet, sail every day out of countless ports to bring back most of the seafood on which the country relies for domestic consumption and export.

Finally, there are marked cultural differences, for the majority of Thailand's estimated two million Muslims—the largest religious minority—live in the southernmost provinces of Narathiwat, Pattani, Yala and Satun, where the domed mosque is as much a part of the landscape as the

RUBBER TAPPERS WORKING IN THE
EARLY MORNING NEAR PHUKET

PREVIOUS PAGES: TWIN BAYS WITH
PALM-FRINGED BEACHES AT KOH PHI PHI
JENNY MILLS

PINEAPPLES ARE ONE OF PHUKET'S MAIN CROPS, OFTEN
GROWN IN ROWS BETWEEN RUBBER TREE SAPLINGS

the daily secretion of valuable latex—Thailand is the
world's third largest producer of natural rubber. By
contrast, sunlight filters through the rustling fronds of
equally numerous coconut palms, and in many plantations trained monkeys scamper up the trunks to select,
pick, and carefully drop those nuts that are ready for
harvest, hundreds of millions of them every year. Particularly on the upper gulf, fields of spiky gray-green pineapple
plants stretch for miles—only the Philippines surpasses
Thailand as a producer of succulent pineapples for can-
ning and export. The sheer limestone cliffs and caves of
southern coasts are a favorite haunt of the tiny, fork-tailed
swift known as *Callocalia esculenta*, which produces the
edible nests so highly prized by Chinese gourmets all
over the world that 1 pound (about 500 grams) of top-
quality specimens sell for about US$100.

A recurrent southern dream has long been the construction of a Panama-type canal across the Kra Isthmus,
the narrowest point of the peninsula, where the two
coasts are separated by a bare 15 miles (24 kilometers).
Such a canal would cut nearly 1000 miles (1600 kilometers) off shipping routes between ports on the Indian
Ocean and the Gulf of Thailand and undoubtedly bring
great economic advantages to the region. Since it would
also have a serious effect on Singapore's prosperity, the
British naturally opposed the scheme, even signing a
secret agreement with the Thais in 1897 promising to
exclude third-power activities—that is, French activities—
on the peninsula in return for a promise not to build. The
dream has never really died, however; it is still revived
from time to time by various business consortiums and
may yet become a reality one day.

Southern food is as distinctive as its people and its
scenery. Not surprisingly, coconut milk plays a very

A FISHERMAN LOWERING ONE OF HIS CRAB TRAPS
INTO THE WATER IN AMONGST THE MANGROVES

multi-tiered roofs of the Buddhist temple, and Malay is the
second language for those who live in areas closest to the
Malaysian border.

The South has wealth, rare natural beauty, and more
than a few oddities among its flora and fauna. Along
many stretches of coast there are all but impenetrable
mangrove swamps, with aerial roots that rise straight out
of the mud. Salt-water crocodiles live in such haunts, as
well as swimming pig-tailed monkeys which forage for
crabs and other shellfish. At other places, especially on
such offshore islands as Koh Samui and Phuket, there are
silvery palm-fringed beaches straight out of an escapist's
dream. A few miles inland, immense rainforest trees,
draped with clambering vines and wild orchids, rise
hundreds of feet in the air to create a humid green
twilight where kingfishers, hornbills, and parakeets flit,
gibbons swing from lofty branches, and some fifty-six
species of snakes, including the deadly king cobra and
banded krait, slither through the ferny undergrowth. In
the more mountainous areas one might come across the
serow, a goat-antelope which according to Thai folklore
can heal a broken leg by simply licking it, the tiny mouse
deer, the flying lemur, and the Malayan porcupine which
charges backwards to repel an enemy.

Perpetual semi-darkness prevails at ground level in
the huge rubber estates, where each tree has a cup to catch

A MAN WITH HIS SON NEGOTIATES HIS SMALL BOAT IN AMONGST
THE BRIGHTLY PAINTED FISHING VESSELS IN THE PORT AT PHUKET

prominent role in numerous dishes, especially soups and curries; the oil is also often used for frying, and the grated meat as a condiment. On both sides of the peninsula, abundant fresh seafood is available in almost every market: marine fish, some of huge size, prawns, crab, squid, scallops, clams, and mussels. Rock lobsters and a larger variety sometimes called the Phuket lobster are now common in more cosmopolitan tourist areas, though traditionally these crustaceans were not regarded by Thais as the delicacies they are in the West. Cashew nuts from local plantations turn up regularly as an appetizer or stir-fried with chicken and dried chilies, while regional fruits include finger-sized bananas, mangosteens, durians, and small pineapples of exceptional sweetness. Raw vegetables are served with almost every meal, and cooked ones appear in countless forms. Every year in October the Chinese residents of Phuket celebrate a ten-day Vegetarian Festival, interesting because not only does it include many exotic culinary treats but there are also demonstrations of fire-walking and other feats by devotees in self-induced trances.

Some specialities of the region reflect the influences of foreign cultures: among them an Indian-style curry known as *gaeng massaman*, involving cardamon, cloves, and cinnamon and either chicken or beef (never pork); several Malayan fish curries, often with a garnish of fresh fruits and salted peanuts; and *satay*, marinated pieces of meat on skewers with a spicy peanut sauce, which originally came from Indonesia and is now a popular snack all over Thailand. On the whole southerners like their food hot—hotter, perhaps, than any other region with the possible exception of the Northeast—and liberally season it with the most pungent chilies. They are also partial to a bitter flavor in their cooking, particularly when it is imparted by a local flat bean called *sa-taw* which, like the durian, is the object of considerable controversy, either being greatly relished (by nearly all southerners) or greatly disliked (by most outsiders). The southern durian, it might be noted, is much more assertive in taste and smell than those found in Bangkok markets.

Several southern cities such as Nakhon Si Thammarat, Songkhla, and Chaiya can look back on an ancient heritage, reflected in deep-seated traditions and the crumbling remains of splendid temples and pagodas. Others like Hat Yai, the country's third largest provincial capital, have the raw energy of frontier towns, thriving on the region's prosperity and more concerned with the promises of tomorrow than the memories of past glory.

Despite its differences and its distance from the central heartland, the South has had a powerful effect on the development of Thai culture, mainly because it acted as a conduit for early Indian influences which proved

449

IN PHANG NGA BAY A STEEP LIMESTONE PILLAR JUTS OUT OF
THE SEA, UNDERCUT BY THE MOVEMENT OF THE WAVES

even more wide-ranging and pervasive than those of China. These began around the first century A.D., initially with Indian sailors who came in search of such valuable commodities as gold, tin, spices, scented woods, and perfumed resins from the interior, and who set up a series of trading ports, especially on the Gulf of Thailand. In the third century A.D. Chinese records mention ten such centers, the most important being one called Dan Sun which stretched all the way across the peninsula near Surat Thani. Later there were others, of increasing size and sophistication, and through them came innumerable Indian ideas of art, architecture, government, and religion. Magnificent statues of Hindu gods and goddesses have been found dating from the earliest part of this period. And after the fifth century southern artisans began producing Buddha images of high quality in both stone and bronze.

Starting in the seventh century, other important influences came from Central Java, crystallizing in the somewhat mysterious kingdom known as Srivijaya. There are various theories as to the extent of this kingdom and even the location of its capital; some historians place the latter in Sumatra, while others favor the site of the southern Thai city of Chaiya, where notable Hindu and Mahayana Buddhist artifacts were created. In any event, Srivijaya dominated the peninsula for several centuries and made cultural contributions that extended much farther to other parts of present-day Thailand and what is now Cambodia.

Java was converted to Islam in the fourteenth century, and the faith may have come to southern Thailand from there or through Arab sailors who joined the Indians in trade along the coast. (According to one student of Thai food, the Arabs may also have been responsible for introducing cilantro, that now-ubiquitous garnish. However, others suggest that it arrived later with the Portuguese, along with the chili pepper.)

Thai penetration of the region came later and was more gradual, though certain southern cities are mentioned in chronicles from the first kingdom of Sukhothai. For instance, Nakhon Si Thammarat (or Ligor, as it was then called) apparently had a Thai ruling house in about the mid-thirteenth century. It was also a major center of Theravada Buddhism, which would eventually replace the Mahayana variety in most of Thailand, and monks from Nakhon Si Thammarat carried the new faith not only to Sukhothai but also to Cambodia and the northern Thai kingdom of Lanna. Other parts of the region remained more or less autonomous, despite Thai claims of sovereignty. Singora (now called Songkhla) was controlled by Chinese pirates, who preyed on traders in the gulf, and Pattani, famed for its brocaded silks, was ruled by a succession of Malay queens.

The kingdom of Ayutthaya (1350–1767 A.D.) established a stronger presence on the peninsula, extending deep into present-day Malaysia—all the way, in fact, to Malacca—though actual power was limited by the distances involved. Nakhon Si Thammarat continued to play an important role, becoming a *monthon*, or province, early in the Ayutthaya period, which was ruled by governors sent from the capital. Artisans from the city were famed for their skill at producing exquisite objects in delicately incised gold and silver nielloware, which were used in the royal palace and traditionally presented as gifts to foreign rulers. Elsewhere other officials looked after royal monopolies in economically important places such as the island of Phuket in the Andaman Sea.

Today Phuket is a celebrated tourist destination, but the lure of its scenic beaches is a relatively recent development in its long history. Under the name of Junkceylon—sometimes rendered Junkcelaon and Janselone—it was widely known among ancient traders for more tangible forms of wealth. Just beneath the surface of the hilly island lay seemingly endless deposits of tin ore, a valuable commodity for which Thailand was virtually the only Asian source until the British opened mines in Malaysia. Moreover, Phuket and the nearby mainland offered a variety of other rare treasures: ambergris, rhinoceros horn, ivory, and, perhaps most enticing of all to Chinese traders, the nests of *Callocalia esculenta* esteemed for their medicinal and alleged aphrodisiac qualities. In theory all these lucrative goods belonged to the Ayutthaya kings, who received royalties on their sale to foreigners willing to brave the pirate-infested waters of the Indian Ocean.

The Bangkok period (commencing in 1782) saw a consolidation of Thai power in the South, though there were various threats for more than a century. In 1785, for instance, a Burmese army laid seige to Thalang, the

ON THE TINY ISLAND OF KOH PHI PHI LA, SEA GYPSIES CLIMB BAMBOO SCAFFOLDING TO REACH BIRDS' NESTS HIGH IN THE CAVES

SPREADING FIELDS OF RICE STRETCH AWAY TOWARDS A DISTANT RANGE OF MOUNTAINS

principal town on Phuket, and might have captured the island had it not been for two redoubtable women, the Governor's widow and her sister, who took charge of the defenses and eventually drove off the enemy. (They were given noble titles for their bravery, and statues in their honor stand not far from the scene of the battle.) The British, too, began to regard the region with acquisitive interest as they expanded into northern Malaya, and in 1909 after protracted negotiations King Chulalongkorn (Rama V) ceded four Malay states—Kelantan, Trengganu, Kedah, and Perlis (now called Perak)—to them, a significant loss of southern territory but one that undoubtedly helped preserve Thailand's unique independence. In December 1941 the Japanese made amphibious landings at seven points on the gulf coast, their main goal being to secure the airfield at Songkhla for use in the capture of Malaya and Singapore. There was brief resistance, but recognizing the clearly superior force, the government eventually agreed to allow passage to the Japanese troops in return for a guarantee of Thai independence. One result, in 1943, was the return of the four Malay states ceded by King Chulalongkorn, although these went back to the British at the end of the war.

Through its rich resources of rubber, minerals, seafood, and agricultural products, the South has long played a significant role in the Thai economy. Until recently, for instance, the residents of Phuket enjoyed an average per capita income exceeding that of any other province in the country. And during the nineteenth and early twentieth centuries, thousands of Chinese and Malay immigrants flocked to the island, most to work in the tin mines but some to amass large fortunes and build imposing mansions in the Sino-Portuguese style of Malacca, from where many of them had come.

A southern railway line linked Bangkok with the Malayan rail system in the late 1920s, making it possible to go all the way to Singapore in two days, compared with four days by sea, and also spurring the development of Thailand's first seaside resort at Hua Hin on the upper gulf coast. King Rama VII built a summer palace at Hua Hin which he called *Klai Klangwol*, "Far From Care". (Ironically, he was staying there in 1932 when he received word that a coup had put an end to Thailand's absolute monarchy.) The southern railway did little to open the peninsula's mountainous heart, however. Good all-weather highways were rare until the past few decades, and relatively few central Thais ventured far inland from the coastal areas.

As in the Northeast, early isolation and a consequent sense of neglect bred a number of problems, though in this case the causes have more often been cultural than economic. The most serious of these problems has been a small but persistent separatist movement which developed among the Sunnite Muslims of the southermost provinces. It was particularly strong in the late 1940s, when rather harsh measures were taken to suppress it, but it lingered for many years afterward. In recent years the government has taken positive steps to relieve the situation, by improving health and education facilities, building more roads to facilitate communications, and encouraging officials to be more sensitive to local customs. One of the most effective

NEON LIGHTS ADVERTIZE THAILAND'S FAMOUS NIGHTLIFE AT PATONG BEACH ON PHUKET

PEASANTS TOILING IN THE SALT BEDS

forces in creating a sense of national unity has been the monarchy. The royal family now maintains a residence in Narathiwat province, near the Malaysian border, and spends several months a year there visiting various communities. The King himself provided funds to translate the Koran into Thai, attends or sends a personal representative to the annual ceremonies commemorating the Prophet's birthday, and also appoints a respected Muslim leader to serve as a counsellor to the Religious Affairs Department for the promotion of the Islamic faith.

A STATUE OF BUDDHA WATCHES OVER THE BEACH
AT THE SEASIDE RESORT OF HUA HIN

The King has also initiated a number of royal projects to benefit the southern population, several of them aimed at making extensive swamp areas available to agriculture and other activities and introducing new technologies. The Phikunthong Development Study Center, not far from Taksin Palace in Narathiwat, conducts research and disseminates the results to local farmers. In addition, universities of a status equal to those in Bangkok have been established in Songkhla and Pattani.

Excellent highways now crisscross the South, and there is regular air service to most provincial capitals. Increasingly since the late 1970s tourism has become an important industry. Malaysians, who constitute the biggest single national group of visitors, flock to the bright lights of free-wheeling Hat Yai, just across the border, while others are drawn to the beaches of Koh Samui, Phuket, and Krabi, as well as to such world-class scenic attractions as Phang Nga Bay where hundreds of spectacular limestone islands rise from the blue waters in an endless variety of formations. Movie-makers, too, have been lured by southern scenery: a James Bond saga was shot on one of Phang Nga's islands, and Phuket has played a role in several films.

Some of the most beautiful parts of the region have been established as national parks to protect their unique environments for future generations. Phang Nga Bay is one such area, and the others include Khao Sam Roi Yot on the east coast of the gulf, which has some three hundred small mountains, along with jungled valleys and secluded beaches; Hat Nai Yang on Phuket's northwest coast, where sea turtles come ashore annually to lay their eggs; Thale Noi, which encompasses a huge freshwater lake and swamp system in the provinces of Phattalung, Songkhla, and Nakhon Si Thammarat and is home to some two hundred species of birds, among them the rare painted stork; Ton Nga Chang Wildlife Sanctuary, in a mountainous part of Songkhla and Satun provinces, providing shelter for such endangered animals as elephants, tigers, and tapirs; and Tarutao (a Malay word meaning old and mysterious), consisting of fifty-one islands with beaches and coral reefs in the Andaman Sea off the extreme southwest coast.

Despite its natural attractions, however, the South is unlikely ever to be dependent on tourism, as its traditional sources of wealth continue to thrive and improve. For example, tin mining has moved offshore in search of fresh deposits, rubber production is expanding thanks to new hybrids that produce higher yields, and fishing fleets are employing modern technology to bring in better catches. Related industries have also emerged in the region, among them smelting plants to process tin ore, and modern food-processing facilities that have made Thailand one of the world's major exporters of canned and frozen seafood.

Increasingly, the South is being "discovered" by outsiders, both foreign and Thai, mainly through tourism. Culturally however it retains an aura of strangeness that gives it an intriguing flavor all its own.

BEATING NUTS WITH A HAMMER TO MAKE A KIND OF CHINESE HARD CAKE

LUCA INVERNIZZI TETTONI/PHOTOBANK

DESSERTS

THAI DESSERTS OFFER a soothing finale to a spicy meal. Usually a simple meal will conclude with fresh fruit of some kind, with the more elaborate desserts reserved for special occasions.

Many of the dessert recipes can double as sweet snacks, for eating at any time. Puréed banana *(gluay guan)*, coconut delight *(ma-prow kaew)*, and crisp sweet taro *(puek chaap)* all fall in this group.

At midday a cold dessert is preferred, such as short noodles rolled in coconut *(kanom duang)*, an attractive tricolored noodle dish. Crispy water chestnuts *(tab-tim grob)* is another particularly refreshing dish, with chilled water chestnuts being topped with coconut cream.

Egg desserts like Thai custard *(sangkaya)* reflect the Portuguese influence on Thai cuisine. Thai custard is probably the best known Thai dessert, but there is a great diversity of desserts in the different regions.

In the Northeast sticky rice squares *(khao neow tad)* are popular, with the rice being steamed with coconut milk. In the North, sweet rice pudding with longan *(khao neow piag lamyai)* is a regional specialty when longans are in season. Sticky, or sweet, rice is a short-grain glutinous rice used all over Thailand for desserts but as a staple in the North and Northeast. In the South, pudding with coconut topping *(ta-gow)* served in banana leaf cups is a favorite. The popular desserts of Bangkok include baked mung bean cake *(kanom naw gaeng)* and black glutinous

JOHN HAY

A CHILD SIPPING COCONUT MILK THROUGH A STRAW—
THE FRESHEST AND SIMPLEST OF DRINKS

PREVIOUS PAGES: SWEET CLAM SHELLS (LEFT, RECIPE PAGE 458)
AND BAKED MUNG BEAN CAKE (RIGHT, RECIPE PAGE 460)

456

rice pudding (*khao neow dam piag*), with its distinctive velvety plum color.

Another favorite dessert combines sticky rice with crescent slices of mango (*khao neow ma-muang*). The fruit makes a tempting, sweetly tart complement to the sticky rice, all presented on a bright green banana leaf.

Dessert can also be as simple as a platter of fresh fruits that are in season. They are peeled, sliced and ready to eat: papayas, watermelons, jackfruits, longans, lychees and mangoes are just some of the huge variety available.

One fruit that disdains the company of any other is the magnificent durian. It makes a strong statement with "a smell like hell and a taste like heaven". Durian, an oval-shaped fruit with spikes, signals its presence with its aroma during Thailand's summer—April through June—when durian is in season. As the fruit ripens, the flavor becomes richer. The choicest durians are found in the province of Nonburi, on the periphery of Bangkok.

Thailand's wealth of fruits, as well as vegetables, also play another role during major celebrations such as national holidays when intricately carved fruit and vegetable sculptures add luster to a banquet setting. The embellishment of dishes with such sculptures is a purely Thai signature.

This style of presentation, which elevates any food to one fit for royalty, is another way of showing special regard for one's guests —and this is always an important part of Thai hospitality.

EXOTIC TROPICAL FRUIT FORMS THE BASIS OF MOST THAI DESSERTS

JOHN HAY

457

FRIED BANANAS

Bangkok and the Central Plains

KRONG KRAENG GROB

ครองแครงกรอบ

Sweet Clam Shells

The "clam shells" are made by using a wooden mold, available in Thailand, which resembles a wooden spatula with fine grooves. The fine teeth of a comb can be used to achieve the same grooves. This dessert should have a sweet and salty taste.

2 cups (8 oz/250 g) all-purpose/plain flour
pinch of salt
1 tablespoon sugar
½ teaspoon baking soda/bicarbonate of soda
1 tablespoon oil
3 eggs
3 cups (24 fl oz/750 ml) oil, for deep-frying

SAUCE

1 teaspoon garlic (*kratiem*)
1 tablespoon cilantro/coriander root (*raak pak chee*)
1 tablespoon cilantro/coriander leaves (*bai pak chee*)
3 tablespoons oil
1 teaspoon white pepper
⅓ cup (2 oz/60 g) palm sugar (*nam taan peep*)
3 tablespoons fish sauce (*nam pla*)

clam shell mold

Mix the flour, salt, sugar and baking soda together. Beat the oil with the eggs and gradually add to the flour mixture until all the ingredients are well blended.

Pinch off a small piece of dough and roll it into a ball about ½ in (1 cm) in diameter. Press the ball onto the clam shell mold. Then press the piece of dough away from you, making it curl. (It should resemble a ridged potato chip, only thicker and more rounded.) Place on a cookie tray/baking tray lined with waxed paper. Continue until all of the dough is used.

Heat the oil in a deep skillet. Deep-fry the pieces of shaped dough until golden brown. Remove and drain well.

In a blender, chop the garlic, cilantro root and leaves. Heat the 3 tablespoons of oil in a small saucepan and sauté the blended ingredients on medium heat for 30 seconds. Add the pepper, sugar and fish sauce, stir to combine, and boil for 3 minutes to the glaze stage. Remove from heat.

Drop the fried "clam shells" into the sauce and remove them immediately. Let them cool and then store in a tightly sealed container.

SERVES 4   *Photograph pages 454–455*

Bangkok and the Central Plains

GLUAY KAEG

กล้วยแขก

Fried Bananas

These treats are found in many areas of Bangkok at street food stalls. They are bought as snacks throughout the day and night.

1 lb (500 g) small green bananas, about 6

BATTER

1 cup (4 oz/125 g) rice flour
1 cup (4 oz/125 g) all-purpose/plain flour
1 teaspoon baking soda/bicarbonate of soda
1 cup (8 fl oz/250 ml) water
½ cup (4 fl oz/125 ml) coconut milk
½ teaspoon salt
¼ cup (1¼ oz/45 g) sesame seeds
3 tablespoons sugar
¾ cup (1¼ oz/40 g) flaked/shredded coconut

4 cups (1 qt/1 l) oil, for deep-frying

Peel and slice each banana lengthwise into four slices. Combine all the batter ingredients and stir just to mix together.

Heat the oil in a wok to 375°F (190°C). Dip each piece of banana into the batter and then deep-fry until golden brown. Remove from the oil and drain. Serve as a snack or dessert.

SERVES 4

Bangkok and the Central Plains

GLUAY GUAN

กล้วยกวน

Puréed Bananas

A sweet to be enjoyed anytime as a snack. The abundance of this fruit encouraged the creation of a variety of different recipes, and bananas are used in many desserts and snacks throughout Thailand. If they are available Thai candied fruits make a good accompaniment.

6 ripe bananas
¾ cup (6 fl oz/185 ml) coconut milk
½ cup (4 oz/125 g) sugar
½ cup (3 oz/90 g) palm sugar (*nam taan peep*)
pinch of salt

Peel the bananas. Use a beater or food processor to process the coconut milk and bananas until creamy.

Spray a large non-stick skillet with a non-stick coating. Sauté the creamy banana mixture on medium-high heat until the mixture is dry, about 10 minutes.

Add both the sugars and the salt and continue to mix and cook until the mixture caramelizes. Spread on a cookie sheet/baking sheet to a thickness of 1 in (2.5 cm) and allow to cool.

Cut into 1-in (2.5-cm) pieces and serve as a snack.

SERVES 4

Bangkok and the Central Plains

KANOM MAW GAENG

ขนมหม้อแกง

Baked Mung Bean Cake

This dessert is a favorite with the people of Bangkok—the best recipe is from Petchaburi province.

1 cup (8 oz/250 g) dried mung beans
¼ cup shallots, sliced
½ cup (4 fl oz/125 ml) oil, for deep-frying
1 cup (8 fl oz/250 ml) water
6 eggs
1½ cups (12 fl oz/375 ml) coconut cream
1 cup (8 oz/250 g) white sugar or ¾ cup (5 oz/155 g) palm
    sugar (*nam taan peep*)

▓ Soak the mung beans overnight in water to cover. Drain.
▓ Using a small saucepan, deep-fry the shallots in the oil until golden brown, then drain and set aside.
▓ Heat the water to boiling in a medium saucepan and simmer the mung beans until they are soft. Drain and put in a blender. Process until smooth.
▓ Add the eggs, coconut cream and sugar to the blender and process with the mung beans for 2 minutes.
▓ Pour the mixture into an 8-in x 8-in (20-cm x 20-cm) baking pan, sprinkle the shallots on top, and bake at 350°F (180°C) for 45 minutes.
▓ Allow to cool, and cut into 2-in (5-cm) squares to serve.

MAKES 16 PIECES   *Photograph pages 454–455*

Bangkok and the Central Plains

GLUAY CHAAP

กล้วยฉาบ

Crisp Sweet Bananas

Green bananas are firmer and so easier to handle for deep-frying. The crispy texture takes the syrup coating readily and makes for a very tasty dessert or snack.

1 lb (500 g) green bananas
4 cups (1 qt/1 l) oil, for deep-frying

SYRUP

1 cup (8 oz/250 g) sugar
1 cup (8 fl oz/250 ml) water
1 drop jasmine flavoring
pinch of salt

▓ Slice the bananas into long pieces about 4 in (10 cm) long and ¼ in (6 mm) thick.
▓ Heat the oil to 375°F (190°C) in a large deep pan. Deep-fry the bananas for 10 minutes or until golden and crispy. Remove and set aside.
▓ Combine all the ingredients for the syrup, heat to boiling and cook the syrup for 3 minutes.
▓ Dip the fried bananas into the syrup and remove immediately
▓ These can be served hot, warm or cool, as either a snack or dessert.

SERVES 4

CRISP SWEET BANANAS

Ma-Prow Kaew

มะพร้าวแก้ว

Coconut Delight

Food coloring can be used to give this any color of the rainbow.

1 cup (8 fl oz/250 ml) water
1½ cups (12 oz/375 g) sugar
⅛ teaspoon salt
1 teaspoon jasmine extract
1–2 drops food coloring
2 cups (3 ½ oz/105 g) flaked/shredded coconut

▨ Place the water in a medium saucepan and add the sugar and salt. Heat on medium-high heat. Stir, and continue cooking until the mixture thickens like syrup.
▨ Add the jasmine extract and food coloring. If desired, divide the mixture and add different colors to each half. Mix in the flaked coconut and stir until all of the syrup is absorbed.
▨ Drop by teaspoonfuls onto a tray lined with a sheet of waxed paper. Allow 2 in (5 cm) space between each piece. Allow to cool, then serve.

SERVES 4

Sangkaya

สังขยา

Thai Custard

One of the best known Thai desserts, this traditional dish is sometimes served with steamed sticky rice (khao neow), on page 350.

6 eggs
1 cup (8 fl oz/250 ml) coconut cream
1 cup (8 oz/250 g) sugar
½ teaspoon jasmine extract

▨ Combine the eggs, coconut cream, sugar and jasmine extract. Beat together with a fork for 2 minutes.
▨ Heat a 9-in (23-cm) cake pan in a steamer. Pour the egg mixture into the cake pan. Cover the steamer and steam for approximately 30 minutes.
▨ Allow the custard to cool and then cut into slices.

SERVES 4

COCONUT DELIGHT

CRISP SWEET TARO (TOP, RECIPE PAGE 212)
AND THAI CUSTARD (BOTTOM)

Bangkok and the Central Plains

PUEK CHAAP

เผือกฉาบ

Crisp Sweet Taro

A favorite among the Thai people, this dessert or snack is readily available in markets and food stalls. The glaze on the outside is almost like candy, complementing the tender taro on the inside.

1 lb (500 g) taro/sweet potato
2½ cups (20 fl oz/625 ml) oil, for deep-frying
1¾ cups (14 oz/440 g) sugar
3 tablespoons water
pinch of salt

▓ Peel the brown outer skin from the taro and discard. Rinse the taro and wipe dry.
▓ Cut the taro in half lengthwise. Slice it lengthwise again, leaving four equal quarters. Slice each quarter diagonally into ¼-in (3-mm) thick pieces, which are about 2 in (5 cm) long by 1–1½ in (2.5–3.5 cm) wide.
▓ Heat the oil and deep-fry the taro slices in small batches at 375°F (190°C) until golden brown on all sides.
▓ Heat the sugar, water and salt to boiling in a small saucepan. Continue to boil for 3 minutes.
▓ Dip the fried taro slices in the sugar solution so that they are coated all over. Set aside to cool.

SERVES 4   *Photograph page 463*

The North

KHAO NEOW PIAG LAMYAI

ข้าวเหนียวเปียกลำไย

Sweet Rice Pudding with Longan

When longans come into season, this dessert tastes extra special. However if fresh longans are not available, canned longans can be substituted, or rambutans.

1 cup (8 oz/250 g) sticky rice
3 cups (24 fl oz/750 ml) water
¾ cup (6 oz/185 g) sugar
1 cup fresh seeded longans
½ cup (4 fl oz/125 ml) coconut cream
pinch of salt

▓ Rinse the sticky rice then place in a medium saucepan and add the water. Cook until the rice is soft, stirring occasionally. Add the sugar and continue to stir.
▓ Add the longans and stir into the rice. Remove from heat and allow to cool.
▓ Add the salt to the coconut cream and stir until the salt is fully dissolved.
▓ Garnish the cooked rice and fruit with the coconut cream mixture.

SERVES 4

SWEET RICE PUDDING WITH LONGAN, GARNISHED WITH RAMBUTAN

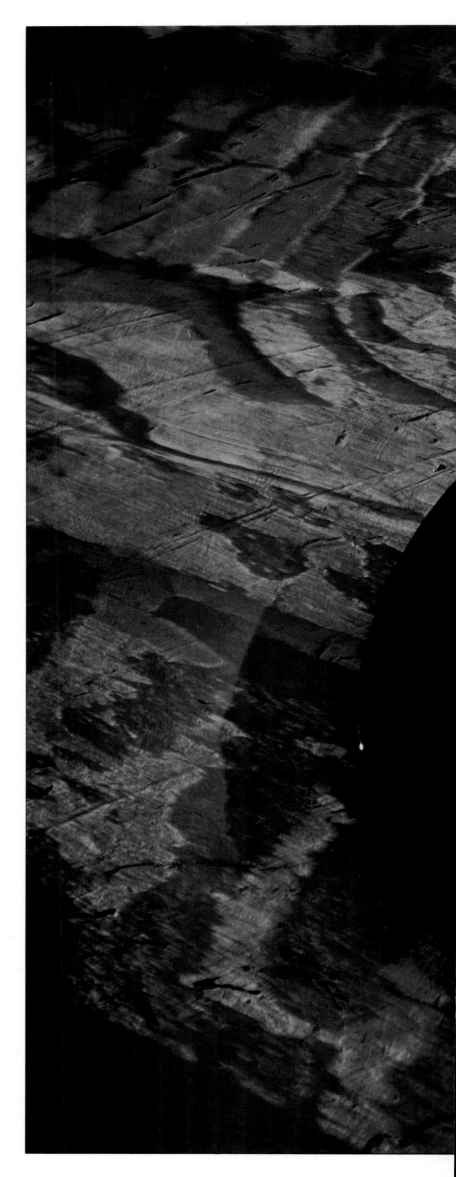

SWEET STICKY RICE

Bangkok and the Central Plains

KANOM DUANG

ขนมด้วง

Short Noodles Rolled in Coconut

In the early morning hours in Bangkok the vendors sell this favorite sweet snack to the waiting customers. This light and tasty dish provides energy for the morning, ready for a day's work. It is also popular as a sweet ending to a meal.

1½ cups (6 oz/185 g) rice flour
1½ cups (6 oz/185 g) tapioca flour
1¼ cups (10 fl oz/310 ml) scented jasmine water (see glossary)
1 drop of pandanus extract for green color
1 drop red coloring
¾ cup (6 fl oz/180 ml) chilled coconut cream
1 cup (1½ oz/45 g) flaked/shredded coconut
½ cup (4 oz/125 g) sugar
pinch of salt
¼ cup (1¼ oz/40 g) toasted sesame seeds

Combine the rice flour and 5 oz (155 g) of the tapioca flour together in a large bowl. Heat the scented jasmine water to boiling in a small saucepan and immediately pour into the bowl of flour. Stir to mix until the flour resembles a very thick dough. Knead until smooth.

Divide the dough into three equal parts. Add the green coloring to one of the portions and knead into the dough until the color is even. Add the red coloring to another portion, leaving one batch white. You should have dough in three colors—green, pink and white.

Dust your hands with the rest of the tapioca flour and pinch off a ball of dough about ½ in (1 cm) in diameter. Roll it in the palm of your hand to form a thin noodle about 2¼ in (5.5 cm long). Repeat until all the dough is used. Heat a large pot of water to boiling and boil the noodles for 1 minute.

Drain the noodles, then place in a bowl containing the chilled coconut cream. Drain, then roll the noodles in the flaked coconut. Set aside the noodles on a serving plate.

Combine the sugar, salt and toasted sesame seeds. Place in a serving bowl. To eat, place a portion of the noodles in a dish and sprinkle the sugar mixture over the noodles.

SERVES 4

Bangkok and the Central Plains

KHAO NEOW KAEW

ข้าวเหนียวแก้ว

Sweet Sticky Rice

Usually fresh pandanus leaves are used to color and flavor the rice for this delicious dessert. Similar results are achieved using pandanus extract or commercial food colorings.

1 cup (8 oz/250 g) sticky rice
3 cups (24 fl oz/750 ml) water
2 teaspoons pandanus extract
⅛ teaspoon salt
¾ cup (6 fl oz/180 ml) coconut cream
⅔ cup (5 oz/155 g) sugar

Soak the rice in the water with the pandanus extract overnight. The next day, drain and place in a steamer. Cover and steam for 20 minutes on high heat.

Combine the salt with the coconut cream and stir into the hot steamed rice. Cover the rice and leave in the steamer for another 10 minutes. Remove to a bowl and thoroughly mix in the sugar. Serve in small cups or bowls.

SERVES 4

Bangkok and the Central Plains

SA-KOO PIAG

สาคูเปียก

Tapioca Pudding

Used to balance the palate after a fiery Thai meal, this dessert is not very sweet. Toasted sesame seeds can be sprinkled on top.

1 cup (6 oz/185 g) small tapioca pearls
6 cups (1½ qt/1.5 l) water
1½ cups (12 oz/375 g) sugar
2 cups (16 fl oz/500 ml) coconut cream
pinch of salt
2 cups assorted sliced canned Thai fruit, such as jackfruit, longan, lychee, coconut meat, rambutan or palm seed

▨ Rinse the tapioca then place in a large saucepan and add the water. Heat to boiling, stirring constantly. Reduce heat to medium and simmer for 15 minutes, or until all the pearls are soft and clear.
▨ Add 1 cup (8 oz/250 g) of the sugar and half the coconut cream and salt. Stir to combine, then add the sliced fruit.
▨ Mix together the rest of the coconut cream and sugar to make a topping. Divide the fruit mixture into individual bowls and pour some of the topping over each. Serve warm.

SERVES 4

Bangkok and the Central Plains

TAB-TIM GROB

ทับทิมกรอบ

Crispy Water Chestnuts

This is a very light and refreshing dessert which is perfect for summer.

8 oz (250 g) peeled water chestnuts (fresh if possible, otherwise use canned)
1 cup (8 fl oz/250 ml) water tinted with red food coloring
½ cup (2 oz/60 g) tapioca starch/tapioca flour
1 cup (8 oz/250 g) sugar
1 cup (8 fl oz/250 ml) water
pinch of salt
½ cup (4 fl oz/125 ml) coconut cream
1 cup ice cubes

▨ Cut each peeled water chestnut into a square by trimming the edges. Place the water chestnuts in the colored water and allow to soak for 30 minutes to pick up the color of the water. Drain and set aside.
▨ Heat a large saucepan of water to boiling. Roll the water chestnuts in the tapioca starch and drop them into the boiling water. Boil until they float to the top, or for 4–5 minutes. Canned water chestnuts will not require boiling. Remove them with a strainer and drop immediately into a large pan of cold water. Hold at this stage until ready to serve.
▨ Dissolve the sugar in the cup of water and heat to boiling. Allow to cool.
▨ Mix the salt with the coconut cream and set aside.
▨ When ready to serve, drain the water chestnuts and place in a glass bowl with the sugar water, and add the ice cubes.
▨ Each guest is served a portion of the chilled water chestnuts in a smaller glass bowl and this is then topped with the coconut cream mixture.

SERVES 4

TAPIOCA PUDDING (LEFT) AND CRISPY WATER CHESTNUTS (TOP RIGHT)

469

SWEET RICE WITH SYRUP

Bangkok and the Central Plains

GAENG BUAD TUA DAM

แกงบวดถั่วดำ

Black Beans in Coconut Milk

These black beans are cooked until tender and combined with a creamy coconut sauce. This sauce can also be served alone or over sticky rice.

1 cup (6 oz/185 g) dried black beans
5 cups (1¼ qt/1.25 l) water

SAUCE

1¾ cups (14 fl oz/440 ml) coconut milk
¼ cup (2 oz/60 g) sugar
¼ cup (1½ oz/45 g) palm sugar (*nam taan peep*)
pinch of salt

▓ Soak the black beans overnight in water. Drain them and cook in the 5 cups of water until soft. Drain.
▓ Combine the remaining ingredients in a large saucepan, and add the beans. Heat to boiling and serve.
▓ If you would like a more creamy texture, add some coconut cream. This will make a richer dessert.

SERVES 4

The North

KANOM NEOW

ขนมเหนียว

Sweet Rice with Syrup

This tasty dessert makes a very nice ending to a Thai meal. It can be made in advance and is a favorite dessert of the North where sticky rice is more popular.

DOUGH

2 cups (8 oz/250 g) sticky rice flour
1 cup (4 oz/125 g) rice flour
1 cup (8 fl oz/250 ml) hot water
1 teaspoon pandanus extract

SYRUP

1 cup (8 fl oz/250 ml) hot water
¾ cup (5 oz/155 g) palm sugar (*nam taan peep*)

extra rice flour for dusting
5 cups (1¼ qt/1.25 l) water
1½ cups (2 1/2 oz/75 g) flaked/shredded coconut
½ cup (4 oz/125 g) sticky rice

▓ Combine the rice flours in a large bowl. Add the hot water and pandanus extract. Knead the dough until smooth. Set aside.
▓ For the syrup, combine the hot water with the sugar and heat to boiling in a small saucepan. Continue to boil until it reaches the syrup stage (just before it sets). Remove and allow to cool. Set aside.
▓ Roll the dough out into a ½-in (1-cm) thick sheet. Cut into ½-in x ½-in x 2-in (1-cm x 1-cm x 5-cm) pieces. Use more rice flour to dust the dough pieces.
▓ Heat the water to boiling. Drop in the pieces of dough and boil until they float to the top. Remove the cooked dough pieces and sprinkle with the flaked coconut.
▓ Sauté the rice in a skillet until golden brown.
▓ Before serving the dumplings, drizzle with the syrup and sprinkle with the roasted rice.

SERVES 4

Bangkok and the Central Plains

KHAO NEOW MOON

ข้าวเหนียวมูล

Sweet Glutinous Rice

This steamed sticky rice is the basis of many Thai desserts. It has the delicate scent of jasmine and imparts a flavor which is enhanced by many of the ingredients in the various dessert recipes.

2 cups (1 lb/500 g) sticky rice

SAUCE

2 cups (16 fl oz/500 ml) coconut milk
pinch of salt
½ cup (4 oz/125 g) sugar

▓ Soak the rice in water overnight, or in warm water for 2 hours. Drain, then place the rice in a steamer and steam for 15 minutes.
▓ Combine the sauce ingredients in a large bowl. Add the steamed sticky rice and stir to combine. Cover the bowl and allow to stand for 10 minutes before serving.

SERVES 4

SWEET GLUTINOUS RICE (BOTTOM) AND
BLACK BEANS IN COCONUT MILK (TOP)

The South

KANOM TUAY FOO

ขนมถ้วยฟู

Puffy Cups

The cake's delicate taste is very similar to a sponge cake and is perfect as a dessert after a spicy Thai meal. It is very pleasing to the eye as well as the palate.

¾ cup (3 oz/90 g) rice flour
⅓ cup (3 oz/90 g) sugar
½ teaspoon baking soda/bicarbonate of soda
1 drop of red or yellow food coloring
½ cup (4 fl oz/125 ml) scented jasmine water (see glossary)

❖ Combine the rice flour, sugar and baking soda thoroughly in a bowl. Add the food coloring to the jasmine water and stir to combine thoroughly, then add to the bowl of dry ingredients and stir until the batter is smooth.

❖ Arrange eight tea cups in a large steamer or use a muffin pan that fits into the steamer. The cups or muffin pan can also be lined with cupcake liners.

❖ Steam the cups uncovered for 2 minutes to heat them then pour in the batter and cover the steamer. Steam on high heat for 15 minutes. Remove them from the steamer and allow to cool for 5 minutes. Turn the steamed cakes out of the cups and serve warm or cool.

SERVES 4

Bangkok and the Central Plains

KANOM TUA-PAEP

ขนมถั่วแปบ

Mung Bean Stuffing

Mung beans are steamed, encased in dough and rolled in shredded coconut for this dish, creating a light dessert or snack.

1 cup (8 oz/250 g) dried mung beans
2 cups (8 oz/250 g) sticky rice flour
1 cup (4 oz/125 g) rice flour
1 cup (8 fl oz/250 ml) boiling water
⅖ cup (1 oz/30 g) flaked/shredded coconut
½ cup (4 oz/125 g) sugar
pinch of salt
¼ cup (1¼ oz/40 g) toasted sesame seeds

❖ Soak the mung beans overnight in water to cover. Drain, and steam the mung beans for 20 minutes or until tender. Set aside.

❖ Combine the sticky rice flour and rice flour in a large bowl. Gradually add the boiling water and knead until a smooth dough forms.

❖ Pinch off a 2-in (5-cm) piece of dough and roll it with a rolling pin until a 3½-in (9-cm) circle is formed. Place 1 tablespoon of cooked mung beans on the dough circle, fold the dough over, then seal the edges by pinching all around to form a filled crescent. Continue until all of the dough is used.

❖ Spray the bottom of a steamer with water and evenly space the filled dough in the steamer. Cover and steam for about 20 minutes.

❖ Remove the dumplings and roll them in the flaked coconut. Place on a tray.

❖ Combine the sugar with the salt. Sprinkle the sugar and salt mixture over the dumplings and then sprinkle with toasted sesame seeds.

SERVES 4

PUFFY CUPS (TOP) AND MUNG BEAN STUFFING (BOTTOM)

The Northeast

KHAO NEOW TAD

ข้าวเหนียวตัด

Sticky Rice Squares

When sticky rice is steamed with coconut milk the resulting flavor combines well with the texture of the steamed rice. This dessert can be cut into decorative shapes for presentation.

⅓ cup (3 oz/90 g) dried black beans
2 cups (1 lb/500 g) sticky rice
1 cup (8 fl oz/250 ml) coconut milk
pinch of salt
¼ cup (2 oz/60 g) sugar

TOPPING SAUCE

1 cup (8 fl oz/250 ml) coconut cream
pinch of salt
½ cup (4 oz/125 g) sugar
1 tablespoon tapioca starch/tapioca flour

▨ Soak the black beans overnight in warm water to cover. Also cover the sticky rice with water and soak overnight.
▨ The next day, drain the black beans then cover them with fresh water and simmer for 1 hour. Drain and set aside. Drain the rice and place it in a square pan 8 in x 8 in x 2 in (20 cm x 20 cm x 5 cm).
▨ Combine the coconut milk, salt and sugar together, stir to dissolve, and pour over the rice in the pan. Place the pan of rice in a steamer, cover, and steam for 30 minutes or until soft throughout.
▨ While the rice is cooking, thoroughly combine all the ingredients for the topping sauce. Pour the sauce over the steamed sticky rice. Then cover the steamer and continue steaming on high heat for 5 minutes.
▨ Uncover the steamer and sprinkle the cooked drained black beans on the surface. Cover the steamer and continue steaming for another 5 minutes.
▨ Allow the sticky rice to cool and then cut into squares before serving.

SERVES 4

The Northeast

GLUAY TAAK

กล้วยตาก

Sun-Dried Bananas

Drying the bananas in the sun was a way of preserving the fruit for later use. A favorite snack food in Thailand.

1 lb (500 g) small bananas, about 6
1 cup (10 oz/315 g) honey

▨ Peel the bananas, slice thinly and lay on a tray. Allow to dry in the sun for 5 days, turning occasionally to allow for even drying. The bananas will be dark when they are ready. On the fifth day, dip into the honey and dry for 1 more day.
▨ A faster way of achieving the same effect is to lay the banana slices on an oven rack and bake at 300°F (150°C) for 40 minutes or until golden brown. Then dip them into the honey and bake for 20 minutes more.
▨ Store in a jar with a tight lid and eat when desired.

SERVES 4

SUN-DRIED BANANAS

Bangkok and the Central Plains

KHAO NEOW DAM
NAA GRACHEEK

ข้าวเหนียวดำหน้ากระฉีก

Black Rice with Coconut

This variety of rice is naturally black and the texture is firm. It is usually grown away from other varieties of rice so that the color does not blend with the other rice grown in nearby fields. This favorite Thai dessert has a rich color.

2 cups (1 lb/500 g) black rice
2 cups (16 fl oz/500 ml) coconut milk
½ cup (4 oz/125 g) sugar
1½ cups (2½ oz/75 g) flaked/shredded coconut
½ cup (3 oz/90 g) palm sugar (*nam taan peep*)
pinch of salt

▨ Soak the black rice in warm water overnight. Drain, place the rice in a steamer and steam for 20 minutes on high heat.
▨ Combine half the coconut milk with the sugar and mix thoroughly into the hot steamed rice. Set aside.
▨ Place the flaked coconut, the rest of the coconut milk, the palm sugar and salt in a medium saucepan and cook on high heat to reduce until almost dry. Use as a topping for the black rice. Serve warm.

SERVES 4

STICKY RICE SQUARES (TOP)
AND BLACK RICE WITH COCONUT (BOTTOM)

The North

KANOM TIEN

ขนมเทียน

Mung Beans in Banana Leaf

Wrapping the sticky rice flour dough filled with mung beans in a banana leaf gives the typical triangular shape. This can be served either as a dessert or snack. The banana leaf is not eaten.

1½ cups (12 oz/375 g) dried mung beans
3 cups (12 oz/375 g) sticky rice flour
½ cup (3 oz/90 g) palm sugar (*nam taan peep*)
2 cups (16 fl oz/500 ml) hot water
3 tablespoons oil
2 tablespoons chopped cilantro/coriander root (*raak pak chee*)
2 garlic cloves (*kratiem*), minced
pinch of salt
1 lb (500 g) banana leaves (available frozen)

Soak the mung beans in water overnight. The next day, drain, then place the mung beans in a steamer and steam for 30 minutes. Remove, allow to cool, and mash to form a paste. Set aside and keep covered.

Combine the sticky rice flour and sugar in a large bowl. Add the hot water and blend well. Mix to form a smooth dough.

Heat a large skillet and add the oil. Sauté the cilantro root, garlic and salt for 30 seconds. Mix in the mashed mung beans.

Cut sections from the banana leaves and cut a 10-in (25-cm) circle from each section.

Pinch off a 2-in (5-cm) ball from the dough. Press the ball out to a 5-in (12.5-cm) diameter circle. Fill with 1 tablespoon of the mung bean filling and enclose the filling with the dough.

Pick up a banana leaf circle using both hands, positioned as if on the numbers 4 and 8 on a clock face. Push both hands together to form a funnel shape, making sure the fold is in the inside of the funnel-shaped container.

Drop the filled dough in the center part of the banana leaf funnel. Holding the folded side close to you, fold this part up. Fold the other two sides in to overlap. Fold the top down and tuck under the first fold. Pin with a piece of bamboo or a toothpick, or tie with twine. It should resemble a triangle.

Repeat until all the dough is used. Place the filled triangles in a steamer and steam for 15 minutes. Allow to cool. Serve at room temperature.

SERVES 4

Bangkok and the Central Plains

BUA LOI

บัวลอย

Floating Lotus Seeds

"Lotus seeds" floating in a pool of coconut milk make a favorite winter dessert. Sometimes an egg is added to the coconut milk to give a richer taste.

1½ cups (6 oz/185 g) sticky rice flour
½ cup (2 oz/60 g) tapioca starch/tapioca flour
2 cups (16 fl oz/500 ml) hot water
2½ cups (20 fl oz/625 ml) coconut milk
½ cup (3 oz/90 g) palm sugar (*nam taan peep*)
1 teaspoon jasmine extract
pinch of salt
5 cups (1¼ qt/1.25 l) water

Combine the rice flour and tapioca starch and gradually add the hot water to the mixture. Continue to mix until the dough is completely blended, using a spoon and kneading with hands. Cover and set aside.

Heat the coconut milk in a large saucepan and add the palm sugar, jasmine extract and salt. Heat to boiling, stirring to dissolve the sugar. Remove from heat and set aside.

FLOATING LOTUS SEEDS (TOP LEFT)
AND MUNG BEANS IN BANANA LEAF (RIGHT)

Divide the dough into two portions and knead until smooth. Roll each into a rod-shaped piece approximately ½ in (1 cm) thick. Cut the rods into shorter lengths for easier handling.

Pinch off pieces of dough to resemble the size and shape of a lotus seed, ½ in (1 cm) in diameter. Roll in the palms of your hands until smooth. Continue until all the dough is used.

Heat the water to boiling in a large saucepan.

When the water is boiling, drop the rounds of dough into the water, one at a time. Reheat the water to boiling, stirring to keep the dough pieces separated. Remove them with a slotted spoon after 30 seconds and add to the coconut milk.

Heat the coconut milk with the rounds just to boiling. Serve hot.

SERVES 4

477

BLACK GLUTINOUS RICE PUDDING

The Northeast

KHAO LAAM

ข้าวหลาม

Sweet Rice in Bamboo

An unusual dish, in which rice is actually baked and served in stalks of bamboo in Thailand. If you can obtain it, bamboo of medium maturity is the best to use.

2 cups (1 lb/500 g) sticky rice
1 cup (6 oz/185 g) dried black beans
2½ cups (20 fl oz/625 ml) coconut milk
1¼ cups (10 oz/310 g) sugar
pinch of salt
4 stalks of bamboo with a joint in the center of each,
    6 in (15 cm) in length and 3 in (7.5 cm) in diameter
banana leaves to use as a stopper for top of bamboo

▩ Soak the rice in water overnight. Soak the black beans overnight.
▩ Mix the coconut milk, sugar and salt together.
▩ Drain the rice and black beans and mix together.
▩ Stuff about a quarter of the rice mixture in each bamboo stalk so that the top ends are three-quarters full. The center notch keeps the rice from going into the bottom section.
▩ Pour in some of the coconut milk mixture and plug with a folded banana leaf.
▩ Using a baking pan 9 in x 12 in (23 cm x 30 cm), arrange the bamboo stalks with the rice end propped up to keep the rice from falling out. Bake at 350°F (180°C) for 30 minutes.
▩ If bamboo is unavailable, cook the drained rice and black beans in boiling water for 5 minutes, then drain well. Combine with the coconut milk mixture in a medium saucepan and continue to cook over medium heat until the rice has absorbed most of the liquid (for about 10 minutes). Serve in a bowl.

SERVES 4

Bangkok and the Central Plains

FOITHONG

ฝอยทอง

Golden Threads

These thin strands of egg yolk resemble bundles of golden thread and thus the name is derived. Foithong is often used as a garnish for desserts or for just enjoying with coffee.

12 eggs
3 cups (24 fl oz/750 ml) water
3 cups (1½ lb/750 g) sugar
1 sheet of foil, 12 in x 12 in (30 cm x 30 cm)

▩ Separate the eggs and reserve the yolks for this dessert. Place the yolks in the refrigerator until ready to make the strands.
▩ Bring the water to a slow boil in a large saucepan. Add the sugar and maintain a slow boil throughout the entire process.
▩ Fold the sheet of foil in half and in half again. Open the foil to form a funnel. Poke two holes 1 in (2.5 cm) apart, about ⅛ in (3 mm) wide, at the bottom of the funnel.
▩ Take the egg yolks out of the refrigerator and gently stir to ensure an even mixture.
▩ Holding the funnel over the saucepan of boiling water, pour the egg yolks into the funnel. The yolk mixture will come out in thin streams. Move the funnel from side to side to form long thin golden threads. As soon as the stream of yolk mixture drops into the water, it will begin to cook. The threads will cook more quickly if they are prepared in small batches, so that each batch has plenty of room to float. When the threads are cooked, use a long skewer to lift the threads out in long strands.
▩ Fold the golden threads into small 2-in (5-cm) long rectangular bundles of threads. Set onto a serving plate.

SERVES 4

Bangkok and the Central Plains

KHAO NEOW DAM PIAG

ข้าวเหนียวดำเปียก

Black Glutinous Rice Pudding

Similar in style to the Western rice pudding, this dish has its own distinctive coloring and flavor.

1 cup (7 oz/220 g) black glutinous rice
6 cups (1½ qt/1.5 l) water
½ cup (4 oz/125 g) sugar
8 fl oz (250 ml) coconut milk

TOPPING

½ cup (4 fl oz/125 ml) coconut cream
pinch of salt
¼ cup (2 oz/60 g) sugar

▩ Rinse the rice and drain. Place the rice in a large saucepan, add the water and heat to boiling. Reduce heat to a slow simmer and cook for 45 minutes, or until the rice is soft, stirring occasionally.
▩ Add the sugar and coconut milk. Stir well and simmer for a further 10 minutes.
▩ Combine the topping ingredients. Pour a small amount over each serving of rice pudding. Serve hot.

SERVES 4

SQUASH IN COCONUT SAUCE (LEFT, RECIPE PAGE 480), SWEET
RICE IN BAMBOO (TOP) AND GOLDEN THREADS (RIGHT)

The South

GAENG BUAD FAK THONG

แกงบวดฟักทอง

Squash in Coconut Sauce

The color of winter squash (fak thong) is similar to that of Thai monks' robes. This dessert is commonly made at home for offering to the monks at temple ceremonies. It also makes a delightful finish to an elegant meal.

2 cups (16 fl oz/500 ml) coconut milk
¼ cup (2 oz/60 g) sugar or coconut sugar
2 cups sliced winter squash/pumpkin, in
    1 in x 1 in x ¼ in (2.5 cm x 2.5 cm x 6 mm) pieces

❀ Heat the coconut milk to boiling and add the sugar. Stir and boil again. Add the sliced squash and simmer for 15 minutes. Serve cold.

SERVES 4
Photograph page 479

The South

TA-GO

ตะโก้

Pudding with Coconut Topping

In Thailand small containers made of banana leaves are used for a beautiful presentation which contrasts green with the white dessert. This is a slightly sweet dessert which can be eaten any time of day.

1 cup (4 oz/125 g) rice flour
¾ cup (6 oz/185 g) sugar
2¼ cups (18 fl oz/560 ml) scented jasmine water (see glossary)

PUDDING WITH COCONUT TOPPING

TOPPING

⅓ cup (1½ oz/45 g) rice flour
2 cups (16 fl oz/500 ml) coconut cream
2 tablespoons sugar
pinch of salt

❀ Combine the rice flour and sugar with the water and set aside for 15 minutes, then heat to boiling in a medium saucepan. Simmer, stirring constantly, for 15 minutes. After cooking, half-fill twelve ⅓-cup capacity molds or small banana leaf cups.
❀ Combine the topping ingredients in a small saucepan and bring to a slow boil. Cook, stirring constantly, on low heat for 20 minutes. Spoon carefully into the molds on top of the first layer and allow to cool. The top layer should be thinner than the bottom layer. If using molds, unmold to serve.

SERVES 4

Bangkok and the Central Plains

KRONG KRAENG GA-THI

ครองแครงกะทิ

Clam Shell Delight

The picture of clams floating in a sea of coconut milk is as appealing to the eye as it is to the palate. Using the proper wooden mold, which resembles a paddle with fine line grooves, makes this dessert much more delightful.

1½ cups (6 oz/185 g) rice flour
¾ cup (3 oz/90 g) tapioca starch/tapioca flour
1 cup (8 fl oz/250 ml) hot water
3 cups (24 fl oz/750 ml) coconut milk
1 cup (8 oz/250 g) sugar
pinch of salt
¼ cup (1¼ oz/40 g) toasted sesame seeds

1-in (2.5-cm) clam mold or a fine-tooth comb (the fine teeth of
    the comb resembles the outside surface of a clam)

❀ Combine the rice flour with ½ cup (2 oz/60 g) of the tapioca starch in a bowl. Add the hot water a little at a time and mix to make a pliable dough. Knead until smooth. Keep the dough covered to prevent it from drying out.
❀ Using the leftover tapioca starch to dust your fingers, pinch off pieces of the dough to form ½-in (1-cm) diameter balls. Dust your fingers and the clam mold, or the fine teeth of the comb, with the starch and press the dough into the mold. Roll the dough off with your thumb, pushing and rolling the dough at the same time into the shape of a clam. Remove onto a surface dusted with tapioca starch.
❀ Heat a large pot of water to boiling and drop in the clam shapes. Try not to crowd them while cooking and stir to keep them separated. Cook in stages if necessary to avoid crowding. Continue to cook until the clam shapes float to the surface (about 30 seconds), then remove them with a slotted spoon and set aside.
❀ Meanwhile, combine the coconut milk, sugar and salt in a medium saucepan. Bring to a simmer and stir intermittently.
❀ Gently drop the clam shapes into the coconut sauce. Simmer to heat through, and serve with a sprinkling of toasted sesame seeds.

SERVES 4

CLAM SHELL DELIGHT

Bangkok and the Central Plains

MED KA-NOON

เม็ดขนุน

Jackfruit Seeds

Although this dessert looks like the jackfruit seeds for which it is named, it also resembles nuggets of gold. This golden appearance makes it a very appealing dessert, which is delicious served with fruit.

8 oz (250 g) split mung beans
4 cups (1 qt/1 l) water
2½ cups (1¼ lb/625 g) sugar
4 egg yolks

❈ Place the mung beans in a medium saucepan and add half the water. Bring to a slow simmer and cook until the beans are soft. Drain, then place the beans in a mortar and grind until smooth. A blender can be used for this process. Mix in thoroughly ½ cup (4 oz/125 g) of the sugar and allow the mixture to cool.

❈ Take about 1 tablespoon of the mixture and shape into an oblong piece resembling a jackfruit seed or nugget. Continue until all of the mixture is used.

❈ Heat the rest of the water to boiling in a large saucepan and add the rest of the sugar. Simmer.

❈ Mix the egg yolks in a bowl and carefully dip a nugget into the egg yolks. Drop the nugget into the simmering syrup and cook for 5 minutes. Repeat with the remaining nuggets. Remove to a rack and allow to cool.

SERVES 4

JACKFRUIT SEEDS

SWEET RICE WITH MANGO

Bangkok and the Central Plains

Khao Neow Ma-Muang

ข้าวเหนียวมะม่วง

Sweet Rice with Mango

A favorite Thai dessert—the firm texture of the sweet rice paired with slices of fresh mango with coconut cream topping is an irresistible taste experience.

2 cups (1 lb/500 g) sticky rice, soaked overnight in water
   to cover
2 mangoes

SAUCE 1

1 cup (8 fl oz/250 ml) coconut cream
½ cup (4 oz/125 g) sugar
pinch of salt

SAUCE 2

1 cup (8 fl oz/250 ml) coconut cream
½ cup (4 oz/125 g) sugar

1 12-in (30-cm) section of banana leaf
1 teaspoon toasted sesame seeds

▨ Drain the rice and place in an even layer in a steamer lined with cheesecloth so the rice does not fall through the holes. Steam the rice on full steam or high heat for 15 minutes.
▨ While the rice is cooking combine the ingredients for Sauce 1. Remove the rice to a bowl and mix with Sauce 1 while the rice is still hot. Set aside.
▨ Peel the mangoes carefully so as not to bruise the fruit. Slice in half as close to the seed as possible, then slice each half into ½-in (1-cm) slices.
▨ Cut the banana leaf attractively and lay it on a serving plate. Arrange the sticky rice and mango slices on top of the leaf.
▨ Combine the ingredients for Sauce 2 and either serve it separately or pour over the sticky rice. Garnish with a sprinkling of sesame seeds and perhaps an orchid or other flower on the side.

SERVES 4

483

Bangkok and the Central Plains

SANGKAYA FAK THONG OR SANGKAYA MA-PROW

สังขยาฟักทอง หรือ สังขยามะพร้าว

Baked Custard in Squash or Coconut

This is a beautiful and delicious dessert served in many Bangkok restaurants. Sometimes a small coconut is hollowed out and used as a container instead of a winter squash: both methods of presentation are equally acceptable.

2 small winter squash/pumpkins

CUSTARD

3 eggs
¾ cup (6 fl oz/180 ml) coconut cream
½ cup (3 oz/90 g) palm sugar *(nam taan peep)*
⅛ teaspoon jasmine extract

Cut the top off each squash, retaining it to act as a lid. Scoop out the seeds and some of the flesh from the squash.
Combine all the custard ingredients. Be careful not to over beat the eggs, causing too much foam. Pour carefully into the squash containers and cover with the lids. Place in a steamer over rapidly boiling water.
Cover the steamer and steam on high heat for 45 minutes. Make sure the steamer has enough water to boil for 45 minutes.Remove the steamer lid carefully and lift out the squash. Allow to cool before serving. Garnish with golden threads *(foithong),* on page 478.

SERVES 2

Bangkok and the Central Plains

KHAO NEOW NAA GOONG

ข้าวเหนียวหน้ากุ้ง

Sweet Yellow Rice with Shrimp

The sticky yellow rice makes this a very colorful dish.

2 cups (1 lb/500 g) sticky rice
4 cups (1 qt/1 l) water
1 teaspoon turmeric
1 cup (8 fl oz/250 ml) coconut milk
½ cup (4 oz/125 g) sugar
4 oz (125 g) shrimp/prawn meat, minced
1 cup (1½ oz/45 g) flaked/shredded coconut
2 drops orange food coloring
1 tablespoon oil
8 garlic cloves *(kratiem),* chopped
pinch of salt
3 tablespoons sugar
½ teaspoon white pepper
2 tablespoons chopped cilantro/coriander leaves *(bai pak chee)*
5 kaffir lime leaves *(bai ma-grood),* thinly slivered

Soak the sticky rice in the water with the turmeric overnight. Drain and steam in a steamer on high heat for 15 minutes. Remove and set aside.
Combine the coconut milk with the sugar and mix into the hot rice. Place on a large serving plate and set aside.
Combine the minced shrimp meat with the flaked coconut and food coloring very thoroughly, so the mixture is even.
Heat the oil in a skillet and fry the garlic, shrimp mixture, salt, sugar, pepper and cilantro until the mixture is reduced so much that it is almost dry. Remove to a serving dish and sprinkle the lime leaves on top.
Spread the shrimp mixture over the sticky rice and serve.

SERVES 4

SWEET YELLOW RICE WITH SHRIMP

BAKED CUSTARD IN SQUASH OR COCONUT

SAUCES, DIPS AND CURRY PASTES

THAI CUISINE relies upon a wealth of sauces and dips to enhance the flavor of any dish. Fish sauce (*nam pla*) is considered an essential ingredient in many of these recipes, imparting a distinctive saltiness. Peppers of different varieties impart the distinctive hotness, and the other herbs and spices provide the varieties of flavors.

NAM PRIK GAENG KEOW WAN

น้ำพริกแกงเขียวหวาน

Green Curry Paste

Green curry paste is used to make the hottest of all Thai curries.

10 green jalapeño peppers (*prik chee fa*)
5 green Thai chili peppers (*prik khee noo*)
1/2 cup sliced cilantro/coriander root (*raak pak chee*) or stems (*pak chee*)
8 garlic cloves (*kratiem*)
1/4 cup chopped shallots or purple onions
1/4 cup chopped lemon grass/citronella (*ta-krai*) or 1 tablespoon dried lemon grass (*ta-krai haeng*)
5 thin slices fresh galangal (*kha*) or 1 teaspoon dried galangal powder (*kha pon*)
1 teaspoon cumin
1 teaspoon shrimp paste (*gapi*)

🍴 Combine all the ingredients in a blender and process until smooth.

MAKES 2½ CUPS

NAM PRIK MA-MUANG

น้ำพริกมะม่วง

Green Mango Dip

A good dip with seafood and fish, fresh vegetables, and boiled eggs.

8 oz (250 g) shredded green mango
6 garlic cloves (*kratiem*), minced
2 tablespoons shrimp paste (*gapi*)
1/4 cup (2 fl oz/60 ml) fish sauce (*nam pla*)

2 tablespoons lime juice
2 tablespoons sugar

🍴 Place the shredded mango, garlic and shrimp paste in a mortar and gently mash with the pestle so that the mango is bruised but is still in shreds. Add the remaining ingredients and stir to combine. Remove to a serving bowl and use as a dip for grilled meats or fresh vegetables.

MAKES 2 CUPS   *Photograph pages 486–487*

NAM PRIK GAENG PED

น้ำพริกแกงเผ็ด

Red Curry Paste

Red and green curry pastes are the basis for most Thai curries.

1/2 cup chopped onions
8 garlic cloves (*kratiem*)
10 dried red jalapeño chilies (*prik chee fa daeng haeng*)
4 thin slices fresh galangal (*kha*)
2 tablespoons chopped lemon grass/citronella (*ta-krai*)
1 tablespoon chopped cilantro/coriander root (*raak pak chee*) or stems (*pak chee*)
1/2 teaspoon cumin
1 teaspoon shrimp paste (*gapi*)
1 teaspoon salt
3 tablespoons oil

🍴 Combine all the ingredients except the oil in a blender and process until smooth.
🍴 Heat a small skillet on medium-high heat and add the oil. Slowly fry the curry paste for 5 minutes until it is fragrant. Remove and store in a jar for future use.

MAKES 2½ CUPS

GREEN CURRY PASTE (TOP) AND RED CURRY PASTE (BOTTOM)

HELL DIPPING SAUCE

Nam Prik Na-Rok

น้ำพริกนรก

Hell Dipping Sauce

Because it keeps well, this sauce was traditionally used by travellers.

2 cups (16 fl oz/500 ml) oil, for deep-frying
2 lb (1 kg) freshwater fish fillets
1 cup dried green Thai chili peppers *(prik khee noo haeng)*
½ cup garlic cloves *(kratiem)*, unpeeled
½ cup whole shallots, unpeeled
2 tablespoons shrimp paste *(gapi)*
¼ cup (2 fl oz/60 ml) fish sauce *(nam pla)*
3 tablespoons palm sugar *(nam taan peep)*

 Heat the oil in a large skillet to 375°F (190°C). Deep-fry the fish fillets until very crispy and golden brown.
Charcoal-broil/grill the chilies, garlic and shallots until their outsides are charred. Remove the garlic and shallot skins.
Place the fried fish, chilies, garlic and shallots in a mortar and mash with the pestle until smooth, or use a blender.
Place the shrimp paste, fish sauce and palm sugar in a small saucepan and cook for about 15 minutes on medium-high heat, so that the mixture is reduced to a paste.
Thoroughly combine the mashed ingredients with the reduced sauce ingredients. Store in a jar with a tight-fitting lid and use as a dipping paste or for cooking.

MAKES 4 CUPS

Nam Jim Satay

น้ำจิ้มสะเต๊ะ

Peanut Sauce

This richly flavored sauce is usually served with satays.

1¾ cups (14 fl oz/440 ml) coconut milk
2 tablespoons red curry paste *(nam prik gaeng ped)* (see page 488)
¼ cup (2 fl oz/60 ml) fish sauce *(nam pla)*
3 tablespoons sugar
1 cup (8 oz/250 g) ground roasted peanuts

Combine all the ingredients in a medium saucepan and simmer for 15 minutes, stirring constantly.

MAKES 2½ CUPS

PEANUT SAUCE

491

NAM PRIK GAENG MASSAMAN

น้ำพริกแกงมัสมั่น

Massaman Curry Paste

A different style of curry paste, this reflects an Indian influence.

5 tablespoons (2½ fl oz/75 ml) oil
4 dried jalapeño peppers (*prik chee fa haeng*)
½ cup chopped onions
½ cup chopped garlic cloves (*kratiem*)
1 tablespoon chopped lemon grass/citronella (*ta-krai*)
2 thin slices galangal (*kha*)
2 shallots
¼ teaspoon kaffir lime skin (*piew ma-grood*)
2 tablespoons dried cilantro/coriander (*pak chee pon*)
1 tablespoon cumin
1 teaspoon cinnamon powder
1 tablespoon star anise powder

▨ Heat a small skillet on medium heat and add the oil. Fry the peppers, onions and garlic until golden brown.
▨ Combine the fried ingredients and all remaining ingredients in a blender and process until thoroughly mixed.

MAKES 2 CUPS

NAM PRIK PANAENG

น้ำพริกพะแนง

Panaeng Curry Paste

The name of this curry paste shows its Malaysian origin.

4 oz (125 g) dried green jalapeño peppers (*prik chee fa haeng*)
¼ cup coriander seed (*med pak chee*)
½ cup chopped onions or shallots
½ cup chopped garlic (*kratiem*)
2 tablespoons chopped galangal (*kha*)
2 tablespoons kaffir lime skin (*piew ma-grood*)
¼ cup chopped lemon grass/citronella (*ta-krai*)
2 tablespoons shrimp paste (*gapi*)
1 teaspoon salt

▨ Place all the ingredients in a mortar and crush with the pestle to form a thick paste, or process in a blender. Store in a jar with a tight-fitting lid for future use—it will keep indefinitely.

MAKES 3 CUPS

NAM PRIK POW

น้ำพริกเผา

Black Chili Paste

This dip will give any food a much richer taste, and add spiciness.

1 cup (8 fl oz/250 ml) oil, for deep-frying
4 oz (125 g) dried green jalapeño peppers (*prik chee fa haeng*)
1 cup chopped shallots
1 cup chopped garlic (*kratiem*)
8 oz (250 g) dried shrimp/prawns

BLACK CHILI PASTE

2 tablespoons shrimp paste (*gapi*)
⅓ cup (3 fl oz/90 ml) fish sauce (*nam pla*)
¼ cup (2 oz/60 g) sugar

▨ Heat a small pan with the oil and deep-fry the dried peppers, shallots and garlic until dark brown. Place the fried ingredients with all the others in a blender, and process until a smooth mixture forms.
▨ Pour the entire mixture into a medium skillet and fry on medium heat for 5 minutes. Remove, cool, and place in a jar with a tight lid and use as needed. It will keep indefinitely.

MAKES 4 CUPS

PRIK DONG

พริกดอง

Chili in Vinegar

This very simple sauce adds flavor to any dish.

6 green jalapeño peppers (*prik chee fa*), sliced in rounds
⅓ cup (3 fl oz/90 ml) vinegar

▨ Combine the peppers with the vinegar. Use as a sauce or dip for noodles or to improve or change the flavor of other dishes.

MAKES ⅔ CUP   *Photograph page 494*

MASSAMAN CURRY PASTE (LEFT) AND PANAENG
CURRY PASTE (RIGHT)

NAM PLA PRIK

น้ำปลาพริก

Fish Sauce with Chili

Most popular of all the sauces, this can be served with most dishes.

¼ cup (2 fl oz/60 ml) fish sauce (*nam pla*)
5 tablespoons (2½ fl oz/75 ml) lemon or lime juice
2 garlic cloves (*kratiem*), minced
5 green Thai chili peppers (*prik khee noo*), chopped

❈ Combine all the ingredients and use as a dipping sauce. This sauce can also be used in curries or stir-fried dishes.

MAKES ¾ CUP

JAEW BONG

แจ่วบอง

Northeast Anchovy Paste

This paste is a very popular dip, used in the Northeast to add flavor to any fresh vegetable or cooked meat.

8 oz (250 g) fresh/frozen anchovy fish (use canned
   if unavailable)
1 banana leaf

SAUCE

¼ cup chopped lemon grass/citronella (*ta-krai*)
¼ cup chopped shallots
¼ cup chopped galangal (*kha*)
2 tablespoons chopped green Thai chili peppers (*prik khee noo*)
¼ cup (2 fl oz/60 ml) tamarind juice (*ma-kaam piag*)
   (see glossary)
5 lime leaves, sliced
4 garlic cloves (*kratiem*)

❈ Remove the head and bones of the anchovy fish. Cut the banana leaf in 12-in (30-cm) pieces. Neatly wrap the anchovy fish together using the banana leaf sections.
❈ Cook the wrapped anchovy fish over charcoal for 4 minutes on each side. The fish can also be broiled/grilled, or baked in the oven at 350°F (180°C) for 15 minutes. If using canned anchovies just drain away the oil.
❈ Remove the fish from the banana leaves and place them in a mortar with the sauce ingredients and mash with a pestle until all ingredients are combined.
❈ Serve the paste as a dip for barbecued fish and steamed or fresh vegetables.

SERVES 4

FISH SAUCE WITH CHILI (LEFT) AND CHILI
IN VINEGAR (RIGHT, RECIPE PAGE 493)

NORTHEAST ANCHOVY PASTE (LEFT), PICKLED FISH DIPPING SAUCE (TOP RIGHT) AND SPICY ANCHOVY DIP (BOTTOM RIGHT)

Nam Prik Jaew

น้ำพริกแจ่ว

Spicy Anchovy Dip

The charcoal-broiled lemon grass and shallots give this dip a richer flavor ideal for barbecued meats such as barbecued chicken (gai yang), *on page 382, and tiger cry beef* (seua rong hai), *on page 386.*

2 cups (16 fl oz/500 ml) water
8 oz (250 g) anchovy fish (2 fish)
¼ cup chopped roasted lemon grass/citronella (*ta-krai*)*
¼ cup chopped roasted shallots*
¼ cup chopped roasted galangal (*kha*)*
15 roasted green Thai chili peppers (*prik khee noo*)*
6 garlic cloves (*kratiem*)
½ cup (4 fl oz/125 ml) tamarind juice (*ma-kaam piag*)
  (see glossary)
2 tablespoons fish sauce (*nam pla*)

▧ Boil the water in a medium saucepan. Add the fish to the pan and boil for 5 minutes, leaving at least ½ cup (4 fl oz/125 ml) of stock.
▧ Place the roasted lemon grass, shallots, galangal, chilies and garlic in a mortar and mash until all ingredients are finely ground.
▧ Strain the fish stock and add to the mashed mixture. Add the tamarind juice and fish sauce and mix all the ingredients together.
▧ Use as a dip for barbecued meats.

* *Charcoal broil/grill, or burn over a gas flame, whole lemon grass, shallots, galangal and chili peppers for a few minutes, until barbecued but not black. Measure required amounts after cooking.*

MAKES 2 CUPS

Nam Prik Pla-Raa

น้ำพริกปลาร้า

Pickled Fish Dipping Sauce

The pickled fish and fresh fish together make this thicker dipping sauce suitable for any selection of fresh vegetables.

8 oz (250 g) pickled fish
2 cups (16 fl oz/500 ml) water
8 oz (250 g) firm-fleshed freshwater fish
2 stalks lemon grass/citronella (*ta-krai*), chopped
6 garlic cloves (*kratiem*), minced
¼ cup chopped green Thai chili peppers (*prik khee noo*)
6 shallots, chopped
2 teaspoons chopped galangal (*kha*)
⅓ cup (3 fl oz/90 ml) fish sauce (*nam pla*)
⅓ cup (3 fl oz/90 ml) lime juice

▧ Boil the pickled fish in the water for 10 minutes. Strain, pressing as much liquid through as possible. Reserve only the liquid, discarding the pickled fish.
▧ Broil/grill the freshwater fish until done, then remove all the bones, reserving the cooked flesh.
▧ Put the lemon grass, garlic, chilies, shallots and galangal in a mortar and pound with a pestle until ground to a coarse mash.
▧ Add the fish sauce, lime juice and strained fish juice. Combine thoroughly with the finely chopped cooked fish flesh and remove to a bowl. Use as a dip for any fresh vegetables.

MAKES 3 CUPS

YOUNG TAMARIND PASTE

🔲 Place the dried shrimp, young tamarind, garlic and shrimp paste in a mortar and gently pound with the pestle until all the ingredients are mashed. Add the fish sauce, lime juice and sugar and carefully stir to combine. Alternatively, all the ingredients can be blended in a blender.

🔲 Heat a medium skillet and add the oil. Stir-fry the mixture on medium heat until it has reduced to a medium-thick paste.

* *Young tamarind is still green and the seeds are not hard so it can be blended to form a paste. Do not use the outer peel.*

MAKES 2 CUPS

MA-MUANG DONG

มะม่วงดอง

Mango Pickle

Not just a condiment, this dish can be eaten as a snack before lunch or dinner and whets the appetite for the remainder of the meal. It can be kept indefinitely.

PICKLING SOLUTION

4 cups (1 qt/1 l) water
1 cup (8 oz/250 g) salt
½ cup (4 oz/125 g) sugar

2½ lb (1.25 kg) green mangoes

🔲 Combine all the ingredients for the pickling solution in a medium enamel or stainless steel saucepan, heat to boiling, then set aside and allow to cool.

🔲 Peel the mangoes and slice into sections, leaving in large pieces.

🔲 Place in a large container (glass is best) and pour the pickling solution over the mango pieces to cover.

🔲 Allow to sit for at least 2 weeks before eating.

MAKES 4 CUPS

KHING DONG

ขิงดอง

Ginger Pickle

If young tender ginger is available, it need not be peeled as its skin is translucent. If using regular ginger the outer skin must be peeled. Pickled ginger can be eaten with roasted meats or poultry.

PICKLING SOLUTION

2 cups (16 fl oz/500 ml) vinegar
2 cups (16 fl oz/500 ml) water
¼ cup (2 oz/60 g) salt
1 lb (500 g) sugar

2 lb (1 kg) fresh ginger
½ teaspoon baking soda/bicarbonate of soda

🔲 Combine the ingredients for the pickling solution in an enamel or stainless steel pan, heat to boiling then allow to cool.

🔲 Peel the ginger if necessary and slice very thinly. Rub the ginger slices with the baking soda and allow to sit for 5 minutes.

🔲 Place the ginger in a jar and pour the pickling solution over the slices to cover. Keep for 2 weeks in the refrigerator and then it is ready to use.

MAKES 4 CUPS

NAM PRIK MA-KAAM

น้ำพริกมะขาม

Young Tamarind Paste

Another of the interesting and flavorful dips that team with the natural flavors of meat and vegetables to give Thai cuisine its variety of tastes.

¼ cup (½ oz/15 g) dried shrimp/prawns
8 oz (250 g) young tamarind,* peeled and chopped
6 garlic cloves (kratiem), peeled
2 tablespoons shrimp paste (gapi)
¼ cup (2 fl oz/60 ml) fish sauce (nam pla)
2 tablespoons lime juice
3 tablespoons sugar
3 tablespoons oil

MANGO PICKLE (TOP), GINGER PICKLE (BOTTOM LEFT)
AND GARLIC PICKLE (RIGHT)

Kratiem Dong

กระเทียมดอง

Garlic Pickle

Whole clusters of garlic cloves are pickled in this solution and allowed to sit for at least a week after which they can be kept indefinitely. These cloves of garlic can be eaten with any dish or used in cooking.

2 cups (16 fl oz/500 ml) water
1 lb (500 g) garlic (*kratiem*)

PICKLING SOLUTION

2 cups (16 fl oz/500 ml) vinegar
1 lb (500 g) sugar
¼ cup (2 oz/60 g) salt

❈ Heat the water to boiling in a medium saucepan and simmer the clusters of garlic for 10 minutes. Drain and set aside to dry for 5 minutes.
❈ Heat the pickling solution to boiling in a medium enamel or stainless steel saucepan, then remove from the heat and drop in the clusters of garlic. When cool transfer to a glass jar and allow to pickle for at least a week. Peel the garlic before eating or using for cooking.

MAKES 5 CUPS

497

GLOSSARY

BAMBOO SHOOTS: A vegetable which is widely used in Thai cooking, canned bamboo shoots are to be found in most Asian food stores. Even in Thailand it is simpler to use the canned shoots. If the fresh vegetable is used it needs considerable boiling to soften.

BASIL

Bai ga-prow: This is the hot form of basil. If it is unavailable then sweet basil can be substituted but the taste will not leave the burning sensation on the palate. It is sometimes called white basil or light green basil.

Bai horapa: The variety which is most commonly used in Thai curries, this type of basil is similar to sweet basil, but it has a slight aniseed flavor and a reddish purple color. Ordinary sweet basil makes a good substitute.

Bai manglak: A plant which has smaller leaves but a similar taste to sweet basil, which can be used as a substitute, it can be sprinkled in soups and salads. It is sometimes called Greek basil or bush basil.

BEAN SPROUTS: The fresh sprouts of the mung bean are very crunchy and are available in most vegetable markets. If unavailable, canned bean sprouts from Asian food stores can be substituted.

BEANS

LONG STRING BEANS or snake beans: These can measure up to 2 feet (60 cm) in length. If unavailable, green string beans can be used.

SOUTHERN BEANS (*sa-taw*): These are small round green beans available only in Thailand. Use ordinary green beans as a substitute.

BLOODY CLAMS: These are sold at Asian seafood shops. If they are not available ordinary clams or mussels may be used instead.

CARDAMON: The pods or large black seeds of the cardamon plant are used to flavor and garnish many Thai dishes. They can be bought fresh or in the spice section of Asian food stores. They are also used in ground form.

CHILI (*prik*)

There are several chilies used in Thai cooking. They come in a number of sizes and colors. If the type of chili specified in a particular recipe is unavailable, substitute with care. The smaller the chili, the hotter it is, and green chilies are hotter than red ones of the same size. The quantity of chili used depends on the palate—always start with a little, and add more.

THAI CHILI PEPPERS (*prik khee noo*): These are tiny red or green chilies used to add heat to the dish.

Dried chilies are also used in cooking and are called *prik khee noo haeng*.

Ground chili pepper is called *prik khee noo pon*.

Tinned chilies may not be as hot as fresh ones, so check after adding.

JALAPEÑO PEPPERS (*prik chee fa*): These are larger red or green chilies used in milder dishes. Remove the seeds to reduce the heat further.

The large pale green chilies are not hot and can be used like capsicums.

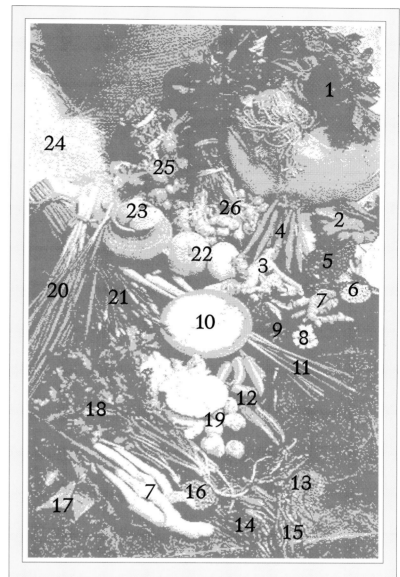

KEY

1	basil	15	Thai chili peppers
2	tamarind pods	16	coriander seeds
3	galangal	17	fresh and dried kaffir
4	lesser ginger		lime leaves
5	green peppercorns	18	coriander
6	white peppercorns	19	mushrooms
7	ginger	20	green onions/scallions/
8	cardamon		spring onions
9	star anise	21	garlic chives
10	jasmine rice	22	brown onions
11	lemon grass	23	palm sugar
12	jalapeño peppers	24	cellophane noodles
13	ground chili	25	shallots
14	dried chilies	26	garlic

CHINESE BROCCOLI: Chinese broccoli has a smaller flower head than broccoli, but the flavors are similar, so that they can be used interchangeably.

CHIVES: Chives belong to the same family as the onion, leek, garlic and shallot. Available in both flat and hollow forms, they are very pungent, and are used as garnishes as well as in cooking.

CILANTRO/CORIANDER (*pak chee*): This herb is essential to Thai cooking and is also known as Chinese parsley. There is no substitute for its distinctive flavor and not only are the leaves used in many dishes but also the stems, roots, and seeds. All have a different flavor and use. The leaves, fresh or dried, are used to garnish many dishes, the roots add flavor to curry pastes, while the seeds are ground into powder.

Cilantro leaves are called *bai pak chee* and the roots are *raak pak chee*.

To grind your own cilantro powder, take whole cilantro seeds and saute lightly in pan until brown and aromatic. Grind in a blender or food processor until a coarse powder is produced. 1 teaspoon of cilantro powder is the equivalent of 2 tablespoons of fresh leaves.

COCONUT
COCONUT MILK: Coconut milk can either be obtained by grating the coconut flesh, soaking it in boiling water and then squeezing out the liquid using a fine sieve, or by using cans of coconut milk from Asian food stores.
COCONUT CREAM: Coconut cream is the thick top layer which forms after making coconut milk. This is also available in Asian food stores and some supermarkets.

EGGPLANT (*ma-khue puang*): These tiny eggplants have a different texture to that of the Western vegetable. There are several forms of Thai eggplants which may be difficult to find outside Thailand. There are small types like a baby green tomato, others are round with stripes. If unavailable, common eggplants or peas can be substituted, but the flavor may vary.

FISH: If the particular fish specified in a recipe is unavailable substitute with any firm-fleshed fish.
ANCHOVIES: If fresh or frozen anchovies are not available drained canned ones can be used.
CRISPY FISH: Prepare crispy fish by deep-frying fish fillets in oil until crisp. Remove from pan and drain well.
DRIED FISH BELLY: Dried fish belly/maw is available from Asian food stores.
PICKLED FISH: Pickled fish are sold in Asian food stores.

FISH SAUCE (*nam pla*): A salty, pale brown liquid used widely in Thai cooking, this is made from fermented small fish or shrimp. The fish are salted and fermented in jars and then the liquid is collected. It adds salt to many dishes and is essential for authentic Thai flavors—and is available from Asian food stores.

GALANGAL (*kha*): A relative of the ginger root, galangal is pale yellow and has a unique, delicate flavor. In Indonesia it is called *laos*. It has rhizomes which are similar to but narrower than those of common ginger, and can be obtained as a root knob or in dried or powdered form from Asian food stores. Fresh young ginger root, but not dried ginger, is an adequate substitute, but does not properly replace the unique flavor.

Kha orn is young galangal, *kha haeng* is dried galangal, *kha pon* is powdered galangal.

GARLIC (*kratiem*): In Thailand the garlic cloves are much smaller and sweeter than the Western variety and have a purple tinge. They can be difficult to find outside the country. These recipes will work with ordinary garlic.

GINGER, LESSER: Another relative of the ginger root, lesser ginger (*krachai*) is milder-flavored than ginger and

galangal. The tubers are yellow with a brown skin, and are shaped like fingers hanging from the main body.

JASMINE WATER: Used to add a delicate flavor to some desserts, scented jasmine water can be made by adding ¼ teaspoon of jasmine extract to 1 cup of water.

KAFFIR LIME (*ma-grood*): This fruit is widely used in Thailand and adds a sour, sharp flavor. Dried and frozen leaves are sold in Asian food stores. If dried kaffir lime leaves are all that are available, soak them in water to prepare them for use. The skin, juice, and leaves of this green lime are all used, the rind especially in curry pastes. If unavailable, there is no real substitute but lemon is the closest flavor.

LEMON GRASS/CITRONELLA (*ta-krai*): This tall plant resembles a grass with a small bulbous root. Its flavor and aroma are very lemony. The bulb and base leaves are chopped and pounded for use in a variety of dishes. It is available fresh in markets and Asian food stores and also comes in frozen and dried forms.

MAGGI SEASONING: A sauce which is used in many Asian and Southeast Asian dishes, Maggi seasoning is found in Asian food stores.

MUSHROOMS
ABALONE OR OYSTER MUSHROOMS: Appropriately named, oyster mushrooms have a distinct oyster flavor. They are available from Asian food stores.
DRIED CHINESE BLACK MUSHROOMS: These are soaked in boiling water for 20 minutes before using in Chinese-style clear soups and stir-fried dishes. Their flavor is a fairly bland mushroom one. Asian food stores stock them.
STRAW MUSHROOMS: These are more delicately flavored and have a small brown round cap. They can be bought in cans from Asian food stores.

NOODLES
CELLOPHANE NOODLES (*woon sen*) or glass noodles: These are made from mung beans and are thin and almost transparent in appearance.
RICE VERMICELLI (*sen mee/sen lek/sen yai*): Rice noodles or rice sticks are made from rice and used in such dishes as mee grob. They have a subtle distinct flavor of their own.
THIN EGG NOODLES (*ba mee*): Egg and wheat noodles are used in soups and stir-fried dishes. Most Asian food stores stock a wide variety.
SOFT NOODLES: Fresh wheat flour noodles are used in soups.

ONIONS
SHALLOTS: Small brown or red onions in a bulb form. Red Spanish onions give a similar taste. In some parts of the world (especially Australia), green onions are mistakenly called shallots.
GREEN ONIONS/SCALLIONS/SPRING ONIONS: Mild, long-stemmed, slim onions. Both the green and the white portions are used.
WHITE, BROWN, RED, OR YELLOW ONIONS: These are the large, bulbous, common variety.

OYSTER SAUCE: A brown salty sauce, oyster sauce is made from oysters boiled in salted water and soya sauce. It adds flavor to a number of dishes and is widely available.

PALM SUGAR (*nam taan peep*): This is obtained from a species of palm tree, the Palmyra tree. It comes in dry cubes and a thick paste form. If unavailable, then demerara, light brown or coconut sugar can be substituted.

PEPPERCORNS: These are hot and pungent and used in many dishes for flavor. Canned peppercorns can be bought at Asian food stores. Dried white and black peppercorns are used whole and also in ground form.

PORK
PORK NECK: A boned pork neck can be obtained by making a special request of your butcher or from a specialist Asian food supplier.
PORK STOMACH: Specialist Asian butcher shops are the best source of supply for this.
SIDE PORK: Side pork is also known as pork flap. Pork belly is a slightly different cut but can be used if necessary.

RICE (*khao*)
BLACK GLUTINOUS RICE: A dark rice, black glutinous rice is most often used in desserts.
JASMINE WHITE RICE: The most popular rice in Thailand is fragrant or jasmine white rice, a long-grain white fluffy rice with a distinctive fragrance.
ROASTED STICKY RICE: Prepared by adding raw sticky rice to a hot skillet and cooking until it is golden brown. Add a tablespoon of water to the pan at occasional intervals.
   Grind in a mortar with a pestle if ground roasted sticky rice is needed.
STICKY OR GLUTINOUS JASMINE RICE: A short-grain rice which becomes very sticky when cooked. This is popular in the North and Northeast and is used in many desserts.

SALTED DRIED TURNIP: Salted turnip is available from Asian food stores. It is available in soft shreds or strips and looks like dried banana.

SHRIMP PASTE (*gapi*): This can be bought in a jar from Asian food stores and has a pungent fish taste. Use in small quantities and keep refrigerated.

STAR ANISE: A spice which is a feature of most Asian cuisines, star anise has a distinctive sweet liquorice taste.

SUN-DRYING: Only attempt to sun-dry foods if the weather is very hot and dry. Otherwise follow the alternative instructions, which use an oven.

SWAMP CABBAGE: A vegetable found in Thailand, swamp cabbage may not be available everywhere. Although not the same taste, English spinach, silverbeet or green chard can be substituted.

TAMARIND (*ma-kaam*): Tamarind juice adds a sharp, sour flavor without the tartness of lemon. It comes from the tamarind tree, which has fine fern-like leaves. The fruit is eaten green, but the brown pulp is used for cooking.
   Tamarind juice can be prepared at home or can be bought in bottles in Asian food stores. Lemon or lime can act as a substitute, but the delicate flavor is lost.
   To make tamarind juice add 1 tablespoon of tamarind paste to $1/2$ cup of hot water and stir.
   Commercial tamarind sauce can be bought in bottles and can be substituted for tamarind juice but the quantity needs to be reduced and then diluted with water to bring back up to the required quantity.

TAPIOCA FLOUR: Cornstarch/cornflour can be substituted for tapioca flour if it is unavailable.

TOFU: Also known as beancurd, tofu is made from soya beans and is very nutritious. It is sold by healthfood stores and Asian food stores in square blocks packed in water.
FRIED TOFU: Chop the tofu into $1/2$-in (1-cm) squares and fry in oil on both sides until it turns golden brown.

TURMERIC: A yellow colored rhizome used for flavor and coloring, it is a perennial plant of the ginger family. The dried root is used in curry powders and is bright yellow in appearance. It has a mellow fragrance.

THE SUN SHINING THROUGH DRIED FISH AT A BANGKOK MARKET

JOHN HAY

ACKNOWLEDGMENTS

The Publishers would like to thank the following people and organizations for their support and assistance in the production of this book.

Thai Airways International
Tourism Authority of Thailand
The Regent of Bangkok
Nestlé Products (Thailand) Inc.
Tetra Pak
AT&T
Italthai
Ogilvy & Mather
Bangkok Post
Presko Public Relations Company

The Editorial Board in Thailand was especially helpful in guiding us through the complexities of Thai cuisine and language. We would like to thank Dr Suvit Yodmani, who chaired the meetings, for the outstanding job he did in selecting the members comprising M. L. Tooi Xoomsai, M. R. Thanadsri Svasti, M. L. Tuang Snidvongs, Mrs Chancham Bunnag, Mrs Charunee Bhumidit, and also for his own generous contribution of time and support.

In addition, we would like to thank those people in Bangkok who assisted in making the book a reality: Adisorn Charanachitta, Chertchai Methanayanonda, Dharmnoon Prachuabmoh, Didier Millet, Garth M. Britton, Glenn R. Nelson, John Englehart, Louie Morales, Nadaprapai Sucharitkul, Nares Howatanakul, Nigel Oakins, Norman Pajasalmi, Rusty Kekuewa, Steve Tsitouris, William D. Black, William L. Zentgraf and Yibpan Promyoti.

A number of companies kindly donated their goods and services to facilitate the location photography in Thailand: Mrs Naphali Areesorn, props, Thai Celadon, 18/7 Sukhumvit 21 Road, Bangkok 10110; Mrs Marisa Viravaidya from the Thai House Co. Ltd for the use of the guesthouse as a location, tel (662) 2589651, fax (662) 2588426; Mr Tinakorn Asvarak, props; Ms Worawon Ongkrutraksa, Chiang Mai Honorary Guide; Siam Exclusive Tours Limited kindly allowed us to use their Bangkok to Ayutthaya river cruise boat, the *Mekhala*, as a photographic platform, tel (662) 2567168-9, fax (662) 2556065. At the Ancient City, or Muang Boran, we were able to photograph the recreated traditional Thai architecture. Visitors can obtain further information from 78 Democracy Monument Circle, Ratchadamnoen Avenue, Bangkok 10200.

We would also like to thank John Dunham and Jimmy Shu. The fruit and vegetables shown in the desserts section were expertly carved by Miss Kuson Japeng.

This book was inspired by Somnuk Phadchan who first introduced us to the joy of Thai cuisine.

MONKS AT WAT THAMMAKAI IN BANGKOK

504

INDEX